GO MATH

Grade 6

Differentiated Instruction

ISBN   978-0-544-06637-3

15 16 17 18   2266 18 17 16 15 14 13 12 11 10

4500567053   B C D E F G

Contents

Module 16 Displaying, Analyzing, and Summarizing Data

Answers

Description of Contents

Using the Differentiated Instruction Worksheets

Practice and Problem Solving: A/B, C, D
There are three worksheets for every lesson. All of these reinforce and practice the content of the lesson.

Level A/B (slightly below/on level students)
Level C (above level students)
Level D (considerably below level students who require modified worksheets)

Reteach (one worksheet per lesson)
Provides an alternate way to teach or review the main concepts of the lesson, and for students to have further practice at a basic level.

Reading Strategies
(one worksheet per lesson)
Provides tools to help students master the math vocabulary or symbols, and comprehend word problems.

Success for English Learners
(one worksheet per lesson)
Provides teaching strategies for differentiated instruction and alternate practice. The worksheets use a visual approach with fewer words, making them ideal for English language learners as well as other students who are having difficulties with the lesson concepts.

Challenge (one worksheet per module)
Provides extra non-routine problem solving opportunities, enhances critical thinking skills, and requires students to apply the math process skills.

Integrating Language Arts

The *Differentiated Instruction* worksheets help students become successful learners by integrating the literacy grade-level expectations.

The worksheets provide opportunities for students to:

- demonstrate independence as they become self-directed learners.
- show their mastery of content through writing.
- justify and defend their reasoning by using relevant evidence.
- view critically and constructively the reasoning of others.
- use technology appropriately.

LACC.68.RST.1.3 Follow precisely a multistep procedure…

LACC.68.RST.2.4 Determine the meaning of symbols, key terms…

LACC.68.RST.3.7 Integrate quantitative or technical information…

LACC.68.WHST.1.1 Write arguments focused on discipline-specific content…

LACC.68.WHST.2.4 Produce clear and coherent writing…

Using the Differentiated Instruction Worksheets	Integrating Language Arts
Practice and Problem Solving: A/B, C, D There are three worksheets for every lesson. All of these reinforce and practice the content of the lesson. Level A/B (slightly below/on level students) Level C (above level students) Level D (considerably below level students who require modified worksheets)	The Differentiated Instruction worksheets help students become successful learners by integrating the literacy grade-level expectations. The worksheets provide opportunities for students to:
Reteach (one worksheet per lesson) Provides an alternate way to teach or review the main concepts of the lesson, and for students to have further practice at a basic level.	• demonstrate independence as they become self-directed learners • show their mastery of content through writing • justify and defend their reasoning by using relevant evidence • view critically and constructively the reasoning of others • use technology appropriately
Reading Strategies (one worksheet per lesson) Provides tools to help students master the math vocabulary of symbols, and comprehend word problems.	LACC.68.RST.1.3 Follow precisely a multistep procedure. LACC.68.RST.2.4 Determine the meaning of symbols, key terms.
Success for English Learners (one worksheet per lesson) Provides teaching strategies for differentiated instruction and alternate practice. The worksheets use a visual approach with fewer words, making them ideal for English language learners as well as other students who are having difficulties with the lesson concepts.	LACC.68.RST.3.7 Integrate quantitative or technical information. LACC.68.WHST.1.1 Write arguments focused on discipline-specific content.
Challenge (one worksheet per module) Provides extra non-routine problem solving opportunities, enhances critical thinking skills and requires students to apply the math process skills.	LACC.68.WHST.2.4 Produce clear and coherent writing.

LESSON
1-1
Identifying Integers and Their Opposites
Practice and Problem Solving: A/B

Name a positive or negative number to represent each situation.

1. depositing $85 in a bank account _____

2. riding an elevator down 3 floors _____

3. the foundation of a house sinking

   5 inches _____

4. a temperature of 98° above

   zero _____

Graph each integer and its opposite on the number line.

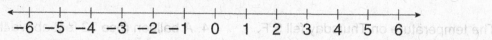

5. –2

6. +3

7. –5

8. +1

Write the correct answers.

9. The average temperature in Fairbanks, Alaska, in February is 4°F below zero. Write this temperature as an integer.

_____

10. The average temperature in Fairbanks, Alaska, in November is 2°F above zero. Write this temperature as an integer.

11. The highest point in the state of Louisiana is Driskill Mountain. It rises 535 feet above sea level. Write the elevation of Driskill Mountain as an integer.

_____

12. The lowest point in the state of Louisiana is New Orleans. The city's elevation is 8 feet below sea level. Write the elevation of New Orleans as an integer.

_____

13. Death Valley, California, has the lowest elevation in the United States. Its elevation is 282 feet below sea level. Mount McKinley, Alaska, has the highest elevation in the United States. Its elevation is 20,320 feet above sea level. Use integers to describe these two locations in the United States.

_____

14. Are there any integers between 0 and 1? Explain.

_____

_____

LESSON 1-1 Identifying Integers and Their Opposites

Practice and Problem Solving: C

Name a positive or negative number to represent each step in each situation.

1. Fabio is climbing a tree. He climbs up
   7 feet.

   _____

   Then he falls back 3 feet.

   _____

2. Roya deposits $30 in her checking account.

   _____

   Then she withdraws $12.

   _____

3. The temperature on Thursday fell 5°F.

   _____

   On Friday, it rose 11°F.

4. A balloon rose 32 feet above the ground.

   _____

   Then it fell to the ground.

Graph the opposite of each integer on the number line. Label each correctly.

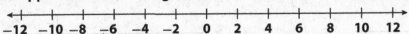

5. –7

6. –11

7. 3

8. 0

Write each temperature and its opposite.

9. The highest temperature ever recorded
   in Texas was 120°F in Seymour on
   August 12, 1936.

   _____

10. The lowest temperature ever recorded
    in Texas was –23°F in Seminole on
    February 8, 1933.

    _____

Solve.

11. The temperature at which water freezes
    on the Celsius scale is 0°C. It freezes at
    32°F on the Fahrenheit scale. Write the
    opposites of these two temperatures as
    integers.

    _____

12. Water boils at 212°F on the Fahrenheit scale
    and 100°C on the Celsius scale, so these
    two temperatures are the same. Write the
    opposites of these temperatures as integers.

    _____

    Are the integers the same? _____

13. Describe an integer and its opposite on the number line. Give an
    example.

    _____

    _____

LESSON
1-1

Identifying Integers and Their Opposites
Practice and Problem Solving: D

Circle the letter that best represents each situation.

1. a gain of 5 yards in football

   A   −5

   B   +5

   C   +50

2. a bank withdrawal of $25

   A   +5

   B   −25

   C   +50

Write the integer that is graphed on each number line. The first one is done for you.

3.

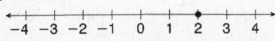

2 or +2

4.

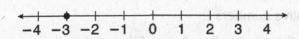

_____

5. Jenny made a deposit of $20 into her bank account. Write this amount as an integer.

_____

6. Mark withdrew $25 from his bank account. Write this amount as an integer.

_____

Write the correct answer. The first one is done for you.

7. Mercury melts at 38°F below zero. Write this temperature as an integer.

   Solution:

   Think: Integers are whole numbers and their opposites.

   The temperature is 38, which is a whole number. The temperature is below zero, so use the opposite of 38. That integer is −38.

   _____**−38**_____

8. The lowest temperature recorded in San Francisco was 20°F. Buffalo's lowest recorded temperature was the opposite of San Francisco's. What was Buffalo's lowest temperature?

LESSON 1-1
Identifying Integers and Their Opposites
Reteach

Positive numbers are greater than 0. Use a positive number to represent a gain or increase. Include the positive sign (+).

an increase of 10 points	+10
a flower growth of 2 inches	+2
a gain of 15 yards in football	+15

Negative numbers are less than 0. Use a negative number to represent a loss or decrease. Also use a negative number to represent a value below or less than a certain value. Include the negative sign (−).

a bank withdrawal of $30	−30
a decrease of 9 points	−9
2° below zero	−2

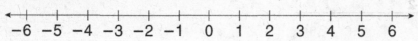

negative numbers   positive numbers

Opposites are the same distance from zero on the number line, but in different directions. −3 and 3 are opposites because each number is 3 units from zero on a number line.

Integers are the set of all whole numbers, zero, and their opposites.

Name a positive or negative number to represent each situation.

1. an increase of 3 points   2. spending $10

_____   _____

3. earning $25   4. a loss of 5 yards

_____   _____

Write each integer and its opposite. Then graph them on the number line.

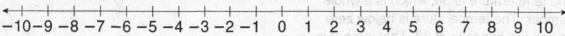

5. −1   6. 9   7. 6   8. −5

_____   _____   _____   _____

Name _____ Date _____ Class _____

LESSON 1-1 Identifying Integers and Their Opposites
Reading Strategies: Use Context

We get information from the numbers we read.

A **positive number** is greater than zero. The plus sign (+) denotes a positive number. If no sign is shown, the number is positive.

- Our car travels 55 miles per hour. ⟶ 55 or +55
- The temperature climbed to 90°. ⟶ 90 or +90

Write the positive number for each of the following situations.

1. Alicia put $25 in her savings account. _____

2. Oklahoma City is 1,195 feet above sea level. _____

3. Our football team gained 12 yards on the last play.

   _____

A **negative number** is less than zero. A negative sign (–) is always used to denote a negative number.

- Death Valley is 282 feet below sea level. ⟶ –282
- The temperature dipped to 12° below zero. ⟶ –12

Write the negative number for each of the following situations.

4. Dave withdrew $50 from his savings account. _____

5. The coldest temperature recorded in Greenland was 87° below zero.

   _____

6. Oarfish live at 3,000 feet below sea level. _____

LESSON 1-1

Identifying Integers and Their Opposites
Success for English Learners

Problem 1

Is the number positive or negative?

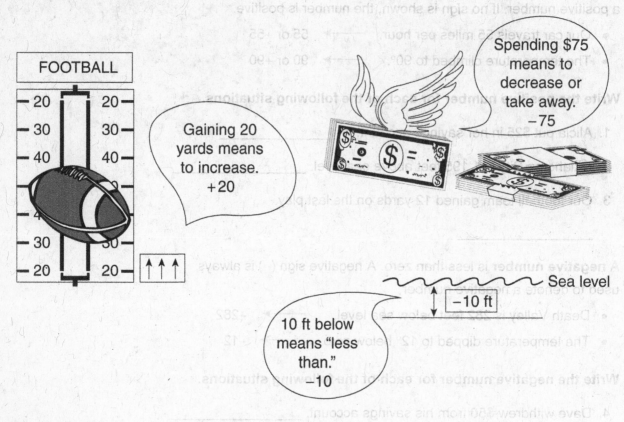

FOOTBALL

Gaining 20 yards means to increase. +20

Spending $75 means to decrease or take away. −75

10 ft below means "less than." −10

Sea level

−10 ft

Problem 2

The opposite of 7 is −7. They are the same distance from 0 on the number line.

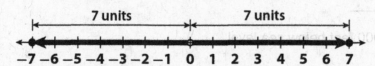

7 units   7 units

−7 −6 −5 −4 −3 −2 −1 0 1 2 3 4 5 6 7

1. If spending money is represented by negative numbers, what would represent positive numbers?

_____

2. The integers are the set of all whole numbers and _____.

LESSON 1-2 Comparing and Ordering Integers
Practice and Problem Solving: A/B

Use the number line to compare each pair of integers. Write < or >.

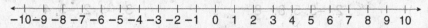

$$-10\ -9\ -8\ -7\ -6\ -5\ -4\ -3\ -2\ -1\quad 0\quad 1\quad 2\quad 3\quad 4\quad 5\quad 6\quad 7\quad 8\quad 9\quad 10$$

1. 10 ◯ −2

2. 0 ◯ 3

3. −5 ◯ 0

4. −7 ◯ 6

5. −6 ◯ −9

6. −8 ◯ −10

Order the integers in each set from least to greatest.

7. 5, −2, 6

8. 0, 9, −3,

9. −1, 6, 1

_____

_____

_____

Order the integers in each set from greatest to least.

10. −1, 1, 0

11. −12, 2, 1

12. −10, −12, −11

_____

_____

_____

13. 205, −20, −5, 50

14. −78, −89, 78, 9

15. −55, −2, −60, 0

_____

_____

_____

16. 28, 8, −8, 0

17. 37, −37, −38, 38

18. −111, −1, 1, 11

_____

_____

_____

Solve.

19. Four friends went scuba diving today. Ali dove 70 feet, Tim went down
50 feet, Carl dove 65 feet, and Brenda reached 48 feet below sea
level. Write the 4 friends' names in order from the person whose depth
was closest to the surface to the person whose depth was the farthest
from the surface.

_____

20. Ted is comparing the temperatures of three days in January.
The temperatures on Monday and Tuesday were opposites.
The temperature on Wednesday was neither positive nor negative.
The temperature dropped below zero on Monday. Write the 3 days
in order from the highest to the lowest temperature.

_____

LESSON
1-2

Comparing and Ordering Integers
Practice and Problem Solving: C

Compare each group of integers. Write < or >.

1. 7, 10, −3, 0

    _____

2. −5, 5, 8, −8

    _____

3. −1, 2, −3, 4

    _____

4. 2, −1, −2, 0

    _____

5. −9, 6, −8, 7

    _____

6. 2, −1, 0, 1, −2

    _____

Order the integers in each set from least to greatest and then from greatest to least.

7. 9, 8, 0, −1

    _____

8. 3, −3, −2, 2, 0

    _____

9. 11, −11, 1, 0, −1

    _____

10. 13, −13, |−7|, 0, −5

    _____

11. |−8|, −8, 0, |7|, −7

    _____

12. |−15|, |16|, −13, 14, −15

    _____

Solve.

13. Five friends were flying kites. Abe's kite flew up to 15 feet, Beth's went to 23 feet, Casey's went to 11 feet, Davio's went to 31 feet, and Eric's never left the ground. Write the friend's names in order from the person whose kite flew the highest to the person whose kite flew the lowest.

    _____

14. An elevator made the following trips: up 5 floors, then down 3 floors, then up 7 floors, then down 2 floors, then up 2 floors, and finally down 4 floors.

    a. Write each of these trips as an integer.

    _____

    b. Which trip was the longest? _____

    c. Which, if any, trips were opposites?

    _____

    d. Was the elevator higher at the finish or at the start?

    _____

    e. If the elevator started on the 18th floor, on which floor did it end up?

    _____

Name _____ Date _____ Class _____

Comparing and Ordering Integers
Practice and Problem Solving: D

Use the number line to compare each pair of integers. Write < or >. The first one is done for you.

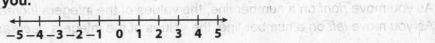

-5 -4 -3 -2 -1 0 1 2 3 4 5

1. 4 (>) 3   2. -5 ( ) -1   3. -2 ( ) 5

Order the integers from least to greatest. The first one is done for you.

4. 2, -3, 4 ___-3, 2, 4___   5. 2, -2, 3 _____

6. 3, -1, 0 _____   7. -1, -3, 1, 3, 0 _____

Circle the letter of the correct answer.

8. Which set of integers is written from least to greatest?

   A 3, -1, 0, 8

   B 0, -1, 3, 8

   C -1, 0, 3, 8

9. Which set of integers is written from greatest to least?

   A 7, 4, -5, 2

   B 7, 4, 2, -5

   C -5, 2, 4, 7

Use the table below to answer each question.

10. What is the lowest point on Earth? What is its elevation?

   Look at the Elevation column. Two numbers have four digits: _____ and

   _____.

   Of those two numbers, the one with the greater digit in the thousands

   place is _____.

   The lowest point on Earth is _____ at an elevation of

   _____ feet.

Location	Elevation (ft)
Lake Assal	-512
Bentley Subglacial Trench	-8,327
Dead Sea	-1,349
Lake Eyre	-52
Caspian Sea	-92

11. Which location on Earth is lower, the Caspian Sea or Lake Eyre?

   _____

LESSON 1-2

Comparing and Ordering Integers
Reteach

You can use a number line to compare integers.

As you move *right* on a number line, the values of the integers *increase*.
As you move *left* on a number line, the values of the integers *decrease*.

Compare –4 and 2.

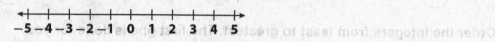

–4 is to the left of 2, so –4 < 2.

Use the number line above to compare the integers. Write < or >.

1. 1 ◯ –4

2. –5 ◯ –2

3. –3 ◯ 2

4. –1 ◯ –4

5. 5 ◯ 0

6. –2 ◯ 3

You can also use a number line to order integers.
Order –3, 4, and –1 from least to greatest.

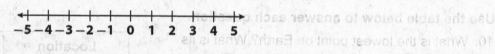

List the numbers in the order in which they appear from left to right.

The integers in order from least to greatest are –3, –1, 4.

Order the integers from least to greatest.

7. –2, –5, –1

8. 0, –5, 5

9. –5, 2, –3

_____

_____

_____

10. 3, –1, –4

11. 3, –5, 0

12. –2, –4, 1

LESSON 1-2   Comparing and Ordering Integers

Reading Strategies: Use a Graphic Aid

Integers include all the **positive whole numbers** and **negative whole numbers** plus zero. Use a number line to help you picture and compare integers.

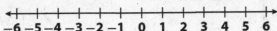

1. Start at the left and move to the right on the number line. As you move from left to right, do integers increase or decrease in value?

   _____

2. Now start at the right and move to the left along the number line. As you move from right to left, do integers increase or decrease in value?

   _____

Compare two numbers by checking their location on a number line.

Compare –4 and –2. –4 is to the left of –2.

    –4 < –2   ⟵   Read: "–4 is less than –2."

    –2 > –4   ⟵   Read: "–2 is greater than –4."

3. Start at –5. Move to –1. Did you move to the right or to the left?

   _____

4. Start at 3. Move to –2. Did you move to the right or to the left?

   _____

5. Compare the locations of –3 and 3 on the number line above.

   _____

6. Use < or > to compare –3 and 3.

   _____

7. Compare the locations of –1 and –4 on the number line above.

   _____

8. Use < or > to compare –1 and –4.

   _____

**LESSON
1-2**

Comparing and Ordering Integers
Success for English Learners

Problem 1

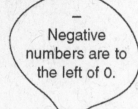

–
Negative numbers are to the left of 0.

```
←--+--+--+--+--+--+--+--+--+--+--+--→
  -5 -4 -3 -2 -1  0  1  2  3  4  5
```

A number is less than all numbers to the right of it.

+
Positive numbers are to the right of 0.

Is −4 < −3? yes

Is −4 < 0? yes

Is −4 < 2? yes

Is −5 < −4? yes

Is −5 < −3? yes

Is −5 < 0? yes

Is −5 < −2? yes

How do you know?
The numbers are less than the numbers to the right of them on a number line.

Problem 2

Who won?

 David Berganio

6
5
4
3
2

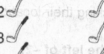 Golfers with more strokes than others lose.

1
0
−1
−2
−3
−4
−5   Ernie Els
−6
−7
−8
−9
−10
−11
−12 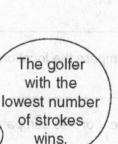 The golfer with the lowest number of strokes wins.
−13
−14
−15
−16 Sergio Garcia

1. How can −3 be greater than −5 if 3 is less than 5?

_____

LESSON 1-3	**Absolute Value**

Practice and Problem Solving: A/B

Graph each number on the number line.

1. –6   2. 3   3. –3   4. 5

$$\begin{array}{c}
\leftarrow\!\!\!+\!-\!\!+\!-\!\!+\!-\!\!+\!-\!\!+\!-\!\!+\!-\!\!+\!-\!\!+\!-\!\!+\!-\!\!+\!-\!\!+\!-\!\!+\!-\!\!+\!-\!\!+\!\!\!\rightarrow \\
-8\,-7\,-6\,-5\,-4\,-3\,-2\,-1\ \ 0\ \ 1\ \ 2\ \ 3\ \ 4\ \ 5\ \ 6\ \ 7\ \ 8
\end{array}$$

Use the number line to find each absolute value.

5. $|-6|$ _____   6. $|3|$ _____   7. $|8|$ _____

8. $|6|$ _____   9. $|-3|$ _____   10. $|5|$ _____

11. What do you notice about the absolute values of 6 and –6?

_____

12. What do you call –6 and 6 or 3 and –3? _____

Use the table for exercises 13–19.

Andrea's Credit-Card Transactions				
Monday	**Tuesday**	**Wednesday**	**Thursday**	**Friday**
Bought $20 shirt	Bought $6 lunch	Made $15 payment	Paid $3 fee	Bought $8 app

Write a negative integer to show the amount spent on each purchase.

13. Monday ____   14. Tuesday ____   15. Friday ____

Find the absolute value of each transaction.

16. Monday ____   17. Tuesday ____   18. Wednesday ____

19. On which day did Andrea spend the most on her card? Explain.

_____

_____

Solve.

20. Show that $|3 + 10| = |3| + |10|$.

_____

_____

21. How many different integers can have the same absolute

value? _____ Give an example. _____

Absolute Value

Practice and Problem Solving: C

Average Deviation from Daily Calorie Standard*				
Rob	**Jorge**	**Elan**	**Pietro**	**Bill**
+540	–125	+610	–220	+125

*Standard: An active 12-year-old male should consume about 2,300 calories a day.

Use the table above to answer the questions.

1. Which number acts like a base or 0 in this situation? _____

2. Whose calorie consumption is farthest from the standard?

   _____ How many calories does he consume?

   _____

3. Who consumes the fewest calories? _____

   How many calories does he consume? _____

4. Which two students' deviations from the standard are opposites?

   _____

5. Who consumes a number of calories closest to the standard?

   _____

6. Who consumes almost 3,000 calories? _____

7. What is the average deviation from the standard among these five

   students? _____

8. What is the average *absolute* deviation from the standard among these

   five students? _____

9. Find two calorie counts whose deviations from the standard are
   opposites. What can you say about their absolute values?

   _____

10. If the standard were reduced to 2,200 calories, how would that affect

    the deviations in the table? _____

    _____

LESSON 1-3

Absolute Value
Practice and Problem Solving: D

Graph each number on the number line. The first one is done for you.

1. –5   2. 4   3. –7   4. 5

$$\xleftarrow{\hspace{0.3cm}} \underset{-8}{|}\,\underset{-7}{|}\,\underset{-6}{|}\,\underset{-5}{\blacklozenge}\,\underset{-4}{|}\,\underset{-3}{|}\,\underset{-2}{|}\,\underset{-1}{|}\,\underset{0}{|}\,\underset{1}{|}\,\underset{2}{|}\,\underset{3}{|}\,\underset{4}{|}\,\underset{5}{|}\,\underset{6}{|}\,\underset{7}{|}\,\underset{8}{|}\xrightarrow{\hspace{0.3cm}}$$

Use the number line to find each absolute value. The first one is done for you.

5. |4| _____4_____   6. |–5| _____   7. |7| _____

8. |5| _____   9. |–4| _____   10. |6| _____

Complete.

11. The absolute values of –5 and 5 are the _____.

12. The integers –5 and 5 are called _____.

Use the table for exercises 13–22.

Temperatures at a Ski Resort				
Monday	**Tuesday**	**Wednesday**	**Thursday**	**Friday**
5°F below zero	2°F below zero	0°F	2°F above zero	3°F below zero

Write a negative integer to show the amount each temperature is below zero. The first one is done for you.

13. 5°F below zero _–5_   14. 2°F below zero ____   15. 3°F below zero ____

16. Can 0°F be written as a negative integer? ____

Find the absolute value of each temperature below zero. The first one is done for you.

17. |–5| = _5_   18. |–2| = ____   19. |–3| = ____

Complete.

20. On which day was the temperature the coldest? _____

21. On which day was the temperature the warmest? _____

22. When a number is negative, its opposite is also its

_____.

LESSON 1-3

Absolute Value
Reteach

The absolute value of any number is its distance from 0 on the number line.

Since distance is always positive or 0, absolute value is always positive or 0.

Find the absolute value of –7 and 7.

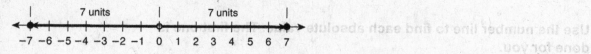

|–7| = 7 |7| = 7

Match. You can use the letters more than once.

1. absolute value of 15 ____   a. –7

2. negative integer ____   b. 7

3. opposite of –7 ____   c. 15

4. opposite of 7 ____   d. –15

5. |–15| ____

Find each absolute value.

6. |–3| _____   7. |5| _____   8. |–7| _____

9. |6| _____   10. |0| _____   11. |–2| _____

12. |–10| _____   13. $\left|-\frac{3}{4}\right|$ _____   14. |0.8| _____

Answer the question.

15. Abby has been absent from class. How would you explain to her what absolute value is? Use the number line and an example in your explanation.

_____

_____

Name _____ Date _____ Class_____

Absolute Value
Reading Strategies: Use Context Clues

In everyday speech, people describe certain situations by using absolute values instead of negative numbers.

When people use numbers with certain words or phrases, we know the numbers they are talking about are *positive numbers.*

> Jackie **deposited** $50 in her checking account.
>
> A mountain is 13,457 feet **above sea level**.
>
> The baseball team **scored** 7 runs in the last inning.

List the words or phrases above that refer to positive numbers.

1. deposited, _____ , _____

However, when people use numbers with certain other terms, we know the numbers they are talking about are actually *negative numbers*. In these contexts, people are using the **absolute value** of the number.

> The temperature was 5° **below zero.**
>
> A stock posted a **loss** of 5 points one week.
>
> New Orleans is about 8 feet **below sea level.**

List the words or phrases above that refer to absolute values.

2. below zero, _____ , _____

Underline each phrase that includes an amount. Then write the positive or negative integer that is being described.

3. a kite rising 17 feet into the air ____

4. drilling a foundation 5 feet below the surface ____

5. losing 6 points in a game ____

6. paying a fee of $35 on a checking account ____

7. a penalty of 5 yards in a football game ____

8. adding 32 MB of storage to a computer ____

9. an award of $50 for perfect attendance ____

10. crediting an account with a gift card of $60 ____

Absolute Value
Success for English Learners

Problem 1

Compare the absolute values of –7 and 7.

The absolute value of a number is its distance from 0 on a number line.

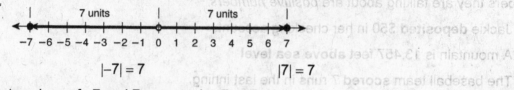

$$|-7| = 7 \qquad\qquad |7| = 7$$

The absolute values of –7 and 7 are equal: $|-7| = |7|$.

Problem 2

When people speak, they often use absolute values instead of negative numbers.

Complete the table.

1.

Situation	Numbers We Write	Absolute Value	Words We Say
bought $30 shoes	–30	$|-30| = 30$	"spent $30"
8-foot drop	–8	$|-8| = 8$	"dropped 8 feet"
5-point loss	____	$|-5| =$ ____	"lost 5 points"

Use the number line above to find the absolute values.

2. absolute value of –6 _____

3. $|-4| =$ _____

4. $|-3|$ _____

5. absolute value of 0 _____

6. absolute value of –2 _____

7. $|2| =$ _____

8. What do you notice about $|-2|$ and $|2|$?

_____

Integers
Challenge

1. The table below shows in both degrees Celsius and degrees Fahrenheit the freezing and boiling points of pure ethanol.

Ethanol	Celsius (°C)	Fahrenheit (°F)
Freezing Point	–114	–173
Boiling Point	78	173

On a separate sheet of paper, draw two number lines without increments. On one, divide the line into even increments, then plot and label the two Celsius temperatures. On the other line, first plot and label the two Fahrenheit temperatures so that they align with the two Celsius temperatures on the first number line. Then divide the second number line into even increments. What do you notice about the size of the Fahrenheit and Celsius degrees?

_____

2. The following table shows average planting depths and flowering heights for several bulbs.

Bulb	Planting Depth (in.)	Height (in.)
Miniature Iris	3	5
Hyacinth	6	9
Trumpet Daffodil	6	18
Peacock Tulip	6	8
Perennial Tulip	7	21
Daffodil	6	12
Bluebell	4	12

a. Write the depths as integers._____

b. List those integers from least to greatest.

_____

c. Write the heights as integers._____

d. List those integers from least to greatest.

_____

e. Identify any opposites on your list.

_____

Greatest Common Factor

Practice and Problem Solving: A/B

List the factors of each number.

1. 5

2. 15

3. 60

_____

4. 6

5. 12

6. 36

_____

Find the *greatest common factor* (GCF) for each pair of numbers.

7. 6 and 9

8. 4 and 8

9. 8 and 12

_____

10. 6 and 15

11. 10 and 15

12. 9 and 12

_____

Write the sum of the numbers as the product of their GCF and another sum.

13. $44 + 40 =$

14. $15 + 81 =$

_____

15. $13 + 52 =$

16. $64 + 28 =$

_____

Solve.

17. A jewelry maker will use 24 jade beads and 30 teak beads to make necklaces. Each necklace will have the same numbers of jade beads and teak beads. What is the greatest number of necklaces she can make? How many beads of each type are on each necklace?

_____

18. The marine-life store would like to set up fish tanks that contain equal numbers of angel fish, swordtails, and guppies. What is the greatest number of tanks that can be set up if the store has 12 angel fish, 24 swordtails, and 30 guppies?

_____

Greatest Common Factor

Practice and Problem Solving: C

Find the factors and the greatest common factor for each set of numbers.

1. 250, 45, 30

_____

_____

_____

2. 375, 66, 33

_____

3. 76, 21, 14

_____

_____

_____

4. 1260, 36, 18

_____

_____

_____

Are the following numbers prime? Explain.

5. 9

_____

_____

6. 15

_____

_____

7. 23

_____

_____

8. 25

_____

_____

9. 29

_____

_____

10. 31

_____

_____

Name _____ Date _____ Class_____

Greatest Common Factor
Practice and Problem Solving: D

Write the factors. The first one is done for you.

1. 6

   <u>**1, 2, 3, and 6**</u>

2. 10

   _____

3. 18

   _____

Write the *greatest common factor* (GCF) of both numbers. First, write the factors. Then, find the *greatest* factor that is common to *both* numbers. The first one is done for you.

4. 12 and 18

   Factors of 12: <u>**1, 2, 3, 4, 6, and 12**</u>

   Factors of 18: <u>**1, 2, 3, 6, 9, and 18**</u>

   Compare the factors:

   <u>**1, 2, 3, 4, 6, and 12**</u>

   <u>**1, 2, 3, 6, 9, and 18**</u>

   Greatest common factor? <u>**6**</u>

5. 6 and 20

   Factors of 6: _____

   Factors of 20: _____

   Compare the factors:

   _____

   _____

   Greatest common factor? _____

6. 25 and 80

   Factors of 25: _____

   Factors of 80: _____

   _____

   GCF: _____

7. 27 and 45

   Factors of 27: _____

   Factors of 45: _____

   _____

   GCF: _____

Write the product as the GCF of both numbers times a sum. Use the distributive principle. The first one is done for you.

8. 9 + 24

   GCF of 9 and 24: <u>**3**</u>

   <u>**3**</u> × (<u>**3**</u> + <u>**8**</u>)

9. 15 + 42

   GCF of 15 and 42: _____

   _____ × (_____ + _____)

Solve using the GCF.

10. A gift shop wants to make gift baskets for its regular customers. There are 24 bottles of shampoo, 36 tubes of hand lotion, and 60 bars of soap. The same number of each item should be in each basket. What is the greatest number of baskets that can be made?

_____

Greatest Common Factor
Reteach

The *greatest common factor*, or GCF, is the largest number that is the factor of two or more numbers.

To find the GCF, first write the factors of each number.

Example

Find the GCF of 18 and 24.

Solution Write the factors of 18 and 24. Highlight the *largest* number that is common to both lists of factors.

Factors of 18: 1, 2, 3, **6**, 9, and 18

Factors of 24: 1, 2, 3, 4, **6**, 8, **12**, and 24

The GCF of 18 and 24 is 6.

This process works the same way for more than two numbers.

Find the GCF.

1. 32 and 48

2. 18 and 36

3. 28, 56, and 84

4. 30, 45, and 75

_____ _____ _____ _____

The *distributive principle* can be used with the GCF to rewrite a sum of two or more numbers.

Example
Write 30 + 70 as the product of the GCF of 30 and 70 and a sum.

Solution

Step 1 Find the GCF of 30 and 70.

Factors of 30: 1, 2, 3, 5, 6, **10**, 15, and 30

Factors of 70: 1, 2, 5, 7, **10**, 14, 35, and 70. The GCF is 10.

Step 2 Write "10 × (? + ?)." To find the questions marks, divide: 30 ÷ 10 = 3; 70 ÷ 10 = 7

Step 3 So, 30 + 70 can be written as 10 × (3 + 7).

Rewrite each sum as a product of the GCF and a new sum.

5. 9 + 15 =

6. 100 + 350 =

7. 12 + 18 + 21 =

_____ _____ _____

LESSON 2-1 **Greatest Common Factor**
Reading Strategies: Follow a Procedure

Numbers you multiply together are called **factors.** When you multiply factors together, the answer is called the **product.**

Answer each question.

1. Is 2 a factor of 8? Why or why not?

_____

2. Is 3 a factor of 8? Why or why not?

_____

The word **common** means "shared." All the students in a class who have blue eyes have eye color in common.
Whole numbers may share the same factors. Shared factors are called **common factors.**

These are the factor pairs for 12 and 18.

12: 1 • 12 2 • 6 3 • 4

18: 1 • 18 2 • 9 3 • 6

The largest factor that two or more whole numbers share is called the **greatest common factor.**

Answer the following questions.

3. List all of the factors for 12._____

4. List all of the factors for 18._____

5. Find the factors that 12 and 18 share in common._____

6. What is the greatest common factor for 12 and 18?

_____

7. List the steps you use to find the greatest common factor of two numbers.

_____

_____

LESSON
2-1

Greatest Common Factor
Success for English Learners

Problem 1

Find the *factors* of 16 and 24.

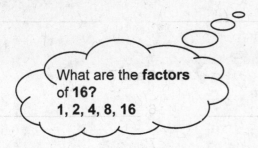
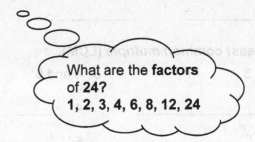

Factors of 16: 1, 2,   4,   **8**, and 16

Factors of 24: 1, 2, 3, 4, 6, **8**, 12,   and 24

Problem 2

Find the *greatest common factor* (or GCF) of 16 and 24.

What are the **common factors**? ⟶ 1, 2, 4, and 8

What is the *greatest* common factor? ⟶ **8**

Answer the questions.

1. What are the three steps in finding the GCF of two numbers?

   Step 1: _____

   Step 2: _____

   Step 3: _____

2. How do you know that 8 is the GCF of 16 and 24?

   _____

3. How would you find the GCF of *three* numbers? Show how using 16, 24, and 32.

   _____

   _____

LESSON 2-2	**Least Common Multiple**

Practice and Problem Solving: A/B

List the first three multiples of each number.

1. 3

2. 7

3. 12

4. 200

_____   _____   _____   _____

Find the *least common multiple* (LCM).

5. 2 and 3

6. 4 and 5

7. 6 and 7

2: _____   4: _____   6: _____

3: _____   5: _____   7: _____

8. 2, 3, and 4

9. 5, 6, and 7

10. 8, 9, and 10

2: _____   5: _____   8: _____

3: _____   6: _____   9: _____

4: _____   7: _____   10: _____

Solve.

11. Sixty people are invited to a party. There are 24 cups in a package and 18 napkins in a package. What is the least number of packages of cups and napkins that can be bought if each party guest gets one cup and one napkin?

_____

12. The science club sponsor is ordering caps and shirts for the boys and girls in the science club. There are 45 science club members. If the caps come in packages of 3 and the shirts come in packages of 5, what is the least number of packages of caps and shirts that will need to be ordered?

_____

13. Some hot dogs come in packages of 8. Why would a baker of hot dog buns package 7 hot dog buns to a package?

_____

14. How are the GCF and the LCM alike and different?

_____

LESSON
2-2

Least Common Multiple
Practice and Problem Solving: C

Find the GCF or LCM.

1. Find the GCF of 12 and 20.

   _____

2. Find the LCM of 12 and 20.

   _____

Solve.

3. 12×20

   _____

4. GCF of 12 and 20 × LCM of 12 and 20

   _____

5. What is the relationship of the product of 12 and 20 to the product of the GCF and the LCM of the two numbers?

   _____

Use the rule you explained in Exercise 5 to solve these problems.

6. The product of two numbers is 36. The GCF of the two numbers is 9. What is the LCM?

   _____

7. The product of the GCF and the LCM of two numbers is 12. Give one possible pair of values for the two numbers.

   _____

Solve.

8. Write 6 multiples of each fraction.

   $\frac{1}{3}$: _____

   $\frac{2}{5}$: _____

9. What is the LCM of $\frac{1}{3}$ and $\frac{2}{5}$? _____

10. Use the result of Exercise 5. What is the GCF of $\frac{1}{3}$ and $\frac{2}{5}$? _____

11. Show that your answer to Exercise 10 gives one of the multiples in Exercise 8. (*Hint*: What would you multiply by your Exercise 10 answer to get $\frac{1}{3}$ and $\frac{2}{5}$?)

   _____

Name _____ Date _____ Class _____

 LESSON 2-2

Least Common Multiple

Practice and Problem Solving: D

List the first 5 multiples. The first one is done for you.

1. 4

   4, 8, 12, 16, 20

2. 13

   _____

3. 250

   _____

Write the multiples of each number until you see the *least common* multiple (LCM) for *all* of the numbers. Then, write the LCM. The first one is done for you.

4. 5 and 8

   Multiples of 5: **5, 10, 15, 20, 25, 30, 35, 40**

   Multiples of 8: **8, 16, 24, 32, 40**

   Least common multiple: **40**

5. 6 and 10

   Multiples of 6: _____

   Multiples of 10: _____

   Least common multiple: _____

6. 3 and 15

   3: _____

   15: _____

   LCM: _____

7. 2, 3, and 5

   2: _____

   3: _____

   5: _____

   LCM: _____

Use the table to solve the problems. The first one is done for you.

8. You want to have an equal number of plastic cups and paper plates. What is the least number of packs of each you can buy?

   Count cups by 15's and plates by 10's.

   Cups: 15, 30; plates: 10, 20, 30

   The least number is 2 packs of cups

   and 3 packs of plates.

9. You want to invite 48 people to a party. What is the least number of invitations and napkins you should buy to have one for each person and none left over?

   _____

   _____

   _____

Party Supplies

Item	Number per Pack
Invitations	12
Balloons	30
Paper plates	10
Paper napkins	24
Plastic cups	15
Noise makers	5

Least Common Multiple
Reteach

The smallest number that is a multiple of two or more numbers
is called the least common multiple (LCM) of those numbers.

To find the least common multiple of 3, 6, and 8, list the multiples
for each number and put a circle around the LCM in the three lists.

Multiples of 3: 3, 6, 9, 12, 15, 18, 21, 24

Multiples of 6: 6, 12, 18, 24, 30, 36, 42

Multiples of 8: 8, 16, 24, 32, 40, 48, 56

So 24 is the LCM of 3, 6, and 8.

**List the multiples of each number to help you find the least common
multiple of each group.**

1. 2 and 9

   Multiples of 2:

   _____

   Multiples of 9:

   _____

   LCM: _____

2. 4 and 6

   Multiples of 4:

   _____

   Multiples of 6:

   _____

   LCM: _____

3. 4 and 10

   Multiples of 4:

   _____

   Multiples of 10:

   _____

   LCM: _____

4. 2, 5, and 6

   Multiples of 2:

   _____

   Multiples of 5:

   _____

   Multiples of 6:

   _____

   LCM: _____

5. 3, 4, and 9

   Multiples of 3:

   _____

   Multiples of 4:

   _____

   Multiples of 9:

   _____

   LCM: _____

6. 8, 10, and 12

   Multiples of 8:

   _____

   Multiples of 10:

   _____

   Multiples of 12:

   _____

   LCM: _____

7. Pads of paper come 4 to a box, pencils come 27 to a box, and erasers
   come 12 to a box. What is the least number of kits that can be made
   with paper, pencils, and erasers with no supplies left over?

   _____

Name _____ Date _____ Class _____

Least Common Multiple
Reading Strategies: Understanding Vocabulary

Least means the smallest in size. The person with the least amount of homework has the smallest amount of work to do.

Common means shared. You may have classes in common with some of your friends.

A **multiple** is the product of a number and an integer.

The multiples of 5 are the answers to multiplying numbers by 5.

$1 \times 5 = 5$ $2 \times 5 = 10$ $3 \times 5 = 15$ $4 \times 5 = 20$

The **least common multiple** is the smallest multiple two numbers have in common.

Follow the steps for finding the least common multiple of 5 and 10.

1. List the first 10 multiples of 5.

    _____

2. List the first five multiples of 10. _____

3. What multiples do 5 and 10 have in common? _____

4. Write the *smallest* multiple that 5 and 10 have in common. _____

5. What is the *least common multiple* (LCM) of 5 and 10? _____

6. What is the first step in finding the LCM of two or more numbers?

    _____

7. What is the second step?

    _____

8. How do you know which of the common multiples is the least common multiple?

    _____

9. Write your own definition of the least common multiple. Use 5 and 7 as examples.

    _____

Least Common Multiple

LESSON 2-2

Success for English Learners

Problem 1

What is the *least common multiple* (LCM) of 6 and 9?

Use a **number line.**

Write the **multiples** of 6 *above* the line.

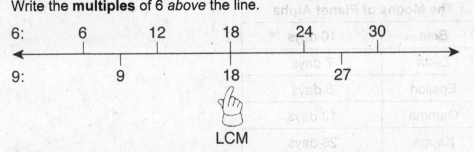

6:          6   12   18   24   30

9:                9   18   27

LCM

Write the **multiples** of 9 *below* the line.

What is the LCM according to the number line?

Problem 2

What is the *least common multiple* (LCM) of 3, 5, and 6?

Use a **table.**

Make a column for each number.

Write the multiples.

3	5	6
3	5	6
6	10	12
9	15	18
12	20	24
15	25	30
18	30	
21	35	
24		
27		
30	LCM = 30	
33		

1. How did you use the number line to find the LCM of 6 and 9?

_____

2. Find the LCM of 8 and 12 using either method.

_____

Factors and Multiples
Challenge

One month is the name for the time it takes the moon to orbit Earth one time. A month is about 30 days. Planet Alpha in another star system has 6 moons, which orbit the planet in the times given in the table.

The Moons of Planet Alpha	
Beta	10 days
Delta	7 days
Epsilon	8 days
Gamma	13 days
Kappa	26 days

Complete the table to show the number of orbits it will take for the moons of Planet Alpha to form a straight line with Planet Alpha and the planetary system's star. See the hint below the table for completing the last row.

Planet Alpha Moons	LCM of Months	Number of Orbits of Each Moon
Beta and Delta	1. _____	2. Beta: _____; 3. Delta: _____
Delta and Epsilon	4. _____	5. Delta: _____; 6. Epsilon: _____
Delta, Gamma, and Epsilon	7. _____	8. Delta: _____; 9. Epsilon: _____; 10. Gamma: _____
Gamma and Kappa	11. _____	12. Gamma: _____; 13. Kappa: _____
All 5 moons	14. _____	15. Beta: _____; 16. Delta: _____; 17. Epsilon: _____; 18. Gamma: _____; 19. Kappa: _____

(*Hint:* To find the LCM of the months of all 5 planets, divide all of the months that are divisible by 2. Keep dividing the months that are divisible by 2 until you get 1. Do the same for all of the months that are divisible by any other numbers, like 7 and 13. When you are unable to divide another number, multiply all of the divisors you used to get the LCM.)

LESSON 3-1

Classifying Rational Numbers

Practice and Problem Solving: A/B

Write each rational number in the form $\frac{a}{b}$, where a and b are integers.

1. 0.3 _____

2. $2\frac{7}{8}$ _____

3. −5 _____

4. 16 _____

5. $-1\frac{3}{4}$ _____

6. −4.5 _____

7. 3 _____

8. 0.11 _____

Place each number in the correct place on the Venn diagram. Then list all the sets of numbers to which each number belongs.

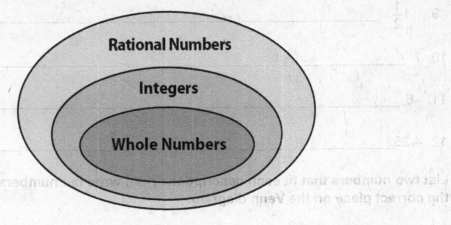

9. −13 _____

10. $\frac{1}{6}$ _____

11. 0 _____

12. 0.99 _____

13. −6.7 _____

14. 34 _____

15. $-14\frac{1}{2}$ _____

LESSON 3-1

Classifying Rational Numbers
Practice and Problem Solving: C

Write each rational number in the form $\frac{a}{b}$, where *a* and *b* are integers.

1. −4

2. 0

3. $5\frac{1}{3}$

4. 6.75

_____   _____   _____   _____

5. $2\frac{1}{8}$

6. −0.35

7. 7.8

8. $-9\frac{3}{5}$

_____   _____   _____   _____

Identify which of the following sets of numbers each number belongs to: rational numbers, integers, whole numbers.

9. $-1\frac{1}{2}$ _____

10. 7 _____

11. −6 _____

12. 4.25 _____

List two numbers that fit each description. Then write the numbers in the correct place on the Venn diagram.

13. Whole numbers greater than 5 _____

14. Integers that are not whole numbers _____

15. Rational numbers less than 0 that are not integers _____

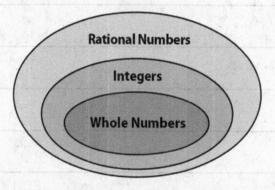

LESSON 3-1 **Classifying Rational Numbers**
Practice and Problem Solving: D

Write each rational number in the form $\frac{a}{b}$, where *a* and *b* are integers.
The first one is done for you.

1. $5\frac{1}{6}$

$\frac{31}{6}$
_____

2. –6

_____

3. 0.97

_____

4. 18

_____

5. 3.3

_____

6. $-2\frac{1}{8}$

_____

Circle the number set(s) to which each number belongs. The first one
is done for you.

7. –9

Whole Numbers   ⟨Integers⟩   ⟨Rational Numbers⟩

8. 0.16

Whole Numbers   Integers   Rational Numbers

9. 146

Whole Numbers   Integers   Rational Numbers

Place each number in the correct place on the Venn diagram.
Then list all the sets of numbers to which each number belongs.
The first one is done for you.

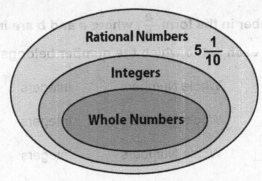

Rational Numbers $5\frac{1}{10}$
Integers
Whole Numbers

10. $5\frac{1}{10}$ rational numbers _____

11. –14 _____

12. 0 _____

Classifying Rational Numbers
Reteach

A rational number is a number that can be written as $\frac{a}{b}$, where a and b are integers and $b \neq 0$. Decimals, fractions, mixed numbers, and integers are all rational numbers.

You can demonstrate a number is rational by writing it in the form $\frac{a}{b}$.

A. $14 = \frac{14}{1}$ Write the whole number over 1.

B. $0.83 = \frac{83}{100}$ Write the decimal as a fraction. Simplify if possible.

C. $5\frac{1}{8} = \frac{41}{8}$ Change the mixed number to an improper fraction.

A Venn diagram is a graphical illustration used to show relationships between various sets of data or groups. Each set or group is represented by an oval, and the relationships among these sets are expressed by their areas of overlap.

- Integers contain the entire set of whole numbers.

- Rational numbers contain the entire sets of integers and whole numbers.

- If a number is a whole number, it is also an integer.

- If a number is an integer, it is to also a rational number.

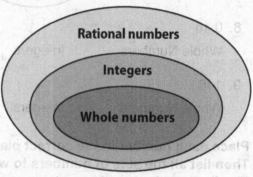

Write each rational number in the form $\frac{a}{b}$, where a and b are integers.

Then circle the name of each set to which the number belongs.

1. −12 _____   Whole Numbers   Integers   Rational Numbers

2. 7.3 _____   Whole Numbers   Integers   Rational Numbers

3. 0.41 _____   Whole Numbers   Integers   Rational Numbers

4. 6 _____   Whole Numbers   Integers   Rational Numbers

5. $3\frac{1}{2}$ _____   Whole Numbers   Integers   Rational Numbers

LESSON 3-1

Classifying Rational Numbers

Reading Strategies: Identify Relationships

You can classify rational numbers when you understand the relationships between number sets.

First, you need to understand the terms *whole numbers, integers* and *rational numbers*.

• A **whole number** is either 0 or a number used when counting.

• An **integer** is either a whole number or the opposite of a whole number.

• A **rational number** is a number that can be written as $\frac{a}{b}$, where a and b are integers and $b \neq 0$.

Use this flowchart to determine to which set(s) a number belongs:

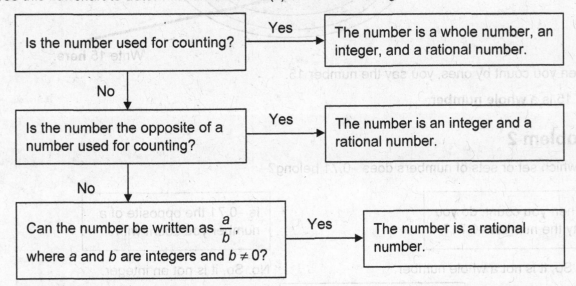

To which number sets does 85 belong?

Because 85 is used for counting, it is a whole number, an integer, and a rational number.

Write the number set(s) to which each number belongs.

1. 0.75

_____

2. −18

_____

3. $\frac{1}{3}$

_____

4. 37

_____

LESSON 3-1

Classifying Rational Numbers
Success for English Learners

Problem 1

Where does the number 15 belong in the diagram?

> The Whole Numbers circle is inside the Integers circle.
> So, whole numbers are integers.

> The Integers circle is inside the Rational Numbers circle.
> So, integers *and* whole numbers are rational numbers.

Rational Numbers

Integers

Whole Numbers

Write 15 **here**.

When you count by ones, you say the number 15.

So, 15 is a **whole number**.

Problem 2

To which set or sets of numbers does −0.71 belong?

> When you count, do you say the number −0.71?

No. So, it is not a whole number.

> Is −0.71 the opposite of a number you count with?

No. So, it is not an integer.

> Can you write the number −0.71 as a fraction?

Yes: $-0.71 = -\dfrac{71}{100}$.

So, −0.71 *is* a rational number.

1. How do you write $5\dfrac{1}{5}$ in the form $\dfrac{a}{b}$?

_____

2. Explain why every whole number is a rational number.

_____

3. Is every integer a whole number? Explain why or why not.

_____

LESSON 3-2 **Identifying Opposites and Absolute Value of Rational Numbers**

Practice and Problem Solving: A/B

Graph each number and its opposite on a number line.

1. 3.5

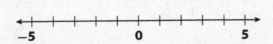

2. −2.5

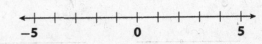

3. $2\frac{1}{2}$

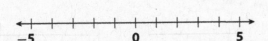

4. $-1\frac{1}{2}$

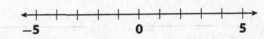

Name the opposite of each number.

5. 4.25 _____

6. $-5\frac{1}{4}$ _____

7. $\frac{1}{2}$ _____

Name the absolute value of each number.

8. $2\frac{1}{3}$ _____

9. −3.85 _____

10. −6.1 _____

The table shows elevations of checkpoints along a marathon route.
Use the table to answer problems 11–13.

Checkpoint	A	B	C	D	E
Elevation (ft)	15.6	17.1	5.2	−6.5	−18.5

11. Write the opposite value of each checkpoint elevation.

_____

12. Which checkpoint is closest to sea level? _____

13. Which checkpoint is furthest from sea level? Explain.

_____

_____

LESSON 3-2

Identifying Opposites and Absolute Value of Rational Numbers

Practice and Problem Solving: C

Write the opposite and the absolute value of each rational number.

1. $-\dfrac{2}{3}$

2. $1\dfrac{1}{7}$

3. -0.89

4. 3.47

_____   _____   _____   _____

5. $\dfrac{7}{5}$

6. $5\dfrac{2}{3}$

7. -4.03

8. -1.11

_____   _____   _____   _____

9. When are the absolute value and the opposite of a rational number equal?

_____

_____

Solve.

10. Ursula says the distance between -5.47 and 5.47 on a number line is equal to $|-5.47|$. Explain her error.

_____

_____

11. The table below shows temperatures of a mixture in a chemistry experiment over 5 days.

Day	Monday	Tuesday	Wednesday	Thursday	Friday
Temperature (°C)	−7.1	−3.4	−1.2	2.1	3.4

On which two days did the mixture's temperature have the same

absolute value? _____

12. Put the integers in the chart above in order from greatest to least and then from greatest to least absolute value.

_____

_____

LESSON 3-2

Identifying Opposites and Absolute Value of Rational Numbers

Practice and Problem Solving: D

Plot each number and its opposite on a number line. The first one is done for you.

1. 1.0

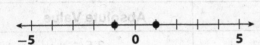

2. –2.0

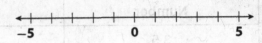

3. $2\frac{1}{2}$

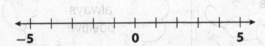

4. $-1\frac{1}{2}$

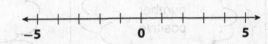

Find the opposite of each number. The first one is done for you.

5. 3 **–3**

6. –4.5 _____

7. $\frac{1}{3}$ _____

Find the absolute value of each number. The first one is done for you.

8. –4.0 **4.0**

9. $-2\frac{1}{2}$ _____

10. $\frac{2}{3}$ _____

Use the table to answer questions 11–14.

Lunch Account Balances					
Student	**Aida**	**BJ**	**Camille**	**Darrin**	**Eric**
Balance	–$1.50	$5.25	$9.00	$7.45	–$0.35

11. Who has the greatest balance? _____

12. What is the opposite of Darrin's balance? _____

13. How much money would Aida need to add to have a

    balance of $0.00? _____

14. How much money would BJ need to spend to have

    a balance of $0.00? _____

LESSON 3-2

Identifying Opposites and Absolute Value of Rational Numbers

Reteach

You can use charts to determine whether the opposites and absolute values of rational numbers are positive or negative.

For positive rational numbers:

Number	Opposite	Absolute Value
3.5	−3.5	3.5
number positive	opposite negative	absolute value always positive

For negative rational numbers:

Number	Opposite	Absolute Value
$-\dfrac{7}{8}$	$\dfrac{7}{8}$	$\dfrac{7}{8}$
number negative	opposite positive	absolute value always positive

Answer each question below.

1. Are the opposite of −6.5 and the absolute value of −6.5 the same?

   Give both. _____

2. Are the opposite of $3\dfrac{2}{5}$ and the absolute value of $3\dfrac{2}{5}$ the same?

   Give both. _____

3. Write a rational number whose opposite and absolute value are

   the same. _____

4. Write a rational number whose opposite and absolute value are

   opposites. _____

Name _____ Date _____ Class_____

Identifying Opposites and Absolute Value of Rational Numbers

Reading Strategies: Use a Graphic Aid

Rational numbers can be decimals or fractions.
They can be positive or negative.

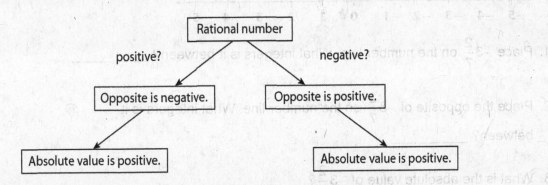

Use the flowchart to determine whether the opposites of the numbers in questions 1 through 4 are positive or negative. Then give the opposite of each number.

1. –2.7 _____

2. $3\frac{1}{8}$ _____

3. $\frac{2}{7}$ _____

4. –0.9 _____

5. Do you need to use a flowchart to determine whether the absolute value of a rational number is positive or negative? Explain.

_____

6. How can you define the absolute value of a rational number using the number line?

_____

_____

Name _____ Date _____ Class _____

Identifying Opposites and Absolute Value of Rational Numbers

Success for English Learners

Problem 1

Use the number line below to answer the questions.

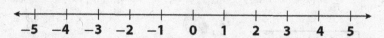

1. Place $-3\frac{2}{7}$ on the number line. What integers is it between? _____

2. Place the opposite of $-3\frac{2}{7}$ on the number line. What integers is it between? _____

3. What is the absolute value of $-3\frac{2}{7}$? _____

4. What is the absolute value of $3\frac{2}{7}$? _____

5. Why do $-3\frac{2}{7}$ and $3\frac{2}{7}$ have the same absolute value?

_____

_____

6. Place a decimal rational number on the number line. Then place its opposite. Give the absolute value for both numbers.

_____

_____

Comparing and Ordering Rational Numbers
Practice and Problem Solving: A/B

Write each fraction as a decimal. Round to the nearest hundredth if necessary.

1. $\frac{3}{8}$ ____

2. $\frac{7}{5}$ ____

3. $\frac{21}{7}$ ____

4. $\frac{5}{3}$ ____

Write each decimal as a fraction or mixed number in simplest form.

5. 0.55 ____

6. 10.6 ____

7. –7.08 ____

Write the numbers in order from least to greatest.

8. 0.5, 0.05, $\frac{5}{8}$ _____

9. 1.3, $1\frac{1}{3}$, 1.34 _____

10. 2.07, $2\frac{7}{10}$, 2.67, –2.67 _____

Solve.

11. Out of 45 times at bat, Raul got 19 hits. Find Raul's batting average as

    a decimal rounded to the nearest thousandth. _____

12. Karen's batting average was 0.444. She was at bat 45 times. How

    many hits did she get? _____

13. To have batting averages over 0.500, how may hits in 45 times at bat

    would Raul and Karen need? _____

14. A car travels at 65 miles per hour. Going through construction, it

    travels at $\frac{3}{5}$ this speed. Write this fraction as a decimal and find the

    speed. _____

15. A city's sales tax is 0.07. Write this decimal as a fraction and tell how

    many cents of tax are on each dollar. _____

16. A ream of paper contains 500 sheets of paper. Norm has 373 sheets
    of paper left from a ream. Express the portion of a ream Norm has as a

    fraction and as a decimal. _____

Comparing and Ordering Rational Numbers
Practice and Problem Solving: C

First, tell whether each fraction will be a decimal greater than, equal to, or less than 1. Then, write each fraction as a decimal. Round to the nearest hundredth, if necessary.

1. $\frac{5}{8}$ _____

2. $\frac{11}{5}$ _____

3. $\frac{17}{17}$ _____

4. $\frac{4}{7}$ _____

First, tell whether each decimal is a fraction or a mixed number. Then, write it in simplest form.

5. 0.85 _____

6. 3.8 _____

7. –11.16 _____

Write the score as a decimal rounded to the nearest thousandth. Then answer the question.

8. On her driver's test, Mrs. Lynch got 26 out of 30 questions correct. The

   passing grade was 0.85. Did Mrs. Lynch pass? _____

9. If she got 25 out of 30 questions correct, would she pass? _____

Write the numbers in order from least to greatest.

10. 5.78, $-5\frac{7}{8}$, –5.9 _____

11. $\frac{3}{7}$, 0.45, $\frac{4}{9}$ _____

12. –0.38, $-\frac{3}{8}$, –0.04 _____

Solve.

13. In the 2008 election, there were 28 "blue" states and 22 "red" states. Express the "red" and "blue" states as fractions, in lowest terms, of the total number of states and also as decimals.

    _____

14. A machine produces 75 widgets an hour. How many widgets does it

    produce in 6 minutes? _____

LESSON 3-3

Comparing and Ordering Rational Numbers

Practice and Problem Solving: D

Write each decimal as a fraction or mixed number. The first one is done for you.

1. 0.5 $\frac{5}{10}$ or $\frac{1}{2}$

2. 0.25 _____

3. 0.75 _____

4. 0.4 _____

5. 0.8 _____

6. 1.2 _____

Write each fraction or mixed number as a decimal. The first one is done for you.

7. $\frac{3}{10}$ _____0.3_____

8. $\frac{3}{5}$ _____

9. $1\frac{2}{5}$ _____

Circle the letter of the best answer.

10. Which of the following sets is written in order from least to greatest?

   A. 0.4, $\frac{7}{10}$, 0.6

   B. $\frac{1}{4}$, 0.5, 0.75

   C. $\frac{7}{10}$, 0.4, 0.6

11. Which of the following sets is written in order from greatest to least?

   A. $\frac{1}{3}$, $1\frac{1}{2}$, $1\frac{3}{4}$

   B. $\frac{2}{5}$, $0.\overline{3}$, 0.3

   C. 0.3, $0.\overline{3}$, $\frac{2}{5}$

Solve.

12. At Franklin Elementary School, $\frac{2}{3}$ of all the students attended the chorus recital on Thursday. On Friday, $\frac{3}{4}$ of all the students attended the basketball game. Which event had the higher attendance?

_____

Comparing and Ordering Rational Numbers
Reteach

You can write decimals as fractions or mixed numbers. A place value table will help you read the decimal. Remember the decimal point is read as the word "and."

To write 0.47 as a fraction, first think about the decimal in words.

Ones	Tenths	Hundredths	Thousandths	Ten Thousandths
0	4	7		

0.47 is read "forty-seven hundredths." The place value of the decimal tells you the denominator is 100.

$$0.47 = \frac{47}{100}$$

To write 8.3 as a mixed number, first think about the decimal in words.

Ones	Tenths	Hundredths	Thousandths	Ten Thousandths
8	3			

8.3 is read "eight and three tenths." The place value of the decimal tells you the denominator is 10. The decimal point is read as the word "and."

$$8.3 = 8\frac{3}{10}$$

Write each decimal as a fraction or mixed number.

1. 0.61 ____

2. 3.43 ____

3. 0.009 ____

4. 4.7 ____

5. 1.5 ____

6. 0.13 ____

7. 5.002 ____

8. 0.021 ____

LESSON
3-3
Comparing and Ordering Rational Numbers
Reading Strategies: Build Vocabulary

The word *repeating* means "something happening over and over." A town hall bell that chimes every hour is an example of a repeating sound.

The word *terminating* means "something that ends." The sixth-grade party will be terminating at 10:00 P.M.

When a fraction is rewritten as a decimal, the result can be a **repeating decimal** or a **terminating decimal**.

In a repeating decimal, sometimes one digit repeats and sometimes more than one digit repeats.

$\dfrac{1}{3}$ ⟶ means $1 \div 3$ $\qquad$ $\dfrac{1}{4}$ ⟶ means $1 \div 4$

$$\begin{array}{r} 0.333 \\ 3\overline{)1.000} \\ -9 \\ \hline 10 \\ -9 \\ \hline 10 \\ -9 \\ \hline 1 \end{array} \qquad \begin{array}{r} 0.25 \\ 4\overline{)1.00} \\ -8 \\ \hline 20 \\ -20 \\ \hline 0 \end{array}$$

$\dfrac{1}{3} = 0.\overline{3}$ $\qquad\qquad$ $\dfrac{1}{4} = 0.25$

The bar over the 3 means the 3 keeps repeating. $\qquad$ 0.25 is a decimal that terminates.

Write each fraction as a decimal. Then identify each decimal as *terminating* or *repeating*.

1. $\dfrac{1}{6}$ $\qquad\qquad\qquad\qquad\qquad\qquad$ 2. $\dfrac{1}{8}$

_____ $\qquad$ _____

3. $\dfrac{1}{11}$ $\qquad\qquad\qquad\qquad\qquad\qquad$ 4. $\dfrac{2}{9}$

_____ $\qquad$ _____

5. $\dfrac{4}{5}$ $\qquad\qquad\qquad\qquad\qquad\qquad$ 6. $\dfrac{5}{9}$

_____ $\qquad$ _____

7. $\dfrac{1}{2}$ $\qquad\qquad\qquad\qquad\qquad\qquad$ 8. $\dfrac{7}{9}$

LESSON 3-3

Comparing and Ordering Rational Numbers

Success for English Learners

Problem 1

How do I write a decimal as a fraction?

Place the number in a place-value chart.

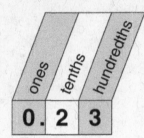 $\Rightarrow$ $\dfrac{23}{100}$

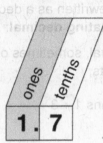 $\Rightarrow$ $1\dfrac{7}{10}$

Problem 2

How do I write a fraction as a decimal?

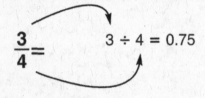

$\dfrac{3}{4} =$ $\qquad$ $3 \div 4 = 0.75$

$5\dfrac{2}{3} =$ $\qquad$ $2 \div 3 = 0.666...$ so $\boxed{5\dfrac{2}{3} = 5.\overline{6}}$

Use 3 dots or a bar over a number to show that it repeats.

1. How can you tell the difference between a terminating decimal and a repeating decimal?

_____

_____

2. Describe one method you can use to write a fraction as a decimal.

_____

MODULE 3

Rational Numbers
Challenge

1. A food processing plant packs oranges into boxes. The weight of the oranges to be packed and the number of boxes available on each day of a week are shown in the table below.

Day	Weight of Oranges (lb)	Number of Boxes
Monday	113	45
Tuesday	116	43
Wednesday	144	50
Thursday	129	40
Friday	109	35

Each day, the oranges are packed so that every box weighs the same. The food processing plant will not ship a box if the weight of the box is greater than 3 pounds.

a. On which of the days in the five-day period shown will the boxes of oranges be too heavy to ship?

_____

b. Of the boxes that ship, the heaviest boxes sell for the highest price. On which day will the boxes packed sell for the highest price?

_____

2. The inequality below is incorrect. The five numbers are not in the correct order.

$$2 \le -\frac{1}{8} \le -10 \le -0.125 \le -\frac{15}{2}$$

You can correct the inequality by swapping the numbers. Each time you swap a pair of numbers, it counts as one "move."

What is the minimum number of "moves" that are required to make the above inequality correct?

_____

What is the correct inequality?

_____

LESSON
4-1

Applying GCF and LCM to Fraction Operations
Practice and Problem Solving: A/B

Multiply. Use the greatest common factor to write each answer in simplest form.

1. $\dfrac{2}{3} \cdot \dfrac{6}{7}$

2. $\dfrac{3}{4} \cdot \dfrac{2}{3}$

3. $\dfrac{8}{21} \cdot \dfrac{7}{10}$

_____ _____ _____

4. $24 \cdot \dfrac{5}{6}$

5. $32 \cdot \dfrac{3}{8}$

6. $21 \cdot \dfrac{3}{7}$

_____ _____ _____

Add or subtract. Use the least common multiple as the denominator.

7. $\dfrac{4}{15} + \dfrac{5}{6}$

8. $\dfrac{5}{12} - \dfrac{3}{20}$

9. $\dfrac{3}{5} + \dfrac{3}{20}$

_____ _____ _____

10. $\dfrac{5}{8} - \dfrac{5}{24}$

11. $3\dfrac{5}{12} + 1\dfrac{3}{8}$

12. $2\dfrac{9}{10} - 1\dfrac{7}{18}$

_____ _____ _____

Solve.

13. Louis spent 12 hours last week practicing guitar. If $\dfrac{1}{4}$ of the time
was spent practicing chords, how much time did Louis spend practicing chords?

_____

14. Angie and her friends ate $\dfrac{3}{4}$ of a pizza. Her brother Joe ate $\dfrac{2}{3}$ of what
was left. How much of the original pizza did Joe eat?

_____

LESSON 4-1

Applying GCF and LCM to Fraction Operations

Practice and Problem Solving: C

Multiply. Use the greatest common factor to write each answer in simplest form.

1. $\dfrac{4}{9} \cdot \dfrac{3}{8}$

2. $\dfrac{7}{9} \cdot \dfrac{3}{14}$

3. $18 \cdot \dfrac{7}{9}$

_____   _____   _____

Add or subtract. Use the least common multiple as the denominator.

4. $\dfrac{7}{15} + \dfrac{5}{6}$

5. $1\dfrac{7}{12} - \dfrac{3}{20}$

6. $\dfrac{2}{5} + \dfrac{7}{20}$

_____   _____   _____

Solve.

7. A recipe calls for the following ingredients.

   3 c flour _____ $\dfrac{1}{2}$ t salt _____

   $\dfrac{3}{4}$ c sugar _____   4 c fruit _____

   2 T butter _____

   To make $\dfrac{2}{3}$ of the recipe, how much of each ingredient should you

   use? Write the revised amount on the line next to each ingredient.

8. Half of a pizza was broccoli and half was mushroom. George ate $\dfrac{2}{3}$

   of the broccoli part and $\dfrac{1}{4}$ of the mushroom part. How much of the

   pizza did he eat?

   _____

9. What else could you call the least common multiple in an addition or subtraction problem involving fractions?

   _____

Applying GCF and LCM to Fraction Operations

LESSON 4-1

Practice and Problem Solving: D

Multiply. Use the greatest common factor to write each answer in simplest form. The first one is done for you.

1. $\frac{2}{3} \cdot \frac{3}{4}$
2. $\frac{12}{15} \cdot \frac{3}{4}$
3. $24 \cdot \frac{5}{8}$

$$\frac{2}{3} \cdot \frac{3}{4} = \frac{6}{12} = \frac{1}{2}$$

_____

Add or subtract. Use the least common multiple as the denominator. The first one is done for you.

4. $\frac{11}{12} - \frac{3}{20}$
5. $\frac{3}{5} + \frac{9}{20}$
6. $\frac{11}{15} + \frac{2}{3}$

_____   _____   _____

Solve. The first one is done for you.

7. Lyza used 24 ounces of spaghetti to make a recipe. If she wanted to make $\frac{1}{4}$ as much, how much spaghetti should she use?

   $$\frac{1}{4} \cdot 24 = 6; \; 6 \text{ ounces}$$

   _____

8. Noah spent 25 hours working on his car. He spent $\frac{4}{5}$ of his time working on the transmission. How much time did Noah spend working on the transmission?

   _____

9. Miguel made lemonade. He mixed $\frac{1}{3}$ cup of lemon juice with $\frac{4}{9}$ cup of water. How much more water than lemon juice did Miguel use?

   _____

LESSON 4-1

Applying GCF and LCM to Fraction Operations

Reteach

How to Multiply a Fraction by a Fraction

$$\frac{2}{3} \cdot \frac{3}{8}$$

$$\frac{2}{3} \cdot \frac{3}{8} = \frac{6}{}$$ Multiply numerators.

$$\frac{2}{3} \cdot \frac{3}{8} = \frac{6}{24}$$ Multiply denominators.

$$\frac{6 \div 6}{24 \div 6} = \frac{1}{4}$$ Divide by the greatest common factor (GCF).

The GCF of 6 and 24 is 6.

How to Add or Subtract Fractions

$$\frac{5}{6} + \frac{11}{15}$$

$$\frac{25}{30} + \frac{22}{30}$$ Rewrite over the least common multiple (LCM).

The least common multiple of 6 and 15 is 30.

$$\frac{25}{30} + \frac{22}{30} = \frac{47}{30}$$ Add the numerators.

$$= 1\frac{17}{30}$$ If the sum is an improper fraction, rewrite

it as a mixed number.

Multiply. Use the greatest common factor.

1. $\frac{3}{4} \cdot \frac{7}{9}$

2. $\frac{2}{7} \cdot \frac{7}{9}$

3. $\frac{7}{11} \cdot \frac{22}{28}$

_____   _____   _____

4. $8 \cdot \frac{3}{10}$

5. $\frac{4}{9} \cdot \frac{3}{4}$

6. $\frac{3}{7} \cdot \frac{2}{3}$

_____   _____   _____

Add or subtract. Use the least common multiple.

7. $\frac{7}{9} + \frac{5}{12}$

8. $\frac{21}{24} - \frac{3}{8}$

9. $\frac{11}{15} + \frac{7}{12}$

_____   _____   _____

LESSON 4-1
Applying GCF and LCM to Fraction Operations
Reading Strategies: Use Graphic Aids

You can find the answer to $6 \cdot \frac{2}{3}$ using fraction strips and multiplication.

$$6 \cdot \frac{2}{3} = \frac{12}{3}$$

1. What fractional part of each fraction strip is shaded? _____

2. How many of these fraction strips are there? _____

3. Write a multiplication equation for this picture. _____

You can use fraction strips to find the least common multiple.

$$\frac{3}{4} + \frac{1}{3}$$

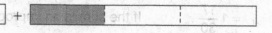

$$\frac{3}{4} + \frac{1}{3} = \frac{9}{12} + \frac{4}{12}$$

So, $\frac{3}{4} + \frac{1}{3} = \frac{13}{12} = 1\frac{1}{12}$.

Find the products. Use the greatest common factor. Write each answer in simplest form.

4. $6 \cdot \frac{1}{9}$

5. $3 \cdot \frac{5}{9}$

6. $2 \cdot \frac{11}{14}$

_____ _____ _____

Find the sums. Use the least common multiple. Write each answer in simplest form.

7. $\frac{1}{4} + \frac{5}{12}$

8. $\frac{2}{9} + \frac{7}{12}$

9. $\frac{9}{10} + \frac{1}{4}$

_____ _____ _____

Applying GCF and LCM to Fraction Operations

Success for English Learners

Problem 1

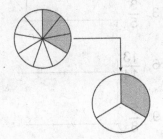

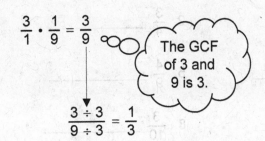

$$\frac{3}{1} \cdot \frac{1}{9} = \frac{3}{9}$$

The GCF of 3 and 9 is 3.

$$\frac{3 \div 3}{9 \div 3} = \frac{1}{3}$$

Problem 2

$$\frac{2}{4} + \frac{2}{3}$$

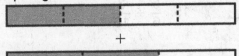

2 of **4 parts**

2 of **3 parts**

THINK:
What is the LCM
of 4 and 3?

$$\frac{2}{4} + \frac{2}{3} = \frac{6}{12} + \frac{8}{12} = \frac{14}{12}$$

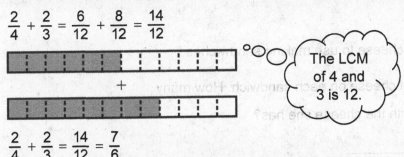

The LCM of 4 and 3 is 12.

$$\frac{2}{4} + \frac{2}{3} = \frac{14}{12} = \frac{7}{6}$$

1. Compare the steps you take to multiply fractions to the steps you take
   to add fractions.

   _____

   _____

   _____

2. Explain how using the greatest common factor and the least common
   multiple helps you to multiply, and add or subtract fractions.

   _____

   _____

   _____

LESSON 4-2

Dividing Fractions

Practice and Problem Solving: A/B

Find the reciprocal.

1. $\dfrac{5}{7}$ _____

2. $\dfrac{3}{4}$ _____

3. $\dfrac{3}{5}$ _____

4. $\dfrac{1}{10}$ _____

5. $\dfrac{4}{9}$ _____

6. $\dfrac{13}{14}$ _____

7. $\dfrac{7}{12}$ _____

8. $\dfrac{3}{10}$ _____

9. $\dfrac{5}{8}$ _____

Divide. Write each answer in simplest form.

10. $\dfrac{5}{6} \div \dfrac{1}{2}$ _____

11. $\dfrac{7}{8} \div \dfrac{2}{3}$ _____

12. $\dfrac{9}{10} \div \dfrac{3}{4}$ _____

13. $\dfrac{3}{4} \div 9$ _____

14. $\dfrac{6}{9} \div \dfrac{6}{7}$ _____

15. $\dfrac{5}{6} \div \dfrac{3}{10}$ _____

16. $\dfrac{5}{6} \div \dfrac{3}{4}$ _____

17. $\dfrac{5}{8} \div \dfrac{3}{5}$ _____

18. $\dfrac{21}{32} \div \dfrac{7}{8}$ _____

Solve.

19. Mrs. Marks has $\dfrac{3}{4}$ pound of cheese to use making sandwiches.

   She uses about $\dfrac{1}{32}$ pound of cheese on each sandwich. How many

   sandwiches can she make with the cheese she has?

   _____

20. In England, mass is measured in units called *stones*. One pound

   equals $\dfrac{1}{14}$ of a stone. A cat weighs $\dfrac{3}{4}$ stone. How many pounds does

   the cat weigh?

   _____

21. Typographers measure font sizes in units called *points*. One point is

   equal to $\dfrac{1}{72}$ inch. Esmeralda is typing a research paper on her

   computer. She wants the text on the title page to be $\dfrac{1}{2}$ inch tall. What

   font size should she use?

   _____

LESSON 4-2

Dividing Fractions

Practice and Problem Solving: C

Find the reciprocal. Tell whether it is greater or less than 1.

1. $\dfrac{3}{7}$ _____

2. $\dfrac{3}{4}$ _____

3. $\dfrac{8}{5}$ _____

4. $\dfrac{1}{11}$ _____

5. $\dfrac{8}{9}$ _____

6. $\dfrac{13}{4}$ _____

7. If a fraction is less than 1, what do you know about its reciprocal?

_____

8. If a fraction is greater than 1, what do you know about its reciprocal?

_____

9. What is the product of a number and its reciprocal? _____

Divide. Write each answer in simplest form.

10. $\dfrac{5}{6} \div \dfrac{2}{3}$ _____

11. $\dfrac{7}{8} \div \dfrac{3}{5}$ _____

12. $\dfrac{8}{9} \div \dfrac{2}{5}$ _____

13. $\dfrac{2}{3} \div \dfrac{4}{5}$ _____

14. $\dfrac{5}{7} \div \dfrac{7}{9}$ _____

15. $\dfrac{3}{5} \div \dfrac{9}{11}$ _____

Answer each question.

16. In problems 10–12, the dividend is greater than the divisor. What do you know about the quotients?

_____

17. In questions 13–15, the divisor is greater than the dividend. What do you know about the quotients?

_____

18. Jonathan has $1\dfrac{3}{4}$ hours to practice guitar. If he spends $\dfrac{1}{8}$ hour on each song, how many songs can Jonathan practice? For how many minutes does he practice each song?

_____

Dividing Fractions
Practice and Problem Solving:

LESSON 4-2

Dividing Fractions

Practice and Problem Solving: D

Find the reciprocal. The first one is done for you.

1. $\dfrac{2}{3}$ ___ $\dfrac{3}{2}$

2. $\dfrac{7}{9}$ _____

3. $\dfrac{8}{5}$ _____

4. $\dfrac{1}{9}$ _____

5. $\dfrac{9}{10}$ _____

6. $\dfrac{3}{10}$ _____

7. $\dfrac{4}{7}$ _____

8. $\dfrac{8}{1}$ _____

9. $\dfrac{6}{7}$ _____

Divide. Write each answer in simplest form. The first one is done for you.

10. $\dfrac{3}{4} \div \dfrac{1}{2}$

$\dfrac{3}{4} \cdot \dfrac{2}{1} = \dfrac{6}{4} = 1\dfrac{1}{2}$

11. $\dfrac{7}{10} \div \dfrac{2}{3}$

12. $\dfrac{5}{6} \div \dfrac{3}{4}$

13. $\dfrac{3}{10} \div \dfrac{5}{6}$

14. $\dfrac{5}{9} \div \dfrac{5}{7}$

15. $\dfrac{7}{10} \div \dfrac{5}{6}$

16. $\dfrac{7}{8} \div \dfrac{3}{4}$

17. $\dfrac{11}{12} \div \dfrac{2}{3}$

18. $\dfrac{5}{7} \div \dfrac{10}{13}$

Solve. The first one has been started for you.

19. Each package of dried fruit contains $\dfrac{3}{16}$ of a pound. Mr. Lopez has 4 pounds of dried fruit. How many packages can he fill?

$4 \div \dfrac{3}{16} = 4 \bullet$ ____ $= \dfrac{\quad}{3} =$ _____ packages

20. One inch is $\dfrac{1}{12}$ of a foot. Eunice has a puppy that is $\dfrac{3}{4}$ of a foot tall. How many inches tall is her puppy?

_____

21. One minute is $\dfrac{1}{60}$ of an hour. What part of an hour is 12 minutes?

_____

LESSON 4-2

Dividing Fractions
Reteach

Two numbers are reciprocals if their product is 1.

$\frac{2}{3}$ and $\frac{3}{2}$ are reciprocals because $\frac{2}{3} \cdot \frac{3}{2} = \frac{6}{6} = 1$.

Dividing by a number is the same as multiplying by its reciprocal.

$$\frac{1}{4} \div \frac{1}{2} = \frac{1}{2} \quad \longrightarrow \quad \frac{1}{4} \cdot \frac{2}{1} = \frac{1}{2}$$

So, you can use reciprocals to divide by fractions.

Find $\frac{2}{3} \div \frac{1}{4}$.

First, rewrite the expression as a multiplication expression.

Use the reciprocal of the divisor: $\frac{1}{4} \cdot \frac{4}{1} = 1$.

$$\frac{2}{3} \div \frac{1}{4} = \frac{2}{3} \cdot \frac{4}{1}$$
$$= \frac{8}{3}$$
$$= 2\frac{2}{3}$$

Think: 6 thirds is 2, and 2 of the 8 thirds are left over.

Rewrite each division expression as a multiplication expression. Then find the value of the expression. Write each answer in simplest form.

1. $\frac{1}{4} \div \frac{1}{3}$

2. $\frac{1}{2} \div \frac{1}{4}$

3. $\frac{3}{8} \div \frac{1}{2}$

4. $\frac{1}{3} \div \frac{3}{4}$

Divide. Write each answer in simplest form.

5. $\frac{1}{5} \div \frac{1}{2}$

6. $\frac{1}{6} \div \frac{2}{3}$

7. $\frac{1}{8} \div \frac{2}{5}$

8. $\frac{1}{8} \div \frac{1}{2}$

LESSON 4-2

Dividing Fractions

Reading Strategies: Use Models

Bar models can help you picture dividing by fractions.

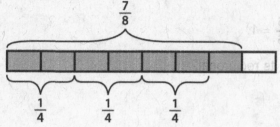

What is $\frac{7}{8} \div \frac{1}{4}$? Think: How many one-fourths are in $\frac{7}{8}$?

Use the picture to answer each question.

1. How many whole groups of $\frac{1}{4}$ are in $\frac{7}{8}$? _____

   What fraction of a group of $\frac{1}{4}$ is left? _____

2. $\frac{7}{8} \div \frac{1}{4}$ = _____

Instead of dividing, multiply by the reciprocal. Think: $\frac{7}{8}$ four times.

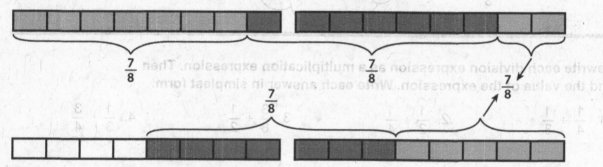

Use the picture to answer each question.

3. How many whole bars are shaded? _____

4. How many additional eighths of a bar are shaded? _____

   What is this fraction in simplest form? _____

5. All together, how many bars are shaded? _____

6. Compare the multiplication and division examples. What do you notice

   about the answer you get when you divide by $\frac{1}{4}$ or multiply by 4?

   _____

LESSON 4-2 Dividing Fractions
Success for English Learners

Problem 1

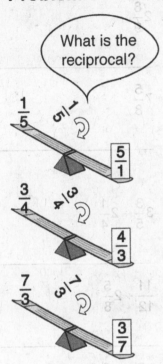

Problem 2

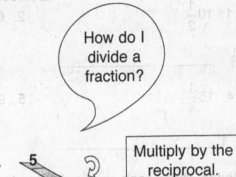

$\frac{4}{5} \div 5$

$\frac{4}{5} \cdot$

$\frac{4}{5} \cdot \frac{1}{5} = \frac{4}{25}$

Multiply by the reciprocal.

1. How do you find the reciprocal of a fraction?

_____

_____

2. Explain the steps you follow to divide $\frac{5}{8}$ by $\frac{1}{3}$.

_____

_____

3. You multiply any fraction times its reciprocal. What is the product?
   Give an example.

_____

_____

LESSON 4-3

Dividing Mixed Numbers

Practice and Problem Solving: A/B

Find the reciprocal. Show that the product of the mixed number and its reciprocal is 1.

1. $10\frac{1}{2}$

2. $6\frac{3}{7}$

3. $2\frac{8}{9}$

_____

_____

_____

4. $15\frac{1}{4}$

5. $9\frac{2}{3}$

6. $7\frac{5}{8}$

_____

_____

_____

Divide. Write each answer in simplest form.

7. $\frac{8}{10} \div 1\frac{5}{6}$

8. $2 \div 1\frac{6}{7}$

9. $3\frac{3}{5} \div 2\frac{1}{4}$

_____

_____

_____

10. $4\frac{1}{2} \div 2\frac{3}{8}$

11. $5\frac{5}{6} \div 3\frac{1}{6}$

12. $\frac{11}{12} \div 2\frac{5}{8}$

_____

_____

_____

13. $1\frac{9}{13} \div \frac{3}{8}$

14. $6\frac{4}{5} \div 3\frac{2}{9}$

15. $9\frac{2}{3} \div 6\frac{8}{9}$

_____

_____

_____

Write each situation as a division problem. Then solve.

16. A concrete patio is $5\frac{2}{3}$ feet wide. It has an area of $36\frac{5}{6}$ square feet.

Is the concrete slab long enough to fit a 7-foot picnic table without placing the table along the diagonal of the patio? Explain.

_____

_____

17. The area of a mirror is 225 square inches, and its width is $13\frac{3}{4}$ inches.

Will the mirror fit in a space that is 15 inches by 16 inches? Explain.

_____

_____

18. Barney has $16\frac{1}{5}$ yards of fabric. To make an elf costume, he needs

$5\frac{2}{5}$ yards of fabric. How many costumes can Barney make?

_____

LESSON 4-3

Dividing Mixed Numbers

Practice and Problem Solving: C

Solve.

1. Vanessa buys a strip of 25 postage stamps. The strip of stamps is $21\frac{7}{8}$ inches long. How long is a strip after Vanessa uses 1 stamp?

   _____

2. Hasan has $18\frac{3}{4}$ yards of fabric. It takes $3\frac{1}{6}$ yards to make a pillowcase. Hasan plans to make as many pillowcases as he can. How many yards of fabric will be left over?

   _____

3. Takafumi is hiking on a path that is $5\frac{7}{8}$ miles long. There are 6 markers evenly posted along the path. Takafumi arrives at the 4th marker. How many miles has he hiked so far?

   _____

4. Yuki has a ribbon that is $11\frac{1}{4}$ feet long. She divides it into pieces that are each $1\frac{7}{8}$ feet long. She uses three pieces to make a bow. How many bows can she make in all?

   _____

5. Mrs. Lemke has $10\frac{2}{3}$ ounces of fertilizer for her plants. She plans to use $\frac{3}{4}$ ounce of fertilizer on each plant. After she puts fertilizer on as many plants as she can, how much fertilizer will be left over?

   _____

6. Gabriel has $15\frac{5}{8}$ pounds of clay. He will use $\frac{7}{10}$ pound to make each bowl. After making 8 bowls, Gabriel wonders how many more bowls he can make. How many more bowls can he make? Explain how you know.

   _____

   _____

   _____

LESSON 4-3

Dividing Mixed Numbers

Practice and Problem Solving: D

Show how to write each mixed number as an improper fraction. Then find the reciprocal. The first one is done for you.

1. $9\frac{1}{2}$

$$\frac{(9 \times 2) + 1}{2} = \frac{19}{2}$$

The reciprocal is $\frac{2}{19}$.

2. $5\frac{3}{7}$

3. $1\frac{8}{9}$

4. $14\frac{1}{4}$

5. $8\frac{2}{3}$

6. $6\frac{5}{8}$

Divide. Write each answer in simplest form. The first one is done for you.

7. $\frac{7}{10} \div 1\frac{2}{6}$

$$\frac{7}{10} \div \frac{8}{6} = \frac{7}{10} \times \frac{6}{8} = \frac{42}{80} = \frac{21}{40}$$

8. $2 \div 1\frac{5}{7}$

9. $4\frac{3}{5} \div 2\frac{2}{5}$

10. $\frac{11}{12} \div 1\frac{3}{4}$

Write a division expression for each problem. Then solve. The first one is done for you.

11. Larry has $9\frac{3}{5}$ yards of fabric. He will use $2\frac{2}{5}$ yards to make each vest. How many vests can Larry make?

$$9\frac{3}{5} \div 2\frac{2}{5} = \frac{48}{5} \div \frac{12}{5} = \frac{48}{5} \times \frac{5}{12} = \frac{48}{12} = 4$$

Larry can make ____4____ vests.

12. A patio has an area of $20\frac{5}{6}$ ft², and the width is $3\frac{1}{2}$ feet. What is the length of the patio?

_____ The patio is _____ feet long.

LESSON 4-3

Dividing Mixed Numbers

Reteach

Two numbers are **reciprocals** if their product is 1.

$\dfrac{7}{3}$ and $\dfrac{3}{7}$ are reciprocals because $\dfrac{7}{3} \times \dfrac{3}{7} = 1$.

Write a mixed number as an improper fraction to find its reciprocal.

$2\dfrac{3}{4}$ and $\dfrac{4}{11}$ are reciprocals because $2\dfrac{3}{4} = \dfrac{11}{4}$ and $\dfrac{11}{4} \times \dfrac{4}{11} = 1$.

To find $2\dfrac{3}{4} \div 1\dfrac{3}{4}$, first rewrite the mixed numbers as improper fractions.

$$\dfrac{11}{4} \div \dfrac{7}{4}$$

Next, rewrite the expression as a multiplication expression and replace the divisor with its reciprocal.

$$\dfrac{11}{4} \times \dfrac{4}{7}$$

Solve. Write your answer in simplest form.

$$2\dfrac{3}{4} \div 1\dfrac{3}{4} = \dfrac{11}{4} \div \dfrac{7}{4} = \dfrac{11}{4} \times \dfrac{4}{7} = \dfrac{11}{7} = 1\dfrac{4}{7}$$

Find the reciprocal.

1. $\dfrac{9}{14}$

_____

2. $3\dfrac{1}{2}$

_____

3. $10\dfrac{2}{3}$

_____

Complete the division. Write each answer in simplest form.

4. $3\dfrac{3}{5} \div 2\dfrac{1}{4}$

$= \dfrac{18}{5} \div \dfrac{}{4}$

$= \dfrac{}{5} \times \dfrac{}{9}$

_____

5. $1\dfrac{1}{2} \div 1\dfrac{1}{4}$

$= \dfrac{3}{2} \div \dfrac{}{4}$

$= \dfrac{}{} \times \dfrac{}{}$

_____

6. $\dfrac{5}{12} \div 1\dfrac{7}{8}$

$= \dfrac{}{12} \div \dfrac{}{8}$

$= \dfrac{}{} \times \dfrac{}{}$

_____

7. $3\dfrac{1}{8} \div \dfrac{1}{2}$

_____

8. $1\dfrac{1}{6} \div 2\dfrac{2}{3}$

_____

9. $2 \div 1\dfrac{1}{5}$

_____

LESSON 4-3 Dividing Mixed Numbers
Reading Strategies: Use a Model

A model is useful for dividing mixed numbers.

The Smith family has a $2\frac{1}{2}$-foot-long sandwich to share. Each $\frac{1}{2}$-foot of the sandwich serves one person. How many $\frac{1}{2}$-foot servings are in this sandwich?

Find $2\frac{1}{2} \div \frac{1}{2}$.

Step 1: Draw a square and label it $\frac{1}{2}$.

$$\boxed{\dfrac{1}{2}}$$

Step 2: Draw a row of these squares until they add up to $2\frac{1}{2}$.

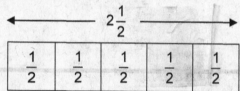

Step 3: Count the number of squares needed to reach $2\frac{1}{2}$.

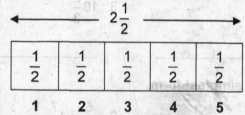

1. How do you represent a single serving?

_____

2. Why draw a row of servings until they add up to $2\frac{1}{2}$?

_____

3. How many $\frac{1}{2}$-foot servings does the Smith family have?

_____

4. What is $2\frac{1}{2} \div \frac{1}{2}$? _____

LESSON
4-3

Dividing Mixed Numbers
Success for English Learners

Problem 1

What is the reciprocal of $2\frac{3}{4}$?

Write the mixed number as an improper fraction.

$$2\frac{3}{4} = 2 + \frac{3}{4}$$
$$= \frac{8}{4} + \frac{3}{4}$$
$$= \frac{11}{4}$$

What is the reciprocal of $\frac{11}{4}$?

Flip it!

$$\frac{11}{4} \qquad \frac{4}{11}$$

How can I tell this is right?

$$\frac{11}{4} \times \frac{4}{11} = \frac{44}{44} = 1$$

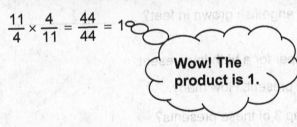

Wow! The product is 1.

Problem 2

How wide is the rectangle?

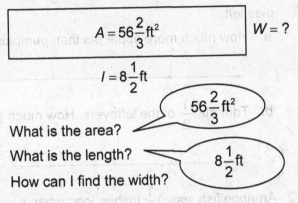

$$A = 56\frac{2}{3} \text{ ft}^2 \qquad W = ?$$

$$l = 8\frac{1}{2} \text{ ft}$$

$56\frac{2}{3} \text{ ft}^2$

What is the area?

What is the length? $8\frac{1}{2}$ ft

How can I find the width?

Divide the area by the length.

$$56\frac{2}{3} \div 8\frac{1}{2} = \frac{170}{3} \div \frac{17}{2}$$
$$= \frac{170}{3} \times \frac{2}{17}$$
$$= \frac{\overset{10}{\cancel{170}} \times 2}{3 \times \underset{1}{\cancel{17}}}$$
$$= \frac{20}{3} \text{ or } 6\frac{2}{3}$$

The width is $6\frac{2}{3}$ ft.

---

1. How is dividing mixed numbers different from multiplying mixed numbers?

_____

_____

2. What is the first step to divide mixed numbers?

_____

3. Why would you expect the width of the rectangle to be about 7 ft?

_____

_____

Solving Multistep Problems with Fractions and Mixed Numbers
Practice and Problem Solving: A/B

Solve. Show your work.

1. After a holiday dinner, there are $3\frac{1}{3}$ apple pies left and $2\frac{5}{6}$ pumpkin pies left.

   a. How much more apple pie than pumpkin pie is left?

   _____

   b. Tom ate $\frac{1}{2}$ of the leftovers. How much pie in all did he eat?

   _____

2. An angelfish was $1\frac{1}{2}$ inches long when it was bought. Now it is

   $2\frac{1}{3}$ inches long.

   a. How much has the angelfish grown? _____

   b. An inch is $\frac{1}{12}$ of a foot. How much has the angelfish grown in feet? _____

3. There was a 6 square-foot piece of wrapping paper for a birthday present.

   It takes $3\frac{3}{8}$ square feet of the paper to wrap the present. How many

   pieces of 6 square-foot paper are needed to wrap 3 of these presents?

   _____

4. Today, a bicycle rider rode her bike $5\frac{1}{2}$ miles. Yesterday, she rode

   $6\frac{1}{4}$ miles. The difference in length between the two rides is what

   fraction of the longer ride?

   _____

5. A survey by the state health department found that the average person

   ate 208 pounds of vegetables last year and $125\frac{5}{8}$ pounds of fruit. What

   fraction of the total pounds of fruit and vegetables do the pounds of

   fruits represent?

   _____

LESSON 4-4
Solving Multistep Problems with Fractions and Mixed Numbers
Practice and Problem Solving: C

Solve. Show your work.

1. One wintry week a ski town got $15\frac{1}{2}$ inches of snow. On Monday the town

   got $2\frac{3}{4}$ inches; on Tuesday it got $1\frac{1}{2}$ times as much; and on Wednesday it

   got $\frac{7}{8}$ inch. How much snow did the town get the rest of the week?

   _____

2. Laura was making a recipe that said the ingredients were for 6 people,

   but she needed to make it for 8 people. The recipe called for $2\frac{2}{3}$ cups

   of milk and $\frac{1}{4}$ cup of oil. How many cups of these liquid ingredients did

   she need for 8 people?

   _____

3. Brian decided to make the same recipe in Exercise 2 for 4 people.
   How many cups of these liquid ingredients did he need? Explain two
   ways you could find the answer.

   _____

   _____

4. A fence around a square garden is made up of 4 equal-sized pieces

   that are each $5\frac{1}{2}$ feet long. Matt decided to make the sides $2\frac{1}{2}$ times

   longer. How much fencing does he need in all?

   _____

5. Pedro spent $2\frac{1}{5}$ hours on his math homework and half as long on his

   science homework one weekend. If his English and social studies

   homework took $\frac{7}{8}$ as long, how much time did he spend on homework

   that weekend?

   _____

6. Ken spent $\frac{1}{5}$ of his allowance on a movie, $\frac{3}{8}$ on snacks, and $\frac{2}{7}$ on

   games. If his allowance was $20, how much did Ken have left?

   _____

LESSON 4-4

Solving Multistep Problems with Fractions and Mixed Numbers
Practice and Problem Solving: D

Solve. Show your work. The first one is done for you.

1. After a party, there is $\frac{1}{3}$ apple pie left and $\frac{5}{6}$ pumpkin pie left.

   a. How much more pumpkin pie than apple pie is left?

   $$\frac{5}{6} - \frac{1}{3} = \frac{5}{6} - \frac{2}{6} = \frac{3}{6} \text{ or } \frac{1}{2} pie$$

   b. Terri ate $\frac{1}{3}$ of the leftover pies. How much pie did she eat?

   _____

2. An angelfish was $1\frac{1}{2}$ inches long when it was bought. Now it is

   $2\frac{1}{2}$ inches long.

   a. How much has the angelfish grown? _____

   b. An inch is $\frac{1}{12}$ of a foot. How much has the angelfish grown in feet? _____

3. There was a 6 square-foot piece of wrapping paper for a present. It

   takes $3\frac{1}{8}$ square feet of paper to wrap the present. How many pieces

   of 6-foot-square paper are needed to wrap 2 presents?

   _____

4. Today, a bicycle rider rode her bike $5\frac{1}{2}$ miles. Yesterday, she rode

   6 miles. What fraction of the total of the two rides is the longer ride?

   _____

5. A survey by the state health department found that the average person

   ate 208 pounds of vegetables last year and $125\frac{5}{8}$ pounds of fruit. How

   many pounds of vegetables and fruits did the average person eat per

   month? [Hint: Remember that 1 month is $\frac{1}{12}$ of a year.]

   _____

LESSON 4-4
Solving Multistep Problems with Fractions and Mixed Numbers
Reteach

In order to solve some problems involving mixed numbers, you will have to rewrite the mixed number as a whole number and an improper fraction. For example, $2\frac{1}{3}$ can be rewritten as $1\frac{4}{3}$. The two numbers are the same because $2\frac{1}{3} = 1 + 1\frac{1}{3} = \frac{3}{3} + 1\frac{1}{3} = 1 + \frac{3}{3} + \frac{1}{3}$.

This step is necessary when subtracting mixed numbers as shown here.

Example

After an office party, $4\frac{1}{3}$ pizzas are left. A day later, there are $1\frac{5}{6}$ pizzas left. How much pizza was eaten during the day after the party? One third of the pizza eaten on the day after the party was pepperoni. How much of the day-old pizza eaten was pepperoni?

Solution:

First, change the denominator to the common denominator of 6:

$4\frac{1}{3} = 4\frac{2}{6}$

Then, write the subtraction problem: $4\frac{2}{6} - 1\frac{5}{6}$

Since the fraction with 4 is less than the fraction with 1, write

$4\frac{2}{6}$ as $1 + 3\frac{2}{6}$ and write 1 as $\frac{6}{6}$ so that the subtraction problem

becomes $3\frac{8}{6} - 1\frac{5}{6}$.

Subtract the whole numbers and subtract the numerators of the fractions:

$3\frac{8}{6} - 1\frac{5}{6} = 2 + \frac{3}{6}$ or $2\frac{1}{2}$; $2\frac{1}{2}$ pizzas were eaten during the next day. Of

these, $\frac{1}{3}$ were pepperoni. So: $2\frac{1}{2} \cdot \frac{1}{3} = \frac{5}{2} \cdot \frac{1}{3} = \frac{5}{6}$.

On the second day, $\frac{5}{6}$ of a pepperoni pizza was eaten.

Solve by rewriting the mixed number that is being subtracted.

1. A deli ordered $6\frac{1}{2}$ wheels of cheese. Over the weekend, $3\frac{5}{8}$ wheels of

cheese were sold. On Tuesday another $1\frac{3}{4}$ wheels were sold. How

much cheese was left for Wednesday?

_____

LESSON 4-4

Solving Multistep Problems with Fractions and Mixed Numbers
Reading Strategies: Compare and Contrast

When you solve problems with fractions, mixed numbers, and whole numbers, it can be helpful to compare and contrast different methods of solving the problems. The example shows two ways to solve a problem involving a mixed number and a whole number.

Example

A carpet store puts 40 square yards of outdoor carpet on sale. After the sale, they have $10\frac{1}{3}$ square yards of carpet left. How much did they sell?

Of the carpet sold, half was green. How many square feet of green carpet did they sell?

Method 1 Estimation can be used to solve this problem without converting the 40 yards to a fraction and a mixed number. Forty yards less 10 yards is 30 yards. However, the real difference is one third of a yard less than 30 yards. Thirty yards less one third of a yard is 29 yards and a fraction. What fraction? One third from one whole leaves two thirds. So, the amount of carpet sold is 29 yards and two thirds of a yard or $29\frac{2}{3}$ square yards. Half of $29\frac{2}{3}$ square yards is about 15 square yards or $14\frac{1}{2}$ square yards plus $\frac{1}{3}$ square yard. So, they sold $14\frac{5}{6}$ square yards of green carpet.

Method 2 Change 40 yards to 39 yards and one yard. Write one yard as thirds: three thirds. So, the problem becomes $39 + \frac{3}{3}$ minus $10\frac{1}{3}$. Subtract the whole numbers: $39 - 10 = 29$. Subtract the fractions. Since the fractions have the same denominators, the numerators can be subtracted:

$$\frac{3}{3} - \frac{1}{3} = \frac{2}{3}.$$

Add 29 and $\frac{2}{3}$ to get $29\frac{2}{3}$ yards.

Then multiply $29\frac{2}{3}$ by $\frac{1}{2}$ to get $14\frac{5}{6}$ square yards.

Answer the question.

1. Which of the two methods of doing the problem in the example do you prefer and why?

_____

_____

Solving Multistep Problems with Fractions and Mixed Numbers
Success for English Learners

Problem 1a

Sarai has a piece of ribbon that is $6\frac{1}{3}$ yards long. She cuts off a piece that

is $2\frac{5}{6}$ yards long. How much ribbon is left?

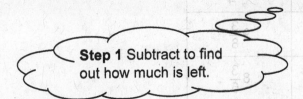

Step 1 Subtract to find out how much is left.

Rewrite the fraction:

$$6\frac{1}{3} - 2\frac{5}{6} = 6\frac{2}{6} - 2\frac{5}{6} = 3\frac{3}{6} \text{ or } 3\frac{1}{2} \text{ yards}$$

Problem 1b

Sarai wants to use $\frac{1}{2}$ of a $3\frac{1}{2}$-yard piece of ribbon to wrap a present.

How much ribbon will she use?

$$3\frac{1}{2} \cdot \frac{1}{2} = \frac{7}{2} \cdot \frac{1}{2}$$

$$= \frac{7}{4} \text{ or}$$

$$= 1\frac{3}{4} \text{ yards}$$

1. Why is 6 the common denominator in Problem 1a?

_____

2. What operations did you use to solve Problems 1a and 1b?

_____

Name _____ Date _____ Class_____

Operations with Fractions
Challenge

The table shows the length and width of 4 rug designs that
a carpet store stocks. Use the table to answer problems 1–2.

Rug Design	Length (ft)	Width (ft)
Classic	$8\frac{1}{2}$	$10\frac{3}{4}$
Deco	$10\frac{3}{4}$	$9\frac{3}{8}$
Solid	$7\frac{2}{5}$	$8\frac{3}{5}$
Modern	$10\frac{3}{5}$	$9\frac{1}{2}$

1. The price of each rug is found by multiplying the area of the rug
   (length times width) by the price per square foot. The price for all 4
   rug designs listed above is $8 per square foot. Which rug is the most
   expensive? How much does it cost?

   _____

2. Pauline orders a custom rug. She wants a rug that is the same final
   price as the Deco but the same width as the Modern. What is the
   length of the rug Pauline wants to purchase? Explain.

   _____

   _____

Solve.

3. $\frac{1}{2}, \frac{2}{3}, \frac{3}{4}, \frac{4}{5}, \frac{5}{6}, \cdots \frac{99}{100}$

   In the list above, each fraction after the first is obtained by adding
   1 to both the numerator and denominator of the fraction before it.

   For example, the first fraction is $\frac{1}{2}$. To get the second fraction, add

   1 to 1 and to 2: $\frac{1+1}{2+1} = \frac{2}{3}$. This pattern continues to $\frac{99}{100}$. What is

   the product of the fractions in the list above? What pattern can help
   you find the product quickly?

   _____

   _____

Dividing Whole Numbers

LESSON 5-1

Practice and Problem Solving: A/B

Estimate each quotient by rounding the dividend and the divisor to the largest place value.

1. $585 \div 13$

2. $2,756 \div 53$

3. $22,528 \div 98$

_____

_____

_____

4. $7,790 \div 210$

5. $17,658 \div 360$

6. $916 \div 320$

_____

_____

_____

Find each quotient using long division. Show your work.

7.

$29\overline{)1,334}$

8.

$92\overline{)20,884}$

9.

$25\overline{)18,175}$

Find each quotient and remainder using long division. Show your work.

10.

$18\overline{)2,902}$

11.

$64\overline{)34,680}$

12.

$215\overline{)52,245}$

Solve.

13. At the museum, there were 4,050 students in attendance from a total of 15 different school districts. What was the average attendance from each school district?

_____

14. The Appalachian Trail is about 2,175 miles long. If a hiker averages 12 miles each day, how long will it take her to hike the length of the trail?

_____

LESSON 5-1

Dividing Whole Numbers
Practice and Problem Solving: C

Estimate each quotient by rounding the dividend and the divisor to the largest place value. Then estimate each quotient by rounding the dividend and divisor to the nearest 10.

1. $585 \div 13$

_____

_____

2. $2,756 \div 53$

_____

_____

3. $22,528 \div 98$

_____

_____

4. $7,790 \div 210$

_____

_____

5. $17,658 \div 360$

_____

_____

6. $916 \div 320$

_____

_____

Answer the question.

7. In Exercises 1–6, which method of estimating usually gave you an estimated quotient closer to the quotient?

_____

Each quotient is given with the remainder in decimal form. What is the remainder for each in fraction form?

8. $18\overline{)2,902} = 161.\overline{2}$

_____

9. $64\overline{)34,680} = 541.875$

_____

10. $215\overline{)52,259} = 243.065116$

_____

Solve.

11. One weekend, 5,780 people saw a new movie at 17 different theaters. Each theater sold tickets at $7.50 a piece. Assuming that each theater received the same number of moviegoers, how much did each theater make?

_____

12. The Appalachian Trail is about 2,175 miles long.

   a. If Katia averages 18 miles each day, how long will it take her to hike the length of the trail?

   _____

   b. Katia's friend Joelle joins her for the last quarter portion of the hike. How many full days will Joelle hike?

   _____

Dividing Whole Numbers
Practice and Problem Solving: D

Estimate the quotients by filling in the blanks. The first one is done for you.

1. $345 \div 28$

    345 rounds to ____**3**____ hundreds.

    28 rounds to ____**3**____ tens.

    Quotient estimate:

    ____**300 ÷ 30, or about 10**____

2. $1,711 \div 105$

    1,711 rounds to _____ thousands.

    105 rounds to _____ hundred.

    Quotient estimate:

    _____

3. $715 \div 24$

    _____

4. $2,315 \div 95$

    _____

Use long division to find the quotients and remainders by writing numbers in the boxes. The first one is done for you.

5.
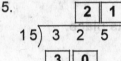

6.
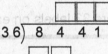
23)7 6 4

7.

4 1)1 8 7 5

8.
3 6)8 4 4 1

LESSON 5-1

Dividing Whole Numbers
Reteach

Division is used to separate a quantity into a given number of equal parts.

It is also used to separate a quantity into parts of a specific size.

A **division algorithm** breaks division with greater numbers into a series of lesser divisions. Follow the steps for each lesser division:

Step 1: Divide and write the number in the first correct place in the quotient.

Step 2: Multiply the divisor by the number in the quotient.

Step 3: Subtract.

Step 4: Bring down the next digit in the dividend.

Repeat these steps until there are no digits from the dividend left to bring down.

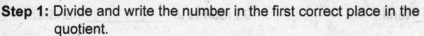

Jon bought a package of 792 labels. There are 24 sheets of labels in the package.

How many labels are on each sheet?

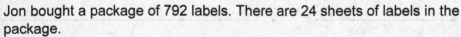

$24\overline{)792}$

Divide to find the number of labels per sheet.

792 labels ÷ 24 sheets

Problem 1

$\boxed{33}$
$24\overline{)792}$
$\underline{-72}\downarrow$

Problem 2

72
$\underline{-72}$
0

Divide. **79 ÷ 24 = 3. Place 3 in the tens place.**

Multiply. **24 × 3 = 72**

Subtract. **79 − 72 = 7**

Bring down the next digit in the dividend: **2**.

Repeat the process.

Divide. **72 ÷ 24 = 3**. Place 3 in the ___ones___ place.

Multiply. **24 × 3 = 72**

Subtract. **72 − 72 = 0**

792 ÷ 24 = 33. There are 33 labels on each sheet.

Use the 4-step process to do the division.

1. The art teacher has a box of 473 markers. She wants to distribute them evenly among 11 tables. How many markers will she put on each table?

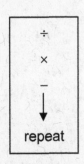

$11\overline{)473}$
$\underline{-44}$
33
$\underline{-33}$
0

Divide: 47 ÷ _____ = _____

Multiply: 11 × _____ = _____

Subtract: 47 − _____ = _____

Bring down the _____.

Repeat the steps.

Divide: _____ ÷ _____ = _____

Multiply: _____ × _____ = _____

Subtract: _____ − _____ = _____

Answer: _____ markers

Dividing Whole Numbers
Reading Strategies: Build Vocabulary

Division is the act of separating something into equal parts. This means that the parts of a problem include a total, the number of groups, and the number of items in one group. These three parts are named the dividend, divisor, and quotient.

The number that represents the total or what is being separated, is the **dividend**.

Identify the number that is the dividend for each situation.

1. Gina has a collection of 645 stamps. She stores the stamps on pages that each holds 15 stamps.

   _____

2. Karl wants to fill a storage case that he uses to hold his miniature toy cars. The case has 5 racks that will hold 120 cars.

   _____

Unlike the dividend, the *divisor* and *quotient* can take on multiple roles. They can each represent the number of groups or the number of items in the group. When the **divisor** is the number of groups, the **quotient** is the number of items in each group. When the **divisor** is the size of the group, the **quotient** is the number of groups. These differences do not change the way you compute the quotient, it simply changes the meaning of the quotient.

Answer each question. Explain your answer.

3. In Question 1, does the number 15 represent the number of groups or the number of items in a group?

   _____

4. In Question 2, does the number 5 represent the number of groups or the number of items in a group?

   _____

Find each quotient. Does the quotient represent the number of groups or the number of items in a group?

5. Gina has a collection of 645 stamps. She stores the stamps on pages that each holds 15 stamps. How many pages are in Gina's collection?

   _____

6. Karl uses a storage case to hold his miniature toy cars. The case has 5 racks that will hold 120 cars. How many cars will each of the 5 racks hold?

   _____

LESSON 5-1
Dividing Whole Numbers
Success for English Learners

Problem 1

Step 1

Estimate 120 ÷ 65

120 ——→ 120

65 ——→ 60

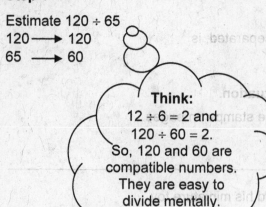

Think:

12 ÷ 6 = 2 and

120 ÷ 60 = 2.

So, 120 and 60 are compatible numbers. They are easy to divide mentally.

Step 2

120 ÷ 65 = 120 ÷ 60

120 ÷ 60 = 2

So, the quotient is **about** 2.

Check your estimate.

120 ÷ 65 = 1.846

So, 1.846 is close to 2.

Problem 2

Divide 235 by 17.

$$
\begin{array}{r}
13 \\
17\overline{)235} \\
-17 \\
\hline
65 \\
-51 \\
\hline
14
\end{array}
$$

Step 1
- Divide **23** by **17**. What do you get?
- **1** with **6** left over.
- Write the **1** in the quotient.
- Multiply **1** times **17**.
- Write **17** below the **23**.
- Subtract **17** from **23**.

Step 2
- Write the **6** and bring down the **5**.
- What do you get? **65**.

Step 3
- Divide **65** by **17**. What do you get?
- **3** with **14** left over.
- Write the **3** in the quotient.

Step 4
- Write the answer:
- **235 ÷ 17 = 13 R 14**

1. In Problem 1, is the estimate an *underestimate* or an *overestimate*?

_____

2. Why are 150 and 50 compatible numbers?

_____

3. In Problem 2, write the answer in Step 4 with a whole number and a fraction.

_____

LESSON 5-2 Adding and Subtracting Decimals

Practice and Problem Solving: A/B

Find each sum or difference.

1. $1.5 + 2.3$

_____

2. $8.9 - 5.1$

_____

3. $2.5 + 1.3 + 4.1$

_____

4. $7.25 + 8.75$

_____

5. $8.16 - 7.72$

_____

6. $3.3 + 4.5 + 2.6$

_____

7. $8.9 + 3.05$

_____

8. $10.64 - 8.8$

_____

9. $4.1 + 0.35 + 6.564$

_____

Solve.

10. Marcus is 1.5 meters tall. His sister is 0.1 meter taller than Marcus.
Their father is 0.2 meter taller than his sister. How tall is their father?

_____

11. Jennifer brought $24.75 to the baseball game. She spent $12.45 on
drinks and snacks. How much money does she have left over?

_____

Find the missing digit.

12.
$$7.089$$
$$+ \; 2.\square13$$
$$\overline{9.502}$$

13.
$$16.594$$
$$- \; \square.175$$
$$\overline{11.419}$$

14.
$$6.2\square67$$
$$+ \; 9.75$$
$$\overline{15.9867}$$

_____

_____

_____

Solve.

15. A gourmet pizza café sells three sizes of pizzas. If you buy all three
sizes, it costs $46.24. A medium pizza costs $15.75 and a large pizza
costs $17.50. How much does the small pizza cost?

_____

16. A carpenter has three sheets of plywood that are each 6.85 feet long.
A 3.4-foot piece is cut from one sheet and 0.5-foot piece is cut from
another sheet. How many feet of plywood is left in all?

_____

LESSON 5-2 Adding and Subtracting Decimals

Practice and Problem Solving: C

Write each fraction as a decimal.

1. $\dfrac{2}{3}$ 2. $\dfrac{7}{6}$ 3. $3\dfrac{1}{9}$ 4. $5\dfrac{5}{18}$

_____   _____   _____   _____

5. What is a common feature of all of the decimals in Exercises 1–4?

_____

Add or subtract as indicated.

6.   0.333…   7.   0.121212…   8.   3.456456…
   $+\ 0.666…$ $+\ 0.454545…$ $-\ 1.345345…$

_____   _____   _____

Solve.

9. Write 0.333… as a fraction.   10. Write 0.666… as a fraction.

   $n =$ _____ $n =$ _____

   $10n =$ _____ $10n =$ _____

   $9n =$ _____ ; $n =$ _____ $9n =$ _____ ; $n =$ _____

11. Write 0.343434… as a fraction.   12. Write 1.432432… as a fraction.

   $n =$ _____ $n =$ _____

   $100n =$ _____ $1,000n =$ _____

   $99n =$ _____ ; $n =$ _____ $999n =$ _____ ; $n =$ _____

13. Why are the decimals in Exercises 11 and 12 multiplied by 100 and 1,000, respectively?

_____

_____

LESSON 5-2 Adding and Subtracting Decimals

Practice and Problem Solving: D

Shade the grid to find each sum. The first one is done for you.

1. $0.3 + 0.34$

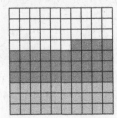

_____0.64_____

2. $0.15 + 0.19$

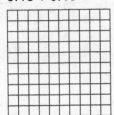

_____

Estimate the answer. The first one is done for you.

3. 12.05 is about __12__
    $+ 27.6$ is about __28__
    39.65 or about __40__

4. 34.5 is about _____
    $- 17.7$ is about _____
    _____   or about _____

Fill in the digits and find the answer. The first one is done for you.

5. $47.65 + 8.059$

	4	7	.	6	5	
+		8	.	0	5	9
	5	5	.	7	0	9

_____55.709_____

6. $77.5 + 23.87$

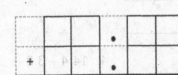

Find the sum or difference. Use any of the methods in this lesson. The first one is done for you.

7. $105.6 - 78.25$

105.60
$- 78.25$
27.35

_____27.35_____

8. $13.2 + 0.5 + 200.6$

_____

LESSON
5-2

LESSON 5-2 Adding and Subtracting Decimals
Reteach

You can use a place-value chart to help you add and subtract decimals.

Add 1.4 and 0.9.

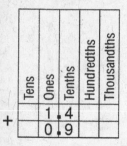

So, 1.4 + 0.9 = 2.3.

Subtract 2.4 from 3.1.

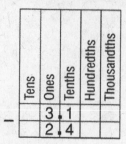

So, 3.1 − 2.4 = 0.7.

Find each sum or difference.

1.

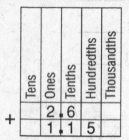

2.

_____

3. 4.3 + 1.4   4. 14.4 − 3.8   5. 7.3 + 8.5   6. 12.34 − 6.9

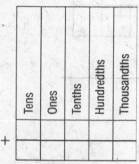 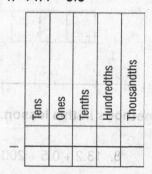 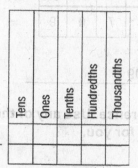 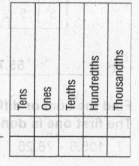

_____   _____   _____   _____

Estimate the answers to Exercises 3–6 by rounding to the nearest whole number. Compare your estimate to the exact answers.

7. 4.3 + 1.4   8. 14.4 − 3.8   9. 7.3 + 8.5   10. 12.34 − 6.9

_____   _____   _____   _____

_____   _____   _____   _____

LESSON 5-2

Adding and Subtracting Decimals

Reading Strategies: Use a Graphic Organizer

Writing decimals in a place-value grid helps you line up decimal points to add or subtract.

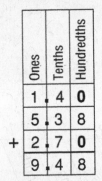

	1.40	Add zeros as place holders.
	5.38	
+	2.70	
	9.48	Place decimal point in answer.

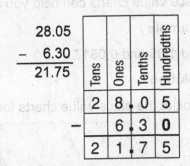

28.05
− 6.30
21.75

1. How does the place-value grid help you add or subtract?

_____

2. Place these numbers on the place-value grid below: 3.25, 1.06, 2.9.

3. Place this problem on the place-value grid below: 23.8–7.2.

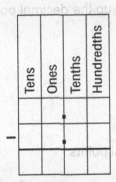

4. Add the numbers on the place-value grid in Exercise 2. What is the sum?

5. Subtract the numbers on the place-value grid in Exercise 3. What is the difference?

_____   _____

6. For which numbers did you add zero as a place holder?

_____

LESSON 5-2

Adding and Subtracting Decimals

Success for English Learners

Problem 1

Place value charts can help you add or subtract decimals.

Example

Add 1.05 and 0.0517.

Solution

Look at the place value charts for the numbers.

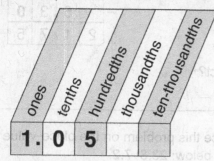
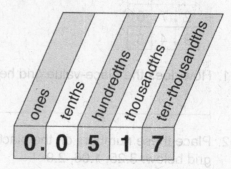

When you add, you line up the decimal points:

1.05
+ 0.0517
1.1017

Problem 2

Add 0.12 and 0.50.

First, line up the decimal points:

0.12
+ 0.50

Second, add the numbers in each place. **0**, **6**, and **2**

Third, write the answer: **0.62**

1. In Problem 1, how would *read* the decimal point if you are saying the number words?

   _____

2. What happens to the value of the sum or difference of numbers if you do not align their decimal points?

   _____

   _____

LESSON 5-3

Multiplying Decimals

Practice and Problem Solving: A/B

Show the decimal multiplication on the grids. Find the product.

1. 0.2×0.6 _____

2. 0.3×0.7 _____

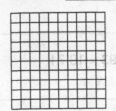   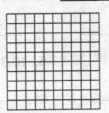

Draw an area model to represent the multiplication problems below. Find the product.

3. $1.2 \times 3.3 =$ _____

4. $4.1 \times 2.1 =$ _____

Multiply.

5. 0.1
   $\underline{\times 0.2}$

6. 0.9
   $\underline{\times 6}$

7. 0.3
   $\underline{\times 0.8}$

8. 1.6
   $\underline{\times 2.9}$

9. $1.5 \times 0.41 =$

10. $0.24 \times 2.68 =$

11. $3.13 \times 4.69 =$

12. $5.48 \times 15.12 =$

_____   _____   _____   _____

Solve.

13. Each basket can hold 2.5 pounds of apples. How many pounds can 7 baskets hold?

_____

14. Canvas cloth costs $7.50 per square meter. How much will 3.5 square meters of canvas cost?

_____

LESSON 5-3 Multiplying Decimals

Practice and Problem Solving: C

Estimate each product to the nearest whole number. Then, find the product.

1. 0.7×0.85

2. 3.05×1.95

3. 0.55×2.3

_____

_____

_____

4. 4.699×1.74

5. 10.37×5.086

6. 5.593×19.71

_____

_____

_____

Compare using < or > without calculating the product.

7. $2.4 \times 3.8 \bigcirc 3.5 \times 2.8$

8. $6.28 \times 3.82 \bigcirc 3.3 \times 6.84$

Solve.

9. A forestry service biologist has time to study insect infestation in an area of 50 square kilometers. On the forest service map, the scale is 1 centimeter equals 1 kilometer. The four possible sectors available for study appear as rectangles on the map. Complete the table by calculating the map area of each sector.

Sector	Map Dimensions (cm)	Map Area (cm^2)
A	2.5×5.8	
B	3.7×2.1	
C	4.7×3.5	
D	4.2×2.8	

a. How can you calculate the actual area of each sector?

_____

b. Does the biologist have time to study all four areas? Explain why or why not?

_____

_____

c. What combinations of three sectors could the scientist study?

_____

d. Which combination of sectors maximizes the area to be studied? Explain why.

_____

LESSON 5-3

Multiplying Decimals

Practice and Problem Solving: D

Multiply. The first one is done for you.

1. 0.5
    × 3
    —
    1.5

2.   4
    × 0.8
    —

3.   9
    × 0.7
    —

4. 0.25
    × 3
    —

Show the decimal multiplication on the grids. Do not solve.

5. 0.1 × 0.7

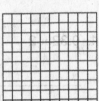

6. 0.4 × 0.8

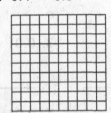

7. 0.3 × 0.7

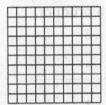

Name the number of decimal places.

8.   2.4 ← _____ decimal places
    × 0.83 ← _____ decimal places
    Answer ← _____ total decimal places

9. 0.456 ← _____ decimal places
    × 2.4 ← _____ decimal places
    Answer ← _____ total decimal places

Multiply. The first one is done for you.

10. 7.15
    × 2.5
    —
    3575
    1430
    —
    17.875

11. 4.36
    ×1.2
    —

Solve.

12. A cabinetmaker buys 3.5 liters of oak varnish. The varnish costs $4.95 per liter.

    a. Write a multiplication expression for this purchase.

    _____

    b. How much does 3 liters of varnish cost? _____

    c. How much does 0.5 liters of varnish cost? _____

    d. What is the total cost of 3.5 liters of varnish? _____

LESSON 5-3 Multiplying Decimals
Reteach

You can use a model to help you multiply a decimal
by a whole number.

Find the product of 0.12 and 4.

Use a 10-by-10 grid. Shade 4 groups of 12 squares.

Count the number of shaded squares. Since you have
shaded 48 of the 100 squares, $0.12 \times 4 = 0.48$.

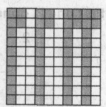

Find each product.

1. 0.23×3 2. 0.41×2 3. 0.01×5 4. 0.32×2

_____   _____   _____   _____

5. 0.15×3 6. 0.42×2 7. 0.04×8 8. 0.22×4

_____   _____   _____   _____

You can also use a model to help you multiply a decimal
by a decimal.

Find the product of 0.8 and 0.4.

Step 1   Shade 8 tenths of the figure.

Step 2   Shade darker 4 tenths of the shaded area.

Step 3   How many squares have you shaded twice?

You have twice shaded 32 of the squares.

So, $0.8 \times 0.4 = 0.32$.

Find each product.

9. 0.2×0.8 10. 0.7×0.9 11. 0.5×0.5 12. 0.3×0.6

_____   _____   _____   _____

13. 0.5×0.2 14. 0.4×0.4 15. 0.1×0.9 16. 0.4×0.7

_____   _____   _____   _____

**LESSON
5-3**
Multiplying Decimals
Reading Strategies: Use Graphic Aids

Each grid has 26 of 100 squares shaded to represent 0.26.

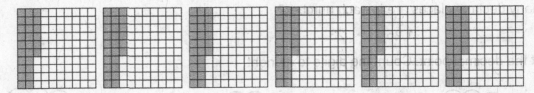

You can add the decimals to
find out how much of the grids
are shaded.

← 0.26 + 0.26 + 0.26 + 0.26 + 0.26 + 0.26 = 1.56

Or, you can multiply the
shading of one grid by 6.

← 0.26 × 6 = 1.56

Use the grids for Exercises 1 to 5.

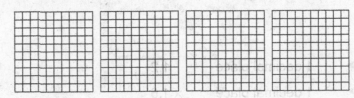

1. Shade the grids so that each one represents 0.89.

2. Write an addition expression to represent the shaded grids.

_____

3. Evaluate your addition expression to find the sum.

_____

4. Write a multiplication expression to represent the shaded grids.

_____

5. Evaluate your multiplication expression to find the product.

_____

LESSON 5-3

Multiplying Decimals

Success for English Learners

Problem 1

How many decimal places are in each number?

2.7   1.25   23

Start at the decimal point. Count the digits to its right.

2.7

one decimal place

1.25

two decimal places

23

no decimal place

Problem 2

Multiply: 1.2×1.6

1.2 ⟶ 1 decimal place   1.2

1.6 ⟶ 1 decimal place $\times$ 1.6

72

+ 120

$1 + 1 = 2$ decimal places ⟶ 1.92

1. How do you find the decimal place in the product of two decimals?

_____

2. To place the decimal point in the product of two decimals, do you move the decimal point to the left or to the right?

_____

3. After you place the decimal point in a product of two decimals, how do you tell if the answer is reasonable?

_____

Is each product reasonable? Write *yes* or *no*. If no, give a reasonable estimate.

4. $0.8 \times 3 = 0.12$ 5. $5.2 \times 6.7 = 34.84$ 6. $2.4 \times 3 = 72$

_____   _____   _____

Name _____ Date _____ Class_____

Dividing Decimals

Practice and Problem Solving: A/B

Use decimal grids to find each quotient. First, shade the grid.
Then, separate the model to show the correct number of equal parts.

1. $3.6 \div 1.2$

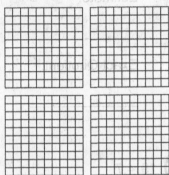

2. $3.27 \div 3$

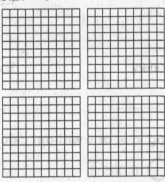

_____

Find each quotient.

3. $9.5\overline{)142.5}$

4. $3\overline{)39.6}$

5. $2\overline{)10.88}$

_____

6. $10.5 \div 1.5$

7. $9.75 \div 1.3$

8. $37.5 \div 2.5$

_____

Estimate each quotient to the nearest whole number. Then, find the actual quotient.

9. $0.9\overline{)3.78}$ 10. $2.5\overline{)36}$ 11. $0.25\overline{)7}$ 12. $9.5\overline{)142.5}$

_____

Solve.

13. A camera attached to a telescope photographs a star's image once
every 0.045 seconds. How many complete images can the camera
capture in 3 seconds?

_____

14. A geologist noticed that land along a fault line moved 24.8 centimeters
over the past 175 years. On average, how much did the land move
each year?

_____

Name _____ Date _____ Class_____

Dividing Decimals

Practice and Problem Solving: C

Estimate the quotient. Then find the exact quotient.

1. $8.4 \div 2.4$ 2. $13.75 \div 2.25$ 3. $5.45 \div 0.5$

   Estimate: Estimate: Estimate:

   _____   _____   _____

   Exact Quotient: Exact Quotient: Exact Quotient:

   _____   _____   _____

Compare using <, >, or = without calculating the quotient.

4. $0.05\overline{)3}$ ◯ $0.005\overline{)3}$ 5. $1.9\overline{)4.7}$ ◯ $19\overline{)4.7}$

6. $0.35\overline{)0.78}$ ◯ $0.35\overline{)7.8}$ 7. $1.2\overline{)34}$ ◯ $0.12\overline{)3.4}$

Solve.

8. Acme Hardware is introducing a new product called Greener Cleaner.
   Complete the table by finding the cost per milliliter for each size based
   on the sales price. One liter is 1,000 milliliters.

Size	Amount of Liquid	Sale Price	Price per Milliliter
Small	250 milliliters	$4.50	
Medium	500 milliliters	$9.95	
Large	1 liter	$16.95	

   a. Write an expression using < or > to compare the three containers by
      price per milliliter.

   _____

   b. What is the least expensive way to buy 1,500 milliliters of Green
      Cleaner? Write an expression to represent your choice and evaluate.

   _____

   c. What is the most expensive way to buy 1,500 milliliters of Green
      Cleaner? Write an expression to represent your choice and evaluate.

   _____

Name _____ Date _____ Class _____

Dividing Decimals
Practice and Problem Solving: D

Find each quotient. The first one is done for you.

1. $2.8 \div 4$

   0.7

2. $1.8 \div 2$

   _____

3. $3.6 \div 6$

   _____

4. $7.2 \div 9$

   _____

5. $0.15 \div 3$

   _____

6. $4.8 \div 8$

   _____

Find each quotient. The first one is done for you.

7. $2.4 \div 0.4$

   6

8. $1.4 \div 0.2$

   _____

9. $4.8 \div 0.6$

   _____

10. $3.3 \div 0.3$

    _____

11. $2.6 \div 1.3$

    _____

12. $7.2 \div 1.2$

    _____

Solve.

13. At the grocery store, a six-pack of bottled water costs $2.88. How much does each bottle cost?

    _____

14. It rained 2.79 inches in July. What was the average daily rainfall in July? (Hint: July has 31 days.)

    _____

15. Over several months, a meteorologist recorded a total snowfall of 8.6 centimeters. During this period, the average monthly snowfall was 4.3 centimeters. For how many months did the meteorologist collect measurements of the snowfalls?

    _____

16. Almonds cost $3.49 per pound. A bag of almonds costs $6.95. To the nearest whole pound, about how many pounds of almonds are in the bag?

    _____

LESSON 5-4

Dividing Decimals
Reteach

You can use decimal grids to help you divide by whole numbers.

To divide 0.35 by 7, first shade in a decimal grid to show thirty-five hundredths.

0.35 ÷ 7 means "divide 0.35 into 7 equal groups." Show this on the decimal grid.

 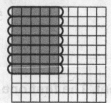

The number of units in each group is the quotient.

So, 0.35 ÷ 7 = 0.05.

Find each quotient.

1. 0.6 ÷ 5

2. 0.78 ÷ 6

3. 0.32 ÷ 4

4. 0.99 ÷ 0.0033

_____ _____

You can use powers of 10 to help you divide a decimal by a decimal.

Divide 0.048 by 0.12.

Notice that 0.12 has two decimal places.
To make this a whole number, multiply by 100.

0.048 ÷ 0.12 ———➤ 0.12 • 100 = 12   0.048 • 100 = 4.8

Then divide.

4.8 ÷ 12

$$\begin{array}{r} 0.4 \\ 12\overline{)4.8} \\ \underline{4\,8} \\ 0 \end{array}$$

Step 1: Divide as you would with a whole number.

Step 2: Think 48 ÷ 12 = 4.

Step 3: Place the decimal point in the quotient.
Add a zero as necessary.

So, 0.048 ÷ 0.12 = 0.4.

Find each quotient.

5. 0.4)0.08

6. 0.9)0.63

7. 0.008)0.4

8. 0.04)0.032

_____ _____ _____ _____

LESSON 5-4

Dividing Decimals
Reading Strategies: Use Graphic Aids

You can use a hundreds grid to show division with decimals.

The grid shows 0.15.   →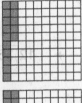

0.15 ÷ 3 means "separate 0.15 into 3 equal groups."   →

0.15 ÷ 3 makes 3 equal groups of 0.05.

0.15 ÷ 3 = 0.05   →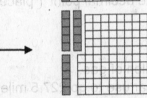

Use the grids to complete 1–8.

1. Shade 0.60 of the grid at right.

2. Divide the shaded area into 3 equal sections.

3. Write a decimal that represents each section. _____

4. Write a division problem for your model.

   _____

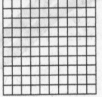

5. Shade 0.72 of the grid at right.

6. Divide the shaded area into 8 equal sections.

7. Write a decimal that represents each section. _____

8. Write a division problem for your model.

   _____

LESSON 5-4
Dividing Decimals
Success for English Learners

Problem 1

Find $3.6 \div 1.2$.

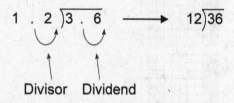

Divisor   Dividend

Remember: To multiply by 10, move the decimal point 1 place to the right.

Problem 2

Sari's car goes 17.5 miles for every gallon of gas.
How many gallons of gas does Sari's car use to go 227.5 miles?

100 miles   227.5 miles

0 miles   200 miles

$$17.5\overline{)227.5}$$ with quotient 13.0

1. What is the quotient in Problem 1?

_____

2. Does the quotient in Problem 1 have a remainder? How do you know?

_____

3. Write another question to go with Problem 2. Solve.

_____

_____

_____

Applying Operations with Rational Numbers

LESSON 5-5

Practice and Problem Solving: A/B

Solve.

1. Four friends equally shared the cost of supplies for a picnic. The supplies cost $12.40. How much did each pay?

   _____

2. Twenty people are going by van to a movie. Each van seats 8 people. How many vans are needed to take everyone?

   _____

3. Plastic forks come in packs of 6. You need 40 forks for a party. How many packs of forks should you buy?

   _____

4. Kesha spent a total of $9.60 on new shoelaces. Each pair cost $1.20. How many pairs of shoelaces did she buy?

   _____

5. Horses are measured in units called hands. One inch equals $\frac{1}{4}$ hand. The average Clydesdale is $17\frac{1}{5}$ hands tall. What is this height in inches? In feet?

   _____

6. A banana bread recipe calls for $\frac{3}{4}$ cup butter. One tablespoon equals $\frac{1}{16}$ cup. How many tablespoons of butter are needed to make the banana bread?

   _____

7. Cindy works part-time and earns $5.75 an hour. One year she worked 50 weeks and averaged 12.4 hours of work per week. About how much money did she earn that year?

   _____

8. At a gymnastics competition, Joey scored 9.4, 9.7, 9.9, and 9.8. Carlos scored 9.5, 9.2, 9.7, and 9.6. Who had the greater average score? By how many points was his score greater?

   _____

9. A granola recipe calls for $2\frac{1}{3}$ cups of almonds. A bag of almonds contains 2 cups. To make $2\frac{1}{2}$ batches of granola, Ali buys 5 bags of almonds. How many cups of almonds will he have left over?

   _____

10. At a zoo, 3 pandas eat a total of $181\frac{1}{2}$ pounds of bamboo shoots each day. The male panda eats 3 times as much as the baby. The female eats twice as much as the baby. How many pounds of bamboo shoots does the female panda eat?

    _____

Name _____ Date _____ Class _____

Applying Operations with Rational Numbers
Practice and Problem Solving: C

Solve.

1. Sandy makes linen scarves that are $\frac{7}{8}$ of a yard long. How many scarves can she make from 156 feet of fabric?

_____

2. A small rug is 36 inches long. Its width is $\frac{2}{3}$ of its length. What is the width of the rug in feet?

_____

3. Four friends split equally a lunch bill of $36.96 plus 20% tip. How much did each person pay?

_____

4. Jade spent $37.60 on groceries. $\frac{4}{5}$ of that total was spent on vegetables. How much was spent on other items?

_____

5. In January, Gene watched 5 movies. Their lengths are shown in the table. How many hours did Gene spend

watching movies? _____

What was the average length of a movie in hours?

_____

Which movies were longer than the average? _____

Movie	Length (min)
A	147.8
B	119.7
C	156.4
D	158.3
E	112.9

6. Derrick's garden is $18\frac{1}{2}$ feet long. He plants bulbs $\frac{3}{8}$ of a

foot apart. How many bulbs can Derrick plant in one row?

_____

Derrick plants three rows of bulbs that cost $0.79 each.
How much does he spend on bulbs? _____

7. Yin's cellphone plan costs $30 a month. She used 12.5 hours in May.

What was her cost per minute? _____

Yin's average call lasted 3.25 minutes. How much did an average

call cost? _____

About how many calls did Yin make in May? _____

Applying Operations with Rational Numbers

LESSON 5-5

Practice and Problem Solving: D

Solve each problem. The first one has been done for you.

1. A hiking trail is $\frac{9}{10}$ mile long. There are 7 markers evenly posted along the trail to direct hikers. This results in 6 spaces of the same length between the markers. How far apart are the markers?

   $\frac{3}{20}$ **of a mile**

2. Tomas is saving $17.00 each week to buy a new sewing machine that costs $175.50. How many weeks will he have to save to have enough money to buy the sewing machine?

   _____

3. Sequins come in packs of 75. Agnes uses 12 sequins on each costume. If she has one pack of sequins, how many costumes can she make?

   _____

4. Jessie pays $2.19 each month for an annual subscription to *Sewing* magazine. She receives 12 magazines annually. How much does Jessie pay for an annual subscription?

   _____

5. Lisa's family drove 830.76 miles to visit her grandparents. Lisa calculated that they used 30.1 gallons of gas. How many miles per gallon did the car average?

   _____

6. Jamal spent $6.75 on wire. Wire costs $0.45 per foot. How many feet of wire did Jamal buy?

   _____

7. In England, mass is measured in units called stones. One pound equals $\frac{1}{14}$ of a stone. A cat has a mass of $\frac{3}{4}$ stone. What is its mass in pounds?

   _____

8. Dan uses $6\frac{1}{4}$ cups of flour to make pita bread for his family. The recipe calls for $2\frac{1}{2}$ cups. How many batches of the pita bread recipe did he make?

   _____

9. Shari used a total of 67.5 yards of cotton material to make costumes for the play. Each costume used 11.25 yards of cloth. How many costumes did Shari make?

   _____

10. Mike earned $11.76 per hour for working 23.5 hours last week. How much money did Mike earn last week?

    _____

Name _____ Date _____ Class_____

Applying Operations with Rational Numbers
Reteach

When a word problem involves fractions or decimals, use these four steps to help you decide which operation to use.

Tanya has $13\frac{1}{2}$ feet of ribbon. To giftwrap boxes, she needs to cut it into $\frac{7}{8}$-foot lengths. How many lengths can Tanya cut?

Step 1	Read the problem carefully. What is asked for?	The number of lengths is asked for.
Step 2	Think of a simpler problem that includes only whole numbers.	Tanya has 12 feet of ribbon. She wants to cut it into 2-foot lengths. How many lengths can she cut?
Step 3	How would you solve the simpler problem?	Divide 12 by 2. Tanya can cut 6 lengths.
Step 4	Use the same reasoning with the original problem.	Divide $13\frac{1}{2}$ by $\frac{7}{8}$. Tanya can cut 15 lengths.

Tell whether you should multiply or divide. Then solve the problem.

1. Jan has $37.50. Tickets to a concert cost $5.25 each. How many tickets can Jan buy?

_____

2. Jon has $45.00. He plans to spend $\frac{4}{5}$ of his money on sports equipment. How much will he spend?

_____

3. Ricki has 76.8 feet of cable. She plans to cut it into 7 pieces. How long will each piece be?

_____

4. Roger has $2\frac{1}{2}$ cups of butter. A recipe for a loaf of bread requires $\frac{3}{4}$ cup of butter. How many loaves can Roger bake?

_____

Name _____ Date _____ Class _____

Applying Operations with Rational Numbers
Reading Strategies: Analyze Information

Word problems contain information that helps you choose which operation
to use. Look for clues to help you decide whether to multiply or divide.

Read the problem carefully.

What is given? What are you asked to find?

Given	Asked to Find	Operation
a whole	a fractional part	Multiply by the fraction.
a whole *and* the **number** of parts	the **size** of the parts	Divide.
a whole *and* the **size** of a part	the **number** of parts	Divide.

Identify the information given and what you are asked to find.
Tell whether to multiply or divide. Then solve the problem.

1. A pumpkin weighs 31.3 pounds. It is split into 3 equal pieces.
   What does each part weigh?

   Given: _____

   Find: _____

   Operation and solution: _____

2. A pumpkin weighs $22\frac{2}{3}$ pounds. What does $\frac{1}{6}$ of it weigh?

   Given: _____

   Find: _____

   Operation and solution: _____

3. A pumpkin weighs $42\frac{1}{3}$ pounds. A grocer wants to cut it into pieces

   weighing $2\frac{1}{2}$ pounds each. How many pieces can he cut?

   Given: _____

   Find: _____

   Operation and solution: _____

LESSON 5-5

Applying Operations with Rational Numbers
Success for English Learners

Problem 1

What does that mean?

$0.75 \div 5.$

It tells you to write the numbers in this format. Then divide.

$5)\overline{0.75}$ ⟹ $\begin{array}{r} 0.15 \\ 5)\overline{0.75} \end{array}$

Problem 2

How do we share the cost?

We have to divide the cost by 3.

We each need to pay $3.87.

$\begin{array}{r} 3.87 \\ 3)\overline{11.61} \end{array}$

Total Cost: $11.61

1. How do you know where to place the decimal point in the quotient in Problem 1?

   _____

2. How can you determine if your answer to Problem 2 is correct?

   _____

Name _____ Date _____ Class _____

Operations with Decimals

Challenge

Divya is cooking dinner. She goes to the market to buy ingredients. The price per pound of different ingredients is shown in the table below.

Ingredient	Price (per lb)
Beef	$10.65
Onions	$2.49
Potatoes	$3.29
Tomatoes	$8.45
Asparagus	$4.99

Divya's recipe calls for 3.25 pounds of beef, 0.65 pounds of onions, 0.2 pounds of potatoes, 0.15 pounds of tomatoes, and 0.33 pounds of asparagus.

1. How much will Divya pay for all the ingredients in the recipe? Show your work.

_____

_____

_____

_____

2. Divya decides to make a vegetarian version of the recipe. To do this she replaces beef with 2.5 pounds of chickpeas and 1.75 pounds of lentils. At the market, chickpeas cost $2.49 per pound and lentils cost $3.59 per pound. How much money does Divya save by making the vegetarian version of her meal? Show your work.

_____

_____

_____

3. Divya also wants to make fruit smoothies for dessert. She purchases a container of rice milk for $3.49, two pounds of strawberries at $4.99 per pound, and six bananas at $0.75 each. How much did Divya spend on dessert? Show your work.

_____

_____

LESSON 6-1

Ratios

Practice and Problem Solving: A/B

The number of animals at the zoo is shown in the table. Write each ratio in three different ways.

1. lions to elephants

   _____

2. giraffes to otters

   _____

3. lions to seals

   _____

4. seals to elephants

   _____

5. elephants to lions

   _____

Animals in the Zoo	
Elephants	12
Giraffes	8
Lions	9
Seals	10
Otters	16

Write three equivalent ratios for the given ratio.

6. $\frac{4}{3}$ _____

7. $\frac{12}{14}$ _____

8. $\frac{6}{9}$ _____

Find three ratios equivalent to the ratio described in each situation.

9. The ratio of cats to dogs in a park is 3 to 4. _____

10. The ratio of rainy days to sunny days is $\frac{5}{7}$. _____

11. The ratio of protein to fiber in a granola bar is $\frac{9}{2}$. _____

12. The ratio of clown fish to angelfish at a pet store is 5:4. The ratio of angelfish to goldfish is 4:3. There are 60 clown fish at the pet store.

    a. How many angelfish are there? _____

    b. How many goldfish are there? _____

**LESSON
6-1**

Ratios

Practice and Problem Solving: C

For centuries, people all over the world have considered a certain rectangle to be one of the most beautiful shapes. Which of these rectangles do you find the most attractive?

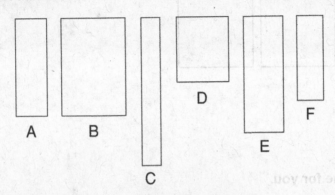

A   B   C   D   E   F

If you are like most people, you chose rectangle B. Why? It's a golden rectangle, of course! In a golden rectangle, the ratio of the length to the width is called the **golden ratio**—about 1.6 to 1.

The golden ratio pops up all over the place—in music, sculptures, the Egyptian pyramids, seashells, paintings, pinecones, and of course in rectangles.

To create your own golden rectangle, just write a ratio equivalent to the golden ratio. This will give you the length and width of another golden rectangle.

Golden Ratio

$$\frac{\ell}{w} = \frac{1.6}{1}$$ $w = 1$ in.

$\ell = 1.6$ in.

Use a ruler to draw a new golden rectangle in the space below. Then draw several non-golden rectangles around it. Now conduct a survey of your family and friends to see if they choose the golden rectangle as their favorite.

LESSON 6-1

Ratios

Practice and Problem Solving: D

The number of square patches compared to circle patches on a quilt is represented by the model below.

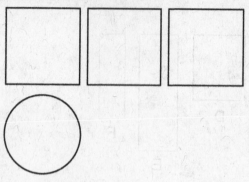

Complete. The first one is done for you.

1. Write a ratio that compares the number of circle patches to the number of square patches.

   _____**1 circle patch to 3 square patches; 1 to 3**_____

2. If there are 9 square patches on the quilt, how many circle patches are there?

   9 ÷ _____ = _____ circle patches

3. How many square patches are there if there are 4 circle patches on a quilt?

   4 × _____ = _____ square patches

The number of Caroline's pet fish is shown in the table. Write each ratio in three different ways. The first one is done for you.

Caroline's Pet Fish	
Tiger Barbs	5
Catfish	1
Angelfish	4

4. tiger barbs to catfish

   5 to 1, 5:1, $\frac{5}{1}$
   _____

5. catfish to angelfish

   _____

6. angelfish to tiger barbs

   _____

Write three equivalent ratios for the given ratio. The first one is done for you.

7. $\frac{2}{3}$ $\frac{4}{6}, \frac{6}{9}, \frac{8}{12}$

8. $\frac{3}{4}$ _____

9. $\frac{1}{6}$ _____

LESSON 6-1 Ratios
Reteach

A ratio is a comparison of two quantities by division.

To compare the number of times vowels are used to the number
of time consonants are used in the word "mathematics," first find each
quantity.

Number of times vowels are used: 4

Number of times consonants are used: 7

Then write the comparison as a ratio, using the quantities in the
same order as they appear in the word expression. There are three
ways to write a ratio.

$\dfrac{4}{7}$ 4 to 7   4:7

Write each ratio.

1. days in May to days in a year

   _____

2. sides of a triangle to sides of a square

   _____

Equivalent ratios are ratios that name the same comparison.

The ratio of inches in a foot to inches in a yard is $\dfrac{12}{36}$. To find

equivalent ratios, divide or multiply the numerator and denominator
by the same number.

$\dfrac{12}{36} = \dfrac{12 \div 3}{36 \div 3} = \dfrac{4}{12}$ $\dfrac{12}{36} = \dfrac{12 \cdot 2}{36 \cdot 2} = \dfrac{24}{72}$

So, $\dfrac{12}{36}$, $\dfrac{4}{12}$, and $\dfrac{24}{72}$ are equivalent ratios.

Write three equivalent ratios to compare each of the following.

3. 8 triangles to 12 circles

   _____

4. 20 pencils to 25 erasers

   _____

5. 5 girls to 6 boys

   _____

6. 10 pants to 14 shirts

   _____

LESSON 6-1

Ratios

Reading Strategies: Use the Context

A **ratio** is a comparison between two similar quantities. The picture below shows geometric figures. You can write ratios to compare the figures.

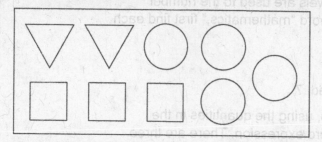

Compare the number of triangles to the total number of figures. This comparison can be written as a ratio in three different ways.

$$\frac{\text{number of triangles}}{\text{total figures}} \longrightarrow \frac{2}{9} \qquad \text{Read: "two to nine."}$$

2 to 9

2:9   Read: "two to nine."

Compare.

1. Write the ratio that compares the number of squares to the number of circles in three different ways.

   _____

2. Write the ratio that compares the number of circles to the total number of figures in three different ways.

   _____

3. Bernie wrote the ratio 2 to 3. What comparison of figures did he make?

   _____

4. Write a ratio that represents the number of polygons to the number of circles.

   _____

LESSON 6-1

Ratios

Success for English Learners

Ways to write ratios

Word form: 3 to 2

Fraction form: $\frac{3}{2}$

Ratio form: 3 : 2
To read all forms, say "3 to 2."

Ways to find equivalent ratios

Multiply the numerator and the denominator by the same number.

OR

Divide the numerator and the denominator by common factors.

Problem 1

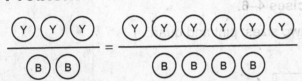

Y	3	6	9	12
B	2	4	6	8

What is happening to the numerator and denominator?

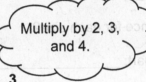
Multiply by 2, 3, and 4.

Equivalent ratios for $\frac{3}{2}$:

Multiply by 2 = $\frac{3 \cdot 2 = 6}{2 \cdot 2 = 4} = \frac{6}{4}$

Multiply by 3 = $\frac{3 \cdot 3 = 9}{2 \cdot 3 = 6} = \frac{9}{6}$

Multiply by 4 = $\frac{3 \cdot 4 = 12}{2 \cdot 4 = 8} = \frac{12}{8}$

Equivalent ratios for $\frac{3}{2}$ are $\frac{6}{4}$, $\frac{9}{6}$, and $\frac{12}{8}$.

Problem 2

40	20	10	5
16	8	4	2

40 : 16 = $\frac{40}{16}$

Divide by 2 = $\frac{40 \div 2 = 20}{16 \div 2 = 8}$

Divide by 2 = $\frac{20 \div 2 = 10}{8 \div 2 = 4}$

Divide by 2 = $\frac{10 \div 2 = 5}{4 \div 2 = 2}$

So, **equivalent ratios** for $\frac{40}{16}$ are $\frac{20}{8}$, $\frac{10}{4}$, and $\frac{5}{2}$.

1. Complete the ratio in the table. Did you multiply or divide to find the equivalent ratio?

Y	3	6	9	12	☐
B	2	4	6	8	10

_____

2. Write a sentence explaining how to find an equivalent ratio for $\frac{5}{2}$.

_____

Name _____ Date _____ Class _____

Rates

Practice and Problem Solving: A/B

Find the unit rate.

1. David drove 135 miles in 3 hours. _____

2. Three medium apples have about 285 calories. _____

3. A 13-ounce package of pistachios costs $5.99. _____

Use the information in the table to solve Exercises 4–6.

Morgan's favorite spaghetti sauce is available in two sizes: pint and quart.
Each size and its price are shown in the table.

Size	Quantity (oz)	Price ($)
pint	16	3.98
quart	32	5.98

4. What is the unit rate to the nearest cent per ounce for each size?

   a. pint: _____   b. quart: _____

5. Which size is the better buy? _____

6. A coupon offers $1.00 off the 16-ounce size. Which size is the better
   buy then?

   _____

Find the unit rate to the nearest cent per ounce. Compare.

7. a. A 24-ounce box of cornflakes costs $4.59. _____

   b. A 36-ounce box of cornflakes costs $5.79. _____

   c. Which is the better buy? _____

Solve.

8. Karyn proofreads 15 pages in 2 hours for $40.

   a. What is her proofreading rate in pages per hour?

   _____

   b. How much does she receive on average for a page?

   _____

LESSON 6-2

Rates
Practice and Problem Solving: C

Find the unit rate. Compare.

1. Jason drives 180 miles in 4 hours and Ali drives 90 miles in 1.7 hours.

   Jason: _____   Ali: _____

   _____ is the faster driver.

2. Five medium apples have about 475 calories. Three medium oranges have about 186 calories.

   apple: _____   orange: _____

   _____ have fewer calories.

Use the information in the table to solve Exercises 3–5.

Paint is available in 3 sizes. Each size and its price are shown in the table.

Size	Quantity (oz)	Price ($)
pint	16	$12.29
quart	32	$19.98
gallon	128	$34.99

3. What is the unit rate to the nearest cent for each size?

   a. pint: _____   b. quart: _____   c. gallon: _____

4. Per ounce, which size paint container costs about twice as much as another size paint container?

   _____

   _____

5. How much larger is a gallon than a quart? _____

Find the unit costs. Solve.

6. a. A 15-inch link of silver chain costs $82.99. _____

   b. A 15-inch link of gold chain costs $112.59. _____

LESSON 6-2	**Rates**

Practice and Problem Solving: D

Find the unit rate. The first one is done for you.

1. Carrie biked 75 miles in 3 days. _____**25 mi per day**_____

2. Twenty emails in 5 minutes. _____

3. A quart (32-ounce) bottle of milk costs $1.19. _____

Use the information in the table to solve the problems. The first one is done for you.

Rob's favorite shampoo is available in two sizes: regular and economy. Each size and its price are shown in the table.

Size	Quantity (oz)	Price ($)
regular	20	$8.00
economy	40	$10.00

4. What is the unit rate to the nearest cent per ounce for each size?

   a. regular: _____**$0.40**_____   b. economy: _____**$0.25**_____

5. Which size is the better buy? _____

6. A coupon offers $1.00 off the regular size. Which size is the better buy then?

   _____

Find the unit rate. The first one is done for you

7. a. A pound (16 ounces) of cheddar cheese costs $8.00 __**$0.50 per oz**__

   b. A half-pound of Swiss cheese costs $8.00 _____

Solve. The first one is done for you.

8. Eric paints 8 rooms in 3 days for $600.

   a. What is his painting rate in dollars per day? __**$200 per day**__

   b. How much does he receive on average for a room? _____

   c. About how many rooms could Eric paint in 6 days? _____

LESSON 6-2

Rates
Reteach

You can divide to find a unit rate or to determine a best buy.

A. Find the unit rate.
Karin bikes 35 miles in 7 hours.
$35 \div 7 = 5$ mph

B. Find the best buy.

| 2 lb $5 | 4 lb $8 | 10 lb $15 |

$5 \div 2 = 2.50 per lb

$8 \div 4 = 2.00 per lb

$15 \div 10 = 1.50 per lb

BEST BUY!

Divide to find each unit rate. Show your work.

1. Jack shells 315 peanuts in 15 minutes. _____

2. Sharmila received 81 texts in 9 minutes. _____

3. Karim read 56 pages in 2 hours. _____

Find the best buy. Show your work.

4.

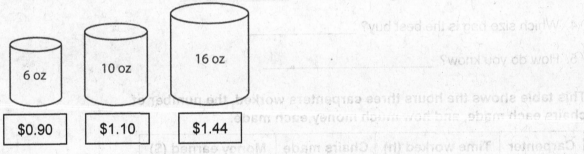

| 6 oz $0.90 | 10 oz $1.10 | 16 oz $1.44 |

_____

_____

5.

Bread	Weight (oz)	Cost ($)
Whole wheat	16	2.24
Pita	20	3.60
7-grain	16	2.56

_____

_____

_____

LESSON
6-2

Rates

Reading Strategies: Read a Table

A table organizes data in rows and columns.

> Column headings tell you what data is below.

> The title tells you what the whole table is about.

> Columns are read up and down.

Rice Prices at Grandee Supermarket

Bag Size	Quantity (lb)	Bag Price ($)	Unit Price ($)
mini	1	1.50	1.50 per lb
small	2	3.40	1.70 per lb
medium	5	7.00	1.40 per lb
large	10	12.50	
extra large	25	26.25	

> Rows are read back and forth.

Find the unit price to the nearest cent per pound. Answer the questions.

1. What is the unit price of the large bag? _____

2. What is the unit price of the extra large bag? _____

3. Which size bag has the highest unit price? _____

4. Which size bag is the best buy? _____

5. How do you know? _____

This table shows the hours three carpenters worked, the number of chairs each made, and how much money each made.

Carpenter	Time worked (h)	Chairs made	Money earned ($)
Dan	38	7	459.80
Flora	35	6	903.00
Chandra	32	5	680.00

6. Which carpenter makes the most money per hour? _____

7. Which makes the least money per hour? _____

8. Based on labor costs alone, which carpenter makes the most

   expensive chairs? _____

LESSON 6-2 Rates
Success for English Learners

Problem 1

Mr. Jackson corrects 56 tests in 3 hours. About how many tests does he correct per hour?

Find the unit rate.
Divide 56 by 3.

$56 \div 3 = 18.7$

Mr. Jackson corrects about 19 tests per hour.

Problem 2

Find the best buy for different size boxes of breakfast bars.

Size	Weight (oz)	Cost ($)
small	8	5.99
medium	16	8.99
large	32	18.99

Divide the cost by the number of ounces.

Small $5.99 \div 8 \approx \$0.75$ per oz

Medium $8.99 \div 16 \approx \$0.56$ per oz

Large $18.99 \div 32 \approx \$0.59$ per oz

To the nearest cent per ounce

Compare. $0.56 < 0.59 < 0.75$.

The unit cost of the medium box of breakfast bars is lowest, so the medium size is the best buy.

1. How would you find the number of miles per hour Mrs. Rodriguez drives if you know she drives 300 miles in 5.2 hours?

_____

2. Is the best buy always the largest size? Explain.

_____

3. Should you always buy the largest size? Explain.

_____

_____

4. Write your own "best buy" problem.

_____

_____

LESSON 6-3

Using Ratios and Rates to Solve Problems

Practice and Problem Solving: A/B

Solve using ratios.

1. Mark is using the ratio of 3 tablespoons of sugar to 2 tablespoons of milk in a recipe. Complete the table to show equivalent ratios if Mark decides to increase the recipe.

sugar	3	6		18	
milk	2		8		20

2. Mark's ratio is 3 tablespoons sugar to 2 tablespoons milk. Sharri is using 4 tablespoons of sugar to 3 tablespoons of milk. Eve is using 9 tablespoons of sugar to 6 tablespoons of milk. Which girl's ratio is

equivalent to Mark's? _____

3. A school cafeteria makes cheese sauce for macaroni using 15 cups of Swiss cheese and 17 cups of cheddar cheese. Perry tries to make the sauce for a family party using 5 cups of Swiss and 7 cups of cheddar.

Is Perry using the correct ratio? Explain. _____

_____

4. The chess club members bought 6 tickets to a tournament for $15. How much would they have paid if all 9 members wanted to go?

_____

5. The Khan's car averages 22 miles per gallon of gas. Predict how far

they can travel on 5 gallons of gas. _____

6. Cafe A offers 2 free bottled waters or juices for every 20 purchased. Cafe B offers 3 free bottled waters or juices for every 25 purchased.

   a. What is Cafe A's ratio of free drinks to purchased drinks?

   _____

   b. What is Cafe B's ratio of free drinks to purchased drinks?

   _____

   c. If you purchased 50 drinks at each café, how many free drinks would you get?

   _____

LESSON 6-3

Using Ratios and Rates to Solve Problems

Practice and Problem Solving: C

Solve using ratios.

1. A water molecule is formed from two hydrogen atoms and one oxygen atom. Fill in the table for 2, 5, 10 and 20 water molecules.

water molecule				
hydrogen atoms				
oxygen atoms				

2. Hydrogen peroxide molecules have two hydrogen atoms and two oxygen atoms.

   How would a table for this compound differ? _____

3. Ammonia molecules have three hydrogen (H) atoms and one nitrogen (N) atom. How many of each atom are in five molecules of ammonia?

   _____

4. Tickets to a science exposition cost $5.75 each for students and $7.00 for adults. How many students and adults went if the ticket charge was

   $42.75? _____

5. The bus to the exposition averaged 18 miles to a gallon of gas. How far away was the exposition if they used 8 gallons of gas for the round trip?

   _____

6. Flyaway airline program offers 5 points for every mile flown, plus a bonus of 20 points for every trip over 500 miles. My Sky airline program offers 7 points for every mile flown plus a bonus of 30 points for each trip. Which program gives more points for this itinerary?

   Trip A 600 mi   Trip D 825 mi   Trip G 1,000 mi

   Trip B 450 mi   Trip E 300 mi   Trip H 545 mi

   Trip C 710 mi   Trip F 300 mi

   _____

7. An appliance store sells lamps at $95.00 for two. A department store sells similar lamps at five for $250.00. Which store sells at a better

   rate? How much better? _____

LESSON 6-3

Using Ratios and Rates to Solve Problems

Practice and Problem Solving: D

Solve using ratios. The first one is done for you.

1. Pam is making fruit punch for a party using the ratio of 2 cups of club soda to 5 cups of juice. Complete the table to show equivalent ratios for increasing numbers of guests.

club soda	2	4	8	10	
juice	5	10			50

2. Pam's ratio is 2 cups club soda to 5 cups juice. Barry is making punch with 3 cups club soda to 8 cups juice. Erin is also making punch with 4 cups of club soda to 10 cups of juice. Whose ratio is the same as Pam's?

_____

3. A restaurant makes vegetable soup using 22 cups of mixed vegetables and 15 cups of stock. Henri tries to make this at home with 5 cups of mixed vegetables and 10 cups of stock. Is Henri using the correct ratio? Explain.

_____

4. Barbara bought 5 amusement park tickets at a cost of $30. If she bought 7 tickets, how much would it cost?

_____

5. Tony bikes 7 miles in one hour. Predict how far he would bike in 4 hours.

_____

6. A sports store sells bicycle baskets at $40.00 for two. Another sports store sells bicycle baskets at $110 for five. Which store sells the baskets at the better rate?

_____

7. Gobbler Stuffing mix has 3 cups of cubed bread and 1 cup of dried vegetables. Perfect Poultry mix has 5 cups of cubed bread to 2 cups of dried vegetables. Which mix has the greater vegetable to bread ratio?

_____

LESSON 6-3

Using Ratios and Rates to Solve Problems
Reteach

You can write a ratio and make a list of equivalent ratios to compare ratios.

Find out who uses more detergent.

Terri's recipe for soap bubble liquid uses 1 cup of dishwashing detergent to 4 cups of water.

Torri's recipe for soap bubble liquid uses 1 cup of dishwashing detergent to 12 cups of water (plus some glycerin drops).

Terri's ratio of detergent to water: 1 to 4 or $\frac{1}{4}$

Torri's ratio of detergent to water: 1 to 12 or $\frac{1}{12}$

List of fractions equivalent to $\frac{1}{4}$: $\frac{1}{4}, \frac{2}{8}, \boxed{\frac{3}{12}}, \frac{4}{16}, \frac{5}{20} \cdots$

List of fractions equivalent to $\frac{1}{12}$: $\boxed{\frac{1}{12}}, \frac{2}{24}, \frac{3}{36}, \frac{4}{48}, \frac{5}{60} \cdots$

You can compare $\frac{3}{12}$ to $\frac{1}{12}$, $\frac{3}{12} > \frac{1}{12}$.

Terri uses much more detergent.

Use the list to compare the ratios. Circle ratios with the same denominator and compare.

1. $\frac{2}{3}$ and $\frac{3}{4}$

   _____

   _____

2. $\frac{4}{5}$ and $\frac{3}{7}$

   _____

   _____

   _____

3. Jack's recipe for oatmeal uses 3 cups of oats to 5 cups of water. Evan's recipe uses 4 cups of oats to 6 cups of water. Thicker oatmeal has a greater ratio of oats to water. Compare the ratios of oats to water to see who makes the thicker oatmeal. Show your work.

   _____

   _____

LESSON 6-3

Using Ratios and Rates to Solve Problems

Reading Strategies: Identify Relationships

To identify a relationship between different units, you can use a table to find a rate. You know that a salad has 6 cups of mixed vegetables.

The Greens Salad Bar provides 3 cups of greens to 2 cups of mixed fresh vegetables.

The Veggie Salad Bar provides 3 cups of mixed fresh vegetables to 2 cups of greens.

The tables below show rates for each salad bar.

Greens (cups)	3	6	9	12	15
Veggies (cups)	2	4	6	8	10

Greens Salad Bar

Greens (cups)	2	4	6	8	10
Veggies (cups)	3	6	9	12	15

Veggie Salad Bar

1. At which salad bar would you get more vegetables in your salad?

   _____

2. Marge really likes lettuce and spinach. To which salad bar should she go?

   _____

3. Rich bought salad for a tailgate party. He had 18 cups of greens and 12 cups of veggies. At which salad bar did he buy the salad?

   _____

4. You know that a salad has 10 cups of mixed vegetables. Can you tell which salad bar it came from? Explain.

   _____

   _____

5. You have 20 cups of veggies in a salad for a large picnic.

   a. How many cups of greens do you have if you bought it at Greens

      Salad Bar? _____

   b. How many cups of greens do you have if you bought it at Veggie

      Salad Bar? _____

LESSON
6-3

Using Ratios and Rates to Solve Problems

Success for English Learners

Problem 1

Mrs. O'Hara frames 5 pictures in 3 hours. Use a table to predict how many pictures she will frame in her workweek of 30 hours.

pictures framed	5	10	15	20	25	. . .	50
hours	3	6	9	12	15		30

Mrs. O'Hara probably frames about 50 pictures in her workweek.

Problem 2

Mr. Suarez plants 6 large trees in 8 hours. Use a double number line to predict how many large trees he will plant in his workweek of 40 hours.

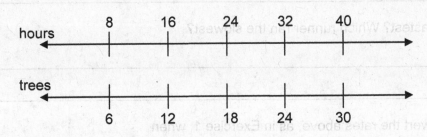

Mr. Suarez will plant 30 large trees in 40 hours.

You can use a table or a double number line. Predict how many sit ups each person can do in 12 seconds.

1. Janet does 3 sit ups in 2 seconds. _____

2. Paulo does 5 sit ups in 6 seconds. _____

3. Shah does 3 sit ups in 4 seconds. _____

4. Which method do you prefer to predict: table or a number line? Explain.

_____

_____

MODULE
6

Representing Ratios and Rates
Challenge

Arabella, Bettina, Chandra, and Divya are runners on the track team.
The distance and time for each runner are shown in the table below.

Runner	Distance	Time
Arabella	7,229 feet	561 seconds
Bettina	3,425 yards	13 minutes, 12 seconds
Chandra	8,214 feet	0.195 hours
Divya	1.62 miles	732 seconds

1. Find the rate for each runner in miles per hour.

_____

_____

2. Which runner ran the fastest? Which runner ran the slowest?

_____

_____

3. Why is it helpful to convert the rates above, as in Exercise 1, when
   comparing the runners?

_____

_____

4. Suppose each runner ran at the rate given in the table above for
   3.1 miles. How much time will elapse between the first place
   finisher and the last place finisher? Show your work.

_____

_____

LESSON 7-1

Ratios, Rates, Tables, and Graphs
Practice and Problem Solving: A/B

Use the table to complete Exercises 1–7.

The table shows information about the packets of flavoring added to an amount of water to make soup.

Packets of Flavoring	2	5		10	
Ounces of Water	24		84		144

1. Find the rate of ounces of water needed for each packet of flavoring. Show your work.

   $$\frac{\text{ounces of water}}{\text{packets of flavoring}} = \underline{\hspace{4cm}}$$

2. Use the unit rate to help you complete the table.

3. Graph the information in the table.

4. How much water should be added to 23 packets of flavoring?

   _____

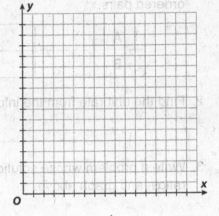

5. Does the point (9.5, 114) make sense in this context? Explain.

   _____

   _____

   _____

6. What are the equivalent ratios shown in the table? Complete the statement.

   $$\frac{24}{2} = \frac{}{3} = \frac{}{5.5} = \frac{108}{} = \frac{}{15}$$

7. Does the relationship shown use addition or multiplication? Explain.

   _____

   _____

LESSON
7-1

Ratios, Rates, Tables, and Graphs
Practice and Problem Solving: C

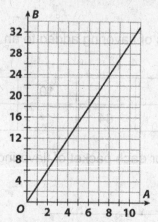

1. Choose several points from the graph and make a table of the ordered pairs.

A					
B					

2. Find the unit rate from the information in the table.

_____

3. Write a problem whose solution could be described by the table, rate, ratios, and graph above.

_____

_____

_____

4. Does the relationship in your problem use addition or multiplication?

_____

5. Does the point (6.5, 19.5) make sense in the context of your problem? Why or why not?

_____

_____

LESSON 7-1

Ratios, Rates, Tables, and Graphs
Practice and Problem Solving: D

Use the table to complete Exercises 1–6.

The table shows information about the number of tires needed for a number of cars.

Number of Tires	8	12		20		
Number of Cars	2	3	4		6	7

1. Complete the table. The first one is done for you.

2. Write the rule for the table.

   _____

3. Find the rate of tires needed for one car. Start with a ratio from the table.

   $\dfrac{tires}{cars}$ = ——— = ——— = ——— tires for every ——— car

4. Write the information in the table as ordered pairs.

   _____

5. Plot the ordered pairs on the graph and draw the line.

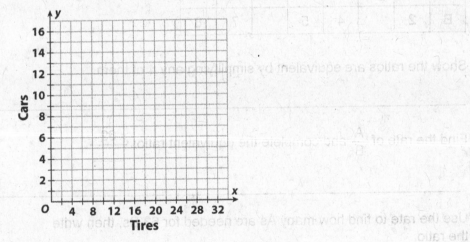

6. Write some equivalent ratios shown by the line of the graph.

   $\dfrac{8}{2}$ = ——— = ——— = ——— = $\dfrac{40}{10}$

LESSON 7-1

Ratios, Rates, Tables, and Graphs
Reteach

A **ratio** shows a relationship between two quantities.

Ratios are **equivalent** if they can be written as the same fraction in lowest terms.

A **rate** is a ratio that shows the relationship between two different units of measure in lowest terms.

You can make a table of equivalent ratios. You can graph the equivalent ratios.

A	4	6	10	12
B	2	3	5	6

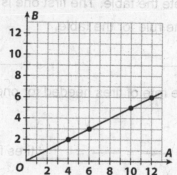

$$\frac{4}{2} = \frac{2}{1} \qquad \frac{6}{3} = \frac{2}{1}$$

$$\frac{10}{5} = \frac{2}{1} \qquad \frac{12}{6} = \frac{2}{1}$$

---

1. Use equivalent ratios to complete the table.

A	6	9			18		
B	2		4	5		7	8

2. Show the ratios are equivalent by simplifying any 4 of them.

_____

3. Find the rate of $\frac{A}{B}$ and complete the equivalent ratio: $\frac{69}{\rule{1cm}{0.4pt}}$.

_____

4. Use the rate to find how many As are needed for 63 Bs, then write the ratio.

_____

LESSON 7-1

Ratios, Rates, Tables, and Graphs
Reading Strategy: Read a Table

Tables help us organize information.

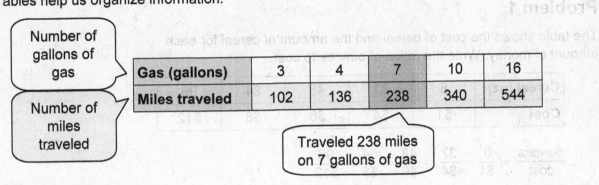

Number of gallons of gas

Gas (gallons)	3	4	7	10	16
Miles traveled	102	136	238	340	544

Number of miles traveled

Traveled 238 miles on 7 gallons of gas

Use the columns to write ratios.

$$\frac{gas}{miles} = \frac{7}{238} \qquad\qquad \frac{miles}{gas} = \frac{238}{7}$$

Use the ratios to write ordered pairs.

$$\frac{7}{238} \longrightarrow (7, 238) \qquad\qquad \frac{238}{7} \longrightarrow (238, 7)$$

1. Read the table. Write all the ordered pairs of cost to pounds. Then write the ordered pairs of pounds to cost.

Cost	$4.50	$7.50	$10.50	$13.50	$16.50
Pounds of Oranges	3	5	7	9	11

_____

_____

2. Find the unit rate. What is the cost of 1 pound of oranges?

   _____

3. Read the table. Write all of the ordered pairs in the order you choose.

Cups of Flour	6	8	10	12	18	24
Teaspoons of Baking Soda	3	4	5	6	9	12

_____

_____

4. Write the unit rate of baking soda to flour.

_____

Name _____ Date _____ Class_____

Ratios, Rates, Tables, and Graphs
Success for English Learners

Problem 1

The table shows the cost of cereal and the amount of cereal for each amount of money. Write the ratios of ounces to cost.

Cereal (oz)	8	32	48	64	96
Cost	$1	$4	$6	$8	$12

$$\frac{\text{ounces}}{\text{cost}} = \frac{8}{\$1} = \frac{32}{\$4} = \frac{48}{\$6} = \frac{64}{\$8} = \frac{96}{\$12}$$

Problem 2

Write the ratios as ordered pairs. Graph the ordered pairs and draw the line.

(8, 1), (32, 4), (48, 6), (64, 8), (96, 12)

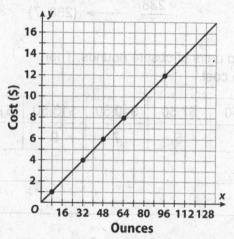

1. How would the ratios change if the problem asked for the ratios of cost to ounces?

_____

2. How would the graph change?

_____

3. Make your own table of ratios of gallons of gas used to the miles traveled. Write the ratios as ordered pairs.

Gas (gal)					
Miles					

_____

Name _____ Date _____ Class_____

LESSON 7-2

Solving Problems with Proportions
Practice and Problem Solving: A/B

Find the unknown value in each proportion. Round to the nearest tenth if needed.

1. $\frac{4}{5} = \frac{}{20}$

2. $\frac{3}{7} = \frac{}{35}$

3. $\frac{4}{3} = \frac{12}{}$

4. $\frac{13}{15} = \frac{52}{}$

Solve using equivalent ratios.

5. Wayne has a recipe on a 3-inch-by-5-inch index card that he wants to enlarge to 15 inches long. How wide will the enlargement be?

_____

6. Sharon is decreasing the size of a diagram of a leaf that is 30 centimeters long by 10 centimeters wide. If the reduced diagram is 4 centimeters wide, how long will it be?

_____

Solve using unit rates. Round to the nearest hundredth if needed.

7. A wood stove burns 4 same-sized logs in 2 hours. How many logs does the stove burn in 8 hours? _____

8. In 2012, five U.S. postal stamps cost $2.20. How much did seven stamps cost? _____

9. a. What is the actual distance between Saugerties and Kingston? _____

   b. Catskill is 15 miles from Saugerties. What would the distance on the map be? _____

   c. On another map, the distance between Saugerties and Kingston is 2 inches. What would the distance from Saugerties to Catskill be on this map? _____

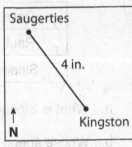

Scale: 1 in. = 2.5 mi.

10. The scale of a map is 1 in. : 250 miles. City A is 378 miles from City B. To the nearest tenth, how far is its distance on the map?

_____

Original content Copyright © by Houghton Mifflin Harcourt. Additions and changes to the original content are the responsibility of the instructor.

133

LESSON 7-2

Solving Problems with Proportions
Practice and Problem Solving: C

Find the unknown value in each proportion. Round to the nearest tenth if needed.

1. $\dfrac{2}{3} = \dfrac{}{7.5}$

2. $\dfrac{7}{100} = \dfrac{3.5}{}$

3. $\dfrac{9}{5} = \dfrac{}{16}$

4. $\dfrac{2}{7} = \dfrac{}{20}$

Solve using equivalent ratios.

5. Suki has a 9 foot by 12 foot oriental rug. She is making a scale drawing of the rug that is 1 foot long. How many inches wide should the diagram be? _____

6. Another rug is 6 feet by 8 feet. For this one, Suki makes a diagram that is $1\dfrac{1}{3}$ feet long. How many inches should its width be? _____

Solve using unit rates. Round to the nearest hundredth if needed.

7. You can buy 4 pounds of peaches for $5.96. What do $4\dfrac{1}{2}$ pounds of peaches cost? _____

8. The table shows the number of miles that Dave, Raul, and Sinead drove on their last trips, as well as the time it took for each drive.

Driver	Distance (mi)	Time (min)
Dave	15	20 min
Raul	15	15 min
Sinead	20	30 min

a. What is Sinead's unit rate in miles per minutes? _____

b. Whose speed was the slowest? _____

c. If all three drivers drove for 2.5 hours at the same speed as their last drive, how many total miles will all three drivers have driven?

_____

9. The scale of a scientific drawing is 1 cm = 2 in. If the actual length of an object in the drawing was 4.5 inches, how long would it be in the drawing? _____

Name _____ Date _____ Class _____

Solving Problems with Proportions

Practice and Problem Solving: D

Find the unknown value in each proportion. The first one has been done for you.

1. $\dfrac{2}{5} = \dfrac{8}{20}$

2. $\dfrac{2}{7} = \dfrac{}{28}$

3. $\dfrac{5}{4} = \dfrac{}{16}$

4. $\dfrac{11}{15} = \dfrac{}{45}$

Solve using equivalent ratios. The first one has been done for you.

5. Jackie has a poster that is 8 inches by 11 inches. She wants to enlarge it so that its length is 33 inches. What should the width be?

   $\dfrac{8}{11} = \dfrac{x}{33}$, $x = 24$; **The width should be 24 in.**

6. Tom has a large photo he wants to shrink to wallet-sized. Its width is 20 centimeters and its length is 30 centimeters. If he wants the width to be 5 centimeters what should the length be? _____

Solve using equivalent ratios. The first one has been done for you.

7. Mr. Sanchez drives 120 miles in 3 hours. At the same rate, how far will he drive in 5 hours? _____ **200 mi** _____

8. Six pounds of apples cost $12.00. How much do 8 pounds cost?

   _____

9. a. What is the actual distance between River City and Pine Bluff?

      _____

   b. White Oak is 15 miles from River City. What would its distance be on the map? _____

   c. On another map, the distance between River City and Pine Bluff is 6 inches. What is the scale of the map?

      _____

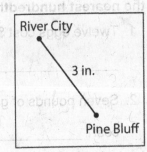

Scale: 1 in. = 3 mi.

10. The scale of a map is 1 in. : 500 miles. City A is 650 miles from City C.

    How far is its distance on the map? _____

**LESSON
7-2**

Solving Problems with Proportions
Reteach

You can solve problems with proportions in two ways.

A. Use equivalent ratios.

Hanna can wrap 3 boxes in 15 minutes.
How many boxes can she wrap in 45 minutes?

$$\frac{3}{15} = \frac{}{45}$$

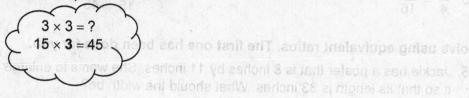

$3 \times 3 = ?$
$15 \times 3 = 45$

$$\frac{3 \cdot 3}{15 \cdot 3} = \frac{9}{45}$$

Hanna can wrap 9 boxes in 45 minutes.

B. Use unit rates.

Dan can cycle 7 miles in 28 minutes.
How long will it take him to cycle 9 miles?

$$\frac{28 \text{ min}}{7 \text{ mi}} = \frac{}{1 \text{ mi}}$$

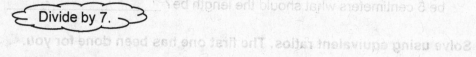

Divide by 7.

$$\frac{28}{7} = \frac{28 \div 7}{1} = \frac{4}{1}, \text{ or 4 minutes per mile}$$

To cycle 9 miles, it will take Dan 9 × 4, or 36 minutes.

Solve each proportion. Use equivalent ratios or unit rates. Round to the nearest hundredth if needed.

1. Twelve eggs cost $2.04. How much would 18 eggs cost?

   _____

2. Seven pounds of grapes cost $10.43. How much would 3 pounds

   cost? _____

3. Roberto wants to reduce a drawing that is 12 inches long by 9 inches
   wide. If his new drawing is 8 inches long, how wide will it be?

   _____

LESSON 7-2

Solving Problems with Proportions

Reading Strategies: Read a Table

> Column headings tell you what data is below.

This table shows the prices for different-sized bottles of fruit juices.

> Rows are read left to right.

Size	Capacity (oz.)	Cost ($)
Small	8	2.80
Medium	12	3.96
Large	16	4.80

> Columns are read up and down.

1. What is the unit cost for each bottle?

   a. Small (8 oz): _____

   b. Medium (12 oz): _____

   c. Large (16 oz): _____

2. Cara drank a 6-ounce glass from the 12-ounce bottle. How much did her drink cost?

   _____

3. Sean drank an 8-ounce glass from the 16-ounce bottle. How much did his drink cost?

   _____

4. Luca had a 4-ounce glass from the 16-ounce bottle. How much did his drink cost?

   _____

This table shows the time three delivery people worked, the miles they drove, and the amount each earned.

Driver	Miles Driven	Hours Driven	Earnings ($)
Jeff	65	7	158.75
Alicia	82	8	180.80
LeShawn	56	6	118.50

5. a. How much did Alicia earn per hour? _____

   b. How much would she earn for 5 hours of work? _____

6. a. On average, how far did LeShawn drive in an hour? _____

   b. On average, how far would she drive in 2 hours? _____

7. Who had the highest earnings per hour? _____

LESSON 7-2

Solving Problems with Proportions
Success for English Learners

Problem 1

Mrs. O'Neill tiles 24 square feet in 3 hours. How many square feet can she tile in 9 hours?

Use a proportion.

$$\frac{24}{3} = \frac{}{9}$$

$3 \times 3 = 9$

$$\frac{24}{3} = \frac{72}{9}$$

$24 \times 3 =$

She can tile 72 square feet in 9 hours.

Problem 2

Which is the better buy: an 18-ounce box of cereal for $4.50 or a 30-ounce box of cereal for $9.00?

Use a unit rate.

$$\frac{4.50}{18} = 0.25$$

$0.25 < 0.30$

$$\frac{9.00}{30} = 0.30$$

The 18-ounce box has a lower unit rate, so it is the better buy.

1. Can you use a unit rate to solve Problem 1? Explain. _____

_____

_____

2. Can you use a proportion to solve Problem 2? Explain. _____

_____

_____

Converting within Measurement Systems
Practice and Problem Solving: A/B

Use proportions to convert.

1. 4 feet to inches

    _____

2. 6 quarts to gallons

    _____

3. 5 kilometers to meters

    _____

4. 2,000 grams to kilograms

    _____

Use conversion factors to convert. Write the factor you used.

5. 5 quarts to cups

    _____

6. 600 centimeters to meters

    _____

Solve.

7. Denver is called the Mile-High City because it is at an altitude of 1 mile.

    How many feet is this? _____

8. The distance from the library to the park is 0.7 kilometers.

    How many meters is this? _____

9. Marcus has three dowels with the lengths shown in the table.
    Complete the table to give each length in inches, feet, and yards.

Dowel	in.	ft	yd
A	36		
B		$5\frac{1}{2}$	
C			$2\frac{1}{2}$

10. Cameron wants to measure a poster frame, but he only has a sheet of
    paper that is $8\frac{1}{2}$ by 11 inches.

    a. He lays the long edge of the paper along the long edge of the frame several times
       and finds the frame is 4 papers long. How long is this in inches?

       _____ In feet? _____

    b. He lays the short edge of the paper along the short edge of the frame several times
       and finds the frame is 3 papers wide. How long is this in inches?

       _____ In feet? _____

11. How would you convert 3 yards 2 feet to inches?

    _____

    _____

LESSON 7-3 Converting within Measurement Systems

Practice and Problem Solving: C

Use proportions to convert.

1. 4.5 feet to inches

   _____

2. 4.5 inches to feet

   _____

3. 543 centimeters to meters

   _____

4. 5.1 kilometers to meters and centimeters

   _____

Use conversion factors to convert.

5. 6.5 quarts to cups

   _____

6. 3.9 meters to centimeters

   _____

Solve.

7. Denver is the Mile-High City. How high is this in feet?_____

   In yards?_____

8. The distance from the porch to the flagpole is 736 centimeters. How far
   is this in meters?

   _____

9. Tammy has 3 chains of different lengths as shown in the table. Complete
   the table. Find the length of the longest and shortest chains and the
   difference between them. Show the difference in inches, feet, and yards.

Chain	yd	ft	in.
gold	$3\frac{1}{2}$		
silver		12.5	
bronze			148

10. a. Pat has a 10-centimeter length of string she is going to use
       to measure a small square table. The side length she measures is
       5 strings. What are the dimensions of the table?

    _____

    b. What is the area of the table? _____

    c. Is that as large as a square meter? Explain.

    _____

LESSON 7-3

Converting within Measurement Systems
Practice and Problem Solving: D

Use proportions to convert. The first one is done for you.

1. 48 inches to feet

   $$\frac{12\text{ in}}{1\text{ ft}} = \frac{48}{x}; 4\text{ ft}$$

2. 2 gallons to quarts

   _____

3. 3,000 meters to kilometers

   _____

4. 1,500 grams to kilograms

   _____

Use conversion factors to convert. Write the factor you used. The first one is done for you.

5. 7 quarts to cups

   4c = 1 qt; 28 c

6. 500 centimeters to meters

   _____

Solve.

7. A bike race takes place over a 3 mile course. How many feet is it?

   _____

8. The distance from the school to the corner is 0.9 kilometers. How many meters is this?

   _____

9. Christina has two pieces of lace trim with lengths as shown in the table. Complete the table to give each length in inches, feet, and yards.

Trim	in.	ft.	yd.
A	24		
B			6

10. a. Lyza has a 9-inch board. She wants to measure the length of a small rug in feet. How can she do this?

    _____

    b. She finds that the 9-inch board fits 4 times along the rug length.

    How many inches is this? _____

    How many feet? _____

11. How would you convert 4 meters 20 centimeters to

    centimeters?_____

LESSON 7-3

Converting within Measurement Systems
Reteach

You can use a bar model to convert measurements.

	1	2	3	4	5
feet					
inches					
	12	24	36	48	60

$\frac{1}{12} = \frac{3}{36}$ so 3 feet = 36 inches

	1,000	2,000	3,000	4,000
grams				
kilograms				
	1	2	3	4

$\frac{1,000}{1} = \frac{4,000}{4}$ so 4,000 g = 4 kg

1. Draw a bar model for converting feet to yards.

2. Draw a bar model for converting cups to fluid ounces.

3. Do you think a bar model would be a good model for converting miles to feet? Explain.

_____

_____

_____

Converting within Measurement Systems

Reading Strategies: Identify Relationships

You can use relationships between customary and metric units to convert within the same measurement system. You can use a table to identify a relationship.

in.	12	24	36
ft	1	2	3

or

in.	18	27	45
ft	1.5	2.25	3.75

1. a. A foot is _____ inches.

   b. An inch is _____ foot.

2. a. To convert feet to inches, _____

   b. To convert inches to feet, _____.

3. If you wanted to show the relationship between meters and centimeters, what would differ in your table?

   _____

   _____

4. Choose a customary and a metric relationship and make a table to show the relationship for each.

LESSON 7-3

Converting within Measurement Systems
Success for English Learners

The two most common systems of measurement used around the world are the **metric system** and the **customary system**. The United States uses the customary system of measurements. Some examples of **customary measurements** are yards (yd), feet (ft), ounces (oz), and pounds (lb).

Problem 1

Nicole bought <u>2 pounds</u> of grapes. <u>How many ounces</u> is this?

How do you **convert,** or change, pounds to ounces?

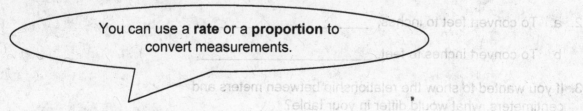

You can use a **rate** or a **proportion** to convert measurements.

1 pound (lb) = 16 ounces (oz)

$$\frac{1\ lb}{16\ oz} = \frac{1\ lb \times 2}{16\ oz \times 2} = \frac{2\ lb}{32\ oz}$$

Two pounds is equal to 32 ounces. So, Nicole bought 32 ounces of grapes.

Problem 2

Joel bought 42 inches of wire. How many yards is that?

Conversion factor: $\dfrac{1\ yd}{36\ in.}$

$$\frac{1\ yd}{36\ in.} = \frac{\frac{7}{6}\ yd}{42\ in.}, \ 42\ in. = \frac{7}{6} \text{ or } 1\frac{1}{6}\ yd$$

42 inches is $1\frac{1}{6}$ yards. Joel bought $1\frac{1}{6}$ yards of wire.

1. Convert 5.5 yards to inches. _____

2. Convert 450 inches to yards. _____

Converting between Measurement Systems

Practice and Problem Solving: A/B

Length	Mass	Capacity
1 inch = 2.54 centimeters 1 foot ≈ 0.305 meter 1 yard ≈ 0.914 meter 1 mile ≈ 1.61 kilometers	1 ounce ≈ 28.4 grams 1 pound ≈ 0.454 kilogram	1 fluid ounce ≈ 29.6 milliliters 1 quart ≈ 0.946 liter 1 gallon ≈ 3.79 liters

Use a conversion factor to convert each measurement. Round your answer to the nearest hundredth.

1. A driveway is 40 yards long. About how many meters long is it?

   _____

2. An ice cube is made of 5 fluid ounces of water. About how many

   milliliters of water does it take to make the ice cube? _____

3. Steven bagged 52 pounds of potatoes. About what is that measure in

   kilograms? _____

4. It is 7 kilometers from Kerry's house to the mall. About what is that

   distance in miles? _____

5. A cooler holds 15 liters of water. About how many gallons does it hold?

   _____

6. Mia's cat weighs 13 pounds, 7 ounces. About what is that weight in

   kilograms? (Hint: 1 kilogram = 1,000 grams) _____

7. D'Quan's grandmother made a quilt for his bed. The quilt is
   2.44 meters long and 1.83 meters wide. What is the area of the quilt in

   square feet? _____

8. It is recommended that an adult drink 64 fluid ounces of water every
   day. Josey has already consumed 700 milliliters of water. How many

   more liters should he drink today? _____

Name _____ Date _____ Class_____

Converting between Measurement Systems
Practice and Problem Solving: C

Some units of measurement are very old and outdated, or used only under certain circumstances.

1 pes ≈ 0.973 foot	1 cubit = 1.5 feet
1 perch = 16.5 feet	1 span = 0.75 foot
1 furlong = 660 feet	1 bamboo ≈ 10.499 feet
1 kick ≈ 3,280.84 feet	1 cabel = 720 feet

1. You have a measure in the units indicated. To which of the measures in the chart would you most likely convert? Why?

    mile _____

    yard _____

    foot _____

    inch _____

    _____

2. How would you convert each unit to feet? How would you convert feet to each unit? Complete the tables below.

Convert to Feet	
Unit	Factor
a. cubit	
b. perch	
c. kick	
d. cabel	

Convert from Feet	
Unit	Factor
e. bamboo	
f. furlong	
g. pes	
h. span	

3. As part of a land grant from General George Washington, a soldier received a parcel of land that measured 108 yards on one side. What is that measure in perches?

    _____

4. In 2004, Xie Qiuping of China held the world's record for the longest hair (female). Her hair measured 5.627 meters. What is that measure in bamboos? (Hint: 1 foot ≈ 0.305 meter)

    _____

Name _____ Date _____ Class _____

Converting between Measurement Systems
Practice and Problem Solving: D

Length	Mass	Capacity
1 inch = 2.54 centimeters 1 foot ≈ 0.305 meter 1 yard ≈ 0.914 meter 1 mile ≈ 1.61 kilometers	1 ounce ≈ 28.4 grams 1 pound ≈ 0.454 kilogram	1 fluid ounce ≈ 29.6 milliliters 1 quart ≈ 0.946 liter 1 gallon ≈ 3.79 liters

To convert customary measurements to metric measurements, multiply by the conversion factor in the table. Round to the nearest hundredth. The first one is done for you.

1. 7 inches × ____**2.54**____ ≈ ____**17.78**____ centimeters

2. 2 pounds × _____ ≈ _____ kilograms

3. 6 fluid ounces × _____ ≈ _____ milliliter

4. 5 gallons × _____ ≈ _____ liters

5. 20 yards × _____ ≈ _____ meters

6. 15 ounces × _____ ≈ _____ grams

To convert metric measurements to customary measurements, write a ratio and multiply. Round to the nearest hundredth. The first one is done for you.

7. 100 grams × $\frac{1}{28.4}$ ≈ ____**3.52**____ ounces

8. 20 liters × _____ ≈ _____ quarts

9. 4 kilometers × _____ ≈ _____ miles

10. 6 kilograms × _____ ≈ _____ pounds

11. 50 centimeters × _____ ≈ _____ inches

12. 81 milliliters × _____ ≈ _____ fluid ounces

Solve.

13. Ashley needs 4.6 yards of chain to hang some flower baskets. The chain is sold by the meter. How many meters does Ashley need?

_____

LESSON 7-4 Converting between Measurement Systems
Reteach

Sometimes you have to convert measurements from one system of measurement to another. You can use this conversion chart to help you change from customary units to metric units.

Length	Mass	Capacity
1 inch = 2.54 centimeters 1 foot ≈ 0.305 meter 1 yard ≈ 0.914 meter 1 mile ≈ 1.61 kilometers	1 ounce ≈ 28.4 grams 1 pound ≈ 0.454 kilogram	1 fluid ounce ≈ 29.6 milliliters 1 quart ≈ 0.946 liter 1 gallon ≈ 3.79 liters

To change from inches to centimeters, multiply the number of inches by the factor in the chart: 1 inch = 2.54 centimeters.

> 8 inches × 2.54 = 20.32 centimeters

Most conversions are approximate. This is shown by the symbol ≈.

Find each conversion factor in the chart.

1. To convert from feet to meters, multiply by _____

2. To convert from quarts to liters, multiply by _____

3. To convert from pounds to kilograms, multiply by _____

4. To convert from gallons to liters, multiply by _____

Use a conversion factor from the chart to change each measurement.

5. 9 yards ≈ _____ meters

6. 4 ounces ≈ _____ grams

7. 12 fluid ounces ≈ _____ milliliters

8. 3 miles ≈ _____ kilometers

9. 24 pounds ≈ _____ kilograms

10. 7 gallons ≈ _____ liters

Name _____ Date _____ Class_____

Converting between Measurement Systems
Reading Strategies: Read a Table

The table below helps you change units of measurement from one system
of measurement to another.

Length	Mass	Capacity
1 inch = 2.54 centimeters 1 foot ≈ 0.305 meter 1 yard ≈ 0.914 meter 1 mile ≈ 1.61 kilometers	1 ounce ≈ 28.4 grams 1 pound ≈ 0.454 kilogram	1 fluid ounce ≈ 29.6 milliliters 1 quart ≈ 0.946 liter 1 gallon ≈ 3.79 liters

Use the table. Find each factor.

1. What is the factor to change pounds to kilograms? _____

2. What is the factor to change quarts to liters? _____

Use the table. Find each measure.

3. 8 yards ≈ _____ meters

4. 2 gallons ≈ _____ liters

5. 6 pounds ≈ _____ kilograms

6. 13 feet ≈ _____ meters

7. 36 fluid ounces ≈ _____ liters

8. 3 miles ≈ _____ kilometers

LESSON 7-4

Converting between Measurement Systems
Success for English Learners

Length	Mass	Capacity
1 inch = 2.54 centimeters		1 fluid ounce ≈ 29.6 milliliters
1 foot ≈ 0.305 meter	1 ounce ≈ 28.4 grams	1 quart ≈ 0.946 liter
1 yard ≈ 0.914 meter	1 pound ≈ 0.454 kilogram	1 gallon ≈ 3.79 liters
1 mile ≈ 1.61 kilometers		

To **convert** a measure means to change the units.

Problem 1

Convert 6 inches to centimeters. Find the factor in the table.

$$6 \text{ inches} \times 2.54 = 15.24 \text{ centimeters}$$

$$6 \text{ inches} = 15.24 \text{ centimeters}$$

Problem 2

Convert 6 centimeters to inches. Find the factor in the table and work backwards.

$$6 \text{ centimeters} \times \frac{1}{2.54} = \frac{6}{2.54} \approx 2.362 \text{ inches}$$

$$6 \text{ centimeters} \approx 2.362 \text{ inches}$$

Find each measurement. Use the factors in the table.

1. 5 miles × _____ ≈ _____ kilometers

2. 4 gallons × _____ ≈ _____ liters.

3. 32 ounces × _____ ≈ _____ grams

4. 15 meters × _____ ≈ _____ yards

5. 9 kilograms × _____ ≈ _____ pounds

6. 8 liters × _____ ≈ _____ quarts

Name _____ Date _____ Class_____

Applying Ratios and Rates
Challenge

A parking lot has three sections. The ratio of the number of cars in the first section to the number of cars in the second section to the number of cars in the third section is 1 : 2 : 3. There are 36 cars in all three sections of the parking lot.

1. How many cars are in each section of the parking lot?

   _____

2. What is one way in which you can move some of the cars between sections so the ratio of cars between sections of the parking lot is 1 : 1 : 1?

   _____

3. Another parking lot with three sections has 80 cars in it. Is it possible for ratio of the number of cars in the first section to the number of cars in the second section to the number of cars in the third section to be 1 : 2 : 3? Explain why or why not.

   _____

   _____

4. Suppose 18 cars are added to the original parking lot of 36 cars in which the ratio of the number cars in the first section to the number of cars in the second section to the number of cars in the third section is 1 : 2 : 3. If all 18 cars are placed in the third section, what will be the new ratio of the number of cars in each section?

   _____

LESSON 8-1

Understanding Percent
Practice and Problem Solving: A/B

Write each percent as a fraction in simplest form and as a decimal to the nearest hundredth.

1. 30% _____

2. 42% _____

3. 18% _____

_____

4. 35% _____

5. 100% _____

6. 29% _____

_____

7. 56% _____

8. $66\frac{2}{3}$% _____

9. 25% _____

_____

Write each decimal or fraction as a percent.

10. 0.03 _____

11. 0.92 _____

12. 0.18 _____

13. $\frac{2}{5}$ _____

14. $\frac{23}{25}$ _____

15. $\frac{7}{10}$ _____

Solve.

16. Bradley completed $\frac{3}{5}$ of his homework. What percent of his homework

    does he still need to complete? _____

17. After reading a book for English class, 100 students were asked whether or not they enjoyed it. Nine twenty-fifths of the class did not like the book. How many students liked the book?

    _____

18. At a concert, 20% of the people are wearing black dresses or suits, $\frac{1}{4}$ are wearing navy, 0.35 are wearing brown, and the rest are wearing a variety of colors (other). Write the percent, fraction, and decimal for each color clothing.

    black _____

    navy _____

    brown _____

    other _____

LESSON
8-1

Understanding Percent
Practice and Problem Solving: C

Write each percent as a fraction in simplest form and as a decimal to the nearest thousandth.

1. 4.5% _____

2. 119% _____

3. 200% _____

_____

_____

_____

4. 0.7% _____

5. 307% _____

6. $5\frac{1}{2}$% _____

_____

_____

_____

Write each decimal or fraction as a percent.

7. $7\frac{1}{7}$ _____

8. $\frac{3}{400}$ _____

9. 0.0054 _____

10. How could you use grids to model percents greater than 100%, such as 217%?

_____

_____

11. How could you use grids to model percents less than 1%, such as 0.7%?

_____

_____

12. In Jeffrey's class, 30% of the students are wearing blue shirts, $\frac{1}{4}$ of the students are wearing green shirts, 0.15 of the students are wearing red shirts and the rest are wearing white shirts. Write the percent, fraction, and decimal for each color shirt.

blue: _____

green: _____

red: _____

white: _____

13. Annabelle's homework is 75% complete. It took her 3 hours. How long should she estimate it will take her to complete her homework?

_____

14. Explain what percent of a dollar a quarter, 2 nickels, a dime and 3 pennies are.

**LESSON
8-1**

Understanding Percent
Practice and Problem Solving: D

Use the 10-by-10 square grids to model each percent. The first one is done for you.

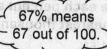

67% means
67 out of 100.

1. 12%

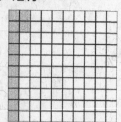

2. 67%

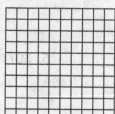

Write each percent as a fraction in simplest form and as a decimal. The first is done for you.

3. 50% $\frac{50}{100} = \frac{1}{2}$

    50 hundredths = 0.50

4. 1% _____

5. 11% _____

6. 10% _____

7. 99% _____

8. 17% _____

9. 73% _____

10. 47% _____

11. 11.5% _____

Write each decimal or fraction as a percent. The first one is done for you.

12. 0.1 $\frac{1}{10} = \frac{10}{100} = 10\%$

13. 0.6 _____

14. 0.02 _____

15. $\frac{1}{2}$ _____

16. $\frac{7}{10}$ _____

17. $\frac{97}{100}$ _____

Solve.

18. A math workbook has 100 pages. Each chapter of the book is 10 pages long. What percent of the book does each chapter make up?

_____

LESSON 8-1 **Understanding Percent**
Reteach

A. A percent is a ratio of a number to 100. Percent means "per hundred."
To write 38% as a fraction, write a fraction with a denominator of 100.

$$\frac{38}{100}$$

Then write the fraction in simplest form.

$$\frac{38}{100} = \frac{38 \div 2}{100 \div 2} = \frac{19}{50}$$

So, $38\% = \frac{19}{50}$.

B. To write 38% as a decimal, first write it as fraction.

$$38\% = \frac{38}{100}$$

$\frac{38}{100}$ means "38 divided by 100."

$$\begin{array}{r} 0.38 \\ 100\overline{)38.00} \\ -300 \\ \hline 800 \\ -800 \\ \hline 0 \end{array}$$

So, 38% = 0.38.

Write each percent as a fraction in simplest form.

1. 43%   2. 72%   3. 88%   4. 35%

_____   _____   _____   _____

Write each percent as a decimal.

5. 64%   6. 92%   7. 73%   8. 33%

_____   _____   _____   _____

LESSON 8-1

Understanding Percent
Reading Strategies: Use Graphic Aids

The word **percent** means "per hundred." It is a ratio that compares a number to 100. A grid with 100 squares is used to picture percents.

Twelve percent is pictured on the grid below.

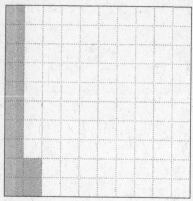

12 percent is a ratio, and means per hundred. $\rightarrow \dfrac{12}{100}$

12 percent can be written with symbols. $\rightarrow$ 12%

Use this figure to complete Exercises 1–4.

1. What is the ratio of shaded squares to total

   squares? _____

2. Write the shaded amount using the %

   symbol. _____

3. What is the ratio of unshaded squares to

   total squares? _____

4. Use the % symbol to write the unshaded

   amount. _____

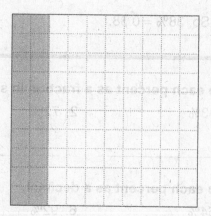

LESSON 8-1

Understanding Percent
Success for English Learners

Problem 1

A percent compares numbers to 100 with the symbol %.

You can rewrite a percent as a decimal or fraction.

$$27\% = \frac{27}{100} = 0.27$$

Problem 2

You can also rewrite a fraction or a decimal as a percent.

For a fraction, first rewrite it as a fraction with a denominator of 100.

$$\frac{3}{4}$$  $$\frac{75}{100}$$

Then write it as a percent.

$$\frac{75}{100} = 75\%$$

For a decimal, first rewrite if necessary as a decimal in hundredths.

$$0.3 = 0.30$$

Then remove the decimal point and write the number as a percent.

$$0.30 = 30\%$$

1. Write each percent as a decimal and as a fraction.

37% _____   6% _____

2. Which way of writing a percent (as a decimal or as a fraction) do you prefer?

_____

_____

Name _____ Date _____ Class_____

Percents, Fractions, and Decimals

Practice and Problem Solving: A/B

Find the percent of each number.

1. 25% of 56

2. 10% of 110

3. 5% of 150

4. 90% of 180

_____

_____

_____

_____

5. 125% of 48

6. 225% of 88

7. 2% of 350

8. 285% of 200

_____

_____

_____

_____

Find the percent of each number. Check whether your answer is reasonable.

9. 55% of 900

10. 140% of 50

11. 75% of 128

12. 3% of 600

_____

_____

_____

_____

13. 16% of 85

14. 22% of 105

15. 0.7% of 110

16. 95% of 500

_____

_____

_____

_____

Solve.

The world population is estimated to be nearly 9 billion by the year 2050.
Use the circle graph to solve Exercises 17–19.

17. What is the estimated population of Africa in

the year 2050? _____

18. Which continent is estimated to have more than
5.31 billion people by the year 2050?

_____

19. What is the combined estimated population for
North and South America in the year 2050?

_____

Estimated 2050 World Population

South America 5.3%
North America 7.9%
Other 0.7%
Europe 7.1%
Asia 59%
Africa 20%

20. In the year 2002, the world population was estimated at 6 billion
people. Based on research from the World Bank, about 20% lived on
less than $1 per day. How many people lived on less than $1 per day?

_____

21. The largest frog in the world is the goliath, found in West Africa. It can
grow to be 12 inches long. The smallest frog in the world is about 2.5%
as long as the goliath. About how long is the smallest frog in the

world?_____

Percents, Fractions, and Decimals
Practice and Problem Solving: C

Tell whether the percent of the number will be greater than, less than, or equal to the number. Explain your reasoning.

1. 25% of 56

   _____

   _____

2. 220% of 35

   _____

   _____

Solve.

3. The price of a shirt was $38. It was reduced by 20% and then again by 10%.

   a. What is the final price of the shirt? _____

   b. What would the price of the shirt be if it were reduced by 30% from

      the original? _____

   c. Explain why the two prices in a. and b. differ.

      _____

      _____

4. In July 2011, about 27% of the population of Texas was under 18 years old. Using the 2011 population figure of 25,674,681, about how many people who lived in

   Texas were under 18? _____

5. The circle graph shows how the Chinn family spends its monthly budget of $5,000.

   a. How much greater is the family's spending on rent than it is on food? Give your answer as a percent and in dollars.

      _____

   b. How much does the family spend on insurance and medical?

      _____

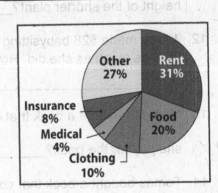

LESSON 8-2

Percents, Fractions, and Decimals
Practice and Problem Solving: D

Find the percent of each number. Check whether your answer is reasonable. The first one is done for you.

1. 20% of 75

   $\dfrac{20}{100} = \dfrac{x}{75}$

   $\dfrac{1}{5} = \dfrac{x}{75}$

   x = 15

2. 25% of 64

   $\dfrac{25}{100} = \dfrac{x}{64}$

   $\underline{\quad\quad} = \dfrac{x}{64}$

   x = _____

3. 4% of 75

   _____

4. 2% of 400

   _____

5. 160% of 80

   _____

6. 12% of 50

   _____

7. 87% of 500

   _____

8. 28% of 250

   _____

9. 500% of 25

   _____

Solve.

10. Frank's Sports Store discounts all sports equipment by 20%. What is the cost of a baseball mitt that originally cost $45?

    _____

11. In a science experiment, two tomato seeds were planted and watered. After six weeks, the plant that was fertilized was 26 centimeters tall. The plant that was not fertilized was only 74% as tall. What was the

    height of the shorter plant?_____

12. Jackie made $28 babysitting last week. Her brother Joe made only 86% as much as she did. How much did Joe make?

    _____

13. Meredith bought a book that cost $18 at a discount of 16%. What did

    she pay for the book?_____

14. Tomás bought a book that cost $18. It was on sale for 84% of its original price. How much did Tomás pay?

    _____

15. Explain why the prices were the same in 13 and 14.

    _____

    _____

LESSON 8-2

Percents, Fractions, and Decimals
Reteach

Percent is a ratio whose second term is 100. The ratio of 27 to 100 is 27%.

To write a fraction as a percent, convert the fraction to an equivalent fraction with a denominator of 100. Then, write it as a percent.

$$\frac{3}{4} = \frac{75}{100} = 75\%$$

with circled ×25 above and ×25 below.

To write a decimal as a percent, move the decimal point two places to the right and write a percent sign.

$$0.89 = 89\%$$

Use the methods above to find the percents.

1. Write the ratio of 41 to 100 as a percent. _____

2. Write 0.23 as a percent. _____

3. Write $\frac{3}{8}$ as a percent. _____

4. How did you change $\frac{3}{8}$ to an equivalent fraction with a denominator of 100?

    _____

    _____

5. Which do you find easier to work with: percents, fractions, or decimals?

    _____

    _____

LESSON 8-2

Percents, Fractions, and Decimals
Reading Strategies: Find a Pattern

You can use decimals to find the percent of a number.

Find 35% of 80.

35% of 80 means 35% times 80.

Step 1: Change the percent to a decimal by using place values.

$$35\% = \frac{35}{100}$$

$$= 0.35$$

Step 2: Multiply the decimal times the number. $\rightarrow 0.35 \times 80$

The answer is 28, so 35% of 80 is 28.

Answer each question.

1. What decimal is equal to 35%? _____

2. How do you change a percent to a decimal?

   _____

3. After the percent is changed to a decimal, what is the next step in

   finding the percent of a number? _____

4. Write 10% as a decimal. _____

5. What is 10% of 60? _____

6. What is 20% of 60? _____

7. What is 30% of 60? _____

8. What is 40% of 60? _____

9. What pattern did you notice in the answers to 10%, 20%, 30%,
   and 40% of 60?

   _____

10. Suppose you know that 10% of 250 is 25. How could you use
    that information to find 30% of 250?

    _____

    _____

LESSON 8-2

Percents, Fractions, and Decimals
Success for English Learners

Problem 1

How much more time will the download take?

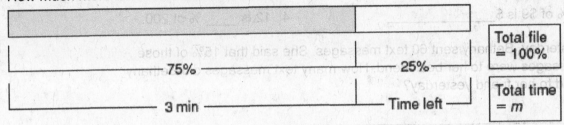

75%	25%

3 min — Time left —

Total file = 100%

Total time = m

$$\frac{75}{100} = \frac{3}{m}$$

$$m = 4$$

It will take 4 minutes for the entire file.

It will take 1 more minute to download the file.

Total time − time passed = time left.
4 min − 3 min = 1 min

Problem 2

What is 20% of 150?

First, write the percent as a decimal.
20% = 20 hundredths
    = 0.20

20

Then multiply the decimal by the number given, 150.

0.20 · 150 = 30

20% of 150 is 30.

1. What is 15% of 84? _____

2. Explain why you represent 75% as $\frac{75}{100}$ in Problem 1.

_____

3. What are two methods of finding the percent of a number?

_____

_____

LESSON 8-3 Solving Percent Problems

Practice and Problem Solving: A/B

Solve.

1. 22 students is ____% of 55.

2. 24 red marbles is 40% of ____ marbles.

3. 15% of $9 is $_____.

4. 12 is ____ % of 200.

5. Yesterday, Bethany sent 60 text messages. She said that 15% of those messages were to her best friend. How many text messages did Bethany send to her friend yesterday?

_____

6. In a survey, 27% of the people chose salads over a meat dish. In all, 81 people chose salads. How many people were in the survey?

_____

7. The sales tax on a $350 computer is $22.75. Find the sales tax rate.

_____

Use the circle graph to complete Exercises 8–12.

8. If 6,000 people voted in the election, how many were from 18 to 29 years old?

_____

9. If 12,000 people voted in the election, how many were from 50 to 64 years old?

_____

10. If 596 people voted in the election, how many were over 65 years old?

_____

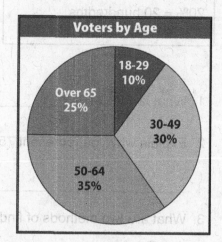

Voters by Age

- Over 65: 25%
- 18-29: 10%
- 30-49: 30%
- 50-64: 35%

11. Suppose that Sahil knows that 45 people with ages of 18 to 29 voted. Without using a calculator, he quickly says then 135 people with ages of 30 to 49 voted. Is he correct? How might Sahil have come up with his answer so quickly?

_____

_____

_____

Solving Percent Problems

LESSON 8-3

Practice and Problem Solving: C

Solve.

1. Selina earns 8% commission on sales. On one sale, her commission was $20.40. What was the amount of that sale?

   _____

2. Bryan bought two shirts for $14.50 each and a pair of shoes for $29.99. The sales tax was 6%. How much did Bryan spend?

   _____

3. Josh created a pattern by using tiles. Twenty tiles were blue. For the rest of the pattern he used equal numbers of red and white tiles. Forty percent of the pattern was made with blue tiles. How many red tiles were used to make the pattern?

   _____

4. Suppose you have a coupon for a 20% discount. You buy a game that costs $38. The sales tax rate is 5.5%. Sales tax applies to the cost after the discount. What is the total cost of the game?

   _____

Use the circle graph to complete Exercises 5–8.

5. Maria spent 40 minutes chatting online. How many minutes did she spend playing games?

   _____

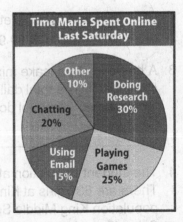

Time Maria Spent Online Last Saturday

Other 10%
Doing Research 30%
Chatting 20%
Using Email 15%
Playing Games 25%

6. How much more time did Maria spend doing research than checking email?

   _____

7. How much time did Maria spend online on Saturday?

   _____

8. Write your own problem using the data from the graph. Your problem should need more than one-step in the solution. Then show how to solve your problem and give the answer.

   Problem: _____

   _____

   Solution: _____

   _____

LESSON 8-3

Solving Percent Problems

Practice and Problem Solving: D

Solve each problem. The first one is done for you.

The world population is estimated to exceed 9 billion by the year 2050. Use the circle graph to solve Exercises 1–2.

1. What is the estimated population of Africa in 2050?

   Solution:

   The graph shows in 2050, Africa will have 20% of the world population. Find 20% of 9 billion.

   Write 20% as a decimal. $20\% = 0.2$

   Multiply 9 by 0.2. $9 \cdot 0.2 = 1.8$

   The estimated population of Africa in 2050

   is about _____ **1.8 billion**

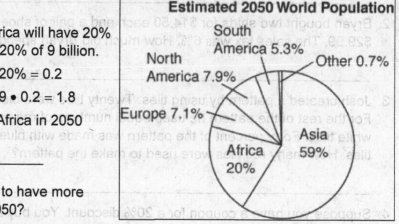

Estimated 2050 World Population

South America 5.3%
North America 7.9%
Other 0.7%
Europe 7.1%
Asia 59%
Africa 20%

2. Which continent is estimated to have more than 5.31 billion people by 2050?

   To solve, find what percent 5.31 billion is of 9 billion.

   Write a ratio of part to whole. $\dfrac{?}{100} = \dfrac{5.31}{9}$

   Solve for ?. Change $\dfrac{\text{your answer for ?}}{100}$ to a decimal and then to a percent. _____%

   Use the graph to complete: In 2050, _____ will have _____% of the population on the graph.

3. A half-cup of pancake mix has 5% of the total daily allowance of cholesterol. The total daily allowance of cholesterol is 300 mg. How much cholesterol does a half-cup of pancake mix have?

   _____

4. The student population at King Middle School is 52% female. There are 637 girls at King Middle School. What is the total student population King Middle School? How many boys go to King Middle School?

   _____

5. Carey needs $45 to buy her mother a gift. She has saved 22% of that amount so far. How much more money does she need?

   _____

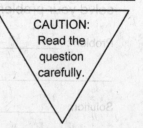

CAUTION:
Read the question carefully.

LESSON 8-3

Solving Percent Problems
Reteach

You can use this proportion to solve percent problems.

$$\frac{part}{total} = \frac{percent}{100}$$

9 is what percent of 12?

Think: part   unknown   total

The number following "of" is the total.

$$\frac{9}{12} = \frac{x}{100}$$

$$12 \cdot x = 9 \cdot 100$$

$$12x = 900$$

$$\frac{12x}{12} = \frac{900}{12}$$

$$x = 75$$

So, 9 is 75% of 12.

30% of what number is 24?

Think: percent   unknown   part

$$\frac{24}{x} = \frac{30}{100}$$

$$30 \cdot x = 24 \cdot 100$$

$$30x = 2,400$$

$$\frac{30x}{30} = \frac{2,400}{30}$$

$$x = 80$$

So, 30% of 80 is 24.

Solve.

1. What percent of 25 is 14?

   a. part = _____

   b. total = _____

   c. percent = _____

   d. Write and solve the proportion.

   Answer: _____ % of 25 is 14.

2. 80% of what number is 16?

   a. part = _____

   b. total = _____

   c. percent = _____

   d. Write and solve the proportion.

   Answer: 80% of _____ is 16.

3. What percent of 20 is 11? _____

4. 18 is 45% of what number? _____

5. 15 is what percent of 5? _____

6. 75% of what number is 105? _____

Name _____ Date _____ Class_____

 LESSON 8-3

Solving Percent Problems
Reading Strategies: Connecting Words and Symbols

You can connect words and symbols to write equations for percent problems.

Ten percent of 190 students are in the band. How many students are in the band?

Use what you know: *n* is 10% of 190

Use symbols: *n* = 10% • 190

Jessica has saved $38. That is 20% of what she wants to save this year. How much does she want to save this year?

Use what you know: $38 is 20% of what number

Use symbols: 38 = 20% • *n*

Bart answered 18 questions correctly. What percent of the 20 questions on the test did he get correct?

Use what you know: 18 is what percent of 20

Use symbols: 18 = *n* • 20

> *Remember*: When finding a percent, your answer will be a decimal that needs to be rewritten as a percent.

Answer each question.

1. What is the symbol for the word "of"? _____

2. What symbol means "is"? _____

3. What symbol in the above examples stands for the unknown

   number? _____

Write an equation for each problem.

4. Mika has completed 5 birdhouses. That is 25% of the number of birdhouses she wants to build. How many birdhouses does she want to build?

   _____

5. A baker made 40 loaves of wheat bread. In all, 160 loaves of bread were made. What percent of the loaves of bread made was wheat bread?

   _____

LESSON 8-3

Solving Percent Problems

Success for English Learners

Problem 1

For Sale $39,500

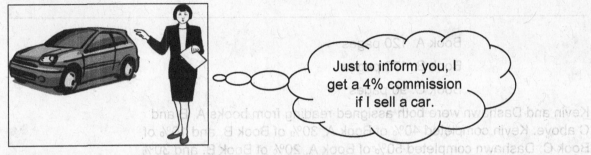

Just to inform you, I get a 4% commission if I sell a car.

Commission   is   Commission Rate   of   Total Sales

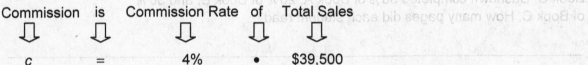

    c =   4%   • $39,500

$c = 4\% \cdot \$39,500$ Write the equation.

$c = 0.04 \cdot \$39,500$ Change the percent to a decimal.

$c = \$1,580$ Multiply.

The salesperson will be paid $1,580 for selling the car.

Problem 2

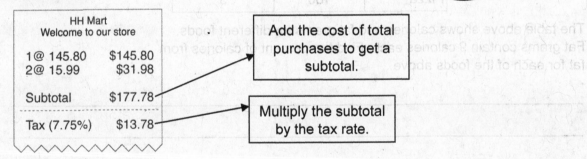

HH Mart	
Welcome to our store	
1 @ 145.80	$145.80
2 @ 15.99	$31.98
Subtotal	$177.78
Tax (7.75%)	$13.78

Add the cost of total purchases to get a subtotal.

Multiply the subtotal by the tax rate.

Find the tax on the sale.

$t = 7.75\% \cdot \$177.78$

$t = 0.0775 \cdot \$177.78$

$t \approx \$13.78$

So, Meka would pay $13.78 in tax for her purchases.

Complete.

1. In Problem 2, what is the total cost, including tax? _____

2. How much is a 6% commission on a sale of $24,000? _____

3. What is the total cost, including tax, of a $48 coat

    with 8% sales tax? _____

Percents

Challenge

1. Anthony found a number that is 20% of 30% of 400. What percent of
   45 is the number that Anthony found?

   _____

2. Book A: 120 pages

    Book B: 170 pages

    Book C: 90 pages

    Kevin and Dashawn were both assigned reading from books A, B and
    C above. Kevin completed 40% of Book A, 30% of Book B, and 10% of
    Book C. Dashawn completed 50% of Book A, 20% of Book B, and 30%
    of Book C. How many pages did each student read?

    _____

Food	Calories	Fat (grams)
Whole Milk	150	8
Egg	80	6
Hamburger	220	15
Pizza	160	3

3. The table above shows calories and fat grams for different foods.
   Fat grams contain 9 calories each. Find the percent of calories from
   fat for each of the foods above.

   _____

   _____

   _____

4. Suppose a food has 300 calories per serving. What is the maximum
   number of grams of fat that the food can contain in order for the
   percent of calories from fat to be 40% or less?

   _____

LESSON 9-1

Exponents

Practice and Problem Solving: A/B

Write each expression in exponential form and find its value.

1. $2 \times 2 \times 2 \times 2$

2. $3 \times 3 \times 3$

3. $\dfrac{3}{5} \times \dfrac{3}{5}$

_____ _____ _____

4. 10×10

5. $\dfrac{1}{6} \times \dfrac{1}{6} \times \dfrac{1}{6} \times \dfrac{1}{6}$

6. $0.5 \times 0.5 \times 0.5$

_____ _____ _____

Find each value.

7. $(1.2)^3$

8. $\left(\dfrac{1}{4}\right)^4$

9. $(2)^6$

10. 2^6

_____ _____ _____ _____

Solve.

11. The volume of a cubic box is 10^6 cubic millimeters.
Write the volume of the box in standard form.

_____

How long is each side of the box? (*Hint*: The length, width, and height of
a cube are equal.)

_____

12. The voltage in an electrical circuit is multiplied by itself each time it is

reduced. The voltage is $\dfrac{27}{125}$ of a volt and it has been reduced three

times. Write the voltage in exponential form. _____

What was the original voltage in the circuit? _____

Compare using >, <, or =.

13. $\left(\dfrac{1}{3}\right)^4$ _____ $\left(\dfrac{1}{3}\right)^0$

14. $(1)^5$ _____ 1^5

15. 5^0 _____ -5^0

16. Use exponents to write 81 three different ways.

$81 =$ _____ ; $81 =$ _____ ; $81 =$ _____

LESSON	**Exponents**
9-1	*Practice and Problem Solving: C*

Use the definitions of exponents to show that each statement is true.

1. $3^5 = (3)^5$

2. $\left(\dfrac{2}{3}\right)^3 < \left(\dfrac{2}{3}\right)^1$

3. $(0.72)^7 > (-7.2)^7$

_____   _____   _____

4. A halogen-lighting manufacturer packs 64 halogen lamps in a cube-shaped container. The manufacturer has been asked by his distributors to package the lamps in a smaller container that holds 8 lamps.

   a. Write the number of lamps in the larger package in exponential

   form. _____

   b. Use the answer to part a. to indicate how many lamps wide, deep, and high the larger shipping container is.

   _____

   c. Write the number of lamps in the smaller package in exponential

   form. _____

   d. How many of the smaller cubic packages fit into the larger cubic package? Explain how you get your answer.

   _____

Simplify each exponential number. Then, multiply the numbers.

5. $\left(\dfrac{2}{3}\right)^4 =$ _____

   $\left(\dfrac{3}{2}\right)^4 =$ _____

   $\left(\dfrac{2}{3}\right)^4 \times \left(\dfrac{3}{2}\right)^4 =$ _____

6. $(0.5)^3 =$ _____ $(2)^3 =$ _____

   $(0.5)^3 \times (2)^3 =$ _____

Use the answers to the third parts of Exercises 5 and 6 to supply the missing number in each problem.

7. $\left(\dfrac{7}{5}\right)^2 \times$ _____ $= 1$ 8. $(4)^3 \times$ _____ $= 1$ 9. $(0.3)^6 \times$ _____ $= 1$

LESSON 9-1

Exponents
Practice and Problem Solving: D

Name the *base* and *exponent*. The first one is done for you.

1. 2^7

2. $\left(\dfrac{5}{6}\right)^4$

3. $(5)^{10}$

Base: ___**2**___

Base: _____

Base: _____

Exponent: ___**7**___

Exponent: _____

Exponent: _____

Write using exponents. The first one is done for you.

4. $10,000 = \mathbf{10 \times 10 \times 10 \times 10} =$

5. $\dfrac{8}{27} = \underline{\quad} \times \underline{\quad} \times \underline{\quad} =$

6. $64 = \underline{\quad} \times \underline{\quad} \times \underline{\quad} =$

_____**10^4**_____

Write as repeated multiplication. The first one is done for you.

7. $(2)^2 =$

8. $(0.25)^3 =$

9. $\left(\dfrac{1}{9}\right)^3 =$

___**$(2) \times (2)$**___

Solve. The first one is done for you.

10. The temperature inside the glazing oven is about 1,000 degrees Fahrenheit. Write 1,000 using exponents.

   Count the number of places from the decimal point on the right to

   the comma between the "1" and the "0" next to it. That number of

   places is the exponent. The base is 10. The answer is $1,000 = 10^3$.

11. A sports memorabilia collector has 3^3 1980 baseball cards and 4^3 1990 football cards. Write the number of baseball cards and football cards in standard form.

12. A long-distance runner ran $4 \times 4 \times 4 \times 4 \times 4 \times 4$ miles last year. How many miles is this?

LESSON 9-1

Exponents

Reteach

You can write a number in exponential form to show repeated multiplication. A number written in exponential form has a **base** and an **exponent**. The exponent tells you how many times a number, the base, is used as a factor.

8^4 ◄——— exponent

│
▼

base

Write the expression in exponential form.

$(0.7) \times (0.7) \times (0.7) \times (0.7)$

0.7 is used as a factor 4 times.

$(0.7) \times (0.7) \times (0.7) \times (0.7) = (0.7)^4$

Write each expression in exponential form.

1. $\dfrac{1}{20} \times \dfrac{1}{20} \times \dfrac{1}{20} \times \dfrac{1}{20}$ 2. 8×8 3. $7.5 \times 7.5 \times 7.5$ 4. (0.4)

_____

You can find the value of expressions in exponential form.
Find the value.
5^6

Step 1 Write the expression as repeated multiplication.
$5 \times 5 \times 5 \times 5 \times 5 \times 5$

Step 2 Multiply.
$5 \times 5 \times 5 \times 5 \times 5 \times 5 = 15{,}625$

$5^6 = 15{,}625$

Simplify.

5. $\left(\dfrac{1}{2}\right)^3$ 6. $(1.2)^5$ 7. 3^6 8. $\left(\dfrac{4}{3}\right)^2$

_____

LESSON 9-1
Exponents
Reading Strategies: Synthesize Information

Exponents are an efficient way to write repeated multiplication.

Read 2^4 $\longrightarrow$ *2 to the fourth power*

2^4 means **2 is a factor 4 times**, or

$2 \times 2 \times 2 \times 2$

Read $2^4 = 16$ $\longrightarrow$ *2 to the fourth power equals 16.*

Exponent	Meaning	Value
10^3 10 to the third power	10 is a factor 3 times: $10 \times 10 \times 10$	$10^3 = 1,000$
6^5 6 to the fifth power	6 is a factor 5 times: $6 \times 6 \times 6 \times 6 \times 6$	$6^5 = 7,776$

Answer each question.

1. Write in words how you would read $(2)^5$.

_____

2. What does $(2)^5$ mean?

_____

3. What is the value of $(2)^5$?

_____

4. Write in words how you would read $\left(\dfrac{3}{5}\right)^4$.

_____

5. Write $\left(\dfrac{3}{5}\right)^4$ as repeated multiplication.

_____

6. Is the value of $\left(\dfrac{3}{5}\right)^4$ equal to $\dfrac{3}{5}$ times four? Explain your answer.

_____

LESSON
9-1

Exponents
Success for English Learners

Problem 1

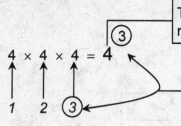

The number you multiply is the **base.**

The number of times you multiply is the **exponent.**

Problem 2

The 7 tells you how many times to multiply the base number.

$2 \times 2 \times 2 \times 2 \times 2 \times 2 \times 2 = 2^7$

1. In Problem 2, what is the base? _____

2. In Problem 2, what is the exponent? _____

3. How do you read the number in Problem 1?

    _____

4. How do you read the number in Problem 2?

    _____

5. a. Write the number 7 raised to the third power. _____

    b. What is the exponent? _____

    c. What is the base? _____

6. a. Write the number 5 raised to the sixth power. _____

    b. What number do you multiply? _____

    c. How many times do you multiply it? _____

Name _____ Date _____ Class_____

Prime Factorization

Practice and Problem Solving: A/B

Fill in the missing information. Add more "steps" to the ladder diagram and more "branches" to the tree diagram, if needed. Then, write the prime factorization of each number.

1.

3 | 36

2.

7 | 42

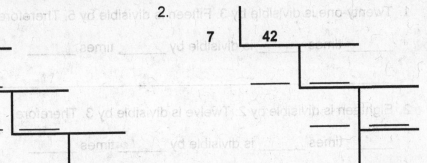

_____   _____

3.   48

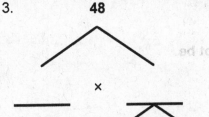

4.   27

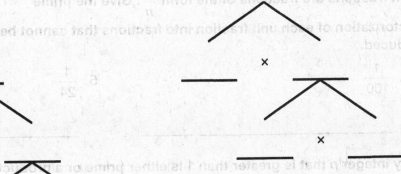

_____   _____

Write the prime factorizations.

5. 44 _____   6. 125 _____   7. 85 _____   8. 39 _____

Prime Factorization
Practice and Problem Solving: C

If 9 is divisible by 3 and 14 is divisible by 2, then 9 × 14 is divisible by 3 × 2. Use this rule to complete Exercises 1–3. Simplify the numbers to prove the result.

1. Twenty-one is divisible by 3. Fifteen is divisible by 5. Therefore,

    _____ times _____ is divisible by _____ times _____

    _____.

2. Eighteen is divisible by 2. Twelve is divisible by 3. Therefore,

    _____ times _____ is divisible by _____ times _____

    _____

3. Ten is divisible by 5. Fourteen is divisible by 7. Therefore,

    _____ times _____ is divisible by _____ times _____

    _____

Unit fractions are fractions of the form $\frac{1}{n}$. Give the prime factorization of each unit fraction into fractions that cannot be reduced.

4. $\frac{1}{100}$

5. $\frac{1}{24}$

Any integer *n* that is greater than 1 is either prime or a product of primes. List the different prime numbers that make up the prime factorization of these composite numbers.

6. 24   7. 105   8. 924

_____   _____   _____

Solve.

9. There are 126 different combinations of soups, salads, and sandwiches available at a café. If there are more choices of sandwiches than choices of salads and fewer choices of soups than salads, how many of each type of food is available at the café?

_____

LESSON
9-2

Prime Factorization
Practice and Problem Solving: D

List all of the factors of each number. Circle the prime factors.
The first one is done for you.

1. 6

      1; ②; ③; 6

2. 9

_____

3. 10

_____

4. 12

_____

5. 21

_____

6. 31

_____

Write the prime factorization of each number. The first one is done for you.

7. 9

      3^2

8. 25

_____

9. 8

_____

10. 14

_____

11. 12

_____

12. 15

_____

13. There are 12 chairs in the meeting hall and an odd number of tables. Each table has the same number of chairs. How many tables are there?

_____

14. What are two different ways that 9 can be written as a product of two numbers?

_____

15. Find the prime factorization of 63 with the factor ladder. The first step is done for you.

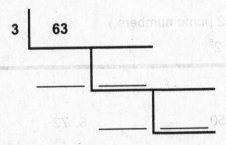

Prime factorization: _____

LESSON 9-2

Prime Factorization

Reteach

Factors of a product are the numbers that are multiplied to give that product.

A factor is also a whole number that divides the product with no remainder.

To find all of the factors of 32, make a list of multiplication facts.

$1 \cdot 32 = 32$

$2 \cdot 16 = 32$

$4 \cdot 8 = 32$

The factors of 32 are 1, 2, 4, 8, 16, and 32.

Write multiplication facts to find the factors of each number.

1. 28 _____

2. 15 _____

3. 36 _____

4. 29 _____

A number written as the product of prime factors is called the **prime factorization** of the number.

To write the prime factorization of 32, first write it as the product of two numbers. Then, rewrite each factor as the product of two numbers until all of the factors are prime numbers.

$32 = 2 \cdot \mathbf{16}$ (Write 32 as the product of 2 numbers.)

$= 2 \cdot \mathbf{4} \cdot \mathbf{4}$ (Rewrite 16 as the product of 2 numbers.)

    ↓   ↓

$= 2 \cdot 2 \cdot 2 \cdot 2 \cdot 2$ (Rewrite the 4's as the product 2 prime numbers.)

So, the prime factorization of 32 is $2 \cdot 2 \cdot 2 \cdot 2 \cdot 2$ or 2^5.

Find the prime factorization of each number.

5. 28 _____

6. 45 _____

7. 50 _____

8. 72 _____

LESSON 9-2

Prime Factorization

Reading Strategies: Use a Graphic Organizer

A graphic organizer can help you "see" how to factor numbers. One of the organizers used in this lesson is the **factor tree**.

Example

Factor 75 using a factor tree.

Start by writing 75 at the top of the tree. Then, think of a prime number that divides 75 evenly.

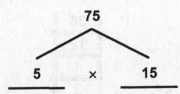

Then, think of a prime number that divides 15 evenly. Add two new "branches" to the tree below 15 as shown.

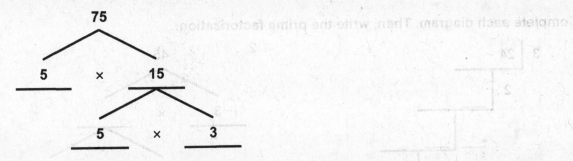

Continue adding "branches" as needed. When the numbers on the last "branch" of the tree are prime numbers, write the prime factorization of the number: $75 = 3 \times 5 \times 5 = 3 \times 5^2$.

Draw a factor tree for each number on the back of this page or on another sheet of paper. Then, write the prime factorization of the number.

1. 360 = _____

2. 378 = _____

_____   _____

LESSON 9-2

Prime Factorization

Success for English Learners

Problem 1

What is the prime factorization of 36?

Factor Tree ← Use → Ladder Diagram

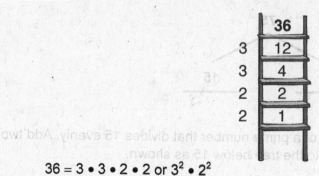

$36 = 3 \cdot 3 \cdot 2 \cdot 2$ or $3^2 \cdot 2^2$

Complete each diagram. Then, write the prime factorization.

1.

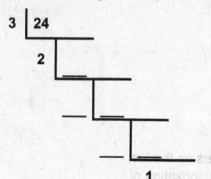

2.

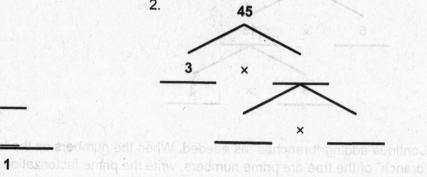

_____   _____

LESSON
9-3

Order of Operations

Practice and Problem Solving: A/B

Name the operation you should perform first.

1. $4 \times 6 - 3$

2. $1 + 8 \div 2$

3. $(2 + 5) - 4^2$

_____

_____

_____

4. $7 \div 7^3 \times 7$

5. $8^2 \div (8 - 4)^2$

6. $-4 + 3^3 \div 5$

_____

_____

_____

Match each expression to its value.

Expression

Value

7. $7 + 8 - 2$ ————— A. 9

8. $9 + (12 - 10)$ B. 40

9. $(20 - 15) \times 2$ C. 12

10. $10 \div 5 + 7$ D. 14

11. $6 + 2 \times 3$ E. 16

12. $(2 \times 4) + 8$ F. 11

13. $14 + 2 \times 0$ G. 13

14. $(5 - 1) \times 10$ H. 10

15. A sixth-grade student bought three cans of tennis balls for $4 each. Sales tax for all three cans was $.95. Write an expression to show the total amount the student paid.

_____

16. The middle-school camera club sold 240 tulip bulbs and 360 daffodil bulbs. Students divided the bulbs into 100 bags to sell at the school fair. Write an expression to show how many bulbs went into each of the 100 bags if students put the same number of each kind of bulb in each bag.

_____

LESSON 9-3

Order of Operations
Practice and Problem Solving: C

Insert +, −, ×, and/or ÷ signs to make each statement true.

1. 1 ◯ 2 < 3 ◯ 4

2. (5 ◯ 6) + 7 = 6 ◯ (5 − 4)

3. 8 + 9 ◯ 10 > (6 × 7) ◯ 5

Evaluate each expression.

4. $(5 + 0) \div 4$

_____

5. $5 + (0 \div 4)$

_____

6. $7 \div (6 + 0)$

_____

7. $(7 + 6) \div 0$

_____

8. $(1 \times 2) \div 3$

_____

9. $1 \div (2 \times 3)$

_____

Write the consecutive integers that make the statements true.

10. _____ $< (15 \div 7) \times 4 <$ _____

11. _____ $> 7 \times (6 \div 4)^2 >$ _____

The Pythagorean Theorem states that sum of the squares of the two legs of a right triangle, *a* and *b*, is equal to the square of the hypotenuse, *c*, of the right triangle: $a^2 + b^2 = c^2$. Use the theorem to complete Exercises 12–14.

12. One leg of a right triangle is 4 less than the other leg. The square of the hypotenuse of the right triangle is 80. How long are the legs of the right triangle? Show your work.

_____

_____

13. Find the square of the leg *b* of this right triangle: $a = 2b$, $c = 10$

_____

14. Find the square of the hypotenuse of a right triangle with *a* and *b* related by the statement $a = b - 5$.

_____

LESSON 9-3

Order of Operations

Practice and Problem Solving: D

Name the operation you should perform first.
The first one is done for you.

	Order of Operations
	1. Parentheses
	2. Exponents
	3. Multiplication
	4. Division
	5. Addition
	6. Subtraction

1. $5 + 6 \times 2$ 2. $18 \div 3 - 1$

__**Multiplication**__   _____

3. $3^2 + 6$ 4. $(15 + 38) \times 6$

_____   _____

Match each expression to its value. The first one
is done for you.

	Expression	Value
__E__	5. $7 + 8 - 2$	A. 9
_____	6. $9 + (12 - 10)$	B. 12
_____	7. $(20 - 15) \times 2$	C. 16
_____	8. $10 \div 5 + 7$	D. 11
_____	9. $6 + 2 \times 3$	E. 13
_____	10. $(2 \times 4) + 8$	F. 10

11. a. Sam bought two CDs for $13 each. Sales tax for both CDs was $3.
    Write an expression to show how much Sam paid in all.

    _____

    b. How much did Sam pay?

    _____

12. Write an expression using multiplication and addition with a sum of 16.

    _____

13. Write an expression using division and subtraction with a difference of 3.

    _____

LESSON 9-3 Order of Operations
Reteach

A mathematical phrase that includes only numbers and operations is called a *numerical expression*.

$9 + 8 \times 3 \div 6$ is a numerical expression.

When you evaluate a numerical expression, you find its value.

You can use the order of operations to evaluate a numerical expression.

Order of operations:

1. Do all operations within *parentheses*.
2. Find the values of numbers with *exponents*.
3. *Multiply* and *divide* in order from left to right.
4. *Add* and *subtract* in order from left to right.

Evaluate the expression.

$60 \div (7 + 3) + 3^2$

$60 \div 10 + 3^2$	Do all operations within parentheses.
$60 \div 10 + 9$	Find the values of numbers with exponents.
$6 + 9$	Multiply and divide in order from left to right.
15	Add and subtract in order from left to right.

Simplify each numerical expression.

1. $7 \times (12 + 8) - 6$

   $7 \times$ _____ $- 6$

   _____ $- 6$

   _____

2. $10 \times (12 + 34) + 3$

   $10 \times$ _____ $+ 3$

   _____ $+ 3$

   _____

3. $10 + (6 \times 5) - 7$

   $10 +$ _____ $- 7$

   _____ $- 7$

   _____

4. $2^3 + (10 - 4)$

   _____

5. $7 + 3 \times (8 + 5)$

   _____

6. $36 \div 4 + 11 \times 8$

   _____

7. $5^2 - (2 \times 8) + 9$

   _____

8. $3 \times (12 \div 4) - 2^2$

   _____

9. $(3^3 + 10) - 2$

   _____

Solve.

10. Write and evaluate your own numerical expression. Use parentheses, exponents, and at least two operations.

    _____

LESSON
9-3

Order of Operations

Reading Strategies: Use a Memory Aid

A memory aid can help you recall the order of operations in simplifying a numerical expression. Just remember the first letter of each operation.

P $\longrightarrow$ **Parentheses**

E $\longrightarrow$ **Exponents**

M $\longrightarrow$ **Multiply**

D $\longrightarrow$ **Divide**

A $\longrightarrow$ **Add**

S $\longrightarrow$ **Subtract**

The six letters form the "word" **PEMDAS**, pronounced "Pem-das". "Pem" rhymes with "Tim", and "das" sounds like "does."

Another way to recall the order of operation is in a sentence.

"<u>P</u>lease <u>E</u>xcuse <u>M</u>y <u>D</u>ear <u>A</u>unt <u>S</u>ally."

You can come up with your own sentence using the first letters of the operations, too.

Fill in the steps in each simplification.

1. $4 + (9 \div 3)^2 \times 5 - 1$

P: _____

E: _____

M: _____

D: _____

A: _____

S: _____

2. $(3 \times 2) + 5^2 - 8 \div 2$

P: _____

E: _____

M: _____

D: _____

A: _____

S: _____

Simplify.

3. $12 \times 4 \div 2 + (7 - 5)^4$

_____

4. $1 + 2^3 - (4 \times 5) \div 10$

_____

**LESSON
9-3**

Order of Operations

Success for English Learners

Problem 1

What did Regina spend on both glass and wooden beads?

Wooden beads   **Glass beads**

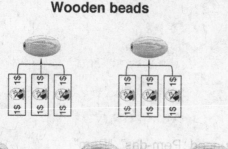

 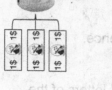   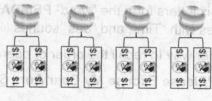

5×3 + 8×2

15   +   16

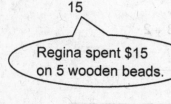

Regina spent $15
on 5 wooden beads.

Regina spent $16
on 8 glass beads.

$31

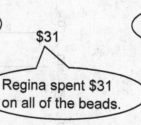

Regina spent $31
on all of the beads.

1. Why do you have to multiply the number of beads by the price before adding?

_____

_____

2. When would you add the number of beads first and then multiply by the price?

_____

_____

MODULE 9 **Generating Equivalent Numerical Expressions**
Challenge

1. Complete the table using the fact that the exponent in a power of 10 is the same as the number of zeros when the number is written out. Then use your observations to explain how you can find the product of any two powers of 10, $10^a \times 10^b$.

Product	Number of Zeros in Product	Product as Powers
100 × 1,000 =		$10^2 \times 10^3 =$
10 × 100,000 =		$10^1 \times 10^5 =$
1,000 × 10 =		$10^3 \times 10^1 =$

_____

2. List all the factors for each of the numbers in the table, which are grouped as perfect square numbers and non-perfect square numbers.

Perfect Square Numbers			Non-Perfect Square Numbers		
9	16	25	6	15	20

a. Count the number of factors for each number. How does the number of factors for perfect square numbers compare to the number of factors for non-perfect square numbers?

_____

b. Use your observation to answer this question: What is the least whole number that has exactly 9 factors, including 1 and itself?

_____

3. Insert parentheses to make each statement true. If parentheses are not needed, then say so.

28 ÷ 4 + 3 × 48 ÷ 6 − 2 = 29 _____

28 ÷ 4 + 3 × 48 ÷ 6 − 2 = 30 _____

28 ÷ 4 + 3 × 48 ÷ 6 − 2 = 43 _____

Name _____ Date _____ Class_____

Modeling and Writing Expressions
Practice and Problem Solving: A/B

Solve.

1. Jessica rode 9 miles farther than Roger rode. Let *r* represent the number of miles Roger rode. Write an expression for the number of miles Jessica rode.

   _____

2. Let *m* represent the number of children playing soccer. Those children are separated into 4 equal teams. Write an expression for the number of children on each team.

   _____

3. Glenda bought some apps for her tablet. Each app cost $5. Let *n* represent the number of apps she bought. Write an expression to show the total amount she spent.

   _____

Write each phrase as a numerical or algebraic expression.

4. 25 multiplied by 3

   _____

5. 3 added to *n*

   _____

6. *r* divided by 8

   _____

7. the product of 7 and *m*

   _____

8. the difference between 48 and 13

   _____

9. the quotient of 18 and 3

   _____

10. 189 subtracted from *t*

    _____

11. the sum of *w* and 253

    _____

Write two word phrases for each expression.

12. $t + 23$ _____

13. $45 - n$ _____

Solve.

14. Write an expression that has two terms. Your expression should have a variable and a constant.

    _____

LESSON 10-1

Modeling and Writing Expressions
Practice and Problem Solving: C

Solve.

1. Cal bought 2 packs of 100 paper plates and 1 pack of 60 paper plates. Write an expression for the total number of plates that he bought.

   _____

2. The temperature dropped 25°. Then the temperature went up 17°. Let *t* represent the beginning temperature. Write an expression to show the ending temperature.

   _____

3. Jill purchased fruit juice boxes for a party. She purchased 1 case of 44 boxes and several packs containing 4 boxes each. Let *p* represent the number of 4-box packs she purchased. Write an expression for the total number of juice boxes Jill purchased.

   _____

Use the figures at the right for Exercises 4–6.

4. Write an expression for the perimeter of the triangle at the right.

   _____

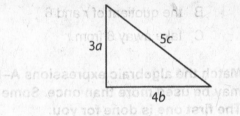

5. Write an expression for the perimeter of the square.

   _____

6. Write an expression for the area of the square.

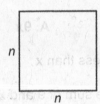

Solve.

7. Write an expression that has four terms. Your expression should have three different variables and a constant.

   _____

8. Josef said that he could represent the amount of money he made last week with the expression: $24d + 8n$. Write a problem about the money Josef made last week.

   _____

   _____

Modeling and Writing Expressions

Practice and Problem Solving: D

Circle the letter of the correct answer. The first one is done for you.

solution: result: answer

1. Which of the following is the **solution** to an addition problem?

   (A) sum

   B plus

   C add

2. Which word phrase represents the following expression $n - 3$?

   A the quotient of n and 3

   B 3 less than n

   C n less than 3

3. Which word phrase represents the following expression $5m$?

   A 5 fewer than m

   B m groups of 5

   C m divided by 5

4. Which of the following is the **solution** to a multiplication problem?

   A quotient

   B factor

   C product

5. Which word phrase represents the following expression $r \div 6$?

   A the product of r and 6

   B the quotient of r and 6

   C take away 6 from r

6. Which word phrase represents the following expression $3 + p$?

   A 3 increased by p

   B 3 decreased by p

   C the difference of 3 and p

Match the algebraic expressions A–E to Exercises 7–12. Some letters may be used more than once. Some letters may not be used at all. The first one is done for you.

A. $9x$	B. $9 + x$	C. $x - 9$	D. $x \div 9$	E. $9 - x$

7. 9 less than x   **C**

8. the quotient of 9 and x ____

9. the sum of 9 and x ____

10. the product of 9 and x ____

11. x more than 9 ____

12. x decreased by 9 ____

Solve.

13. Nicole had 38 beads. She lost some of them. This can be modeled by the expression $38 - x$. What does x represent?

_____

14. Wilhelm bought some shirts. He paid $12 for each shirt. This can be modeled by the expression $12x$. What does x represent?

_____

LESSON
10-1

Modeling and Writing Expressions
Reteach

Write an expression that shows how much longer the Nile River is than
the Amazon River.

NILE RIVER

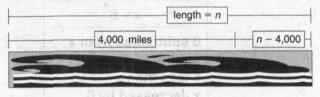

The expression is **_n_ – 4,000**.

AMAZON RIVER

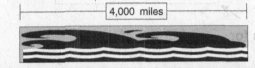

Each state gets the same number of senators. Write an expression for
the number of senators there are in the United States Congress.

There are
50 states.

There are *s*
senators from
each state.

50*s*

The total number of
senators is **50 times *s***.

Solve.

1. Why does the first problem above use subtraction?

_____

2. Why does the second problem above use multiplication?

_____

3. Jackson had *n* autographs in his autograph book. Yesterday he got 3
   more autographs. Write an expression to show how many autographs
   are in his autograph book now.

_____

4. Miranda earned $*c* for working 8 hours. Write an expression to show
   how much Miranda earned for each hour worked.

_____

LESSON 10-1

Modeling and Writing Expressions

Reading Strategies: Use a Visual Map

Identifying word phrases for different operations can help you understand and write algebraic expressions. This visual map shows the four different operations with key word phrases in boldface.

$x + 13$
x **plus** 13
add 13 **to** x
the sum of x **and** 13
13 **more than** x
x **increased by** 13

$x - 6$
6 **subtracted from** x
subtract 6 **from** x
6 **less than** x
x **decreased by** 6
take away 6 **from** x

Word Phrases for Algebraic Expressions

$5x$ or $(5)(x)$ or $5 \bullet x$
5 **times** x
x **multiplied by** 5
the product of 5 **and** x

$\dfrac{x}{2}$ or $x \div 2$
x **divided by** 2
the quotient of x
with a divisor of 2

Write a word phrase for each algebraic expression.

1. $t - 8$ _____

2. $\dfrac{n}{6}$ _____

3. $4w$ _____

4. $z + 8$ _____

5. $9 \bullet m$ _____

Write an algebraic expression for each word phrase.

6. the sum of p and 12

7. i decreased by 7 _____

8. the quotient of r with a divisor of 3 _____

9. z decreased by 1

10. the product of y and 19 _____

Modeling and Writing Expressions

LESSON 10-1

Success for English Learners

Problem 1

There are key words and phrases that tell you which operations to use for mathematical expressions.

Addition (combine)	Subtraction (compare, take away)	Multiplication (put together equal groups)	Division (separate into equal groups)
add plus sum total increased by more than	minus difference subtract less than decreased by take away	product times multiply	quotient divide divide by

Translate **words** and **phrases** into mathematical expressions:

3 **plus** 5 $\longrightarrow$ $3 + 5$

4 **less than** p $\longrightarrow$ $p - 4$

15 **times** n $\longrightarrow$ $15n$

h **divided by** 4 $\longrightarrow$ $h \div 4$

Problem 2

You can use key words to write word phrases for mathematical expressions. You can write different word phrases for the same expression.

$7k \rightarrow$ the **product of** 7 and k $8 - 2 \rightarrow$ 2 **less than** 8 $n + 10 \rightarrow$ 10 **more than** n

$\rightarrow$ 7 **times** k $\rightarrow$ **8 minus** 2 $\rightarrow$ the **sum of** n and 10

Write each phrase as a numerical or algebraic expression.

1. m increased by 5

2. 18 divided by 2

3. the difference between t and 7

_____

4. r multiplied by 4

5. x decreased by 9

6. the quotient of 21 and 7

_____

Write a phrase for each expression.

7. $a - 2$

8. $8 \cdot 6$

_____

_____

9. $p \div 8$

10. $v + 10$

_____

_____

LESSON
10-2
Evaluating Expressions
Practice and Problem Solving: A/B

Evaluate each expression for the given value(s) of the variable(s).

1. $a - 4$ when $a = 16$

_____

2. $2b + 9$ when $b = 3$

_____

3. $c \div 2$ when $c = 26$

_____

4. $5(9 + d) - 6$ when $d = 3$

_____

5. $g^2 + 23$ when $g = 6$

_____

6. $3h - j$ when $h = 8$ and $j = 11$

_____

7. $(n - 2) \cdot m$ when $n = 5$ and $m = 9$

_____

8. $r(s^2)(t)$ when $r = 2$, $s = 3$, and $t = 5$

_____

Use the given values to complete each table.

9.

p	2(13 − p)
2	
3	
4	

10.

v	w	3v + w
4	2	
6	3	
8	4	

11.

x	y	x² ÷ y
2	1	
6	2	
8	4	

Solve.

12. The sales tax in one town is 8%. So, the total cost of an item can be written as $c + 0.08c$. What is the total cost of an item that sells for $12?

_____

13. To change knots per hour to miles per hour, use the expression $1.15k$, where k is the speed in knots per hour. A plane is flying at 300 knots per hour. How fast is that plane flying in miles per hour?

_____

14. Lurinda ordered some boxes of greeting cards online. The cost of the cards is $6.50n + $3 where n is the number of boxes ordered and $3 is the shipping and handling charge. How much will Lurinda pay if she orders 8 boxes of cards?

_____

Evaluating Expressions

LESSON 10-2

Practice and Problem Solving: C

Use the given values to complete each table.

1.

r	$3.14 \cdot r^2$
2	
3	
4	

2.

z	a	$2z - a$
–4	2	
0	2	
4	2	

3.

x	y	$10x^2 \div (y + 1)$
2	1	
–1	3	
–4	4	

Solve.

4. Melinda is hauling water in her pickup truck. An old bridge has a maximum weight limit of 6,000 pounds. To find the weight of her truck, Melinda uses the expression $5,275 + 8.36g$, where g is the number of gallons of water she is hauling. Can Melinda safely drive her pickup across the bridge if she is hauling 120 gallons of water? Explain.

_____

5. A certain machine produces parts that are rectangular prisms. The surface area of each part is found by using the expression $2s^2 + 4sh$, where s is the length of a side of the base and h is the height. What is the surface area of that part when s is 0.5 mm and h is 2 mm? _____ mm²

Three students incorrectly evaluated $4x^2 + 2y$ for $x = 3$ and $y = -2$. Use the table below to complete Exercises 6–9.

Grayson	Emily	Pat
$4x^2 + 2y = 4(3)^2 + 2(-2)$	$4x^2 + 2y = 4(3)^2 + 2(-2)$	$4x^2 + 2y = 4(3)^2 + 2(2)$
$= 144 + (-4)$	$= 36 + 2(-2)$	$= 36 + 4$
$= 140$	$= 38(-2)$	$= 40$
	$= -76$	

6. What error did Grayson make?

_____

7. What error did Emily make?

_____

8. What error did Pat make?

_____

9. Show the correct way to complete the evaluation of $4x^2 + 2y$ for $x = 3$ and $y = -2$.

_____

_____

LESSON
10-2

Evaluating Expressions
Practice and Problem Solving: D

Evaluate each expression for the given value of the variable.
Show each step you used. The first one is done for you.

1. $3n + 4^2$ when $n = 2$

   $3 \times \mathbf{2} + 4^2 \quad \rightarrow \quad$ Substitute 2 for n.

   $3 \times 2 + \mathbf{16} \quad \rightarrow \quad$ Evaluate exponents.

   $\mathbf{6} + 16 \quad\quad \rightarrow \quad$ Multiply.

   $\mathbf{22} \quad\quad\quad \rightarrow \quad$ Add.

2. $2 \times (a + 3)$ when $a = 5$

   $2 \times (5 + 3) \quad \rightarrow$ Substitute values.

   $2 \times \underline{} \quad\quad \rightarrow$ Clear the parentheses.

   $\underline{} \quad\quad\quad \rightarrow$ Multiply.

3. $r + r \div 2 \times 4$ when $r = 8$

   $8 + 8 \div 2 \times 4 \quad \rightarrow$ Substitute values.

   $8 + \underline{} \times 4 \quad \rightarrow$ Multiply or divide from left to right, so divide first.

   $8 + \underline{} \quad\quad \rightarrow$ Multiply.

   $\underline{} \quad\quad\quad \rightarrow$ Add.

Use the given values to complete each table. The first one is done for you.

4.

w	6(3 + w)
2	30
3	36
4	42

5.

c	2c + 7
4	
6	
8	

6.

w	$w^2 - 3$
2	
3	
4	

Solve. Show your work.

7. The height of horses is measured in *hands*. To find the
   height of a horse in inches, use the expression $4h$,
   where h is the number of hands. Rosa has a horse that
   is 15 hands tall. How tall is Rosa's horse in inches?

   Rosa's horse is _____ inches tall.

LESSON 10-2

Evaluating Expressions
Reteach

A **variable** is a letter that represents a number that can change in an expression. When you **evaluate** an algebraic expression, you substitute the value given for the variable in the expression.

- Algebraic expression: $x - 3$

  The value of the expression depends on the value of the variable x.

  If $x = 7 \rightarrow 7 - 3 = 4$
  If $x = 11 \rightarrow 11 - 3 = 8$
  If $x = 25 \rightarrow 25 - 3 = 22$

- Evaluate $4n + 5$ for $n = 7$.

  Replace the variable n with 7. $\rightarrow 4(7) + 5$

  Evaluate, following the order of operations. $\rightarrow 4(7) + 5 = 28 + 5 = 33$

Evaluate each expression for the given value. Show your work.

1. $a + 7$ when $a = 3$

   $a + 7 = 3 + 7 = $ ____

2. $y \div 3$ when $y = 6$

   $y \div 3 = $ ____ $\div 3 = $ ____

3. $n - 5$ when $n = 15$

   $n - 5 = $ ____ $- 5 = $ ____

4. $(6 + d) \cdot 2$ when $d = 3$

   $(6 + d) \cdot 2 = (6 + $ ____ $) \cdot 2$

   $= $ ____ $\cdot 2 = $ ____

5. $3n - 2$ when $n = 5$

   $3n - 2 = 3($ ____ $) - 2 = $ ____

6. $6b$ when $b = 7$

7. $12 - f$ when $f = 3$

8. $\dfrac{m}{5}$ when $m = 35$

9. $2k + 5$ when $k = 8$

10. $10 - (p + 3)$ when $p = 7$

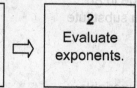

Evaluating Expressions

Reading Strategies: Use a Flowchart

A flowchart gives you a plan. You can use a flowchart to evaluate expressions.

1 Substitute for each variable.	⇨	2 Evaluate exponents.	⇨	3 Eliminate parentheses.	⇨	4 Multiply and divide from left to right.	⇨	5 Add and subtract from left to right.

Evaluate $x^2 - 3(4 + 1)$ when $x = 7$.

$7^2 - 3(4 + 1)$

$49 - 3(4 + 1)$

$49 - 3(5)$

$49 - 15$

34

Plan
1 Substitute for each variable.
2 Evaluate exponents.
3 Eliminate parentheses.
4 Multiply and divide from left to right.
5 Add and subtract from left to right.

Evaluate $(2n + 8) \div t - 2$ when $n = 6$ and $t = 5$.

$(2 \cdot 6 + 8) \div 5 - 2$

There are no exponents.

$(12 + 8) \div 5 - 2$
$20 \div 5 - 2$

$4 - 2$

2

Use the flowchart to evaluate each expression.

1.

Plan	Evaluate $(5 + y) - 3^2$ when $y = 14$.
1 Substitute for each variable.	
2 Evaluate exponents.	
3 Eliminate parentheses.	
4 Multiply and divide from left to right.	
5 Add and subtract from left to right.	

2.

Plan	Evaluate $m^2 - 2(3p + 6)$ when $m = 10$ and $p = 4$.
1 Substitute for each variable.	
2 Evaluate exponents.	
3 Eliminate parentheses.	
4 Multiply and divide from left to right.	
5 Add and subtract from left to right.	

LESSON 10-2

Evaluating Expressions
Success for English Learners

Problem 1

Find the missing values in the table.

Step 1: Substitute for the variables.

Step 2: Compute. Follow the order of operations.

Evaluate $4 \times n + 6^2$ for each value of n.

n	$4 \times n + 6^2$	
2	$4 \times \mathbf{2} + 6^2 \rightarrow$	Substitute 2 for n.
	$4 \times \mathbf{2} + \mathbf{36} \rightarrow$	Evaluate exponents.
	$\mathbf{8} + 36 \rightarrow$	Multiply.
	$44 \rightarrow$	Add.
5	$4 \times \mathbf{5} + 6^2 \rightarrow$	Substitute 5 for n.
	$4 \times \mathbf{5} + \mathbf{36} \rightarrow$	Evaluate exponents.
	___ $+ 36 \rightarrow$	Multiply.
	___ $\rightarrow$	Add.
9	$4 \times \mathbf{9} + 6^2 \rightarrow$	Substitute 9 for n.
	$4 \times \mathbf{9} + \mathbf{36} \rightarrow$	Evaluate exponents.
	___ $+ 36 \rightarrow$	Multiply.
	___ $\rightarrow$	Add.

Fill in the missing values in the table above.

Check your work.

Did you get a result of 56 when $n = 5$?

Did you get a result of 72 when $n = 9$?

Problem 2

Find the missing values in the table.

Step 1: Substitute for the variables.

Step 2: Compute. Follow the order of operations.

Evaluate $2l + 2w$ for the given values.

l	w	$2l + 2w$	
4	3	$2 \times 4 + 2 \times 3 \rightarrow$	Substitute values.
		$8 + 6 \rightarrow$	Multiply first.
		$14 \rightarrow$	Add.
5	2	$2 \times 5 + 2 \times 2 \rightarrow$	Substitute values.
		___ $+$ ___ $\rightarrow$	Multiply first.
		___ $\rightarrow$	Add.
9	6	$2 \times$ ___ $+ 2 \times$ ___ $\rightarrow$	Substitute.
		___ $+$ ___ $\rightarrow$	Multiply first.
		___ $\rightarrow$	Add.

Fill in the missing values in the table above.

Check your work.

Did you get a result of 14 when $l = 5$ and $w = 2$?

Did you get a result of 30 when $l = 9$ and $w = 6$?

Use the given values to complete each table.

1.

r	$2(3 + r)$
2	
3	
4	

2.

c	t	$2c + t$
4	2	
6	3	
8	4	

3.

w	k	$w^2 - k$
2	1	
5	2	
8	3	

Generating Equivalent Expressions
Practice and Problem Solving: A/B

Justify each step used to simplify the expression.

1. $3x + 2y - 2x + 2 = 3x - 2x + 2y + 2$ _____

2. $ = (3x - 2x) + 2y + 2$ _____

3. $ = (3 - 2)x + 2y + 2$ _____

4. $ = x + 2y + 2$ _____

Simplify.

5. $3r + n^2 - r + 5 - 2n + 2$ _____

6. $8v + w + 7 - 8v + 2w$ _____

7. $4c^2 + 6c - 3c^2 - 2c - 3$ _____

8. $z^3 + 5z + 3z^2 + 1 - 4 - 2z^2$ _____

Write and simplify an expression for the perimeter of each figure.

9.

$2d - 3$

$3c 3c$

$2d - 3$

_____

10.

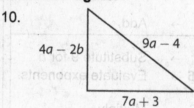

$4a - 2b$ $9a - 4$

$7a + 3$

_____

11. A square has sides of $10x$. Write and simplify an expression for the perimeter of that square.

_____

12. A rectangle has a length of $2x + 7$ and a width of $3x + 8y$. Write and simplify an expression for the perimeter of that rectangle.

_____

13. In the space at the right, draw a triangle. Use an algebraic expression to label the length of each side. Write an expression for the perimeter of your triangle. Then simplify that expression.

_____

Name _____ Date _____ Class _____

Simplify.

1. $3a + a^2 + 5(a - 2)$ _____

2. $8(v + w) - 7(v + 2w)$ _____

3. $4c^2 + 6(c - c^2) - 2c$ _____

4. $z^3 + 5(z + 3) - 4(2 - 2z^2)$ _____

Write and simplify an expression for the perimeter of each figure.

5.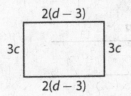

6.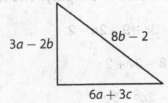

_____ _____

7. A square has sides of $x - 0.4$. Write an expression for the perimeter of that square. Simplify the expression.

_____

8. A rectangle has a length of $2(x + y)$ and a width of $3(x - y)$. Write an expression for the perimeter of that rectangle. Simplify the expression.

_____

Solve.

9. Peter collected soup for the food pantry. He packed 6 small boxes with n cans of soup in each box. He packed 4 boxes with twice as many cans as in the small boxes. Write and simplify an expression for the number of cans that Peter packed.

_____

10. Netta faxed n pages from the library. The library charges $1.50 per page. Later the same day, Netta faxed n more pages from a local copy shop. The copy shop charges $1.25 per page plus a $2 convenience fee. Write and simplify an expression for the amount Netta spent on faxes that day.

_____

LESSON 10-3 Generating Equivalent Expressions
Practice and Problem Solving: D

Identify like terms in each list. The first one is done for you.

1. $5a$ b 43 $2a$ b^2 $2b$ 4 $\underline{\text{5a and 2a; b and 2b; 43 and 4}}$

2. n $4n^3$ $2m$ $6m$ $5n$ $2n$ $\underline{\hspace{5cm}}$

3. $2d$ $5f$ $2g$ 7 $3g$ g $\underline{\hspace{5cm}}$

4. $7x^2$ x $3x^2$ 2 y^2 3 $3x$ $\underline{\hspace{5cm}}$

Combine like terms to simplify. The first one is done for you.

5. $4r + 5n^2 - 3r + 9 - 2n - 2$ $\underline{\hspace{1cm} r + 5n^2 + 7 - 2n \hspace{1cm}}$

6. $3v + w + 8 - 2v + 2$ $\underline{\hspace{5cm}}$

7. $8c^2 + 6c - 2c^2 - 5c$ $\underline{\hspace{5cm}}$

8. $z + 5e + 3z + 13 - 8 - 2e$ $\underline{\hspace{5cm}}$

Perimeter is the distance around a figure. Write an expression for the perimeter of each figure. Be sure to combine like terms. The first one is done for you.

9.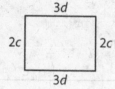

10.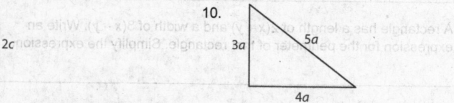

$\underline{\hspace{2cm} 6d + 4c \hspace{2cm}}$ $\underline{\hspace{5cm}}$

Circle the letter of the correct answer.

11. A square has sides of $6x$. Which expression shows the perimeter of that square?

    A $6x$

    B $12x$

    C $24x$

    D $36x$

12. A rectangle has a length of $4x + 5$ and a width of $8x - 4$. Which expression shows the perimeter of that rectangle?

    A $4x + 1$

    B $12x - 2$

    C $12x + 1$

    D $24x + 2$

LESSON 10-3

Generating Equivalent Expressions
Reteach

Look at the following expressions: $x = 1x$

$$x + x = 2x$$
$$x + x + x = 3x$$

The numbers 1, 2, and 3 are called **coefficients** of x.

Identify each coefficient.

1. $8x$ ____

2. $3m$ ____

3. y ____

4. $14t$ ____

An algebraic expression has terms that are separated by + and −.
In the expression $2x + 5y$, the **terms** are $2x$ and $5y$.

Expression	Terms
$8x + 4y$	$8x$ and $4y$
$5m - 2m + 9$	$5m, -2m,$ and 9
$4a^2 - 2b + c - 2a^2$	$4a^2, -2b, c,$ and $-2a^2$

Sometimes the terms of an expression can be combined.
Only **like terms** can be combined.

$2x + 2y$ NOT like terms, the variables are different.

$4a^2 - 2a$ NOT like terms, the exponents are different.

$5m - 2m$ Like terms, the variables and exponents are both the same.

$n^3 + 2n^3$ Like terms, the variables and exponents are both the same.

To **simplify** an expression, combine like terms by adding or subtracting
the coefficients of the variable.

$$5m - 2m = 3m$$

$$4a^2 + 5a + a + 3 = 4a^2 + 6a + 3 \quad \text{Note that the coefficient of } a \text{ is 1.}$$

Simplify.

5. $8x + 2x$

6. $3m - m$

7. $6y + 6y$

8. $14t - 3t$

_____

_____

_____

9. $3b + b + 6$

10. $9a - 3a + 4$

11. $n + 5n - 3c$

12. $12d - 2d + e$

_____

_____

_____

Name _____ Date _____ Class_____

Generating Equivalent Expressions
Reading Strategies: Organization Patterns

An algebraic expression is made up of parts called **terms**.

constants	variables	constants and variables
$3.2 \quad \frac{1}{2} \quad 12$	$m \quad s \quad x$	$4x \quad \frac{n}{2} \quad 3m^2 \quad \frac{2}{3}y$

A **coefficient** is a value multiplied by a variable.

Term	Value of Coefficient	Meaning
$7x$	7	$7 \cdot x$
y	1	$1 \cdot y$
$\frac{n}{2}$	$\frac{1}{2}$	$\frac{1}{2} \cdot n$

The expression below has 6 terms.

Term	Term	Term	Term	Term	Term
↓	↓	↓	↓	↓	↓
$2x$ +	$5b$ +	7 −	b +	$3x$ +	$2x^2$

Like terms have **both** the same variable **and** the same exponent.
Like terms can have different coefficients.

Like Terms			Unlike Terms	
$2y$ and $3y$	$4b$ and b	$4n^2$ and $2n^2$	$3x$ and $2x^2$	$4x$ and b	$7n$ and $7m$

You can **simplify** an algebraic expression. To do that, you **combine** like terms.

    First, reorganize the terms so like terms are together: $2x + 3x + 5b - b + 7 + 2x^2$
    Then add or subtract coefficients to combine like terms: $5x \ + \ 4b + 7 + 2x^2$

Solve.

1. How many terms are there in this expression: $6b + b^2 + 5 + 2b - 3f$? _____ terms

2. $6b$ and b^2 are unlike terms. Explain why. _____

_____

Use $5a^2 + 6b + a^2 - 3b - 2 + 4c$ for Exercises 3–5.

3. How many terms are there in the expression? _____ terms

4. Reorganize the terms so like terms are together. _____

5. Combine like terms to rewrite the expression. _____

LESSON 10-3	**Generating Equivalent Expressions**

Success for English Learners

Problem 1

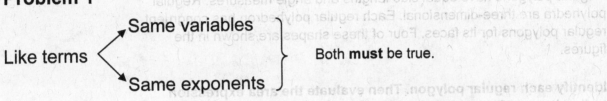

Like terms
- Same variables
- Same exponents

Both **must** be true.

$6x^2$ and $2x^3$ ⟶ Same variables, different exponents, so **NOT like terms**

$4x^4$ and $5y^4$ ⟶ Different variables, same exponents, so **NOT like terms**

$3a^3$ and $6a^3$ ⟶ Same variables, same exponents, so **like terms**

Problem 2

Combining like terms

$8w + 9w$	Like terms		$7n^3 - n^3$	Like terms
$8w + 9w$	Identify coefficients.		$7n^3 - 1n^3$	Identify coefficients.
$17w$	Add ONLY the coefficients.		$6n^3$	Subtract ONLY the coefficients.

Answer the questions below.

1. Can you combine the terms $6x^2$ and $2x^3$ shown in Problem 1? If you can, then combine the terms. If you cannot, explain why not.

_____

2. Can you combine the terms $4x^4$ and $5y^4$ shown in Problem 1? If you can, then combine the terms. If you cannot, explain why not.

_____

3. Can you combine the terms $3a^3$ and $6a^3$ shown in Problem 1? If you can, then combine the terms. If you cannot, explain why not.

_____

4. When a term has no number in front of the variable, what is the coefficient of that variable?

_____

Generating Equivalent Algebraic Expressions
Challenge

Areas of Regular Figures

Regular polygons have equal side lengths and angle measures. Regular polyhedra are three-dimensional. Each regular polyhedron has congruent regular polygons for its faces. Four of these shapes are shown in the figures.

Identify each regular polygon. Then evaluate the area expression to find its area for a side length *s* of 5 centimeters.

	Number of Sides	Name	Area Expression	Area for $s = 5$ cm
1.	3		$\dfrac{s^2}{4}\sqrt{3}$	
2.	4		s^2	
3.	5		$\dfrac{s^2}{4}\sqrt{25 + 10\sqrt{5}}$	
4.	6		$\dfrac{3s^2}{2}\sqrt{3}$	
5.	8		$2s^2(\sqrt{2} + 1)$	
6.	10		$\dfrac{5s^2}{2}\sqrt{5 + 2\sqrt{5}}$	

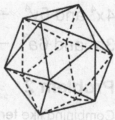

icosahedron

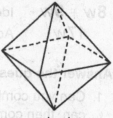

octahedron

Use the figures to identify each regular polyhedra. Then write an expression for its surface area for an edge length *s*.

	Number of Faces	Name	Surface Area for Edge Length *s*
7.	4 triangles		
8.	6 squares		
9.	8 triangles		
10.	12 pentagons		
11.	20 triangles		

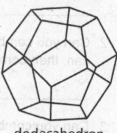

dodecahedron

tetrahedron

LESSON
11-1

Writing Equations to Represent Situations
Practice and Problem Solving: A/B

Determine whether the given value is a solution of the equation. Write *yes* or *no*.

1. $x + 11 = 15$; $x = 4$ _____

2. $36 - w = 10$; $w = 20$ _____

3. $0.2v = 1.2$; $v = 10$ _____

4. $15 = 6 + d$; $d = 8$ _____

5. $28 - w = 25$; $w = 3$ _____

6. $4t = 32$; $t = 8$ _____

7. $\dfrac{12}{s} = 4$; $s = 3$ _____

8. $\dfrac{33}{p} = 3$; $p = 11$ _____

Circle the letter of the equation that each given solution makes true.

9. $m = 19$

   A $10 + m = 20$ C $7m = 26$

   B $m - 4 = 15$ D $\dfrac{18}{m} = 2$

10. $a = 16$

   A $2a = 18$ C $24 - a = 6$

   B $a + 12 = 24$ D $\dfrac{a}{4} = 4$

Write an equation to represent each situation.

11. Seventy-two people signed up for the soccer league. After the players were evenly divided into teams, there were 6 teams in the league and *x* people on each team.

_____

12. Mary covered her kitchen floor with 10 tiles. The floor measures 6 feet long by 5 feet wide. The tiles are each 3 feet long and *w* feet wide.

_____

Solve.

13. The low temperature was 35°F. This was 13°F lower than the daytime high temperature. Write an equation to determine whether the high temperature was 48°F or 42°F.

_____

_____

14. Kayla bought 16 bagels. She paid a total of $20. Write an equation to determine whether each bagel cost $1.50 or $1.25.

_____

15. Write a real-world situation that could be modeled by the equation $\dfrac{24}{y} = 3$. Then solve the problem.

_____

_____

_____

_____

LESSON 11-1

Writing Equations to Represent Situations
Practice and Problem Solving: C

Circle the letter of the value that makes each equation true.

1. $\dfrac{18}{m} = 15 - 12$

   A $m = 6$ C $m = 9$

   B $m = 3$ D $m = 2$

2. $6d = 8(12 - 6)$

   A $d = 18$ C $d = 8$

   B $d = 48$ D $d = 4$

3. $x = \dfrac{14 - 6}{2}$

   A $x = 6$ C $x = 16$

   B $x = 8$ D $x = 4$

4. $\dfrac{a}{4} = 3(10 \div 2)$

   A $a = 15$ C $a = 40$

   B $a = 60$ D $a = 20$

For Exercises 5–7, use the table at the right that shows how many minutes certain mammals can stay under water.

5. A sperm whale can stay under water 7 times as long as *x* minutes more than a platypus can. Write an equation that states the relationship of the minutes these two mammals can stay under water.

Animal	Min
Hippopotamus	15
Platypus	10
Sea Cow	22
Seal	22
Sperm Whale	112

_____

6. A sea cow can stay under water *y* minutes. This is 11 minutes longer than one-third the time a hippopotamus can. Write an equation that states the relationship of the minutes these two mammals can stay under water. Complete the table with 16 or 56.

_____

7. Write an equation that includes division that relates the number of minutes a seal can stay under water to the number of minutes a sperm whale can stay under water.

_____

Solve.

8. Mr. Sosha teaches 4 math classes, with the same number of students in each class. Of those students, 80 are sixth graders and 40 are fifth graders. Write an equation to determine whether there are 22, 25, or 30 students in each class. How many are in each class?

_____

9. Write an equation that involves multiplication, addition, contains a variable, and has a solution of 8.

_____

LESSON 11-1

Writing Equations to Represent Situations
Practice and Problem Solving: D

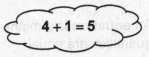

Is the given value of the variable a solution of the equation?
Write *yes* **or** *no***. The first one is done for you.**

1. $x + 1 = 5$; $x = 4$ ___**yes**___   2. $13 - w = 10$; $w = 2$ _____

3. $2v = 12$; $v = 10$ _____   4. $\dfrac{14}{p} = 2$; $p = 7$ _____

5. $8 + w = 11$; $w = 3$ _____   6. $4t = 20$; $t = 5$ _____

Circle the letter of the equation that each given solution makes true.
The first one is done for you.

7. $x = 5$
   (A) $2 + x = 7$
   B $9 - x = 3$
   C $3x = 18$

$2 + 5 = 7$

8. $g = 7$
   A $9g = 16$
   B $8 - g = 1$
   C $11 + g = 17$

9. $y = 2$
   A $7 - y = 1$
   B $3y = 6$
   C $\dfrac{10}{y} = 20$

10. $m = 9$
   A $m - 4 = 13$
   B $7m = 36$
   C $\dfrac{18}{m} = 2$

11. $z = 4$
   A $5z = 20$
   B $\dfrac{12}{z} = 4$
   C $z - 3 = 7$

12. $a = 8$
   A $2a = 10$
   B $a + 12 = 20$
   C $\dfrac{a}{4} = 4$

13. Rhonda has $13. She has one $5 bill, three $1 bills, and one
    other bill. Is the other bill a $1 bill or a $5 bill? Explain.

   ___(1)$5___   +   (3) _____   +   Other bill   = $ _____

   _____

   _____

LESSON
11-1

Writing Equations to Represent Situations
Reteach

An **equation** is a mathematical sentence that says that two quantities are equal.

Some equations contain variables. A **solution** for an equation is a value for a variable that makes the statement true.

You can write related facts using addition and subtraction.

$7 + 6 = 13$ $13 - 6 = 7$

You can write related facts using multiplication and division.

$3 \cdot 4 = 12$ $\dfrac{12}{4} = 3$

You can use related facts to find solutions for equations. If the related fact matches the value for the variable, then that value is a solution.

A. $x + 5 = 9$; $x = 3$

    Think: $9 - 5 = x$
                $4 = x$
                $4 \neq 3$

    3 is **not** a solution of $x + 5 = 9$.

B. $x - 7 = 5$; $x = 12$

    Think: $5 + 7 = x$
                $12 = x$
              $12 = 12$

    12 is a solution of $x - 7 = 5$.

C. $2x = 14$; $x = 9$

    Think: $14 \div 2 = x$
                $7 = x$
               $7 \neq 9$

    9 is **not** a solution of $2x = 14$.

D. $\dfrac{x}{5} = 3$; $x = 15$

    Think: $3 \cdot 5 = x$
              $15 = x$
             $15 = 15$

    15 is a solution of $x \div 5 = 3$.

Use related facts to determine whether the given value is a solution for each equation.

1. $x + 6 = 14$; $x = 8$

2. $\dfrac{s}{4} = 5$; $s = 24$

3. $g - 3 = 7$; $g = 11$

_____   _____   _____

4. $3a = 18$; $a = 6$

5. $26 = y - 9$; $y = 35$

6. $b \cdot 5 = 20$; $b = 3$

_____   _____   _____

7. $15 = \dfrac{v}{3}$; $v = 45$

8. $11 = p + 6$; $p = 5$

9. $6k = 78$; $k = 12$

_____   _____   _____

Name _____ Date _____ Class _____

Writing Equations to Represent Situations

Reading Strategies: Build Vocabulary

You can see part of the word **equal** in **equation**. In math, an equation indicates that two expressions have the same value, or are equal. The = **sign** in an equation separates one expression from the other. The value on each side of the = sign is the same.

Look at the equations below. Notice how the value on each side of the = sign is the same for each equation:

$$5 + 7 = 8 + 4 \qquad 19 - 7 = 12 \qquad 42 = 3 \bullet 14$$

If an equation contains a variable, and the variable is replaced by a value that keeps the equation equal, that value is called a **solution** of the equation.

Determine whether 80 or 60 is a solution to $\dfrac{y}{4} = 15$

$$\dfrac{y}{4} = 15 \qquad\qquad\qquad \dfrac{y}{4} = 15$$

$$\dfrac{80}{4} \stackrel{?}{=} 15 \qquad\qquad\qquad \dfrac{60}{4} \stackrel{?}{=} 15$$

$$20 \stackrel{?}{=} 15 \qquad\qquad\qquad 15 \stackrel{?}{=} 15$$

"20 is **not** equal to 15."   "15 is equal to 15."

Which are equations? Write *yes* or *no*.

1. $7 + 23 \stackrel{?}{=} 9 + 21$ _____

2. $35 + 15 \stackrel{?}{=} 45$ _____

3. $28 - 7 \stackrel{?}{=} 15 + 6$ _____

Replace the given value for the variable. Is it a solution? Write *yes* or *no*.

4. $d + 28 = 45$; $d = 17$

5. $\dfrac{84}{s} = 28$; $s = 3$

_____

6. $17 = 56 - t$; $t = 40$

7. $86 = 4w$; $w = 24$

_____

Solve.

8. Use the numbers 2, 11, 13, and 15 to write an equation.

_____

9. Replace one of the numbers in your equation in Exercise 8 with the variable *y*. Determine whether 2, 11, 13, or 15 is a solution of your equation.

_____

_____

Name _____ Date _____ Class _____

Writing Equations to Represent Situations

Success for English Learners

Problem

Determine whether 61 or 59 is a solution of the equation $a + 23 = 82$.

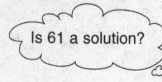

$a + 23 = 82$

$61 + 23 \overset{?}{=} 82$ Replace a with 61.

$84 \neq 82$

These are NOT equal.
61 is NOT a solution.

$a + 23 = 82$

$59 + 23 \overset{?}{=} 82$ Replace a with 59.

$82 = 82$

These are equal.
59 is a solution.

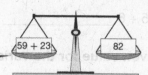

1. How do you know that 61 is not a solution of $a + 23 = 82$?

   _____

   _____

2. How can you find out whether 65 is a solution of $a + 23 = 82$?

   _____

3. Write a real-world situation that could be modeled by $a + 23 = 82$.

   _____

   _____

LESSON 11-2

Addition and Subtraction Equations

Practice and Problem Solving: A/B

Solve each equation. Graph the solution on the number line.

1. $6 = r + 2$ $r =$ ____

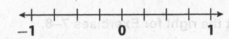

2. $26 = w - 12$ $w =$ ____

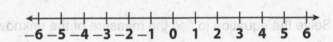

3. $\dfrac{1}{2} = m - \dfrac{1}{8}$ $m =$ ____

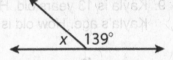

4. $t + 1 = -3$ $t =$ ____

Use the drawing at the right for Exercises 5–6.

5. Write an equation to represent the measures of the angles.

_____

6. Solve the equation to find the measure of the unknown angle.

_____

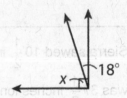

Use the drawing at the right for Exercises 7–8.

7. Write an equation to represent the measures of the angles.

_____

8. Solve the equation to find the measure of the unknown angle.

_____

Write a problem for the equation $3 + x = 8$. Then solve the equation and write the answer to your problem.

9. _____

_____

_____

Addition and Subtraction Equations
LESSON 11-2

Practice and Problem Solving: C

Solve each equation.

1. $b + 2.3 = 5.7$ $b =$ ____

2. $s - \dfrac{1}{3} = \dfrac{4}{9}$ $s =$ ____

3. $6\dfrac{1}{2} + n = 12$ $n =$ ____

4. $15.35 = z - 1.84$ $z =$ ____

5. $d + (-3) = -7$ $d =$ ____

6. $12 = g + 52$ $g =$ ____

Use the drawing at the right for Exercises 7–8.

7. Write an equation to represent the measures of the angles.

   _____

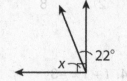

8. Solve the equation to find the measure of the unknown angle.

   _____

Write and solve an equation to answer each question.

9. Kayla is 13 years old. Her uncle says that his age minus 22 is equal to Kayla's age. How old is Kayla's uncle?

   _____

10. Gavin wants to buy a jacket that sells for $38.95. An advertisement says that next week that jacket will be on sale for $22.50. How much will Gavin save if he waits until next week to buy the jacket?

   _____

11. Sierra sawed $10\dfrac{1}{2}$ inches off the end of a board. The remaining board

   was $37\dfrac{1}{2}$ inches long. How long was the board that Sierra started with?

   _____

Write a problem for the equation $4.65 = x - 2.35$. Then solve the equation and write the answer to your problem.

12. _____

   _____

   _____

   _____

LESSON 11-2

Addition and Subtraction Equations

Practice and Problem Solving: D

Solve each equation. Graph the solution on the number line. The first one is done for you.

1. $5 = r - 1$ $r =$ __**6**__

   $5 = r - 1$

   $\underline{+1 \quad +1}$

   $6 = r$

   ◄─┼─┼─┼─┼─┼─┼─┼─┼─┼─┼─┼─●─►
   −6 −5 −4 −3 −2 −1 0 1 2 3 4 5 6

2. $2 = w + 3$ $w =$ ____

   ◄─┼─┼─┼─┼─┼─┼─┼─┼─┼─┼─►
   −5 −4 −3 −2 −1 0 1 2 3 4 5

3. $5 = m + 2$ $m =$ ____

   ◄─┼─┼─┼─┼─┼─┼─┼─►
   −8 −6 −4 −2 0 2 4 6 8

4. $t - 5 = 0$ $t =$ ____

   ◄─┼─┼─┼─┼─┼─┼─┼─┼─┼─┼─┼─►
   −6 −5 −4 −3 −2 −1 0 1 2 3 4 5 6

Use the drawings at the right for Exercises 5–6. The first one has been done for you.

5. Write an equation to represent the measures of the angles.

   $x + 100 = 180$
   _____

   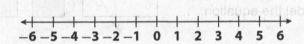

6. Solve the equation to find the measure of the unknown angle.

   _____

7. Mayumi has the boxes shown at the right. The total number of objects in two of the boxes is the same as the number of objects in the third box. Write an equation to show the relationship of the number of objects in the boxes.

   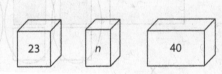

   _____

8. How many objects are in the box marked n? ____ objects

Write a problem for the equation $x - 5 = 2$. Then solve the equation and write the answer to your problem.

9. _____

   _____

   _____

LESSON 11-2

Addition and Subtraction Equations
Reteach

To solve an equation, you need to get the variable alone on one side of the equal sign.

You can use tiles to help you solve subtraction equations.	Addition undoes subtraction, so you can use addition to solve subtraction equations.	Zero pair: $+1 + (-1) = 0$ 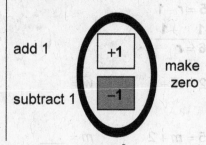

Variable   add 1   subtract 1

One positive tile and one negative tile make a **zero pair**.

To solve $x - 4 = 2$, first use tiles to model the equation.

X   –   4   =   2

To get the variable alone, you have to add positive tiles. Remember to add the same number of positive tiles to each side of the equation.

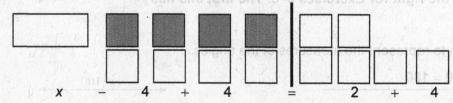

x   –   4   +   4   =   2   +   4

Then remove the greatest possible number of zero pairs from each side of the equal sign.

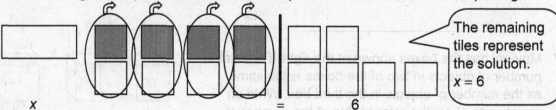

x   =   6

The remaining tiles represent the solution. $x = 6$

Use tiles to solve each equation.

1. $x - 5 = 3$

   $x =$ ____

2. $x - 2 = 7$

   $x =$ ____

3. $x - 1 = 4$

   $x =$ ____

4. $x - 8 = 1$

   $x =$ ____

5. $x - 3 = 3$

   $x =$ ____

6. $x - 6 = 2$

   $x =$ ____

LESSON 11-2 Addition and Subtraction Equations
Reading Strategies: Use a Visual Clue

You can picture balanced scales to solve subtraction equations.
Picture balanced scales for this equation.

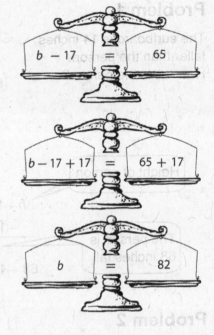

Step 1: To find the value of *b*, get *b* by itself on the left side of the equation. So, add 17 to the left side of the equation.

Step 2: To keep the equation balanced, add 17 to the right side of the equation as well.

Step 3: Check to verify that $b = 82$ is the solution.

$$b - 17 = 65$$
$$82 - 17 \overset{?}{=} 65$$
$$65 \overset{?}{=} 65 \checkmark$$

To get the variable by itself in a subtraction equation, add the same value to both sides of the equation.

Use $n - 21 = 32$ to answer Exercises 1–4.

1. On which side of the equation is the variable? _____

2. What will you do to get the variable by itself? _____

3. What must you do the other side of the equation to keep it balanced? _____

4. What is the value of *n*? _____

Use $12 = p - 25$ to answer Exercises 5–8.

5. On which side of the equation is the variable? _____

6. What will you do to get the variable by itself? _____

7. What must you do the other side of the equation to keep it balanced? _____

8. What is the value of *p*? _____

Name _____ Date _____ Class_____

LESSON 11-2 Addition and Subtraction Equations
Success for English Learners

Problem 1

The surfboard is 14 inches taller than the person. How tall is the person?

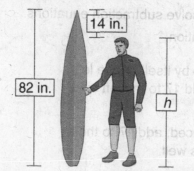

14 in.

82 in.

h

Height of person

Surfboard height

Think: This is an addition equation. I subtract to undo the addition.

$h + 14 = 82$
$\underline{-14 \quad -14}$
$h = 68$

The person is 68 inches tall.

Subtract 14 from both sides.

$68 + 14 = 82$ ✓   Check your answer.

Problem 2

Think: This is a subtraction equation. I add to undo the subtraction.

$x - 21 = 36$
$\underline{+21 \quad +21}$
$x = 57$

Add 21 to both sides.

1. Why do you use an addition equation to find the surfer's height?

_____

_____

2. How can you check the answer to Problem 2?

_____

_____

3. Write an addition or a subtraction equation. Explain how to solve your equation. Give the solution to your equation.

_____

_____

LESSON 11-3

Multiplication and Division Equations
Practice and Problem Solving: A/B

Solve each equation. Graph the solution on the number line.
Check your work.

1. $\dfrac{e}{2} = 3$ $e =$ ____

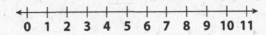

_____

_____

2. $20 = 2w$ $w =$ ____

_____

_____

3. $\dfrac{1}{2} = 2m$ $m =$ ____

_____

_____

4. $\dfrac{k}{5} = 2$ $k =$ ____

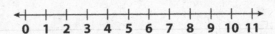

_____

_____

Use the drawing at the right for Exercises 5–6.

5. Write an equation you can use to find the length of the rectangle.

_____

6. Solve the equation. Give the length of the rectangle.

8 m | Area = 72 m² | x m

_____

Solve.

7. Alise separated her pictures into 3 piles. Each pile contained
9 pictures. How many pictures did she have in all? Write and solve an
equation to represent the problem. State the answer to the problem.

_____

_____

LESSON
11-3
Multiplication and Division Equations
Practice and Problem Solving: C

Solve each equation.

1. $8b = 5.6$ $b =$ ____

2. $9 = \dfrac{s}{3}$ $s =$ ____

3. $2\dfrac{1}{2} = 5n$ $n =$ ____

4. $15 = 0.2z$ $z =$ ____

5. $3.5d = 70$ $d =$ ____

6. $\dfrac{t}{3} = \dfrac{4}{9}$ $t =$ ____

7. The perimeter of the square at the right is 48 inches. What is the area of the square at the right? Explain how you found your answer.

_____

_____

_____

s | perimeter $= 48$ in.

s

Write and solve an equation to answer each question.

8. Jose is making model SUVs. Each SUV takes 5 tires. He used 85 tires for the models. How many model SUVs did Jose make?

_____

9. Renee talked for 6 minutes on the phone. Nathan talked for n minutes. Nathan talked three times as long as Renee. How long did Nathan talk?

_____

10. Sylvia rented a boat for $16.50 per hour. Her total rental fee was $49.50. For how many hours did Sylvia rent the boat?

_____

Write a problem for the equation $0.5n = 12.5$. Then solve the equation and write the answer to your problem.

11. _____

_____

_____

_____

Name _____ Date _____ Class _____

LESSON 11-3

Multiplication and Division Equations

Practice and Problem Solving: D

Solve each equation. Graph the solution on the number line.
Check your work. The first is done for you.

1. $8 = 2m$ $m = \underline{\ 4\ }$

   $\dfrac{8}{2} = \dfrac{2m}{2}$

   $4 = m$ $8 = 2 \cdot 4\checkmark$

   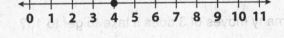

2. $\dfrac{a}{4} = 2$ $a = \underline{\ \ \ }$

   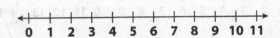

   _____

   _____

3. $12 = 3s$ $s = \underline{\ \ \ }$

   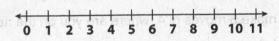

   _____

   _____

4. $\dfrac{u}{2} = 5$ $u = \underline{\ \ \ }$

   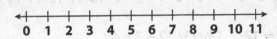

   _____

   _____

Use the situation below to complete Exercises 5–8.
The first one is done for you.

Jim knows the length of his garden is 12 feet. He knows the area of the
garden is 60 ft². What is the width of Jim's garden?

5. Fill in the known values in the picture at the right.

6. Write an equation you can use to solve the problem.

   _____

7. Solve the equation. $w = \underline{\ \ \ }$

8. Write the solution to the problem.

   _____

w ft $\boxed{\quad A = \quad \text{ft}^2 \quad}$

____ ft

LESSON 11-3

Multiplication and Division Equations
Reteach

Number lines can be used to solve multiplication and division equations.

Solve: $3n = 15$

How many moves of 3 does it take to get to 15?

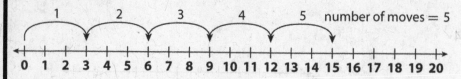

$n = 5$ Check: $3 \cdot 5 = 15$✓

Solve: $\dfrac{n}{3} = 4$

If you make 3 moves of 4, where are you on the number line?

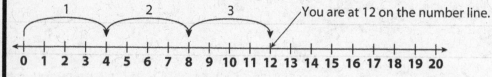

You are at 12 on the number line.

$n = 12$ Check: $12 \div 3 = 4$✓

Show the moves you can use to solve each equation. Then give the solution to the equation and check your work.

1. $3n = 9$

$$\longleftrightarrow$$
$$0 \quad 1 \quad 2 \quad 3 \quad 4 \quad 5 \quad 6 \quad 7 \quad 8 \quad 9 \quad 10 \quad 11$$

Solution: $n =$ ___

Show your check:

2. $\dfrac{n}{2} = 4$

$$\longleftrightarrow$$
$$0 \quad 1 \quad 2 \quad 3 \quad 4 \quad 5 \quad 6 \quad 7 \quad 8 \quad 9 \quad 10 \quad 11$$

Solution: $n =$ ___

Show your check:

Multiplication and Division Equations

LESSON 11-3

Reading Strategies: Use a Flowchart

A flowchart gives you a plan. You can use a flowchart to solve equations.

1 Decide how to get the variable by itself.	⇒	**2** Do the same on both sides of the equation.	⇒	**3** Solve the equation.	⇒	**4** Check the solution.

Solve: $\dfrac{x}{6} = 4$

Think: Multiplying by 6 undoes dividing by 6.

$\dfrac{x}{6} \cdot 6 = 4 \cdot 6$

$x = 24$

$\dfrac{24}{6} = 4 \checkmark$

Plan

1 Decide on what operation to use.

2 Do the same on both sides.

3 Solve the equation.

4 Check the solution.

Solve: $4n = 12$

Think: Dividing by 4 undoes multiplying by 4.

$\dfrac{4n}{4} = \dfrac{12}{4}$

$n = 3$

$4 \cdot 3 = 12 \checkmark$

Use the flowchart to solve each equation.

1.

Plan	**Solve:** $3r = 24$
1 Decide on what operation to use.	
2 Do the same on both sides.	
3 Solve the equation.	
4 Check the solution.	

2.

Plan	**Solve:** $\dfrac{b}{8} = 16$
1 Decide on what operation to use.	
2 Do the same on both sides.	
3 Solve the equation.	
4 Check the solution.	

LESSON 11-3

Multiplication and Division Equations
Success for English Learners

Problem 1

Some armadillo mothers had these babies.

Each mother had 4 babies. How many mothers were there?

4 babies for each mother

$4m = 32$

32 babies

To undo multiplication, use division.

$4m = 32$

$$\frac{4m}{4} = \frac{32}{4}$$

$m = 8$

There are 8 mothers.

Problem 2

Think: This is a division equation. I multiply to undo the multiplication.

$$\frac{x}{6} = 12$$

$$\frac{x \cdot 6}{6} = 12 \cdot 6 \quad \text{Multiply each side by 6.}$$

$x = 72$

$72 \div 6 = 12 \checkmark$ The answer checks.

1. Explain how to check the solution to Problem 1.

_____

_____

2. Solve $\frac{n}{3} = 2$. Show your work.

Check your work.

3. Solve $5t = 20$. Show your work.
   Check your work.

Name _____ Date _____ Class _____

Complete the graph for each inequality.

1. $a > 3$

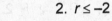

2. $r \le -2$

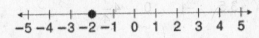

Graph the solutions of each inequality. Check the solutions.

3. $w \ge 0$

Check: _____

4. $b \le -4$

Check: _____

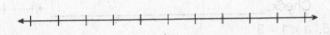

5. $a < 1.5$

Check: _____

Write an inequality that represents each phrase. Draw a graph to represent the inequality.

6. The sum of 1 and x is less than 5.

_____

7. 3 is less than y minus 2.

_____

Write and graph an inequality to represent each situation.

8. The temperature today will be at least 10°F. _____

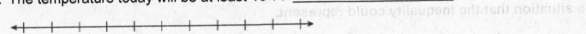

9. Ben wants to spend no more than $3. _____

Write an inequality that matches the number line model.

10. _____

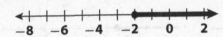

11. _____

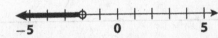

LESSON 11-4

Writing Inequalities

Practice and Problem Solving: C

Circle the values that are solutions for each inequality.

1. $a > -2$

    -3.5 -1 0 $4\frac{1}{4}$

2. $r \leq 2$

    -3.5 -1 0 $4\frac{1}{4}$

Graph the solutions of each inequality. Check the solutions.

3. $4 \geq y$

    Check: _____

4. $b \leq 0.5$

    Check: _____

5. $a < 1 - 3$

    Check: _____

Write and graph an inequality to represent each situation. Then determine if 36 is a possible solution. Write *yes* or *no*.

6. The temperature today will be at least 35°F. _____

7. Monica wants to spend no more than $35. _____

Write an inequality that matches the number line model. Then write a situation that the inequality could represent.

8. _____

    0 5 10 15 20 25 30 35 40 45 50

_____

_____

9. _____

    -4 -3 -2 -1 0 1

_____

_____

_____

LESSON
11-4

Writing Inequalities
Practice and Problem Solving: D

Complete the graph for each inequality. The first one is done for you.

1. $a > 2$

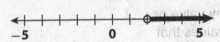

2. $r \leq -1$

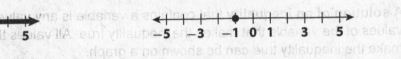

Graph the solutions of each inequality. Check the solutions. The first one is done for you.

3. $m \geq -2$

Check: ___**0 ≥ −2; this is true**___

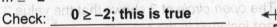

4. $d \leq 3$

Check: _____

5. $s < -3$

Check: _____

Write an inequality that represents each phrase. Draw a graph to represent the inequality. The first one is done for you.

6. x is less than 4

7. -1 is greater than y

_____**x < 4**_____   _____

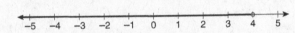

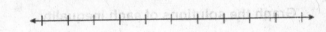

Write and graph an inequality to represent each situation. The first one is done for you.

8. Today's temperature is greater than 0°F. ___**t > 0**___

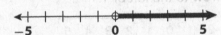

9. Lyle paid more than $2 for lunch. _____

LESSON 11-4 Writing Inequalities
Reteach

An equation is a statement that says two quantities are equal. An **inequality** is a statement that says two quantities are **not** equal.

A **solution of an inequality** that contains a variable is any value or values of the variable that makes the inequality true. All values that make the inequality true can be shown on a graph.

Inequality	Meaning	Solution of Inequality
$x > 3$	All numbers *greater than* 3	-5 -4 -3 -2 -1 0 1 2 3 4 5 The *open circle* at 3 shows that the value 3 is **not** included in the solution.
$x \geq 3$	All numbers *greater than or equal to* 3	-5 -4 -3 -2 -1 0 1 2 3 4 5 The *closed circle* at 3 shows that the value 3 **is** included in the solution.
$x < 3$	All numbers *less than* 3	-5 -4 -3 -2 -1 0 1 2 3 4 5
$x \leq 3$	All numbers *less than or equal to* 3	-5 -4 -3 -2 -1 0 1 2 3 4 5

Graph the solutions of each inequality.

1. $x > -4$
   - Draw an open circle at -4.
   - Read $x > -4$ as "x is greater than -4."
   - Draw an arrow to the right of -4.

   -5 -4 -3 -2 -1 0 1 2 3 4 5

2. $x \leq 1$
   - Draw a closed circle at 1.
   - Read $x \leq 1$ as "x is less than or equal to 1."
   - Draw an arrow to the left of 1.

   -5 -4 -3 -2 -1 0 1 2 3 4 5

3. $a > -1$

   -5 -4 -3 -2 -1 0 1 2 3 4 5

4. $y \leq 3$

   -5 -4 -3 -2 -1 0 1 2 3 4 5

Write an inequality that represents each phrase.

5. the sum of 2 and 3 is less than y

   _____

6. the sum of y and 2 is greater than or equal to 6

   _____

LESSON 11-4

Writing Inequalities

Reading Strategies: Understand Symbols

An **inequality** is a comparison of two unequal values. This chart will help you understand both words and symbols for inequalities.

The team has scored fewer than 5 runs in each game. "Fewer than 5" means **"less than 5."** Symbol for "less than 5": < **5**	No more than 8 people can ride in the elevator. "No more than 8" Means **"8 or less than 8."** Symbol for "less than or equal to 8": ≤ **8**

Inequalities

More than 25 students try out for the team each year. "More than 25" means **"a number greater than 25."** Symbol for "greater than 25": > **25**	There are at least 75 fans at each home game. "At least 75" means "75 or more" or **"a number greater than or equal to 75."** Symbol for "greater than or equal to 75": ≥ **75**

Use the chart to answer each question.

1. What is an inequality?

   _____

2. Explain the difference between the symbols < and ≤.

   _____

   _____

3. Explain the difference between the symbols > and ≥.

   _____

   _____

4. Write an inequality to describe the number of students in each homeroom: There is a limit of 30 students for each homeroom.

   _____

5. Is 28 a solution to the inequality you wrote in Exercise 4? How do you know?

   _____

   _____

LESSON 11-4

Writing Inequalities
Success for English Learners

Problem 1

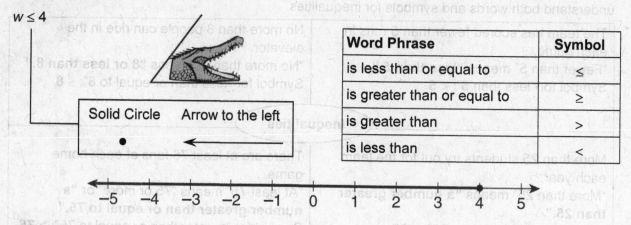

$w \le 4$

Word Phrase	Symbol
is less than or equal to	$\le$
is greater than or equal to	$\ge$
is greater than	$>$
is less than	$<$

Solid Circle   Arrow to the left

●   ←

Problem 2

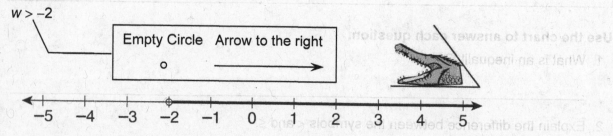

$w > -2$

Empty Circle   Arrow to the right

○   →

1. In Problem 1, is 4 part of the solution set? How do you know?

_____

2. In Problem 2, is −2 part of the solution set? How do you know?

_____

3. When graphing an inequality with a $\ge$ sign, should you use an empty or a solid circle? Why?

_____

4. Graph the solutions of $x \le -2$.

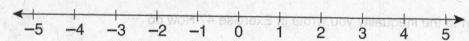

MODULE 11

Equations and Relationships
Challenge

Write and solve an equation to find the unknown measurement. Then use your answer to find the perimeter of each field or court.

Remember
Area = length • width or $A = l \cdot w$
Perimeter is the distance around
or $P = 2l + 2w$

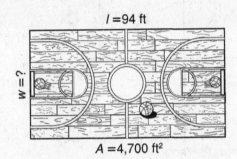

$l = 94$ ft

$w = ?$

$A = 4,700$ ft²

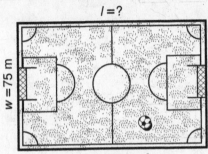

$l = ?$

$w = 75$ m

$A = 8,250$ m²

1. Equation to find area: _____

   Unknown measurement: _____

   Equation to find perimeter:

   $P =$ _____

   Perimeter of court: _____

2. Equation to find area: _____

   Unknown measurement: _____

   Equation to find perimeter:

   $P =$ _____

   Perimeter of field: _____

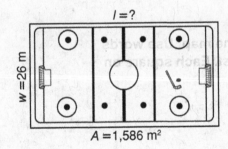

$l = ?$

$w = 26$ m

$A = 1,586$ m²

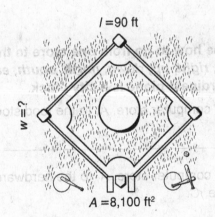

$l = 90$ ft

$w = ?$

$A = 8,100$ ft²

3. Equation to find area: _____

   Unknown measurement: _____

   $P =$ _____

   Perimeter of rink: _____

4. Equation to find area: _____

   Unknown measurement: _____

   $P =$ _____

   Perimeter of diamond: _____

Name _____ Date _____ Class_____

Graphing on the Coordinate Plane
Practice and Problem Solving: A/B

Give the coordinates of the points on the coordinate plane.

1. A (____ , ____)

2. B (____ , ____)

3. C (____ , ____)

4. D (____ , ____)

5. E (____ , ____)

6. F (____ , ____)

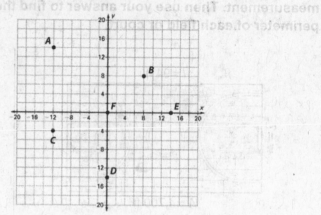

Plot the points on the coordinate plane.

7. G (2, 4)

8. H (–6, 8)

9. J (10, –12)

10. K (–14, –16)

11. M (0, 18)

12. P (–20, 0)

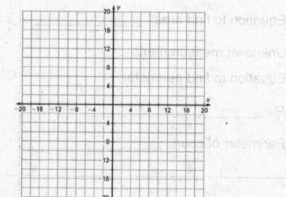

Describe how to go from one store to the next on the map. Use words like *left, right, up, down, north, south, east,* and *west*. Each square on the coordinate plane is a city block.

13. The computer store, *A*, to the food store, *B*.

_____

14. The computer store, *A*, to the hardware store, *C*.

_____

15. The hardware store, *C*, to the food store, *B*.

_____

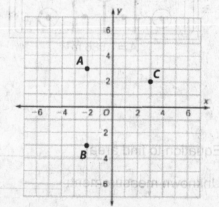

LESSON 12-1

Graphing on the Coordinate Plane
Practice and Problem Solving: C

Label the axes to locate the points on the coordinate planes.

1. A(–6, 15), B(3, –9), C(–9, –9)

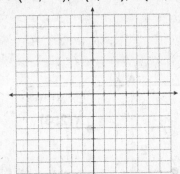

2. D(0, 6), E(–12, 6), F(18, 0)

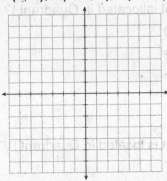

Start with the given point. Give the quadrant in which you end up after following the directions. Then, give the coordinates of the point where you end up.

3. X(5, –8) Go down 5, left 7, and down 6 more.

   Quadrant: _____ ; Point: X(_____, _____)

4. Y(–2, 6) Go up 3, right 5, and up 4 more.

   Quadrant: _____; Point: Y(_____, _____)

5. Z(0, –5) Go left 5, up 4, right 7, and down 3.

   Quadrant: _____; Point: Z(_____, _____)

Give the coordinates of a point that would form a right triangle with the points given. Use the grids for reference. Tell what you know about one of the coordinates of your new point.

6. P(2, 4), Q(2, 8), R(_____, _____)

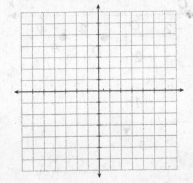

7. S(–3, –5), T(4, –5), U(_____, _____)

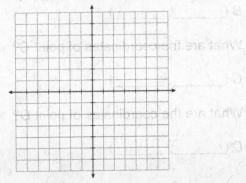

LESSON
12-1

Graphing on the Coordinate Plane
Practice and Problem Solving: D

Use the coordinate plane for Exercises 1–3. Give the letter of the correct answer. The first one is done for you.

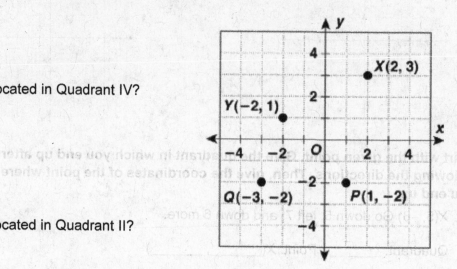

1. Which point is located in Quadrant I?

   A   point *Q*

   B   point *P*

   C   point *X*

   __C__

2. Which point is located in Quadrant IV?

   A   point *X*

   B   point *Y*

   C   point *P*

   ___

3. Which point is located in Quadrant II?

   A   point *Q*

   B   point *Y*

   C   point *X*

   ___

Use the coordinate plane for Exercises 4–7. The first one is done for you.

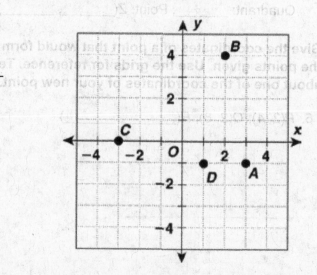

4. What are the coordinates of point *A*?
   **Go over 3 to the right and down 1,
   so the *x*-coordinate is 3 and the
   y-coordinate is –1, or *A*(3, –1).**

5. What are the coordinates of point *B*?

   B (_____, _____)

6. What are the coordinates of point *C*?

   C (_____, _____)

7. What are the coordinates of point *D*?

   D (_____, _____)

LESSON 12-1

Graphing on the Coordinate Plane
Reteach

Each quadrant of the coordinate plane has a unique combination of positive and negative signs for the *x*-coordinates and *y*-coordinates as shown here.

Quadrant	*x*-coordinate	*y*-coordinate
I	+	+
II	–	+
III	–	–
IV	+	–

Use these rules when naming points on the coordinate plane.

Example 1

Draw the point *A*(1, –3) on the coordinate grid.

Solution

According to the table, this point will be in Quadrant IV.

So, go to the *right* (+) one unit, and go *down* (–) three units.

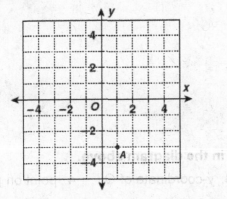

Example 2

What are the coordinates of point *B*?

Solution

According to the table, this point will have a negative *x*-coordinate and a positive *y*-coordinate.

Point *B* is 3 three units to the *left* (–) and four units *up* (+). So the coordinates of point *B* are (–3, 4).

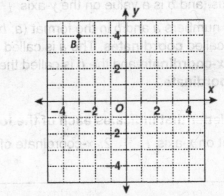

Add the correct sign for each point's coordinates.

1. (____ 3, ____ 4) in

   Quadrant II

2. (____ 2, ____ 5) in

   Quadrant IV

3. (____ 9, ____ 1) in

   Quadrant I

4. In which quadrant is the point (0, 7) located? Explain your answer.

_____

Name _____ Date _____ Class_____

Graphing on the Coordinate Plane
Reading Strategies: Build Vocabulary

This lesson introduces words used to graph numbers. Mathematics uses these words to build new concepts. It is important to remember and to use them. Look at this example. Read each definition, and find it on the picture.

A. The **coordinate plane** includes all of the parts marked on the picture.

B. The **axes** are the darker number lines.

C. The **x-axis** goes left to right, whereas the **y-axis** goes up and down.

D. The axes intersect at the **origin**, which is marked with an "O".

E. The **scale** on the number line is always important in using a coordinate plane. Here, every square on the grid is 2 units.

F. The axes divide the coordinate plane into four **quadrants**. **Quadrant I** is upper right, **Quadrant II** is upper left, **Quadrant III** is lower left, and **Quadrant IV**, which is read "quadrant four," is lower right.

G. Pairs of numbers, called **ordered pairs**, are represented on the coordinate plane as points and in the format *P(a, b)*, where *P* is the point's label, *a* is a value on the x-axis, and *b* is a value on the y-axis.

H. The numbers *a* and *b* in the format (*a*, *b*) are called **coordinates**. The *a* is called the **x-coordinate** and the *b* is called the **y-coordinate**.

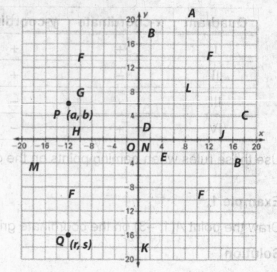

Write a letter that indicates each of the following in the diagram above.

1. point on *x*-axis   2. *x*-coordinate of *Q*   3. *y*-coordinate of *Q*   4. point on *y*-axis

_____   _____   _____   _____

5. point in Quadrant I   6. ordered pair for *Q*   7. point in Quadrant III   8. origin

_____   _____   _____   _____

Graphing on the Coordinate Plane
Success for English Learners

Problem

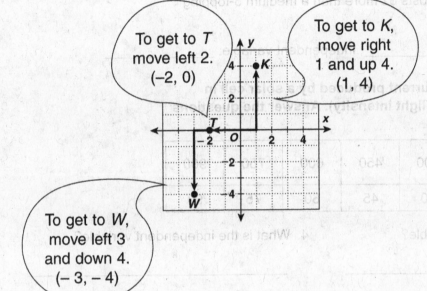

This number shows how many units to move right or left.

This number shows how many units to move up or down.

(x, y)

To get to *T* move left 2. (−2, 0)

To get to *K*, move right 1 and up 4. (1, 4)

To get to *W*, move left 3 and down 4. (−3, −4)

Moves up or to the right are positive values.

Moves down or to the left are negative values.

1. If an ordered pair has an *x*-value of 0, which direction do you move from the origin?

_____

2. A negative *y*-coordinate means that a point may lie in which two quadrants?

_____

3. Does it matter which number comes first in an ordered pair? Explain.

_____

_____

LESSON
12-2

Independent and Dependent Variables in Tables and Graphs
Practice and Problem Solving: A/B

Name the *dependent variable* and the *independent variable* in each problem.

1. A food service worker earns $12 per hour. How much money, *m*, does the worker earn on a shift of *h* hours?

   Dependent variable: _____; independent variable: _____

2. A large 2-topping pizza, *L*, costs $2 more than a medium 3-topping pizza, *M*.

   Dependent variable: _____; independent variable: _____

The table shows the electric current produced by a solar cell in different amounts of sunlight (light intensity). Answer the questions using the data.

Light intensity	150	300	450	600	750	900
Current	10	30	45	60	75	90

3. What is the dependent variable?   4. What is the independent variable?

   _____   _____

5. What do you predict the current will be in the absence of sunlight? Explain.

   _____

6. What do you predict the current will be if the light intensity is 1,000? Explain.

   _____

A race car driver's time in seconds to complete 12 laps is plotted on the graph.

7. Which axis shows the dependent variable?

   _____

8. Why does the graph begin at *x* = 1?

   _____

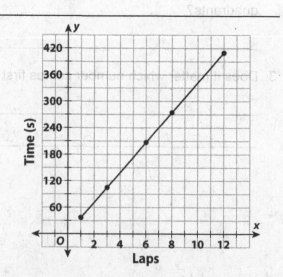

LESSON 12-2

Independent and Dependent Variables in Tables and Graphs
Practice and Problem Solving: C

Use the situation below to complete Exercises 1–4.

The commuter bus system collected the data in the table below. All of the data were collected under the same conditions: dry roads, no accidents or traffic jams, same distance each trip, and no mechanical problems with the bus on each trip.

Number of passengers per trip, *n*	30	35	40	45	50
Average speed, km per hour, *s*	60	58	55	55	52
Liters of biodiesel fuel used, *f*	45	48	50	52	54

1. Assume that more passengers cause the bus to travel slower. Of these two factors, which would be the dependent and independent variables?

   Dependent variable: _____; independent variable: _____

2. Assume that an average slower speed causes the bus to consume more fuel. Describe the relationship between bus speed and fuel consumption.

   _____

3. What can you say about the relationship between the number of passengers and the fuel consumption?

   _____

4. What effect does the number of passengers have on bus speed *and* fuel consumption?

   _____

In the graph, the independent variable is the *x*-axis and the dependent variable is the *y*-axis. Use the graph to answer Exercises 5–6.

5. Describe and compare how the dependent variables shown by lines *A* and *B* change as the independent variables change.

   _____

6. Describe and compare how the dependent variables shown by lines *B* and *C* change as the independent variables change.

   _____

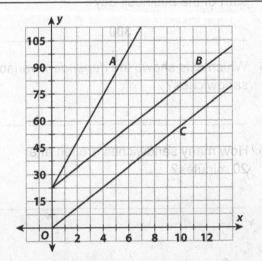

**LESSON
12-2**

Independent and Dependent Variables in Tables and Graphs
Practice and Problem Solving: D

Answer the questions for each real-world situation. The first one is done for you.

1. The table gives the amount of water in a water tank as it is being filled.

Gallons	50	100	150	200	250
Time (min)	10	20	30	40	50

a. Why is gallons the *dependent* variable?

   It depends on how long the water has been filling the tank.

b. Divide gallons by time in each pair of cells. What do you get?

   50 ÷ 10 = 100 ÷ 20 = 150 ÷ 30 = 200 ÷ 40 = 250 ÷ 50 = 5; 5

c. If the time is 60 minutes, how would you get the gallons? What would you get?

   Multiply 60 times 5, which gives 300 gallons.

2. The table shows how to change miles to kilometers. Divide kilometers by miles for each of the four mileage numbers. How many kilometers per mile do you get?

(km)	3.22	4.83	6.44	8.05
(mi)	2	3	4	5

_____

Answer each question using the graph. The first one is done for you.

3. How many sandwiches are available at the start of the business day?

   _____ **300** _____

4. Which axis shows the *dependent* variable, sandwiches?

   _____

5. How many sandwiches are left after 20 minutes?

   _____

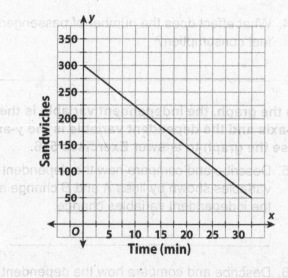

LESSON 12-2

Independent and Dependent Variables in Tables and Graphs

Reteach

In a table, the *independent variable* is often represented by x. The *dependent variable* is often represented by y. Look at this example.

x	0	1	2	3	4	5	6	7
y	4	5	6	7	8	9	10	?

What y value goes for the question mark?

Step 1 Notice that 4 is added to each value of x to give the y value.

Step 2 So, add 4 to 7. What does this give? $4 + 7 = 11$

On a chart or graph,

- the x-axis is usually used for the *independent variable*, and

- the y-axis is usually used for the *dependent variable*.

Look at the example. ⟶

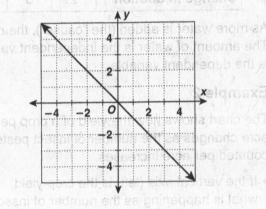

How does y depend on x?

Step 1 Each value of y is the opposite of the value of x.

Step 2 What equation shows this fact?
$y = -x$

Give the relationship between x and y.

1.

x	1	2	3	4	5
y	3	4	5	6	7

_____

2.

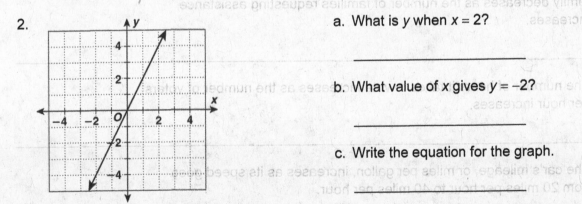

a. What is y when $x = 2$?

_____

b. What value of x gives $y = -2$?

_____

c. Write the equation for the graph.

_____

LESSON 12-2

Independent and Dependent Variables in Tables and Graphs
Reading Strategies: Cause and Effect

It can sometimes be useful to think of the **independent variable** as the *cause* of an event. This cause has an *effect* on the **dependent variable**. This type of thinking can be helpful in doing some real-world problems.

Example 1

A middle-school science student did an experiment in which different amounts of water were added on a one-time basis to a solution to see what effect it would have on the solution's concentration. Here are the results.

Water (milliliters)	5	10	15	20
Change in dilution	2	5	10	15

As more water is added (the "cause"), the concentration dilutes. The amount of water is the independent variable. The amount of dilution is the dependent variable.

Example 2

The chart shows how the yield of a crop per acre changes as the number of insect pests counted per acre increases.

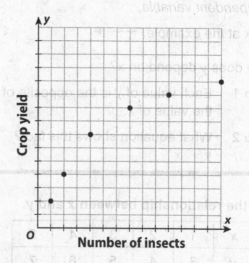

- If the vertical axis (left) is the crop yield, what is happening as the number of insects (horizontal axis) increases?

- The crop yield continues to increase but not as fast as at the beginning.

- The number of insects is the independent variable (the cause), and the crop yield is the dependent variable (the effect).

Identify the cause and the effect in each problem.

1. After a storm, the number of bottles of drinking water available per family decreases as the number of families requesting assistance increases.

   _____

2. The number of hours it takes to vote increases as the number of voters per hour increases.

   _____

3. The car's mileage, or miles per gallon, increases as its speed goes from 20 miles per hour to 40 miles per hour.

   _____

LESSON 12-2

Independent and Dependent Variables in Tables and Graphs
Success for English Learners

Problem 1

Let ℓ = length.

Let w = width.

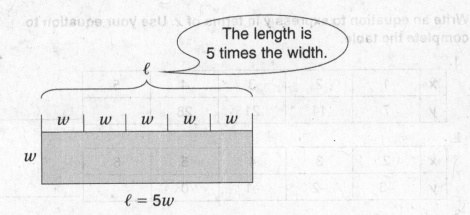

The length is 5 times the width.

$$\ell = 5w$$

Problem 2

In Problem 1, the length, *l*, "depends" on the width, *w*.

Independent variable ⟶ width, *w*

Dependent variable ⟶ length, *l*

The variables are related by the formula, *l = 5 w.*

1. Suppose the width of the rectangle in Problem 1 is 10 inches. What is the length of the rectangle?

   _____

2. The table shows the money the school band members collected for washing cars on four different days.

Cars washed	12	15	20	30
Money collected	$120	$150	$200	?

What is the **dependent variable**? _____

What is the **independent variable**? _____

How much money is collected for washing 30 cars?

_____

LESSON 12-3

Writing Equations from Tables
Practice and Problem Solving: A/B

Write an equation to express y in terms of x. Use your equation to complete the table.

1.

x	1	2	3	4	5
y	7	14	21	28	

_____

2.

x	2	3	4	5	6
y	−3	−2	−1	0	

_____

3.

x	20	16	12	8	4
y	10	8	6	4	

4.

x	7	8	9	10	11
y	11	12	13	14	

Solve.

5. Henry records how many days he rides his bike and how far he rides each week. He rides the same distance each time. He rode 18 miles in 3 days, 24 miles in 4 days, and 42 miles in 7 days. Write and solve an equation to find how far he rides his bike in 10 days.

Number of days, d	3	4	7	10
Number of miles, m	18			

Equation relating d and m is _____.

The number of miles Henry rides his bike in 10 days is _____.

6. When Cabrini is 6, Nikos is 2. When Cabrini is 10, Nikos will be 6. When Cabrini is 16, Nikos will be 12. When Cabrini is 21, Nikos will be 17. Write and solve an equation to find Nikos' age when Cabrini is 40.

Cabrini's age, x	6	10	16	21	40
Nikos' age, y	2				

Equation relating x and y is _____.

When Cabrini is 40 years old, Nikos will be _____.

LESSON 12-3

Writing Equations from Tables

Practice and Problem Solving: C

Write an equation to express *y* in terms of *x*. Use your equation to complete the table.

1.

x	1	2	3	4	5
y	1	4	9	16	

_____

2.

x	32	28	24		16
y	−8		−6	−5	−4

_____

3.

x		8	6	4	2
y	4	3.2		1.6	0.8

_____

4.

x	1		3	4	5
y	7	12	17	22	

_____

Solve.

5. $F = \dfrac{9}{5}C + 32$ is an equation that models the relationship in the table.

Equivalent Temperatures					
Celsius, (°C)	−15	−10	−5	0	5
Fahrenheit, (°F)	5	14	23	32	41

What does each variable represent?_____.

What is the temperature in °F when it is 20°C? _____.

Is the ordered pair (30, 86) a solution for the equation? Justify your answer.

_____

6. Use the table of values and the equation in Exercise 5 to write an equation for which *F* is the independent variable and *C* is the dependent variable.

An equation relating *F* and *C* is _____.

What is the temperature in °C when it is 59°F? Justify your answer.

_____

LESSON 12-3

Writing Equations from Tables

Practice and Problem Solving: D

Write an equation to express *y* in terms of *x*. The first one is done for you.

1.

x	0	1	2	3
y	2	3	4	5

_____ **y = x + 2** _____

2.

x	5	10	15	20
y	1	2	3	4

_____

3.

x	3	4	5	6
y	9	12	15	18

_____

4.

x	7	8	9	10
y	5	6	7	8

_____

Solve. The first one is done for you.

5. When George works 8 hours he earns $80. When George works
   10 hours he earns $100. When George works 12 hours he earns $120.
   Complete the table. Circle the letter of the equation that relates the
   dollars George earns, *y*, to the number of hours he works, *x*.

Number of hours, x	8	10	12
Dollars earned, y	80	100	120

A $y = x \div 10$ Ⓒ $y = 10x$

B $y = x + 72$

6. When Javier is 2, Arianna is 5. When Javier is 3, Arianna is 6.
   When Javier is 8, Arianna will be 11. When Javier is 20, Arianna is 23.
   Complete the table. Circle the letter of the equation that relates the age
   of Arianna, *y*, to the age of Javier, *x*.

Javier's age, x	2	3	8	20
Arianna's age, y	5			

A $y = x \div 2$ C $y = 2x$

B $y = x + 3$

When Javier is 30 years old, Arianna will be _____.

LESSON 12-3

Writing Equations from Tables
Reteach

The relationship between two variables in which one quantity depends
on the other can be modeled by an equation. The equation expresses
the dependent variable y in terms of the independent variable x.

x	0	1	2	3	4	5	6	7
y	4	5	6	7	8	9	10	?

To write an equation from a table of values, first
compare the x- and y-values to find a pattern.

In each, the y-value is 4 more than the x-value.

Then use the pattern to write an equation expressing y in terms of x.
$y = x + 4$

You can use the equation to find the missing value in the table.
To find y when $x = 7$, substitute 7 in for x in the equation.

$y = x + 4$
$y = 7 + 4$
$y = 11$
So, y is **11** when x is 7.

**Write an equation to express y in terms of x. Use your equation to find
the missing value of y.**

1.

x	1	2	3	4	5	6
y	3	6	9	12	15	?

_____

2.

x	18	17	16	15	14	13
y	15	14	13	?	11	10

_____

To solve a real-world problem, use a table of values and an equation.

When Todd is 8, Jane is 1. When Todd is 10, Jane will be 3. When
Todd is 16, Jane will be 9. What is Jane's age when Todd is 45?

Todd, x	8	10	16	45
Jane, y	1	3	9	?

Jane is 7 years younger than Todd.

So $y = x - 7$. When $x = 45$, $y = 45 - 7$. So, $y = 38$.

Solve.

3. When a rectangle is 3 inches wide its length is 6 inches. When it is
4 inches wide its length will be 8 inches. When it is is 9 inches wide its
length will be 18 inches. Write and solve an equation to complete the table.

Width, x	3	4	9	20
Length, y	6			

When the rectangle is 20 inches wide, its length is _____.

LESSON
12-3

Writing Equations from Tables
Reading Strategies: Analyze Information

A table is useful for changing cups to ounces.

Cups	Ounces
1	8
2	16
3	24
4	32
5	40

Use the table above to complete Exercises 1–3.

1. How many ounces are in 1 cup?

   _____

2. How many ounces are in 3 cups?

   _____

3. If "6 cups" were added to the table, how many ounces would be listed?

   _____

An equation shows the relationship between cups and ounces.

ounces = 8 • cups

↓

$y = 8x$

Independent Variable ⟶

Dependent Variable ⟶

x	1	2	3	4	5
y	8	16	24	32	40

The number of ounces depends on the number of cups. The value of y depends on the value of x.

Use the table above to complete Exercises 4–6.

4. Which variable stands for ounces? for cups?

   _____

5. What is the value of y when $x = 2$?

   _____

6. Use the equation to find the number of ounces when the number of cups is 15.

   _____

LESSON 12-3

Writing Equations from Tables
Success for English Learners

Problem 1

The number of inches is 12 times the number of feet.

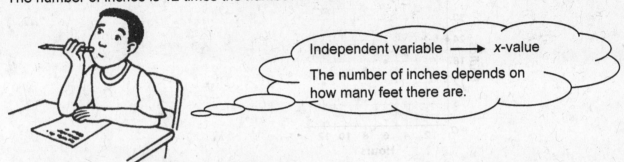

Independent variable ⟶ x-value

The number of inches depends on how many feet there are.

The <u>independent</u> variable is the <u>x-value</u> of the equation.

The <u>dependent</u> variable is the <u>y-value</u> of the equation.

<u>Write an equation</u> to show the relationship between x and y.

number of feet ⟶ x

number of inches ⟶ y

$y = 12x$

Problem 2

Mike has 8 feet of rope. How many inches of rope does he have?

<u>Solve an equation</u> to find a value.

<u>Substitute</u> the value for x into the equation, then <u>solve for y</u>.

y = 12x		
x = 8	Substitute 8 for x.	y = 12(8) = 96

Mike has 96 inches of rope.

1. What does an equation with x and y show?

_____

_____

2. What does it mean to substitute a value into the equation?

_____

3. Suppose Mike has 5 feet of rope. How many inches of rope does he have?

_____

LESSON
12-4

Representing Algebraic Relationships in Tables and Graphs
Practice and Problem Solving: A/B

An antiques dealer has 24 clock radios to sell at a 12-hour-long antique-radio sale. Use the graph to complete the table.

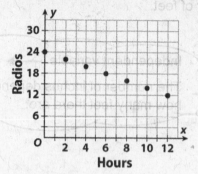

1. Complete the table with the data from the graph.

Radios remaining	24	?	?	?	?	?	?
Hours completed	0	2	4	6	8	10	12

2. What are the dependent (*y*) and independent (*x*) variables?

   dependent: _____; independent: _____

3. Write ordered pairs for the points on the graph and in the table.

   _____

4. How many radios are sold every two hours? _____

5. What happens to the *total* number of radios every two hours?

   _____

6. If *h* is hours and *n* is the number of radios remaining, complete the equation:

   n = _____ × *h* + _____

7. Why is the sign of the number that is multiplied by hours, *h*, negative?

   _____

   _____

LESSON 12-4

Representing Algebraic Relationships in Tables and Graphs

Practice and Problem Solving: C

Use the graph to answer the questions.

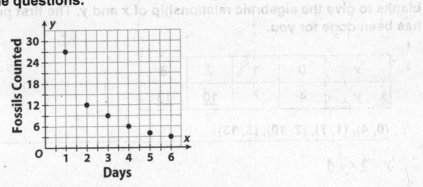

1. A paleontologist is counting fossilized remains of extinct plants at a geological site. Complete the table with data from the graph.

Plant fossils counted, *f*	___	___	___	___	___	___
Elapsed days of dig, *d*	1	2	3	4	5	6

2. There are three rates at which the fossils are being counted: Rate *A* for Days 1 and 2, Rate *B* for Days 2 – 4, and Rate *C*: for Days 5 – 6. What is happening to the number of fossils counted as each day passes?

_____

3. Which rate describes the period of time over which the number of fossils counted decreases at the *greatest* rate? Explain your answer.

_____

4. Give the numerical value of each of the rates, *A*, *B*, and *C*. Your answer should be negative and expressed in units of "fossils counted per day" or "fossils/day."

Rate *A*: _____; Rate *B*: _____; Rate *C*: _____

LESSON 12-4

Representing Algebraic Relationships in Tables and Graphs
Practice and Problem Solving: D

Complete the tables. Then, write the ordered pairs. Finally, fill in the blanks to give the algebraic relationship of *x* and *y*. The first problem has been done for you.

1.

x	0	1	2	3
y	4	7	**10**	**13**

 (0, 4), (1, 7), (2, 10), (3, 13)

 $y = \underline{3} x + \underline{4}$

2.

x	0	1	2	4
y	0	−4	___	−16

 _____

 $y = \underline{\qquad} x + \underline{\qquad}$

3.

x	0	2	___	6
y	5	11	17	___

 _____

 $y = \underline{\qquad} x + \underline{\qquad}$

Write the ordered pairs of two points on the graph. Then, write the algebraic relationship of *x* and *y*. The first one is done for you.

4.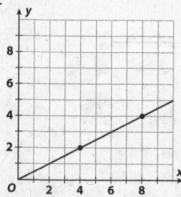

5.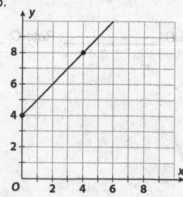

6.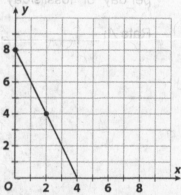

 (4, 2), (8, 4)

 _____

 _____

 $y = \underline{0.5} x + \underline{0}$

 $y = \underline{\qquad} x + \underline{\qquad}$

 $y = \underline{\qquad} x + \underline{\qquad}$

LESSON 12-4

Representing Algebraic Relationships in Tables and Graphs
Reteach

The *x*- and *y*-values in an algebraic relationship should be related in the same way when new values of *x* or *y* are used. This pattern should be seen in a table of values and from a graph of the *x* and *y* values.

Example 1

What is the relationship of the *x* and *y* values in the table?

x	2	4	6	8	10
y	6	12	18	24	30

Solution

First, check to see if there is a simple addition, multiplication, division, or subtraction relationship between the *x* and *y* values.

Here, the *y* values are 3 times the *x* values.

This means that the algebraic relationship is $y = 3x$.

Example 2

What is the relationship between *x* and *y* represented by the graph.

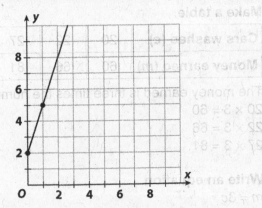

Solution

First, notice that the line through the points crosses the *y*-axis at $y = 2$. This means that part of the relationship between *x* and *y* is given by $y = $ ____ $ + 2$.

Next, notice that the line through the points goes over to the right by one unit as it "rises" by 3 units. This means that any *x* value is multiplied by 3 over 1 or 3 units as the line goes from one point to another. This is written as $y = 3x$.

Combine these two observations:
$y = 3x$ and $y = 2$ give $y = 3x + 2$.
Both parts are needed to completely describe the relationship shown.

1. Find the relationship of *x* and *y* in the table.

x	0	1	3	6	7
y	1.5	2	3	4.5	5

$y = $ _____ $x + $ _____

2. Find the relationship of *x* and *y* from a graph of a line that crosses the *y*-axis at $y = 6$ and that goes to the left 2 units and rises 3 units.

$y = $ _____ $x + $ _____

LESSON 12-4

Representing Algebraic Relationships in Tables and Graphs

Reading Strategies: Reading a Table

In order to write a rule that gives an algebraic relationship, you sometimes need to use a table.

Car washers tracked the number of cars they washed and the total amount of money they earned. They charged the same price for each car they washed. They earned $60 for 20 cars, $66 for 22 cars, and $81 for 27 cars. Use the information to make a table and write an equation.

Make a table.

Cars washed (c)	20	22	27
Money earned (m)	60	66	81

The money earned is three times the number of cars washed.

$20 \times 3 = 60$
$22 \times 3 = 66$
$27 \times 3 = 81$

Write an equation.

$m = 3c$

1. What is the value of m when there are no cars washed?

   _____

2. What is the value of m when 100 cars are washed?

   _____

3. Complete the table. Then write an equation to represent the table.

Tickets (t)	8	10	12	14	16
Total cost (c)	40	50	60		

   _____

4. Complete the table. Then write an equation to represent the table.

x	4	8	12	16	20	24
y	1	2	3	4		

   _____

LESSON 12-4 Representing Algebraic Relationships in Tables and Graphs
Success for English Learners

Problem 1

Find the algebraic rule from a table.

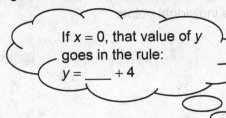

If $x = 0$, that value of y goes in the rule:
$y = $ ____ $+ 4$

What happens to x before it is added to 4 to give 6? Multiplied by 2: 2×1
$y = 2x$

x	0	1	2	3
y	4	6	8	10

Combine the two steps: ⟶ $y = 2x + 4$

Problem 2

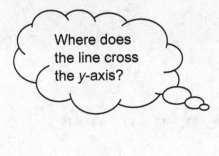

Where does the line cross the y-axis?

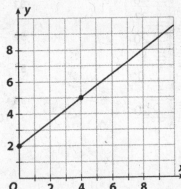

How far over and how far up?

The line crosses the y-axis at 2.

$y = $ _____ $+ 2$

The line goes over 4 and up 3.

$y = \dfrac{3}{4}x + 2$

Give the algebraic rule.

1. (0, 2), (1, 3), (2, 4)

_____

2. (0, 1), (2, 5), (4, 9)

_____

Name _____ Date _____ Class_____

MODULE 12

Relationships in Two Variables
Challenge

Exploring Temperature Data

This activity illustrates the difference between experimental and theoretical data.

1. Complete the tables. Graph the Table 1 data as individual points.
   Show the data in Table 2 as a straight line.

Table 1

data read from
the thermometer

°C	°F
10	
11	
12	
13	
14	
15	

Table 2

data computed
from the equation

$$F = C \times \frac{9}{5} + 32$$

°C	°F
10	
11	
12	
13	
14	
15	

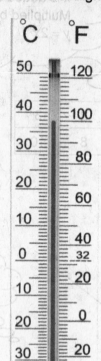

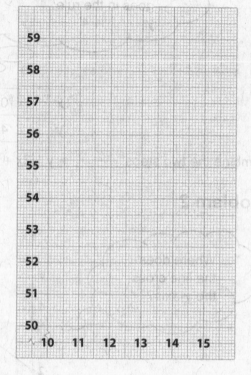

2. Describe the difference between the two data sets and explain why they differ.

_____

_____

_____

Name _____ Date _____ Class _____

Area of Quadrilaterals

Practice and Problem Solving: A/B

Find the area of each parallelogram.

1.

2.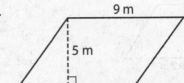

_____   _____

Find the area of each trapezoid.

3.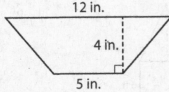

4.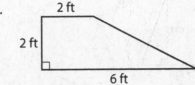

_____   _____

Find the area of each rhombus.

5.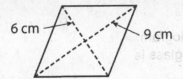

6.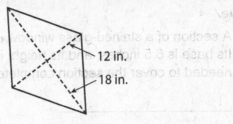

_____   _____

Solve.

7. A desktop in the shape of a parallelogram has a base of 30 inches and a height of 40 inches. What is the area of the desktop?

_____

8. A rhombus has one diagonal that is 14 centimeters long and one diagonal that is 12 centimeters long. What is the area of the rhombus?

_____

9. The bases of a trapezoid are 24 feet and 16 feet. The height of the trapezoid is 12 feet. What is the area of the trapezoid?

_____

LESSON 13-1

Area of Quadrilaterals

Practice and Problem Solving: C

Find the area of each figure.

1.

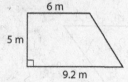

6 m

5 m

9.2 m

2.

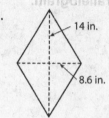

14 in.

8.6 in.

_____

3.

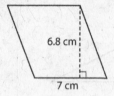

6.8 cm

7 cm

4.

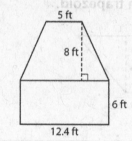

5 ft

8 ft

6 ft

12.4 ft

_____

Solve.

5. A section of a stained-glass window is shaped like a parallelogram. Its base is 6.5 inches, and its height is 4 inches. How much glass is needed to cover the section completely?

_____

6. The base of a statue is in the shape of a trapezoid. The bases of the trapezoid are 7.5 feet and 4.75 feet. Its height is 6 feet. What is the area of the base of the statue?

_____

7. The front view of a piece of art is in the shape of a rhombus. The front view of the art has diagonals that are 1.4 yards long and 0.8 yard long. What is the area of the front view of the piece of art?

_____

8. A decorative pillow is in the shape of a parallelogram. Its base is 28 centimeters, and its height is 24.5 centimeters. What is the area of the front surface of the pillow?

_____

LESSON 13-1

Area of Quadrilaterals
Practice and Problem Solving: D

Find the area of each parallelogram. The first one is done for you.

1.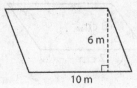

   6 m

   10 m

   $A = 10 \cdot 6 = 60 \text{ m}^2$

2.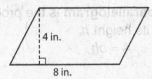

   4 in.

   8 in.

Find the area of each trapezoid. The first one is done for you.

3.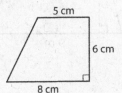

   5 cm

   6 cm

   8 cm

   $A = \dfrac{1}{2} \cdot 6 \cdot (8 + 5) = 39 \text{ cm}^2$

4.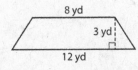

   8 yd

   3 yd

   12 yd

Find the area of each rhombus. The first one is done for you.

5.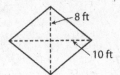

   8 ft

   10 ft

   $A = \dfrac{1}{2} \cdot 8 \cdot 10 = 40 \text{ ft}^2$

6.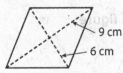

   9 cm

   6 cm

Solve.

7. A countertop in the shape of a parallelogram has a base of 90 centimeters and a height of 50 centimeters. What is the area of the countertop?

   _____

8. A rhombus has one diagonal that is 10 inches long and one diagonal that is 15 inches long. What is the area of the rhombus?

   _____

9. The bases of a trapezoid are 4 yards and 6 yards. The height of the trapezoid is 5 yards. What is the area of the trapezoid?

   _____

Name _____ Date _____ Class_____

LESSON
13-1

Area of Quadrilaterals
Reteach

You can use formulas to find the areas of quadrilaterals.

The area A of a **parallelogram** is the product
of its base b and its height h.
$$A = bh$$

$$A = bh$$
$$= 3 \cdot 7$$
$$= 21 \text{ cm}^2$$

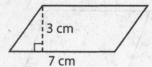

The area of a **trapezoid** is half its height
multiplied by the sum of the lengths of its
two bases.
$$A = \frac{1}{2}h(b_1 + b_2)$$

$$A = \frac{1}{2}h(b_1 + b_2)$$
$$= \frac{1}{2} \cdot 6(5 + 9)$$
$$= \frac{1}{2} \cdot 6(14)$$
$$= 3 \cdot 14$$
$$= 42 \text{ m}^2$$

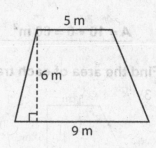

The area of a **rhombus** is half of the product
of its two diagonals.
$$A = \frac{1}{2}d_1 d_2$$

$$A = \frac{1}{2}d_1 d_2$$
$$= \frac{1}{2}(5)(8)$$
$$= 20 \text{ in}^2$$

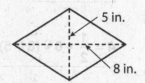

Find the area of each figure.

1.
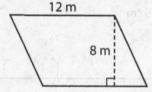

2.
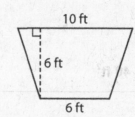

_____

3.

4.
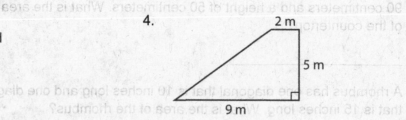

_____

LESSON 13-1 Area of Quadrilaterals
Reading Strategies: Follow a Procedure

Parallelograms and trapezoids are two different types of quadrilaterals.
You can follow a procedure to help you find the area of each type
of quadrilateral.

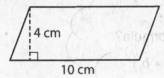

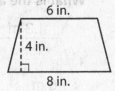

Step 1: Use the formula $A = bh$.	**Step 1:** Use the formula $A = \frac{1}{2}h(b_1 + b_2)$.
Step 2: Substitute the length of the base for b.	**Step 2:** Substitute the length of the height for h.
Step 3: Substitute the length of the height for h.	**Step 3:** Substitute the length of the bases for b_1 and b_2 and add.
Step 4: Multiply.	**Step 4:** Multiply.

Solve.

1. What is the first step in finding the area of the parallelogram above?

   _____

2. What are the second and third steps in finding the area of the
   parallelogram above?

   _____

   _____

3. What is the area of the parallelogram above?

   _____

4. What is the first step in finding the area of the trapezoid?

   _____

5. What are the second and third steps in finding the area of the
   trapezoid above?

   _____

   _____

6. What is the area of the trapezoid above?

   _____

LESSON 13-1	**Area of Quadrilaterals**

Success for English Learners

Problem 1

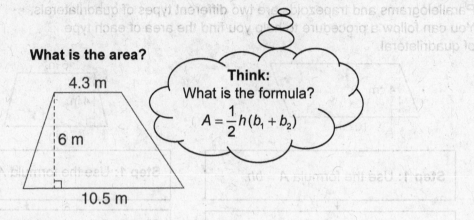

What is the area?

4.3 m

6 m

10.5 m

Think:
What is the formula?
$A = \frac{1}{2}h(b_1 + b_2)$

Remember

A = Area h = height

b_1 = base on top b_2 = base on bottom

What is the height? h = 6 m

What is the base on top? b_1 = 4.3 m

What is the base on the bottom? b_2 = 10.5 m

$A = \frac{1}{2}h(b_1 + b_2)$ Use formula.

$A = \frac{1}{2}(6)(4.3 + 10.5)$ Substitute.

$A = (3)(4.3 + 10.5)$ Multiply.

$A = (3)(14.8)$ Add.

$A = 3 \cdot 14.8 = 44.4$ Multiply.

$A = 44.4\,\text{m}^2$

So, the area is 44.4 m².

1. Does it matter which length you use for b_1 and which you use for b_2? Explain.

_____

2. Describe another way to find the area of a trapezoid.

_____

3. Find the area of the trapezoid shown.

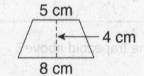

5 cm

4 cm

8 cm

_____

LESSON
13-2

Area of Triangles

Practice and Problem Solving: A/B

Find the area of each triangle.

1.
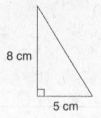

8 cm

5 cm

_____

2.
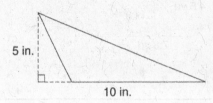

5 in.

10 in.

_____

3.
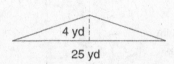

4 yd

25 yd

_____

4.

4 ft

3.5 ft

_____

Solve.

5. The front part of a tent is 8 feet long and 5 feet tall. What is the area of the front part of the tent?

_____

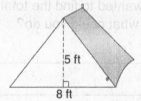

5 ft

8 ft

6. Kathy is playing a board game. The game pieces are each in the shape of a triangle. Each triangle has a base of 1.5 inches and a height of 2 inches. What is the area of a game piece?

_____

7. A triangular-shaped window has a base of 3 feet and a height of 4 feet. What is the area of the window?

_____

8. Landon has a triangular piece of paper. The base of the paper is $6\frac{1}{2}$ inches. The height of the paper is 8 inches. What is the area of the piece of paper?

_____

LESSON 13-2

Area of Triangles

Practice and Problem Solving: C

Find the area of each triangle.

1.

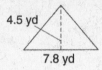

4.5 yd

7.8 yd

_____

2.

$4\frac{1}{2}$ ft

$3\frac{3}{4}$ ft

_____

3.

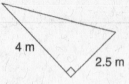

4 m

2.5 m

_____

4.

5 in.

3.2 in.

_____

Solve.

5. If you wanted to find the total area of the triangles in Exercises 1, 2, and 4, what could you do?

_____

_____

6. A scale model of a street sign is in the shape of a triangle. The base is 4.25 centimeters and the height is 8.8 centimeters. What is the area of the street sign?

_____

7. Rachel's earrings are in the shape of a triangle. The height of the earrings is $1\frac{1}{2}$ inches and the base is $\frac{3}{5}$ inch. What is the area of both of Rachel's earrings?

_____

8. The face of a watch is in the shape of a triangle with a base of 6 centimeters and a height of 7.75 centimeters. What is the area of the face of the watch?

_____

9. A flag in the shape of a triangle has an area of 25.2 square inches. The base of the flag is 6 inches. What is the height of the flag?

_____

Name _____ Date _____ Class_____

LESSON 13-2

Area of Triangles

Practice and Problem Solving: D

Find the area of each triangle. The first one is done for you.

1.

1 cm

3 cm

$$A = \frac{1}{2} \cdot 3 \cdot 1 = 1.5 \text{ cm}^2$$

2.

4 in.

7 in.

3.

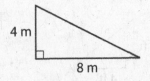

4 m

8 m

_____

4.

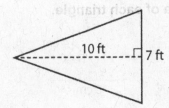

10 ft   7 ft

_____

5.

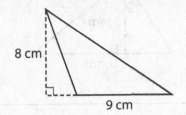

8 cm

9 cm

_____

6.

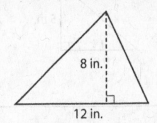

8 in.

12 in.

_____

Solve each problem. The first one is done for you.

7. A triangular-shaped rug has a base of 8 feet and a height of 7 feet. What is the area of the rug?

$$A = \frac{1}{2} \cdot 8 \cdot 7 = 28 \text{ ft}^2$$

_____

8. The sail on a sailboat is in the shape of a triangle that has a base of 12 feet and a height of 14 feet. What is the area of the sail?

_____

9. The front view of a square pyramid is in the shape of a triangle that has a base of 30 yards and a height of 40 yards. What is the area of the front view of the square pyramid?

_____

LESSON 13-2 · Area of Triangles · Practice and Problem Solving: D

LESSON 13-2

Area of Triangles

Reteach

To find the area of a triangle, first turn your triangle into a rectangle.

Next, find the area of the rectangle. 6 • 3 = 18 square units

The triangle is half the area of the formed rectangle or $A = \frac{1}{2}bh$, so

divide the product by 2.

18 ÷ 2 = 9 So, the area of the triangle is 9 square units.

Find the area of each triangle.

1.

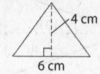

4 cm
6 cm

_____

2.

3 ft
4 ft

_____

3.

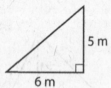

5 m
6 m

_____

4.

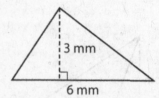

3 mm
6 mm

_____

5.

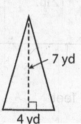

7 yd
4 yd

_____

6.

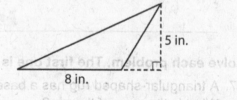

5 in.
8 in.

_____

Name _____ Date _____ Class_____

Area of Triangles

Reading Strategies: Follow a Procedure

You can follow a procedure to help you find the area of a triangle.

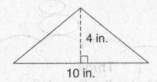

4 in.

10 in.

Step 1: Use the formula $A = \dfrac{1}{2}bh$.

↓

Step 2: Substitute the length of the base for b.

↓

Step 3: Substitute the length of the height for h.

↓

Step 4: Multiply.

Answer each question.

1. What is the first step in finding the area of the triangle?

   _____

2. What are the second and third steps in finding the area of the triangle?

   _____

3. What is the area of the triangle?

   _____

4. What is the area of a triangle with base 18 meters and height
   6 meters?

   _____

5. What is the area of a triangle with base 3.6 feet and height 2.5 feet?

   _____

6. How would you vary this procedure if you were given the area and
   base of a triangle and asked to find its height?

   _____

Area of Triangles

LESSON 13-2

Success for English Learners

Problem 1

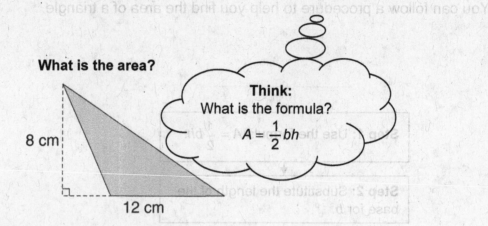

What is the area?

8 cm

12 cm

Think:
What is the formula?
$A = \frac{1}{2}bh$

Remember:
A = Area   **b** = base   **h** = height
Examples of square units: ft², yd², cm²

The base is 12 cm.

The height is 8 cm.

$A = \frac{1}{2}bh$ Use formula.

$A = \frac{1}{2}(12 \cdot 8)$ Use measurements.

$A = \frac{1}{2}(96)$ Multiply. $12 \cdot 8 = 96$

$A = \frac{1}{2}(96) = 48$ Divide. $96 \div 2 = 48$

$A = 48$ cm²

So, the area is 48 cm².

1. Does it matter which side of the triangle you use as the base and
which you use as the height? Explain.

_____

2. Why is the expression $\left(\frac{1}{2} \cdot 12\right) \cdot 8$ the same as $\frac{1}{2} \cdot (12 \cdot 8)$?

_____

3. Find the area of the triangle shown.

_____

8 ft

4 ft

Name _____ Date _____ Class_____

Solving Area Equations

Practice and Problem Solving: A/B

Solve.

1. The front of an A-frame house is in the shape of a triangle. The height of the house is 20 feet. The area of the front of the A-frame is 600 square feet. Write and solve an equation to find the base of the A-frame house.

   _____

2. A countertop is in the shape of a trapezoid. The lengths of the bases are $70\frac{1}{2}$ and $65\frac{1}{2}$ inches long. The area of the countertop is 1,224 square inches. Write and solve an equation to find the height of the countertop.

   _____

3. The top of a coffee table is in the shape of a rectangle. The length of the top of the coffee table is 3.5 feet and the area is 10.5 square feet. What is the width of the top of the coffee table?

   _____

4. Jacob made a banner for a sporting event in the shape of a parallelogram. The area of the banner is $127\frac{1}{2}$ square centimeters. The height of the banner is $4\frac{1}{4}$ centimeters. What is the base of the banner?

   _____

5. McKenzie has enough paint to paint 108 square feet. She wants to paint her garage door, which has a height of 12 feet. The garage door is in the shape of a rectangle. If McKenzie has just enough paint to cover the garage door, what is the width of the door?

   _____

LESSON 13-3

Solving Area Equations

Practice and Problem Solving: C

Solve.

1. The front of a podium is in the shape of a trapezoid with base lengths 4 and 8.5 feet. The height is 2 feet. A gallon of paint covers about 350 square feet. How many front frames of a podium can Lillian paint with 2 gallons of paint?

   _____

2. Kenneth's back yard is in the shape of a rectangle with a length of 12 yards and a width of 10 yards. A bag of grass seed costs $25.99 and covers 400 square feet. How much will Kenneth spend on grass seed to cover his back yard?

   _____

3. The area of a triangular piece of stained glass is 50 square centimeters. If the height of the triangle is four times the base, how long are the height and base of the piece of stained glass?

   _____

4. A park is in the shape of a parallelogram. The park has an area of $776\frac{1}{4}$ square yards. The base of the park is $34\frac{1}{2}$ yards. Marta wants to jog 10 sprints. Each sprint is the same distance as the height of the park. How far will Marta sprint?

   _____

5. A quilt contains cuts of congruent right triangular pieces with a base of $8\frac{1}{2}$ centimeters and a height of $8\frac{1}{2}$ centimeters. How many triangular pieces are needed to make a rectangular quilt with an area of 4,335 square centimeters?

   _____

LESSON 13-3

Solving Area Equations
Practice and Problem Solving: D

Solve each problem. The first one is done for you.

1. Jennifer has a picture frame in the shape of a rectangle. The area of the picture frame is 35 square inches. The length of the picture frame is 7 inches. What is the width of the frame?

$$A = lw$$
$$35 = 7w$$
$$5 = w$$

5 in. _____

2. Christopher's back yard is in the shape of a trapezoid. The bases of his back yard are 30 and 40 feet long. The area of his back yard is 525 square feet. Write and solve an equation to find the height of Christopher's back yard.

_____

3. Cindy made a triangular shaped sculpture with an area of 63 square inches. The height of the sculpture is 9 inches. What is the base length of the sculpture?

_____

4. A floor mat is in the shape of a parallelogram. The mat has an area of 480 square inches. If the base of the mat is 24 inches, what is the height of the mat?

_____

5. A trading token is in the shape of a trapezoid and has an area of 25 square centimeters. If the bases are 3 and 7 centimeters, what is the height of the token?

_____

6. The back frame of a dog house is in the shape of a triangle with an area of 6 square feet. The height of the frame is 4 feet. What is the width of the frame?

_____

LESSON
13-3
Solving Area Equations
Reteach

You can use area formulas to find missing dimensions in figures.
The formula for area of a parallelogram is $A = bh$.

The formula for area of a trapezoid is $A = \frac{1}{2}h(b_1 + b_2)$.

The formula for area of a rhombus is $A = \frac{1}{2}d_1d_2$.

The formula for area of a triangle is $A = \frac{1}{2}bh$.

Suppose you know the area of a triangle is 28 square feet. You also know the length of the base of the triangle is 7 feet. What is the height of the triangle?

Use the formula for area of a triangle. $A = \frac{1}{2}bh$

Substitute known values. $28 = \frac{1}{2}(7)h$

Multiply both sides by 2. $56 = 7h$

Divide both sides by 7. $8 = h$

The height of the triangle is 8 feet.

Solve.

1. The area of a parallelogram is 150 square meters. The height of the parallelogram is 15 meters. What is the length of the parallelogram?

   _____

2. The length of one diagonal of a rhombus is 8 cm. The area of the rhombus is 72 square centimeters. What is the length of the other diagonal of the rhombus?

   _____

3. The area of a triangle is 32 square inches. The height of the triangle is 8 inches. What is the length of the base of the triangle?

   _____

4. The area of a rectangle is 34 square yards. The length of the rectangle is 17 yards. What is the width of the rectangle?

   _____

5. The area of a trapezoid is 39 square millimeters. The height of the trapezoid is 6 millimeters. One of the base lengths of the trapezoid is 5 millimeters. What is the length of the other base of the trapezoid?

   _____

LESSON 13-3 Solving Area Equations
Reading Strategies: Draw a Diagram

You can find missing measurements of figures when you know the formula for the figure and when you are given other information about the figure.

First, you need to know the different area formulas for common figures.

Figure	Area Formula
Parallelogram	$A = bh$
Trapezoid	$A = \frac{1}{2}h(b_1 + b_2)$
Rhombus	$A = \frac{1}{2}d_1d_2$
Triangle	$A = \frac{1}{2}bh$

First, you should draw a diagram. Be sure to label the diagram with all the information you are given.

For example, a triangular-shaped poster has an area of 16 square meters and a base length of 8 meters. What is the height of the poster?

Draw a diagram. Label the diagram with the given information.

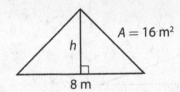

$$A = 16\,m^2$$
$$h$$
$$8\,m$$

Now, use the given information with the formula for area of a triangle.

$A = \frac{1}{2}bh$ Write the formula for area of a triangle.

$16 = \frac{1}{2}(8)(h)$ The area is 16 and the base is 8.

$16 = 4h$ Multiply $\frac{1}{2}$ and 8.

$4 = h$ Divide both sides by 4.

The height of the poster is 4 meters.

Solve.

1. A parallelogram has an area of 60 square inches. If the base of the parallelogram is 12 inches, what is the height of the parallelogram?

_____

2. A trapezoid and has an area of 45 square centimeters. If the bases are 10 and 5 centimeters, what is the height of the trapezoid?

_____

LESSON 13-3

Solving Area Equations
Success for English Learners

Problem 1

If you are given the length of the base and the area, you can find the height of a parallelogram.

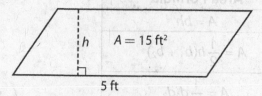

$A = bh$ Write the formula for area.

$15 = 5h$ The area is 15 and the length of the base is 5.

$3 = h$ Divide both sides by 5.

Problem 2

If you are given the height and the area, you can find the length of the base of a triangle.

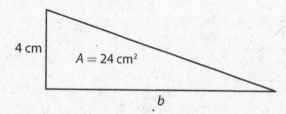

$A = \dfrac{1}{2}bh$ Write the formula for area.

$24 = \dfrac{1}{2}(b)(4)$ The area is 24 and the height is 4.

$24 = 2b$ Multiply $\dfrac{1}{2}$ and 4.

$12 = b$ Divide both sides by 2.

1. When given the area and known dimensions, what is the first step in finding an unknown measure in a figure?

   _____

2. What is the next step?

   _____

LESSON 13-4

Area of Polygons

Practice and Problem Solving: A/B

Find the area of each polygon.

1.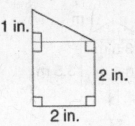

2.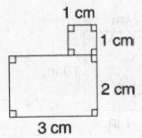

_____

3.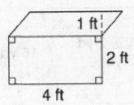

4.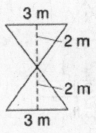

_____

5.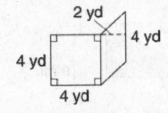

6.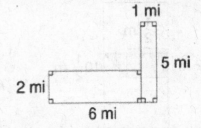

_____

Solve.

7. The shape of Nevada can almost be divided into a perfect rectangle and a perfect triangle. About how many square miles does Nevada cover?

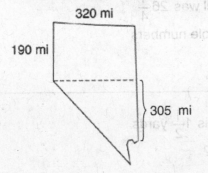

8. The shape of Oklahoma can almost be divided into 2 perfect rectangles and 1 triangle. About how many square miles does Oklahoma cover?

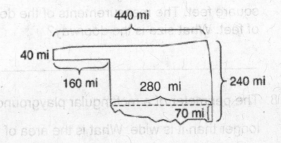

_____

LESSON 13-4

Area of Polygons

Practice and Problem Solving: C

Find the area of each figure. The shaded parts are cut out of the figures.

1.

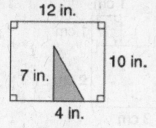

12 in.

7 in.   10 in.

4 in.

_____

2.

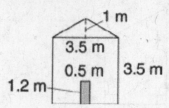

1 m

3.5 m

0.5 m   3.5 m

1.2 m

_____

3.

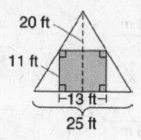

20 ft

11 ft

├─13 ft─┤

25 ft

_____

4.

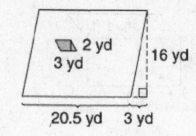

2 yd

3 yd   16 yd

20.5 yd   3 yd

_____

5.

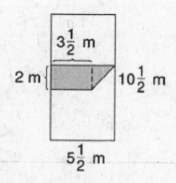

$3\frac{1}{2}$ m

2 m { $10\frac{1}{2}$ m

$5\frac{1}{2}$ m

_____

6.

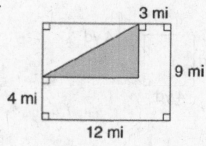

3 mi

9 mi

4 mi

12 mi

_____

Solve.

7. The front wall of the shed that Rita built is 9 feet tall and $5\frac{1}{4}$ feet wide.

   After she cut out a section for a door, the area of that wall was $26\frac{1}{4}$

   square feet. The measurements of the doorway were whole numbers
   of feet. What size is the doorway?

_____

8. The perimeter of a rectangular playground is 40 yards. It is $1\frac{1}{2}$ yards

   longer than it is wide. What is the area of the playground?

_____

LESSON 13-4

Area of Polygons

Practice and Problem Solving: D

Find the area of each polygon. The first one is done for you.

1.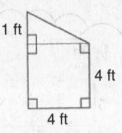

   1 ft
   4 ft
   4 ft

   $$\frac{1}{2}(1 \times 4) + (4 \times 4) = 2 + 16 = 18 \text{ ft}^2$$

2.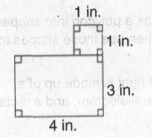

   1 in.
   1 in.
   3 in.
   4 in.

   _____

3.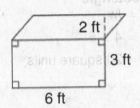

   2 ft
   3 ft
   6 ft

   _____

4.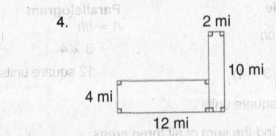

   2 mi
   10 mi
   4 mi
   12 mi

   _____

Solve.

5. A rectangular painting is made up of two congruent squares with sides that are 2 feet long. What is the area of the entire painting?

   _____

6. A carpet is made up of two congruent triangles. The base of each triangle is 3 meters long, and the height is 6 meters. What is the area of the entire carpet?

   _____

LESSON 13-4

Area of Polygons
Reteach

Sometimes you can use area formulas you know to help you find the area of more complex figures.

You can break a polygon into shapes that you know. Then use those shapes to find the area.

The figure at right is made up of a triangle, a parallelogram, and a rectangle.

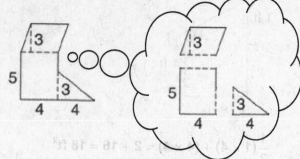

Triangle

$A = \dfrac{1}{2}bh$

$= \dfrac{1}{2}(3 \times 4)$

$= 6$ square units

Parallelogram

$A = bh$

$= 3 \times 4$

$= 12$ square units

Rectangle

$A = lw$

$= 4 \times 5$

$= 20$ square units

Finally, find the sum of all three areas.

$6 + 12 + 20 = 38$

The area of the whole figure is 38 square units.

Find the area of each figure.

1.

_____

2.

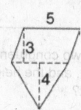

_____

3.

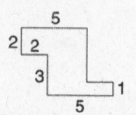

_____

4.

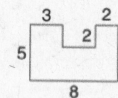

_____

Name _____ Date _____ Class _____

Area of Polygons

Reading Strategies: Use a Flowchart

To find the area of a rectangle, multiply its length by its width.

$A = l \cdot w$

$= 4 \cdot 5$

$= 20$ square units

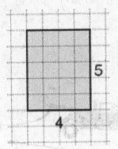

If a polygon is made up of more than one rectangle, you can find its area by following the steps in the flowchart below.

Step 1: Separate the polygon into rectangles.

↓

Step 2: Label the length and width of each rectangle.

↓

Step 3: Find the area of each rectangle.

↓

Step 4: Find the sum of all the areas.

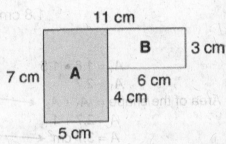

Answer the questions. Refer to the six-sided polygon above.

1. What are the length and width of rectangle A? _____

2. What is the formula for the area of a rectangle? _____

3. What is the area of rectangle A? _____

4. What is the area of rectangle B? _____

5. What do you do with the areas of rectangles A and B to find the area of the polygon?

    _____

6. What is the area of the polygon? _____

LESSON 13-4

Area of Polygons
Success for English Learners

Problem 1

Find the area.

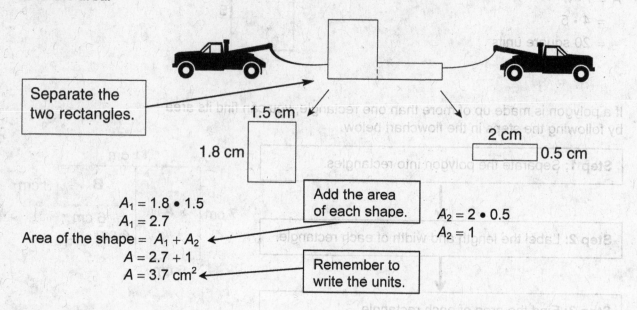

Separate the two rectangles.

1.5 cm

1.8 cm

2 cm

0.5 cm

Add the area of each shape.

$A_1 = 1.8 \cdot 1.5$
$A_1 = 2.7$
Area of the shape = $A_1 + A_2$
$A = 2.7 + 1$
$A = 3.7 \text{ cm}^2$

$A_2 = 2 \cdot 0.5$
$A_2 = 1$

Remember to write the units.

Problem 2

Find the area.

$A_1 = 8 \cdot 10$ $A_2 = \frac{1}{2} \cdot 8 \cdot 3$

$A_1 = 80$ $A_2 = 12$

$A \text{ (shape)} = 80 + 12$
$A \text{ (shape)} = 92 \text{ cm}^2$

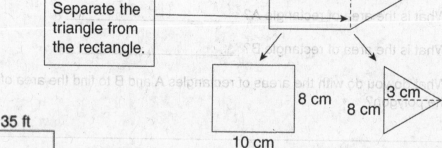

Separate the triangle from the rectangle.

$h = 13 \text{ cm}$

8 cm   3 cm

10 cm   8 cm

Find the area.

1.

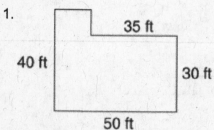

35 ft

40 ft

30 ft

50 ft

MODULE
13

Area and Polygons

Challenge

Answer the questions about the figure. Explain your answers and show your work.

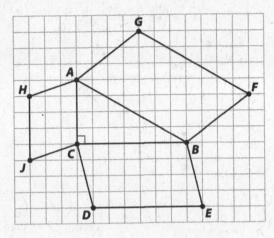

1. What are the areas of parallelograms *ACJH* and *BCDE*? (*Hint*: Use the grid to find the areas.)

   _____

2. What is the sum of the areas of parallelograms *ACJH* and *BCDE*?

   _____

3. Draw auxiliary lines to form triangles inside or outside of parallelogram *ABFG*. How does the area of *ABFG* compare *to* the sum of the areas of parallelograms *ACJH* and *BCDE*?

   _____

4. Use the Pythagorean Theorem, $a^2 + b^2 = c^2$, to find the length of side *AB* of right triangle *ABC*.

   _____

5. How does the length of *AB* affect the area of *ABFG* as it relates to the sum of the areas of parallelograms *ABFG*, *ACJH*, and *BCDE*?

   _____

Distance in the Coordinate Plane
Practice and Problem Solving: A/B

Name the coordinates of each reflection.

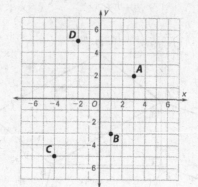

1. Point *A* across the *x*-axis

   New point: (_____, _____)

2. Point *B* across the *y*-axis

   New point: (_____, _____)

3. Point *C* across the *x*-axis

   New point: (_____, _____)

4. Point *D* across the *y*-axis

   New point: (_____, _____)

Name the coordinates of each reflection of the given point.

5. *M*(–2, –6)

   Across the *y*-axis: (_____, _____)

   Across the *x*-axis: (_____, _____)

6. *N*(4, 1)

   Across the *x*-axis: (_____, _____)

   Across the *y*-axis: (_____, _____)

Find the distance between the points.

7. *A* and *B*: _____

8. *A* and *C*: _____

9. *B* and *D*: _____

10. *C* and *G*: _____

11. *D* and *F*: _____

12. *E* and *F*: _____

13. *E* and *B*: _____

14. *E* and *A*: _____

15. *E* and *G*: _____

16. *F* and *G*: _____

Solve.

17. A taxi travels 25 kilometers east of an airport. Then, it travels from that
point to a point that is 40 kilometers west of the airport. Finally, the taxi
returns to the airport. How far did the taxi travel? Show your work.

_____

LESSON 14-1 — Distance in the Coordinate Plane

Practice and Problem Solving: C

Name the coordinates of the point that results from the transformations described.

1. Start at (4, 7).

   Reflect the point across the x-axis.

   Reflect again across the y-axis.

   Coordinates: (_____, _____)

2. Start at (–3, –5).

   Reflect the point across the y-axis.

   Reflect again across the x-axis.

   Coordinates: (_____, _____)

If a and b are whole numbers, what is the distance between the two points? Show your work.

3. X(a, –b) and Y(a, 5b)

   _____

4. C(–3a, 3b) and D(–6a, 3b)

   _____

Use the graph to answer the questions.

5. Explain why points A and B do **not** result from reflections of the same point across the x-axis and y-axis, respectively.

   _____

   _____

   _____

6. Show how point B can be reflected across the y-axis so that it bisects the distance between points A and C.

   _____

   _____

   _____

   _____

7. What is the shortest distance from point B to the midpoint of the line between points A and C?

   _____

   _____

   _____

8. The distance of point A to the x-axis is given by the expression 4a. The distance of the reflection of point A across the x-axis to the y-axis is given by the expression 3b. What is the total distance from point A to its reflection across the x-axis *and* the y-axis? Explain.

   _____

   _____

**LESSON
14-1**

Distance in the Coordinate Plane

Practice and Problem Solving: D

Use the coordinate plane for Exercises 1–5. The first one is done for you.

1. The *x*-coordinate of point *X* is ___3___.

   The *y*-coordinate of point *X* is ___3___.

2. Reflect point *X* across the *x*-axis. What are the coordinates of the reflected point?

   x-coordinate: _____

   y-coordinate: _____

3. Reflect point *X* across the *y*-axis. What are the coordinates of the reflected point?

   x-coordinate: _____   *y*-coordinate: _____

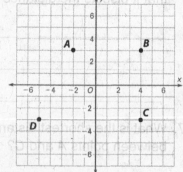

4. The *x*-coordinate of point *Y* is _____.

   The *y*-coordinate of point *Y* is _____.

   Reflect point *Y* across the *x*-axis. Give coordinates of the reflected point.

   x: _____; *y*: _____

5. The *x*-coordinate of point *Z* is _____.

   The *y*-coordinate of point *Z* is _____.

   Reflect point *Z* across the *x*-axis. Give the the coordinates of the reflected point.

   x: _____; *y*: _____

Use the coordinate plane for Exercises 6–8. Find the distance between the points. The first one is done for you.

6. point *A* and point *B*

   What is the *x*-coordinate of point *A*? ___–2___

   What is the *x*-coordinate of point *B*? ___4___

   Subtract the *x*-coordinates. ___|4 – (–2)| = 6___

   The distance is ___6___ units.

7. point *B* and point *C*

   The *y*-coordinate of point *B* is _____.

   The *y*-coordinate of point *C* is _____.

   Subtract the *y*-coordinates.

   |_____ – _____| = _____

   The distance is _____ units.

8. point *C* and point *D*

   The *x*-coordinate of point *C* is _____.

   The *x*-coordinate of point *D* is _____.

   Subtract the *x*-coordinates.

   |_____ – _____| = _____

   The distance is _____ units.

LESSON 14-1
Distance in the Coordinate Plane
Reteach

Reflecting a Point

In this lesson, a point on a coordinate plane is reflected across the axes of the coordinate plane. The points *B* and *C* are reflections of point *A* across the *x*- and *y*-axes.

The coordinates of point *A* are (3, 1).

Point *B* is the reflection of point *A* across the *x*-axis.

Point *C* is the reflection of point *A* across the *y*-axis.

The following rules can help you find the coordinates of a reflected point by looking at the signs of the coordinates.

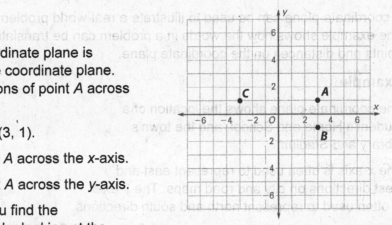

Reflecting across the *x*-axis	Reflecting across the *y*-axis
"Reflect across *x*. ⟶ Change the *y*."	"Reflect across *y*. ⟶ Change the *x*."
In this example, point *A*'s *x*-coordinate, +3, stays the same when point *A* is reflected across the *x*-axis to become point *B*. Point *A*'s *y*-coordinate, +1, switches to –1 to become point *B*. So, point *B*'s coordinates are (3, –1).	In this example, point *A*'s *y*-coordinate, +1, stays the same when point *A* is reflected across the *y*-axis to become point *C*. Point *A*'s *x*-coordinate, +3, switches to –3 to become point *C*. So, point *C*'s coordinates are (–3, 1).

Name the coordinates of each point after it is reflected across the given axis.

1. *A*(1, 3)
   x-axis

   (____, ____)

2. *B*(–4, 5)
   y-axis

   (____, ____)

3. *C*(6, –7)
   y-axis

   (____, ____)

4. *D*(–8, –9)
   x-axis

   (____, ____)

Distance between Points

The distance between two points on a coordinate plane depends on whether their *x*- or *y*-coordinates are different. Look at the points on the grid above to solve the problems.

The distance between points *A* and *B* is the absolute value of the difference of the *y*-coordinates of the points.	The distance between points *A* and *C* is the absolute value of the difference of the *x*-coordinates of the points.

Find the distance between the two points.

5. points *A* and *B*

   _____ units

6. points *A* and *C*

   _____ units

Distance in the Coordinate Plane
Reading Strategies: Use Graphic Aids

A coordinate plane can be used to illustrate a real-world problem.
The example shows how the words in a problem can be translated into
points and distances on the coordinate plane.

Example

The coordinate plane shows the location of a
student's Home and School, and the town's
Library and Stadium.

The *x*-axis is often used to represent east and
west directions on city and road maps. The *y*-axis
is often used to represent north and south directions.

Positive distances are often defined as being
"east" or "north" of an agreed-upon "center,"
such as the origin on a coordinate plane.

Negative distances are defined as being "west"
or "south" of the center.

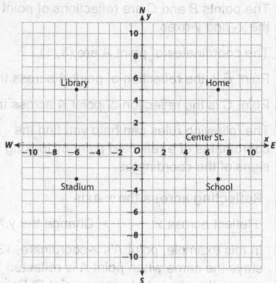

Problem

How far north of School is Home?

Solution

"North" is the vertical distance between School and Home. School is
3 blocks south of Center Street; Home is 5 blocks north of Center Street.

To find the distance from Home to School count the blocks.

_____ blocks.

But the question asked was, "How far "north" of School is Home?" A more
precise answer would be 8 blocks north.

Solve. Show your work.

1. How far west of Home is the Library?

_____

_____

2. How far south of the Library is the Stadium?

LESSON 14-1

Distance in the Coordinate Plane
Success for English Learners

Problem 1

Which point is a reflection of point *A* across the *y*-axis?

Point *B* or Point *C*?

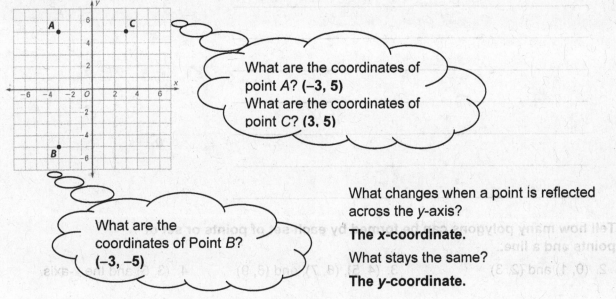

What are the coordinates of point *A*? **(–3, 5)**
What are the coordinates of point *C*? **(3, 5)**

What are the coordinates of Point *B*?
(–3, –5)

What changes when a point is reflected across the *y*-axis?

The x-coordinate.

What stays the same?

The y-coordinate.

Point *C* is the reflection of point *A*, across the *y*-axis because:

Point *A*'s *x*-coordinate changes to become point *C*'s *x*-coordinate: **–3 to +3.**

Point *A*'s *y*-coordinate stays the same to become point *C*'s *y*-coordinate: **+5.**

The answer is point *C* (3, 5).

Problem 2

What is the distance between points *A* and *C*?

Point *A*: **(–3, 5)**
Point *C*: **(3, 5)**

Count the squares.
Distance?

The distance from point *A* to point *C* is 6 units.

1. What kind of reflection of point *A* is represented by point *B*?

_____

2. What is the distance from point *A* to point *B*?

_____

LESSON 14-2

Polygons in the Coordinate Plane

Practice and Problem Solving: A/B

List all of the polygons that can be formed by using some or all of the lettered vertices shown in the coordinate plane.

1. _____

_____

_____

_____

_____

_____

_____

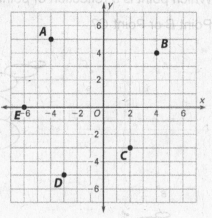

Tell how many polygons can be formed by each set of points or set of points and a line.

2. (0, 1) and (2, 3)   3. (4, 5), (6, 7), and (8, 9)   4. (3, 5) and the *x*-axis.

_____

Find the perimeter and area of each polygon. Show your work.

5.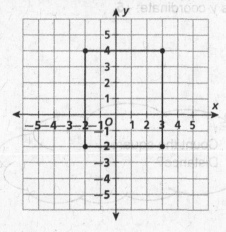
     6.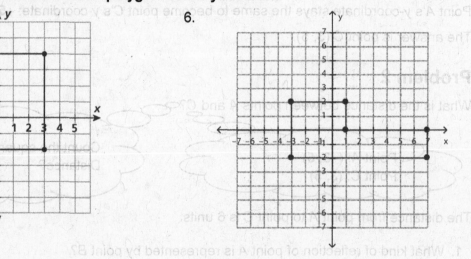

Perimeter: _____   Perimeter: _____

_____   _____

Area: _____   Area: _____

_____   _____

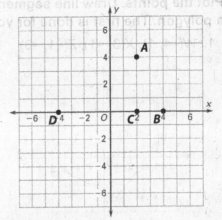

LESSON 14-2

Polygons in the Coordinate Plane

Practice and Problem Solving: C

Use the coordinate plane for Exercises 1–11.

Write an expression for the perimeter of each triangle. For the distance between points *A* and *B*, use *x*. For the distance between points *A* and *D*, use *y*.

1. triangle *ABC* _____

2. triangle *ABD* _____

3. triangle *ACD* _____

Answer each question.

4. What is an expression for the sum of the perimeters for triangles *ABC* and *ACD*?

_____

5. Compare your answer to Exercises 2 and 4. How does the perimeter of the largest triangle compare with the sum of the perimeters of the smaller triangles?

_____

_____

The formula for the area of a triangle is $A = \frac{1}{2}bh$, where *b* is the

length of its base and *h* is the triangle's height. Any side of a triangle can be its base. The height is the vertical distance from the base to the vertex opposite the base. Find the areas of each triangle.

6. triangle *ABC*   7. triangle *ACD*   8. triangle *ABD*

_____   _____   _____

Answer each question.

9. What is the sum of the areas of the triangles *ABC* and *ACD*? _____

10. Compare your answers to Exercises 8 and 9. How does the area of the largest triangle compare with the sum of the areas of the smaller triangles?

_____

11. Consider your answers to Exercises 5 and 10. How do the sums of the perimeters and the sum of the areas differ for these triangles?

_____

_____

Polygons in the Coordinate Plane

LESSON 14-2

Practice and Problem Solving: D

Plot the points. Draw line segments to connect them to form a polygon. The first is done for you.

1. $W(-4, 1)$, $X(3, -1)$, $Z(-1, -3)$

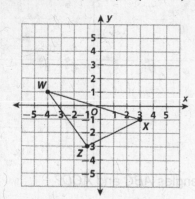

2. $A(-2, 3)$, $B(1, 3)$, $C(1, 0)$, $D(-2, 0)$

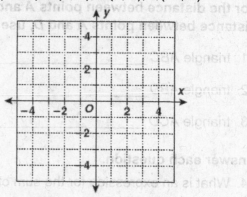

Find the area and perimeter of each figures. The first one is done for you.

3.

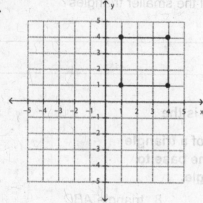

Name the coordinates of the vertices.

(1, 4), (4, 4), (4, 1), and (1, 1)

Find the lengths of the sides.

3, 3, 3, and 3

Find the perimeter.

3 + 3 + 3 + 3 = 12; 12 units

Find the area.

3 × 3 = 9; 9 square units

4.

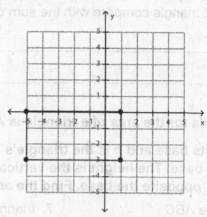

Name the coordinates of the vertices.

_____

Find the lengths of the sides.

_____

Find the perimeter.

_____

Find the area.

_____

LESSON 14-2

Polygons in the Coordinate Plane
Reteach

Polygons are formed from three or more points, called *vertices*, that are connected by line segments and that enclose an area.

If the lengths of the sides are known, the area and perimeter of a polygon can be found. They can also be found if the coordinates of the vertices are known.

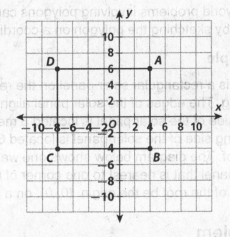

Find the Perimeter

First, identify the coordinates of the points that form the vertices of the polygon.

  A: (4, 6); B: (4, –4); C: (–8, –4); D: (–8, 6)

Next, find the lengths of the sides.

  AB = 10 units

  BC = 12 units

  CD = 10 units

  DA = 12 units

Finally, add the lengths of the sides.

  10 + 12 + 10 + 12 = 44

The perimeter of the polygon is 44 units.

Find the Area

First, identify the polygon. The figure is a rectangle, so its area is the product of its length and width.

Next, use the coordinates of the points to find the length and width.

  AB = 10 units

  BC = 12 units

Finally, multiply the length and width.

  10 × 12 = 120

The area of the polygon is 120 square units.

In this case, the area can also be found by counting the squares enclosed by the polygon. There are 30 squares.
How much area is represented by each square? 2 × 2, or 4 square units.
The area is 30 cubes × 4, or 120 square units.

Find the perimeter and area of the polygon enclosed by the points.

1. (8, 6), (2, 6), (8, –5), and (2, –5)

  Side lengths: _____

  Perimeter: _____

  Area: _____

2. (0, 0), (0, 7), (7, 7), and (7, 0)

  Side lengths: _____

  Perimeter: _____

  Area: _____

Polygons in the Coordinate Plane

LESSON 14-2

Reading Strategies: Analyze Information

Real-world problems involving polygons can sometimes be solved more easily by sketching the polygon on a coordinate plane.

Example

There is a rectangular solar panel on the rectangular roof of an office building. The edges of the solar panel align with the edges of the roof. The short side of the solar panel is located 3 meters from one edge of the roof. The long side of the solar panel is located 6 meters from another edge of the roof. The diagram below shows one way of drawing the corner of the solar panel that is nearest to one corner of the roof. Let the vertex of the corner of the roof be the origin, (0, 0), on a coordinate plane.

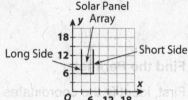

Problem

What are one possible set of coordinates for this corner of the solar panel? (*Hint:* Remember, the corner of the building is (0, 0).)

Solution

The word *corner* is being used in place of the math term, *vertex*. The long side of the solar panel is 3 meters from one edge of the building. If we let the *y*-axis represent that side of the building, the *x*-coordinate of this corner of the solar panel is 3. The short side of the solar panel is 6 meters from one edge of the building. If we let the *x*-axis represent that side of the building, the *y*-coordinate of this corner of the solar panel is 6. So, the coordinates of this corner of the solar panel would be (3, 6).

Note: Alternately, we could have drawn the diagram so that the short side of the solar panel is parallel instead to the *x*-axis. In that case, the coordinates of this corner of the solar panel would be reversed: (6, 3).

The long side of the solar panel measures 8 meters, and the short side measures 4 meters. Answer the questions.

1. As shown in the example, one corner of the solar panel has coordinates (3, 6). What are the coordinates of the other corner of this side that is 3 meters from the edge? Show your work.

_____

_____

2. What are the coordinates of the other two corners of the solar panel? (*Hint:* Find the length of the side of the array that is 6 meters from the edge of the roof as shown in the diagram.) Show your work.

_____

_____

Polygons in the Coordinate Plane

LESSON 14-2

Success for English Learners

Problem 1

What is the perimeter of rectangle *ABDC*?

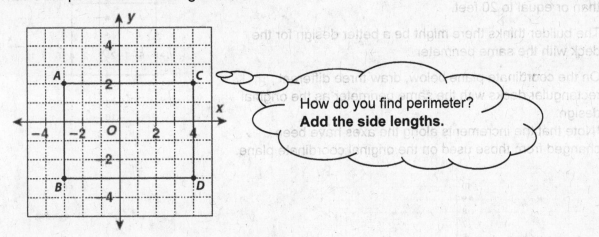

How do you find perimeter?
Add the side lengths.

Perimeter of rectangle *ABDC* = 5 + 7 + 5 + 7

= 24 units

Problem 2

Find the area of a rectangle using the sides.

How do you find the area?
Multiply length times width.

What is the length?
The length is *AC* or *BD*. Why?
They are the same: **7 units.**

What is the width?
The width is *AB* or *CD*. Why?
They are the same: **5 units.**

Area of rectangle *ABDC* = 5 × 7

= 35 square units

Answer the questions.

1. Why is the rectangle labeled *ABDC*, and not *ABCD*?

   _____

2. Find the area of *ABDC* by counting the squares inside the polygon.

MODULE 14

Distance and Area in the Coordinate Plane
Challenge

Mrs. Chirag plans to have a new deck built on the back of her house. The coordinate plane shows plans for the deck in feet. The width of the deck along the *x*-axis has to be less than or equal to 20 feet.

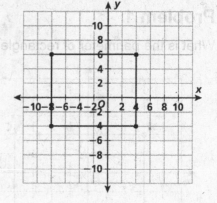

The builder thinks there might be a better design for the deck with the same perimeter.

On the coordinate plane below, draw three different rectangular decks with the same perimeter as the original design.

*Note that the increments along the axes have been changed from those used on the original coordinate plane.

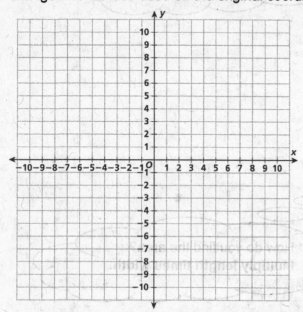

If the builder charges by the square foot, which design will cost the least to build? Explain your answer by answering the questions below.

1. Area of 1st design

2. Area of 2nd design

3. Area of 3rd design

_____   _____   _____

4. Given the fact that the width has to be less than 20 feet, what are the dimensions of the deck that will result in the least area of all? Explain your answer.

_____

5. In the real world, what dimensions of the deck with the given perimeter would be practical?

_____

LESSON 15-1

Nets and Surface Area

Practice and Problem Solving: A/B

Find the surface area of each net.

1. Each square is one square meter.

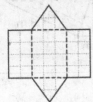

_____ square meters

2. Each square is one square yard

_____ square yards

3. A square pyramid has _____ square base

and _____ triangular faces.

Find its surface area.

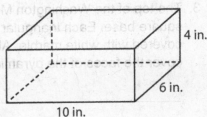

a. The area of the base is _____ square centimeters.

b. The area of the four faces is _____ square centimeters.

c. The surface area is _____ square centimeters.

4. Josef makes wooden boxes for jewelry. He made 5 boxes like the one shown, and wants to cover all the outside faces with fabric.

a. Find the surface area of one box.

_____

b. Find the total surface area of 5 boxes.

_____

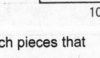

c. The fabric Josef is using comes in 100 square-inch pieces that cost $6.25 each. What will his fabric cost?

_____

Calculate the surface area for each figure.

5. The base is a square.

7.8 m

6.4 m

_____

6.

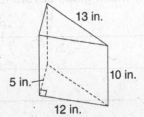

_____

Name _____ Date _____ Class_____

LESSON
15-1
Nets and Surface Area
Practice and Problem Solving: C

LESSON
15-1
Nets and Surface Area
Practice and Problem Solving: C

Solve.

1. What is the surface area of this isosceles triangular prism? Show your work.

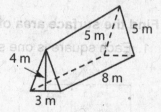

_____

_____

_____

Surface area: _____

2. The volume of the pyramid is 48 cubic feet. What is its surface area if the pyramid's height is 4 feet and the base is a square? Show your work.

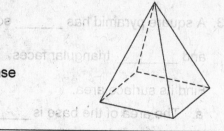

_____

_____

_____

Surface area: _____

3. The top of the Washington Monument is a triangular pyramid with a square base. Each triangular face is 58 feet tall and 34 feet wide and covered with white marble. About how many square feet of marble cover the faces of the pyramid?

_____

_____

_____

4. A glass triangular prism for a telescope is 5.5 inches long. Each side of the prism's triangular bases is 4 inches long and about 3.46 inches high. About how much glass covers the surface of the prism?

_____

_____

_____

LESSON 15-1

Nets and Surface Area

Practice and Problem Solving: D

Find the total surface area of the figures by completing the steps.
The first one is done for you.

1.

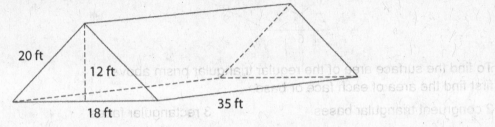

20 ft   12 ft

18 ft   35 ft

Height of the base: ___12___ feet   Length of the base: ___18___ feet

Area of the base: $\frac{1}{2} \times$ base $\times$ height $= \frac{1}{2} \times$ __18__ $\times$ __12__ $=$ __108__ square feet

Number of bases $\times$ area of a base $=$ __2__ $\times$ __108__ $=$ __216__ square feet

Area of first face: __20__ $\times$ __35__ $=$ __700__ square feet

Area of second face: __20__ $\times$ __35__ $=$ __700__ square feet

Area of third face: __18__ $\times$ __35__ $=$ __630__ square feet

Surface area: __700__ $+$ __700__ $+$ __630__ $+$ __216__ $=$ __2246__ square feet

2. The base is a square.

16 m

6 m

Height of a face: _____ meters   Base of a face: _____ meters

Area of a face: $\frac{1}{2} \times$ base $\times$ height $= \frac{1}{2} \times$ _____ $\times$ _____ $=$ _____ square meters

Number of faces $\times$ area of a face $=$ _____ $\times$ _____ $=$ _____ square meters

Area of the base: _____ $\times$ _____ $=$ _____ square meters

Surface area: _____ $+$ _____ $=$ _____ square meters

Complete.

3. The total surface area is the sum of the areas of the _____ and the

areas of the _____

LESSON 15-1

Nets and Surface Area
Reteach

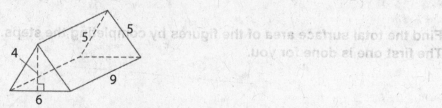

To find the surface area of the regular triangular prism above, first find the area of each face or base.

2 congruent triangular bases   3 rectangular faces

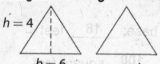 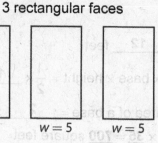

$w = 6$ $w = 5$ $w = 5$

$A = \dfrac{1}{2}bh$ $A = lw$ $A = lw$

$= \dfrac{1}{2}(6 \cdot 4)$ $= (9 \cdot 6)$ $= (9 \cdot 5)$

$= 12$ square units $= 54$ square units $= 45$ square units

Then, find the sum of all of the faces of the prism.

$SA = 12 + 12 + 54 + 45 + 45$

$\quad = 168$ square units

The same procedure can be used to find the surface area of a **pyramid**. The areas of the faces are added to the area of the base to give the total surface area.

Solve each problem.

1. A prism has isosceles triangle bases with leg lengths of 5 inches, 5 inches, and 8 inches, and a height of 3 inches. The distance between the bases is 12 inches. Find the surface area. Show your work.

_____

2. A square pyramid has a base edge of 1 meter. The height of each triangular face is 1 meter. What is the pyramid's surface area? Show your work.

_____

LESSON 15-1

Nets and Surface Area

Reading Strategies: Follow a Procedure

To find the surface area of a solid figure, follow a procedure. The procedures for a triangular prism and a triangular pyramid are different, but they share many of the same steps.

Step 1 The bases of the figure are right triangles, so one leg of the triangle is the base height, h, and the other leg is the base length, b:

$h = 3.8$ centimeters and $b = 5$ centimeters

Example

Find the lateral and total surface area.

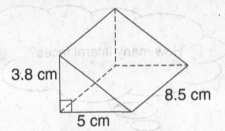

3.8 cm

8.5 cm

5 cm

Step 2 The area of the triangular base can be computed with the formula for the area, A, of a triangle, which is $A = \dfrac{1}{2}bh$. Substitute the values for b and h: $A = \dfrac{1}{2}(5)(3.8) = 9.5$ square centimeters

Step 3 Next, find the areas of the other faces. The first two are easy:

- For the first face, multiply 5 times 8.5, the length of the prism:
  $5 \times 8.5 = 42.5$ square centimeters

- For the second face, multiply 3.8 times 8.5:
  $3.8 \times 8.5 = 32.3$ square centimeters

Step 4 The third face requires that the Pythagorean Theorem be used to find the third side of the triangular base: $(3.8)^2 + 5^2 = x^2$

This gives $x^2 = 39.44$, or x is about 6.3 centimeters.

Multiply 6.3 by 8.5 to get the area of the third face: $6.3 \times 8.5 = 53.55$.

Step 5 Find the sum of the areas in Steps 3 and 4:

$42.5 + 32.3 + 53.55 = 128.35$ square centimeters.

Step 6 To find the total area, add the areas of the bases to Step 5:
$9.5 + 9.5 + 128.35 = 147.35$, or about 147 square centimeters.

1. Modify the procedure above to find the surface area of a pyramid with a square base of area 16 square inches and a triangular face height of 5 inches. Show your work.

_____

_____

_____

_____

_____

LESSON
15-1

Nets and Surface Area
Success for English Learners

Problem 1

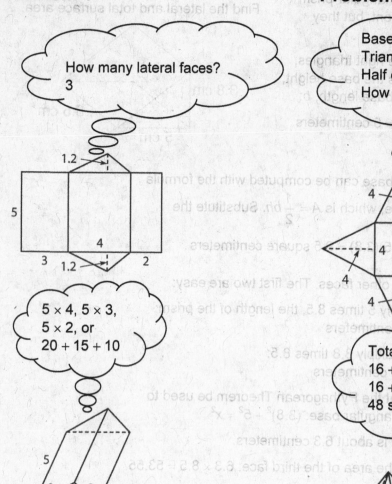

How many lateral faces?
3

$5 \times 4, 5 \times 3,$
$5 \times 2,$ or
$20 + 15 + 10$

Lateral area = 45 square units

Problem 2

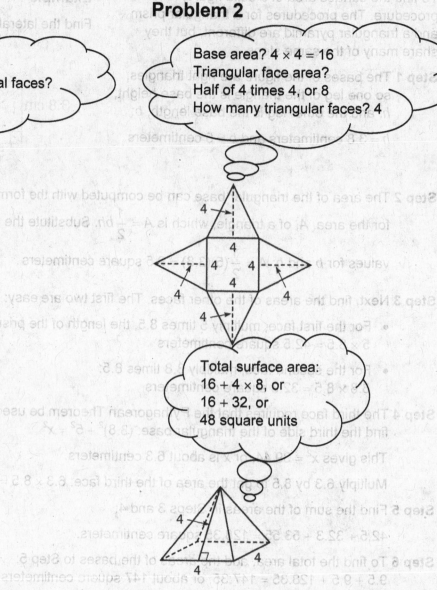

Base area? $4 \times 4 = 16$
Triangular face area?
Half of 4 times 4, or 8
How many triangular faces? 4

Total surface area:
$16 + 4 \times 8,$ or
$16 + 32,$ or
48 square units

1. What measurements are needed to find the base area in Problem 1?

_____

2. In Problem 1, find the base area. Show your work.

_____

3. In Problem 2, how does the net help you find surface area?

_____

**LESSON
15-2**

Volume of Rectangular Prisms

Practice and Problem Solving: A/B

**Use the formula for the volume of a rectangular solid
to find the volume of each solid in cubic meters.**

1.

5 cubes = 1 meter

2.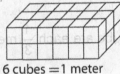

6 cubes = 1 meter

Length:	Length:
_____ cubes = _____ meter	_____ cubes = _____ meter
Width:	Width:
_____ cubes = _____ meter	_____ cubes = _____ meter
Height:	Height:
_____ cubes = _____ meter	_____ cubes = _____ meter
Volume: _____	Volume: _____

Solve.

3. A student made a toy chest for his baby sister's square building blocks.
   Six layers of blocks can fit in the box, and each layer has 15 blocks.
   How many building blocks can the toy chest hold? Show your work.

_____

**Find the volume of each figure. Show your work. Simplify your
answers.**

4.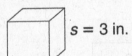

$s = 3$ in.

5.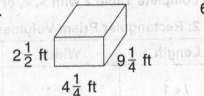

$2\frac{1}{2}$ ft $9\frac{1}{4}$ ft

$4\frac{1}{4}$ ft

6.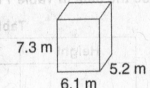

7.3 m

5.2 m

6.1 m

_____   _____   _____

_____   _____   _____

LESSON 15-2

Volume of Rectangular Prisms
Practice and Problem Solving: C

In this lesson, there are several examples of rectangular solids that have heights, lengths, and widths that are less than one unit.

Example

The edges of a cube are each $\frac{1}{3}$ meter in length. What is its volume?

$V = lwh$

Because the figure is a cube, all three dimensions are the same.

So, $V = \left(\frac{1}{3}\right)^3 = \frac{1}{27}$ cubic meter.

To find the dimensions of such prisms may require finding a cube root for a cube or dividing fractions for non-cubic rectangular prisms. Complete Table 1 for these solids with fractional dimensions.

Table 1: Rectangular Prism Sides and Volumes

Height	Length	Width	Volume
$\frac{1}{4}$ ft	$\frac{2}{3}$ ft	$\frac{3}{5}$ ft	1. _____ ft³
0.1 m	2. _____ m	0.01 m	0.0005 m³
$\frac{4}{3}$ in.	$\frac{3}{4}$ in.	1 in.	3. _____ in³
1.1 km	4. _____ km	0.9 km	9.9 km³

Use the data in Table 1 to complete Table 2 with >, <, or =.

Table 2: Rectangular Prism Volumes

Height	Length	Width	Volume
$h < 1$	$l < 1$	$w < 1$	5. $V \bigcirc 1$
$h > 1$	$l > 1$	$w > 1$	6. $V \bigcirc 1$
h	$\frac{1}{h}$	$w = 1$	7. $V \bigcirc 1$

LESSON 15-2

Volume of Rectangular Prisms
Practice and Problem Solving: D

Answer the questions to find the volume of each solid in cubic inches. The first one is started for you.

1.
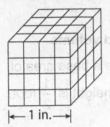
|← 1 in. →|

2.
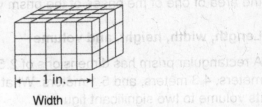
|← 1 in. →|
Width

How many cubes per inch? __4__

Height in cubes: __4__

Height in inches: __1__

Width in cubes: _____

Width in inches: _____

Depth in cubes: _____

Depth in inches: _____

Volume = height × width × depth

Volume = _____ cubes

Volume = _____ cubic inches

How many cubes per inch? _____

Height in cubes: _____

Height in inches: _____

Width in cubes: _____

Width in inches: _____

Depth in cubes: _____

Depth in inches: _____

Volume = height × width × depth

Volume = _____ cubes

Volume = _____ cubic inches

Solve. The first one is done for you.

3. The government plans to build a new dam shaped like a rectangular prism. The base is 1,224 feet long and 660 feet wide. The dam will be 726 feet high. Ignore the spaces within the dam that will be hollow to hold machinery. If the dam were made of solid concrete, how many cubic feet of concrete would be needed? Show your work.

   $V = l \times w \times h$; $V = 1{,}224 \times 660 \times 726 = 586{,}491{,}840$ ft³ or about 590,000,000 ft³

   __of concrete__

4. The world's largest chocolate bar is a rectangular prism weighing more than a ton! The bar is 9 feet long, 4 feet tall, and 1 foot wide. How many cubic feet of chocolate does it contain? Show your work.

_____

_____

LESSON 15-2
Volume of Rectangular Prisms
Reteach

The volume of a rectangular prism is found by multiplying its length, width, and height. In some cases, instead of the length and width, the area of one of the bases of the prism will be known.

Length, width, height, and volume

A rectangular prism has dimensions of 2.5 meters, 4.3 meters, and 5.1 meters. What is its volume to two significant figures?

Solution

$V = l \times w \times h$

$V = 2.5 \times 4.3 \times 5.1$

$= 54.825$

To two significant figures, the volume of the prism is 55 cubic meters.

Base area, height, and volume

A rectangular prism has a base area of $\frac{2}{3}$ of a square foot. Its height is $\frac{1}{2}$ foot. What is its volume?

Solution

$V = A_{base} \times h$

$V = \frac{2}{3} \times \frac{1}{2} = \frac{1}{3}$

The volume of the prism is $\frac{1}{3}$ cubic foot.

Find the volume of a rectangular prism with the given dimensions.

1. length: $\frac{2}{3}$ yd; width: $\frac{5}{6}$ yd; height: $\frac{4}{5}$ yd _____

2. base area: 12.5 m²; height: 1.2 m _____

The density of a metal in a sample is the mass of the sample divided by the volume of the sample. The units are mass per unit volume.

Problem The mass of a sample of metal is 2,800 grams. The sample is in the shape of a rectangular prism that measures 5 centimeters by 7 centimeters by 8 centimeters. What is the volume of the sample?

$V = 5 \times 7 \times 8$

$= 280 \text{ cm}^3$

What is the density of the sample?

$2,800 \div 280 = 10 \text{ g/cm}^3$

3. A sample of metal has a mass of 3,600 grams. The sample is in the shape of a rectangular prism that has dimensions of 2 centimeters by 3 centimeters by 4 centimeters. What is the density of the sample?

_____

Volume of Rectangular Prisms

LESSON 15-2

Reading Strategies: Identify Key Terms and Vocabulary

To solve mathematical problems, it is important to identify and interpret terms and vocabulary.

Example

A cube has a volume of 27 cubic meters. A rectangular prism that is not a cube has a height that is twice the length of the edge of the cube. The volume of the rectangular prism is twice that of the cube. What other dimensions of the rectangular prism can be calculated?

Step 1 Start with what is given: A cube has a volume of 27 cubic meters. The key terms are "**cube**" and "**volume**." Since the length, width, and height of a cube are all the same, the length of the edge of the cube can be calculated by taking the cube root of the volume. The cube root of 27 is 3.

Step 2 Move on to the second sentence of the problem: The rectangular prism has a height that is twice the length of the edge of the cube. The key terms here are "**height**" and "**twice**." Since the cube has a side of 3 meters, the prism has a height of 2 × 3, or 6.

Step 3 The third sentence has one key fact: The volume of the prism of "**twice**" the volume of the cube. Since the volume of the cube is 27 cubic meters, the volume of the prism is 2 × 27, or 54 cubic meters.

Step 4 The last sentence contains the phrase "other **dimensions** of the prism." To find those other dimensions requires the volume formula for the prism, $V = l \times w \times h$. Substitute the numbers found in Steps 2 and 3 into this formula.

$$54 = l \times w \times 6$$

Divide both sides of the formula by 6.

$$9 = l \times w$$

Since no other information is given about the dimensions l and w, the conclusion is that the area of the base of the prism is 9 square meters.

Identify some of the key terms and vocabulary in each problem. Then solve.

1. A cube-shaped container has twice the volume of a container shaped like a rectangular prism that has dimensions of 3 feet by 4 feet by 9 feet. What is the length of the cube's edge?

_____

2. The edge of a cube-shaped container is doubled. By how much is its volume increased?

_____

LESSON 15-2
Volume of Rectangular Prisms
Success for English Learners

Problem 1

The **volume** of a prism is the number of cubic units it holds.

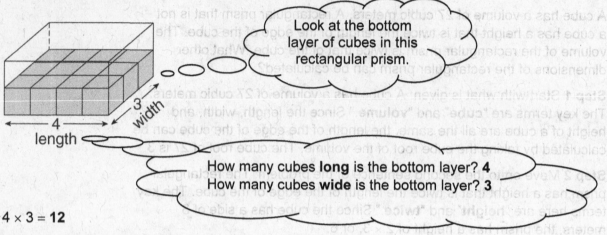

Look at the bottom layer of cubes in this rectangular prism.

How many cubes **long** is the bottom layer? **4**
How many cubes **wide** is the bottom layer? **3**

$4 \times 3 = 12$

So, there are **12 cubes** in the bottom layer of the prism.

Now, look at the top layer of cubes.

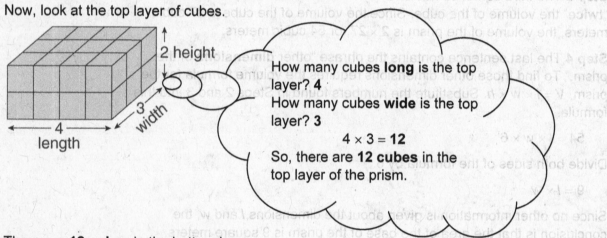

How many cubes **long** is the top layer? **4**
How many cubes **wide** is the top layer? **3**

$4 \times 3 = 12$

So, there are **12 cubes** in the top layer of the prism.

There are **12 cubes** in the bottom layer.
There are **12 cubes** in the top layer.

$12 + 12 = 24$

So, there are 24 cubes in the prism. The volume of the prism is 24 cubic units.

Solve.

1. A rectangular prism is 5 cubes long, 4 cubes wide, and 3 cubes high.
   What is the volume of this prism?

_____

LESSON 15-3

Solving Volume Equations

Practice and Problem Solving: A/B

Find the volume of each figure.

1.

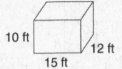

10 ft

12 ft

15 ft

_____

2.

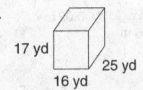

17 yd

25 yd

16 yd

_____

3.

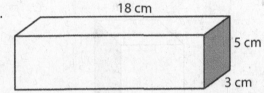

18 cm

5 cm

3 cm

_____

4.

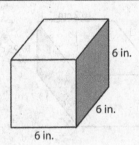

6 in.

6 in.

6 in.

_____

Solve.

5. Fawn built a sandbox that is 6 feet long, 5 feet wide, and $\frac{1}{2}$ foot tall.

   How many cubic feet of sand does she need to fill the box?

   _____

6. A pack of gum is in the shape of a rectangular prism with a length of 8 centimeters and width of 2 centimeters. The volume of the pack of gum is 48 cubic centimeters. What is the height of the pack of gum?

   _____

7. A block of cheese is in the shape of a rectangular prism with a width of 2.5 inches and a height of 5 inches. The volume of the block of cheese is 75 cubic inches. What is the length of the block of cheese?

   _____

8. A tissue box is in the shape of a rectangular prism with an area of 528 cubic inches. The length of the box of tissues is 12 inches and the

   height is $5\frac{1}{2}$ inches. What is the width of the box of tissues?

   _____

LESSON
15-3

Solving Volume Equations

Practice and Problem Solving: C

Find the volume of each figure.

1.   4 m ⟋⟍ 0.02 m
        6 m

2.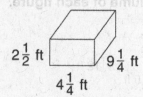
     $2\frac{1}{2}$ ft $9\frac{1}{4}$ ft
         $4\frac{1}{4}$ ft

   _____   _____

3.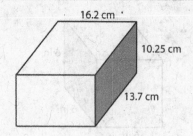
     16.2 cm
     10.25 cm
     13.7 cm

4.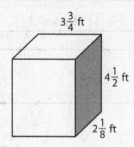
     $3\frac{3}{4}$ ft
     $4\frac{1}{2}$ ft
     $2\frac{1}{8}$ ft

   _____   _____

Solve.

5. If you changed the measures in Exercises 1 and 3 to fractions and

   mixed numbers, would you get the same volumes? _____

6. A rectangular prism's base is 8 feet long. It is $2\frac{1}{2}$ times taller than it is

   long and $\frac{1}{2}$ as wide as it is tall. What is the volume of that prism?

   _____

7. A box of mashed potato flakes has a volume of 220 in^3. The box is
   8 inches long and 11 inches tall. What is the width of the box of
   mashed potato flakes?

   _____

8. A building shaped like a rectangular prism is 42 yards long, 30 yards
   wide, and 120 yards tall. On average, it cost $0.02 per cubic yard to
   provide heat and electricity for one month. What is the heat and electric
   bill for one month?

   _____

9. A 12 inches by 12 inches by 12 inches container of water was placed in the
   freezer. Water expands 4% when it is frozen. What is the volume of the
   container when it is frozen? Give your answer in cubic inches and cubic feet.

   _____

**LESSON
15-3**
Solving Volume Equations
Practice and Problem Solving: D

Find the volume of each figure. The first one is done for you.

1.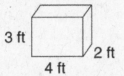
3 ft
2 ft
4 ft

$V = 3(4)(2) = 24; 24 \text{ ft}^3$

2.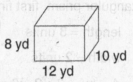
8 yd
10 yd
12 yd

3.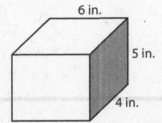
6 in.
5 in.
4 in.

4.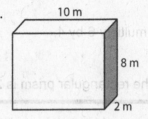
10 m
8 m
2 m

Solve each problem. The first one is done for you.

5. Tim made a toy chest for his little sister's square building blocks. If 6 layers of blocks can fit in the box, and each layer has 15 blocks, how many building blocks can the toy chest hold in all?

   $V = 15(6) = 90; 90 \text{ blocks}$

6. Kathy bought a jewelry box in the shape of a rectangular prism. The volume of the jewelry box is 192 cubic inches. The length and width of the jewelry box are 8 and 6 inches respectively. What is the height of the jewelry box?

   _____

7. A filing cabinet has a height of 4 feet and a length of 2 feet. The volume of the filing cabinet is 24 cubic feet. What is the width of the filing cabinet?

   _____

8. A box of business cards is in the shape of a rectangular prism. The volume of the box of cards is 360 cubic centimeters. The length of the box is 12 centimeters and the height of the box is 5 centimeters. What is the width of the box of business cards?

   _____

LESSON
15-3

Solving Volume Equations
Reteach

Volume is the number of cubic units needed to fill a space. To find the volume of a rectangular prism, first find the area of the base.

length = 3 units

width = 2 units

$A = lw = 3 \cdot 2 = 6$ square units

The area of the base tells you how many cubic units are in the first layer of the prism.

The height is 4, so multiply 6 by 4.

$6 \cdot 4 = 24$

So, the volume of the rectangular prism is 24 cubic units.

Find each volume.

1.

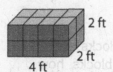

4 ft   2 ft   2 ft

_____

2.

5 m   2 m   3 m

_____

3.

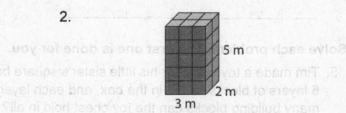

15 cm   3 cm   2 cm

_____

4.

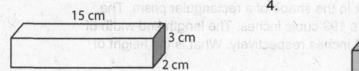

10 yd   10 yd   10 yd

_____

5.

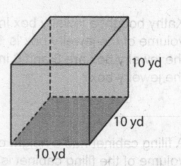

3 mm   3 mm   3 mm

_____

6.

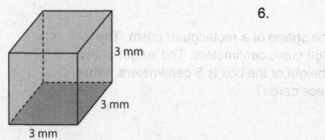

5 in.   4 in.   6 in.

_____

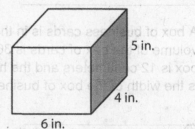

LESSON 15-3

Solving Volume Equations

Reading Strategies: Analyze Information

You can think of the **volume** of a prism as the number of unit cubes it contains.

Look at the first layer of cubic units in this rectangular prism.

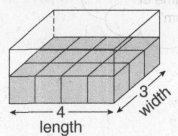

1. How many cubes long is the first layer?   _____

2. How many cubes wide is the first layer?   _____

3. How many cubes are in the first layer?   _____

Now look at the next layer of cubes.

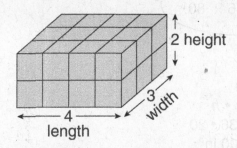

4. How many cubes long is the top layer?   _____

5. How many cubes wide is the top layer?   _____

6. How many cubes are in the top layer?   _____

7. What is the total number of cubes in both layers?   _____

8. What is the total volume of the rectangular prism?   _____

9. Add another layer and find the volume for the new figure.
   Show your work.

   _____

   _____

LESSON 15-3

Solving Volume Equations

Success for English Learners

Problem 1

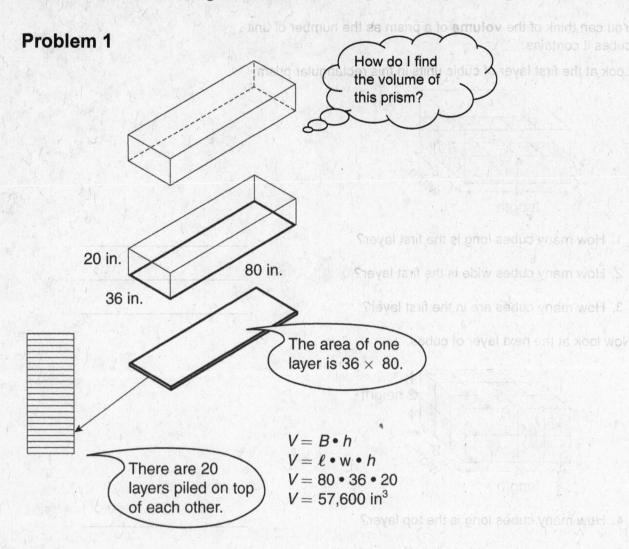

How do I find the volume of this prism?

20 in.

80 in.

36 in.

The area of one layer is 36 × 80.

There are 20 layers piled on top of each other.

$V = B \cdot h$
$V = \ell \cdot w \cdot h$
$V = 80 \cdot 36 \cdot 20$
$V = 57,600 \text{ in}^3$

1. Describe how to find the volume of a rectangular prism.

_____

2. How are units for volume different from units for area?

_____

Surface Area and Volume of Solids

Challenge

Which rectangular prism has the greatest surface area? Which rectangular prism has the greatest volume? The answers to both questions depend on the dimensions of the prisms you are comparing.

The surface area of a rectangular prism can be found by using the formula below, where *h* is a prism's height, *l* is its length, and *w* is its width.

S.A. = 2*hl* + 2*lw* + 2*wh*

The volume of a rectangular prism can be found by using the formula
V = *l* × *w* × *h*.

Suppose the sum of the height, length, and width of a rectangular prism is 30 meters. The table shows three possible sets of length, width, and height whose sum is 30 meters. Complete the table. Then answer the questions that follow.

Height	Length	Width	S.A.	Volume
10 m	10 m	10 m	1. _____	2. _____
15 m	5 m	3. _____	4. _____	5. _____
20 m	6. _____	5 m	7. _____	8. _____

9. Based on the data in the table, what conclusion can you draw about the shape of a rectangular prism that will yield the greatest volume?

_____

10. How does the surface area of the figure with the greatest volume compare to the surface areas of the other shapes?

_____

11. Describe the shape of the rectangular-prism boxes that are commonly used to package dry cereal and dry detergent.

_____

12. Are these boxes designed to hold the maximum amount of product? If not, why do you think the packaging has the shape it does?

_____

_____

_____

LESSON 16-1

Measures of Center

Practice and Problem Solving: A/B

Use the situation below to complete Exercises 1–4.

The heights (in inches) of the starting players on a high school basketball team are as follows: 72, 75, 78, 72, 73.

1. How many starting players are there? _____

2. What is the mean height? _____

3. What is the median height? _____

4. Does one measure describe the data better than the other? Explain.

_____

In Exercises 5–7, find the mean and median of each data set.

5. Daily high temperatures (°F): 45, 50, 47, 52, 53, 45, 51

   Mean: _____   Median: _____

6. Brian's math test scores: 86, 90, 93, 85, 79, 92

   Mean: _____   Median: _____

7. Players' heart rates (beats per minute): 70, 68, 70, 72, 68, 66, 65, 73

   Mean: _____   Median: _____

8. Hikers spent the following amounts of time (in minutes) to complete a nature hike: 48, 46, 52, 57, 58, 52, 61, 56.

   a. Find the mean and median times.

      Mean: _____   Median: _____

   b. Does one measure describe the data better than the other? Explain.

      _____

   c. Suppose another hiker takes 92 minutes to complete the hike. Find the mean and median times including this new time.

      Mean: _____   Median: _____

   d. Does one measure describe the data better than the other now? Explain.

      _____

      _____

Name _____ Date _____ Class_____

Measures of Center

Practice and Problem Solving: C

Find the mean and median of each data set.

1. Monthly rainfall (in inches): 7.6, 6.7, 8.1, 6.2, 6.0, 6.2

   Mean: _____   Median: _____

2. Dylan's weekly earnings (in dollars): 200, 167, 185, 212, 195, 193, 188, 140

   Mean: _____   Median: _____

3. Fundraising calendars sold per person: 22, 13, 47, 11, 8, 16, 15, 14, 13, 17

   Mean: _____   Median: _____

The line plot below shows the number of kilometers Clara ran each day for 14 days. Use the line plot for Exercises 4 and 5.

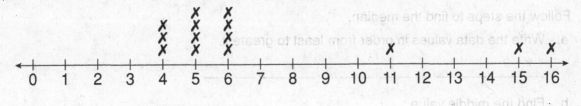

4. Find the mean and median for the data.

   _____

5. Does one measure describe the data better than the other? Explain.

   _____

   _____

In Exercises 6 and 7, use the given measure to find the missing value in each data set.

6. The mean of the ages of 5 brothers is 13 years.

   12, 16, ☐ , 14, 8

7. The median number of students in each music class is 19 people.

   16, ☐ , 24, 17, 20, 21

8. Write a data set where both the mean and the median describe the data equally well. Explain your reasoning.

   _____

   _____

Name _____ Date _____ Class_____

LESSON
16-1

Measures of Center

Practice and Problem Solving: D

Use the situation below to complete Exercises 1 and 2. The first step in Exercise 1 is done for you.

The heights (in meters) of the trees in a park are as follows:
7, 11, 9, 7, 6, 8.

1. Follow the steps to find the mean.

   a. Find the sum of the data values.

      __48__

   b. Divide to find the mean.

      $$\text{Mean} = \frac{\text{sum of data values}}{\text{number of data values}} = \frac{\boxed{}}{\boxed{}} = \boxed{}$$

      The mean height is _____.

2. Follow the steps to find the median.

   a. Write the data values in order from least to greatest.

      _____, _____, _____, _____, _____, _____

   b. Find the middle value.

      The data set has two middle values: _____ and _____.

      $$\text{Median} = \frac{\boxed{} + \boxed{}}{\boxed{}} = \frac{\boxed{}}{\boxed{}} = \boxed{}$$

      The median height is _____.

The points scored by a football team in each game are shown in the table. Use this data to complete Exercises 3–5. The first one is done for you.

3. How many data values are there?

   __6__

4. What is the mean and median?

   Mean: _____

   Median: _____

5. Does one measure describe the data better than the other? Explain.

   _____

   _____

Game	Points Scored
1	7
2	20
3	24
4	17
5	28
6	24

LESSON 16-1
Measures of Center
Reteach

When calculating the mean, you can use *compatible numbers* to find the sum of the data values. Compatible numbers make calculations easier. For example, adding multiples of 5 or 10 is easier than adding all of the individual data values.

A group of students are asked how many hours they spend watching television during one week. Their responses are: 15, 7, 12, 8, 4, 13, 11. What is the mean?

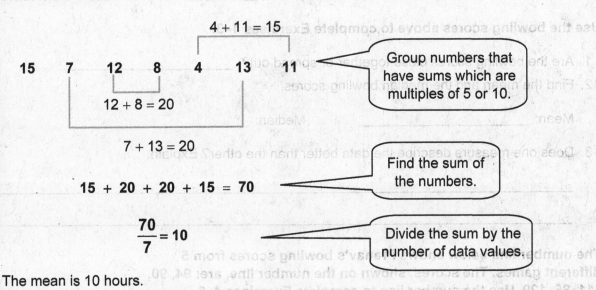

$$4 + 11 = 15$$

15   7   12   8   4   13   11

Group numbers that have sums which are multiples of 5 or 10.

$$12 + 8 = 20$$

$$7 + 13 = 20$$

$$15 + 20 + 20 + 15 = 70$$

Find the sum of the numbers.

$$\frac{70}{7} = 10$$

Divide the sum by the number of data values.

The mean is 10 hours.

Use compatible numbers to find the mean.

1. The costs (in dollars) of items on a lunch menu are 9, 14, 11, 6, 16, 10.

   Mean: _____

2. The numbers of students in Mr. Silva's math classes are 19, 18, 22, 24, 20, 18, 26.

   Mean: _____

3. In the television viewing data above, is there more than one way to pair the data values to form compatible numbers? Explain.

   _____

   _____

Measures of Center
Reading Strategies: Use Graphic Aids

Tim's bowling scores from 5 different games are 89, 98, 110, 98, 105. The
scores are shown on the number line below. The number line is a graphic
aid that lets you see whether the scores are close together or spread apart.

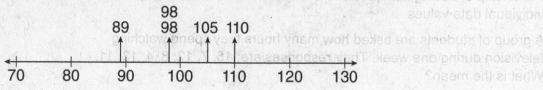

Use the bowling scores above to complete Exercises 1–3.

1. Are the bowling scores close together or spread out? _____

2. Find the mean and the median bowling scores.

   Mean: _____   Median: _____

3. Does one measure describe the data better than the other? Explain.

   _____

   _____

**The number line below shows Pranav's bowling scores from 5
different games. The scores, shown on the number line, are: 94, 90,
111, 86, 129. Use the number line to complete Exercises 4–6.**

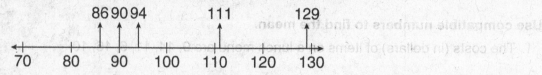

4. Are the bowling scores close together or spread out? _____

5. Find the mean and the median bowling scores.

   Mean: _____   Median: _____

6. Does one measure describe the data better than the other? Explain.

   _____

   _____

7. Explain why you think the mean and median are called "measures
   of center."

   _____

   _____

LESSON
16-1

Measures of Center
Success for English Learners

Problem 1

Steps to find the mean, or average, of a data set.

Add.

Each number

1. Find the sum of the data values.

2. Divide the sum by the number of data values.

Count each number.

Problem 2

Use a visual model to examine the data.

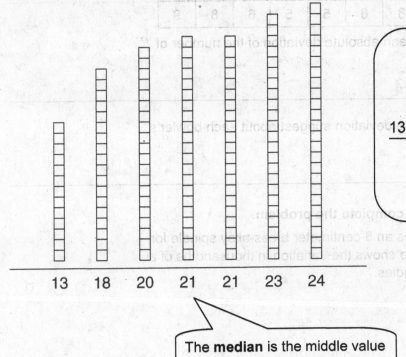

The **mean** is the average.

$$\frac{\text{sum of data values}}{\text{number of data values}} =$$

$$\frac{13+18+20+21+21+23+24}{7} =$$

$$\frac{140}{7} = 20$$

| 13 | 18 | 20 | 21 | 21 | 23 | 24 |

The **median** is the middle value of an ordered data set.

1. What is an "ordered data set"?

_____

2. How do you find the median if there are an even number of data values?

_____

Name _____ Date _____ Class_____

Mean Absolute Deviation
Practice and Problem Solving: A/B

Find the *mean absolute deviation* for each data set.

1. The number of kittens in 10 litters: 4, 5, 5, 6, 6, 7, 8, 8, 8, and 9

   _____

2. The number of approved soy-based containers produced in 10
   stamping runs of 240 containers: 225, 227, 227, 228, 230, 230,
   231, 238, 238, and 240

   _____

3. Two bowlers bowl the following number of strikes in 9 games.

1st bowler	8	5	5	6	8	7	4	7	6
2nd bowler	10	6	8	8	5	5	6	8	9

   What is the mean and the mean absolute deviation of the number of
   strikes of each bowler?

   _____

   What does the mean absolute deviation suggest about each bowler's
   consistency?

   _____

Use a spreadsheet program to complete the problem.

4. A tool manufacturer machines an 8-centimeter brass-alloy spindle for
   one of its tools. The first table shows the variation in thousandths of a
   centimeter in nine of the spindles.

A2		ƒx							
	A	B	C	D	E	F	G	H	I	J
1	8.002	8.002	8	7.997	8.004	7.999	8.002	8.001	7.997	
2										
3										
4										

   Complete the spreadsheet as shown to find the mean spindle length.

DATE		X ✓ ƒx	=AVERAGE(A1:I1)						
	A	B	C	D	E	F	G	H	I	J
1	8.002	8.002	8	7.997	8.004	7.999	8.002	8.001	7.997	
2	mean =	=AVERAGE(A1:I1)								
3										

   Mean: _____

5. Use the spreadsheet to find the mean absolute deviation of the spindle lengths.

DATE		X ✓ ƒx	=AVEDEV(A1:I1)						
	A	B	C	D	E	F	G	H	I	J
1	8.002	8.002	8	7.997	8.004	7.999	8.002	8.001	7.997	
2	mean =									
3	MAD =	=AVEDEV(A1:I1)								
4										

   MAD: _____

Mean Absolute Deviation

LESSON 16-2

Practice and Problem Solving: C

Use the description below to complete Exercises 1–2.

A charcoal producer needs to make sure that his manufacturing process on average does not use more than one ton more or less of the average amount of biomass in order to make most efficient use of his equipment, labor, time, and other resources. The table lists the number of tons of biomass used per day over a 10-day period.

Biomass (tons)	15	12	14	14	13	15	17	18	12	13

1. Are the results of this 10-day production run within the limits the producer wants? Use the mean absolute deviation to support your answer.

2. Which value(s) could be or should be changed in order to achieve the limits on production the producer requires? Use the mean absolute deviation to support your answer.

_____

_____

Use the description below to complete Exercise 3.

In a cross-country bicycle race, the amount of time that elapsed before a rider had to stop to make a bicycle repair on the first day of the race had a mean of 4.25 hours after the race start and a mean absolute deviation of 0.5 hour. On the second day of the race, the mean had shifted to 3.5 hours after starting the race, with a mean absolute deviation of 0.75 hour.

3. Interpret the change in the *mean* and the *mean absolute deviation* from the first to the second day of the race.

_____

Use the description below to complete Exercises 4–6.

A bakery sells the following number of fruit pies over a 10-day period: 234, 215, 222, 240, 239, 241, 256, 225, 230, and 240 pies per day.

4. Use a spreadsheet program to calculate the mean absolute deviation.

_____

5. Change one of the daily sales values so that the mean absolute deviation increases to 10. Describe the change you made to one of the values.

6. Add an extra day so that the value of the mean absolute deviation increases to 10. Give the amount of the extra day's sale.

_____

_____

**LESSON
16-2**

Mean Absolute Deviation
Practice and Problem Solving: D

Fill in the blanks. The first one is done for you.

1.

Data	15	11	12	10	12
Distance from the mean	3	1	0	2	0

$$Mean = \frac{15 + 11 + 12 + 10 + 12}{5} = \underline{12}$$

How far is each number from the mean?

Find the absolute value of the difference of the number and the mean.

Fill in the second row of the table.

$$Mean \ absolute \ deviation \ (MAD) = \frac{3 + 1 + 0 + 2 + 0}{5} = \underline{1.2}$$

2.

Data	1.5	1.4	1.7	1.6	1.8
Distance from the mean	____	____	____	____	____

$$Mean = \frac{\_\_\_ + \_\_\_ + \_\_\_ + \_\_\_ + \_\_\_}{\_\_\_} = \_\_\_$$

How far is each number from the mean? Fill in the amount for each number in the table.

$$Mean \ absolute \ deviation = \frac{\_\_\_ + \_\_\_ + \_\_\_ + \_\_\_ + \_\_\_}{\_\_\_} = \_\_\_$$

<table>
<tr><td>LESSON
16-2</td><td># Mean Absolute Deviation
Reteach</td></tr>
</table>

The *mean absolute deviation*, or *MAD*, is the average of how far the elements in a data set are from the *mean* of the data set.

If you think of MAD as a distance, it will always be a positive number. For two or more comparable data sets, the larger the MAD is, the more "spread out" the elements of a data set are, such as in the example.

Example

Step 1 Find the mean.

The mean of these two data sets of the number of eggs in 10 nests of two birds of the same species over several breeding cycles:

• Bird *A*: 3, 3, 4, 2, 3, 4, 5, 1, 2, and 2

• Bird *B*: 1, 1, 3, 6, 2, 2, 3, 5, 4, and 1

For Bird *A*: mean = 29 ÷ 10 = 2.9 or about 3 eggs
For Bird *B*: mean = 28 ÷ 10 = 2.8 or about 3 eggs

Step 2 Find the mean absolute deviation. First, find the deviation of each element from the mean by subtracting the element's value from the mean or vice versa. This gives these deviations for the 10 elements in each data set.

Bird *A*: 0.1, 0.1, 1.1, 0.9, 0.1, 1.1, 2.1, 1.9, 0.9, and 0.9
Bird *B*: 1.8, 1.8, 0.2, 3.2, 0.8, 0.8, 0.2, 2.2, 1.2, and 1.8

Then add the deviations for each bird and divide by the number of breeding cycles.

For Bird *A*: MAD = 9.2 ÷ 10 = 0.92
For Bird *B*: MAD = 14 ÷ 10 = 1.4

In this example, the mean number of eggs in each bird's nest is almost the same. However, the mean absolute deviations, or MAD, of the two data sets are different. The number of eggs in Bird *B*'s nests over 10 breeding cycles show more **variability**, or the "number of eggs varied more" than did the number of eggs in Bird *A*'s nests over 10 cycles.

Notice that both MAD values round to one egg. What do you think will happen to these MAD values over a larger number of breeding cycles?

Find the mean absolute deviation by hand calculations or with a spreadsheet program.

1. Data:
   0.1, 0.15, 0.09, 0.11, and 0.13

   MAD: _____

2. Data:
   250, 249, 251, 253, and 253

   MAD: _____

Mean Absolute Deviation
Reading Strategies: Analyze Information

To analyze the information in a data set, tools such as the *mean* and the *mean absolute deviation* can be used. These tools are related, but they differ. They also give different kinds of information about a data set.

In its simplest form, the *mean* is an average. There are different kinds of means, some of which are beyond the scope of this lesson. However, the mean presented here is an average that is found by adding the values of the elements in a data set and dividing that sum by the *number* of elements in the data set.

The *mean absolute deviation* is an average, too. It is the average of the deviations, or differences, of each data element from the mean of the data set. There are as many deviations as there are elements, but there is only one mean *absolute* deviation for the data set.

Example 1

Find the *mean* of these data elements:

60, 65, 66, 67, 67, 68, 68, 68, 70, and 75

Solution First, add the values of the elements. The sum is 674. Next, divide by the number of elements, which is 10. This gives a mean of 67.4.

Example 2

Find, the *mean absolute deviation* of the data elements in Example 1.

Step 1 How "far" is *each* data element from the mean? Find the *absolute value* of the difference of the data element and the mean. So, the deviation of 60 is $|67.4 - 60|$ or 7.4. The other numbers' deviations are 2.4, 1.4, 0.4, 0.4, 0.6, 0.6, 0.6, 2.6, and 7.6.

Step 2 To find the mean of these deviations, add them and divide by the number of elements in the data set. In this example, the sum of the deviations is 24, so the *mean absolute deviation* is 2.4.

It is possible for two data sets to have the same mean but different mean absolute deviations and vice versa.

Answer the questions below.

1. Two data sets have a mean of 56, but the first data set has a MAD of 2 and the second data set has a MAD of 1. Describe how the values of the data elements differ.

_____

2. Two data sets have means of 40 and 50, but both have a MAD of 0.5. Describe how the values of the data elements differ.

_____

LESSON 16-2
Mean Absolute Deviation
Success for English Learners

Problem 1

Data set: 5, 5, 5, 6, 7, 7, 8, 9, 9, and 9

What is the *mean*?

Mean = 7

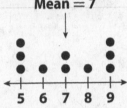

Add the numbers:
$5 + 5 + 5 + 6 + 7 + 7 + 8 + 9 + 9 + 9 = 70$
Divide by the "number of numbers," 10.
Mean = $70 \div 10 = 7$

Problem 2

What is the *mean absolute deviation* (MAD) of the numbers in Problem 1?

Mean = 7

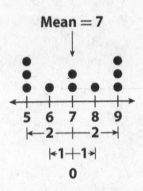

How far is each number from the mean? 2, 2, 2, 1, 0, 0, 1, 2, 2, 2
Add the distances. Sum: 14
Divide by "number of numbers," 10.
MAD = $14 \div 10 = 1.4$

⟶ The MAD *is how "spread out" the data is from the* mean.

Use the data to find each measure: 2, 2, 3, 4, 4, 4, 5, 6, 8, and 12.

1. Calculate the mean.

   _____

2. Calculate how far each number is from the mean.

   _____

3. Calculate the mean absolute deviation (MAD).

   _____

Name _____ Date _____ Class_____

Box Plots

Practice and Problem Solving: A/B

The high temperatures for 2 weeks are shown at the right. Use the data set for Exercises 1–7.

High Temperatures						
69	73	72	66	64	64	61
70	78	78	74	69	61	62

1. Order the data from least to greatest.

   _____

2. Find the median. _____

3. Find the lower quartile. _____

4. Find the upper quartile. _____

5. Make a box plot for the data.

```
  +--+--+--+--+--+--+--+--+--+--+--+
  60 62 64 66 68 70 72 74 76 78 80
```
Daily High Temperatures, °F

6. Find the IQR. _____   7. Find the range. _____

Use the situation and data given below to complete Exercises 8–10.

Two classes collected canned food for the local food bank. Below are the number of cans collected each week.

   Class A: 18 20 15 33 30 23 38 34 40 28 18 33

   Class B: 18 27 29 20 26 26 29 30 24 28 29 28

8. Arrange the data for each class in order from least to greatest.

   Class A: _____

   Class B: _____

9. Find the median, the range, and the IQR of each data set.

   Class A: median:_____   range:_____   IQR:_____

   Class B: median:_____   range:_____   IQR:_____

10. Compare and contrast the box plots for the two data sets.

   _____

   _____

LESSON 16-3

Box Plots

Practice and Problem Solving: C

Use the data set at the right for Exercises 1–3.

A math test had 50 questions. The data set shows how many questions were answered correctly in one class.

Questions Correctly Answered
48 50 48 40 42 42 47 48 48 41
40 48 43 49 50 43 47 43 42 44

1. What is the first step you need to do to make a box plot? Complete that step now.

   _____

   _____

2. Find the median, the range, and the IQR of the data set.

   median:_____   range:_____   IQR:_____

3. Make a box plot for the data.

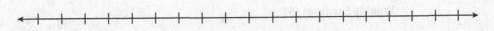

Questions Correctly Answered

Use the situation below to complete Exercises 4–7.

Below are the prices of various rooms at two different resort city hotels.

   Hotel A: 360   100   180   220   240   200

   Hotel B: 300   250   180   80   120   340   220

4. Make box plots for each set of data.

   Hotel A

   Hotel B

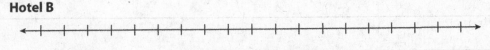

Comparative Room Rates

5. Which hotel has the greater median room price? _____

6. Which hotel has the greater interquartile range of room prices? _____

7. Which hotel appears to have more predictable room prices? Explain.

   _____

   _____

Box Plots

Practice and Problem Solving: D

Weekly Earnings ($)
20 12 10 6 12 15 8 15

The data set at the right shows the money Joe earned in 8 weeks. Use the data set to complete Exercises 1–7. The first one is done for you.

1. Order the data from least to greatest.

   _____ **6, 8, 10, 12, 12, 15, 15, 20** _____

2. Find the median. _____

3. Find the lower quartile. _____

4. Find the upper quartile. _____

5. Complete the box plot for the data.

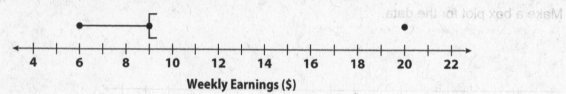

Weekly Earnings ($)

6. Find the IQR. _____

7. Find the range. _____

Use the situation and data given below to complete Exercises 8–11.

Below are the number of books read each week for Juan and Mia.

   Juan: 2, 6, 4, 1, 2, 6, 8, 4, 3

   Mia: 6, 6, 2, 5, 2, 2, 4, 5, 6

8. Arrange the data for each person in order from least to greatest.

   Juan: _____

   Mia: _____

9. Who had the higher median number of books read? _____

10. Who had the greater range in number of books read? _____

11. Who had the higher IQR in number of books read? _____

Box Plots
Reteach

A **box plot** gives you a visual display of how data are distributed.

Here are the scores Ed received on 9 quizzes: 76, 80, 89, 90, 70, 86, 87, 76, 80.

Step 1: List the scores in order from least to greatest.

Step 2: Identify the least and greatest values.

Step 3: Identify the median.
If there is an odd number of values, the median is the middle value.

Step 4: Identify the lower quartile and upper quartile. If there is an even number of values above or below the median, the lower or upper quartile is the average of the two middle values.

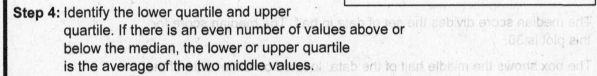

Step 5: Draw a number line that includes the values in the given data.

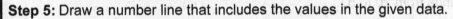

68 70 72 74 76 78 80 82 84 86 88 90 92

Step 6: Place dots above the number lines at each value you identified in Steps 2–4. Draw a box starting at the lower quartile and ending at the upper quartile. Mark the median, too.

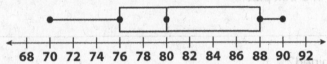

68 70 72 74 76 78 80 82 84 86 88 90 92

Use the data at the right for Exercises 1–5. Complete each statement.

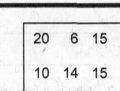

20	6	15
10	14	15
8	10	12

1. List the data in order: _____

2. Least value: _____ Greatest value: _____

3. Median: _____

4. Lower quartile: _____ Upper quartile: _____

5. Draw a box plot for the data.

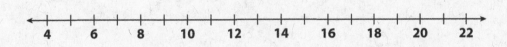

4   6   8   10   12   14   16   18   20   22

LESSON 16-3

Box Plots
Reading Strategies: Use Graphic Aids

A **box plot** shows a set of data divided into four equal parts called **quartiles**.

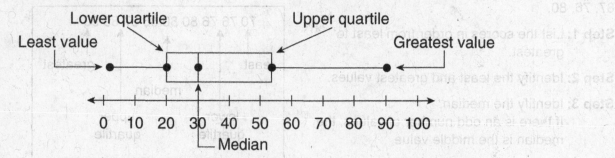

- The median score divides the set of data in half. The median score for this plot is 30.

- The box shows the middle half of the data, located on either side of the median. The box extends from 20 to 53.

- The two "whiskers" identify the remaining half of the data. One whisker extends from the box to the greatest value: from 53 to 90. The other whisker extends from the box to the least value: from 2 to 20.

Answer each question.

1. What does the box stand for in a box plot?

_____

2. How are the whiskers determined?

_____

3. Why is it important to find the median score?

_____

Describe where these scores are located in the box plot above.

4. 18 is between the _____ and the _____.

5. 75 is between the _____ and the _____.

6. 45 is between the _____ and the _____.

**LESSON
16-3**

Box Plots

Success for English Learners

A **box plot** shows a set of data divided into four equal parts.

Problem 1

A box plot shows how the values in a data set are distributed or spread out.

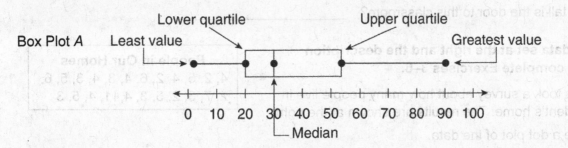

Box Plot A Least value Lower quartile Upper quartile Greatest value Median

0 10 20 30 40 50 60 70 80 90 100

Problem 2

To make a box plot, start by putting the data in order from least to greatest.

Identify the least and greatest values. In box plot *A*, the least value is 2 and the greatest value is 90.

Identify the middle value. This is the **median**. The median for box plot *A* is 30.

Identify the lower quartile. The **lower quartile** is the middle value between the least value and the median. In box plot *A*, the lower quartile 20.

Identify the upper quartile. The **upper quartile** is the middle value between the median and the greatest value. In box plot *A*, the upper quartile 53.

Plot each identified value on a number line and draw a box from the lower quartile to the upper quartile with a line drawn at the median. Draw a line segment from the least value to the lower quartile and from the upper quartile to the greatest value.

Use box plot *B* and box plot *C* to complete the table.

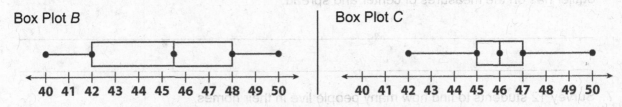

Box Plot *B*

40 41 42 43 44 45 46 47 48 49 50

Box Plot *C*

40 41 42 43 44 45 46 47 48 49 50

		Median	Least Value	Greatest Value	Lower Quartile	Upper Quartile
1.	**Box Plot *B***					
2.	**Box Plot *C***					

3. Which box plot has the middle half of the data closer together? _____

LESSON 16-4 Dot Plots and Data Distribution

Practice and Problem Solving: A/B

Tell whether each question is a statistical question. If it is a statistical question, identify the units for the answer.

1. How far do you travel to get to school? _____

2. How tall is the door to this classroom? _____

Use the data set at the right and the description below to complete Exercises 3–6.

The class took a survey about how many people live in each student's home. The results are shown at the right.

People in Our Homes
4, 2, 5, 4, 2, 6, 4, 3, 4, 3, 5, 6, 2, 7, 3, 2, 5, 3, 4, 11, 4, 5, 3

3. Make a dot plot of the data.

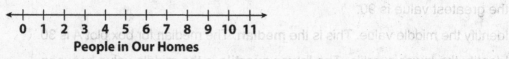

0 1 2 3 4 5 6 7 8 9 10 11
People in Our Homes

4. Find the mean, median, and range of the data.

   mean:_____; median:_____; range:_____

5. Describe the spread, center, and shape of the data distribution.

   _____

   _____

6. Which number is an outlier in the data set? Explain what effect the outlier has on the measures of center and spread.

   _____

   _____

7. Survey 12 students to find how many people live in their homes. Record the data below. Make a box plot at the right.

   _____

   _____

LESSON 16-4

Dot Plots and Data Distribution
Practice and Problem Solving: C

Use the data set at the right and the description below to complete Exercises 1–4.

The class counted the cars in the parking lot each hour from 9 A.M. to 4 P.M. for 3 days. The results are shown in the data set.

> **Cars in the Parking Lot**
> 30, 22, 33, 22, 26, 24, 33, 8,
> 30, 33, 40, 28, 38, 30, 38, 33,
> 33, 28, 22, 28, 30

1. Make a dot plot of the data.

```
←+—+—+—+—+—+—+—+—+—+—+—+—+—+—+—+—+→
  8  10 12 14 16 18 20 22 24 26 28 30 32 34 36 38 40
```
Cars in the Parking Lot

2. Find the mean, median, and range of the data.

   mean:_____; median:_____; range:_____

3. Describe the spread, center, and shape of the data distribution.

   _____

   _____

4. Which number is an outlier in the data set? Explain what effect the outlier has on the measures of center and spread.

   _____

   _____

Answer the questions below.

5. Write a survey question that you can ask at least 15 people.

   _____

6. Complete your survey. List the results.

   _____

   _____

7. In the blank space at the right, make a dot plot to show the results of your survey.

8. Find each of the following.

   mean:____ ; median:____ ; range:____

Dot Plots and Data Distribution

LESSON 16-4

Practice and Problem Solving: D

Use the data set at the right and the description below for Exercises 1–3. The first one is done for you.

The class took a survey about how many dogs and cats each student has. The results are shown in the data set.

Dogs and Cats in Our Homes
1, 0, 3, 5, 1, 3, 2, 4, 2, 1, 2, 0, 5, 3, 1, 2, 0, 0, 2, 3

1. Make a dot plot of the data.

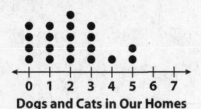

Dogs and Cats in Our Homes

2. Find the mean, median, and range of the data.

   mean:_____; median:_____; range:_____

3. Choose the best description of shape of the data distribution.

   A. symmetric   B. not symmetric

Answer the questions below.

4. The data set at the right shows the hours that a group of students spent volunteering each weekend. Make a dot plot of the data. Then use your dot plot to complete Exercises 5–7.

Hours Spent Volunteering on Weekends
5, 3, 2, 6, 5, 4, 2, 14, 1, 2

Hours Spent Volunteering on Weekends

5. Find the mean, median, and range of the data.

   mean:_____; median:_____; range:_____

6. Choose the best description of shape of the data distribution.

   A. symmetric   B. not symmetric

7. 14 is far away from the other data. What is 14 called? _____

LESSON 16-4

Dot Plots and Data Distribution
Reteach

A **dot plot** gives you a visual display of how data are distributed.

Example: Here are the scores Yolanda received
on math quizzes: 6, 10, 9, 9, 10, 8, 7, 7, and 10.
<u>Make a dot plot for Yolanda's quiz scores.</u>

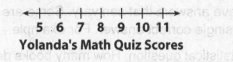

Yolanda's Math Quiz Scores

Step 1: Draw a number line.

Step 2: Write the title below the number line.

Step 3: For each number in the data set, put a dot
above that number on the number line.

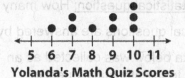

Yolanda's Math Quiz Scores

<u>Describe the dot plot by identifying the **range,** the
mean, and the **median.**</u>

Step 4: Identify the range. 10 − 6 = 4

Step 5: Find the mean. 76 ÷ 9 = 8.4

Step 6: Find the median. 9

Range: Greatest value − least value

Mean: $\dfrac{\text{Sum of data values}}{\text{Number of data values}}$

Median: Middle value

Use the data set at the right to complete Exercises 1–4.

1. Draw a dot plot for the data.

Game Scores			
12	6	15	10
14	15	8	10
12	21	15	8

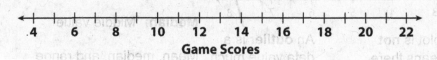

Game Scores

2. Find the range. _____

3. Find the mean. _____

4. Find the median. _____

LESSON 16-4

Dot Plots and Data Distribution
Reading Strategies: Build Vocabulary

When people study data, they are often asked questions that have a mathematical answer. Some such questions are **statistical**, meaning they have answers that can vary. Some are **not statistical**, meaning they have a single correct answer. For example:

<u>Statistical question:</u> How many books does a typical student read in a week?

<u>Not a statistical question:</u> How many books did Dave read last week?

Statistical questions are answered by collecting and analyzing data.

The data below was collected as an answer to the statistical question above. The data is shown in the dot plot at the right.

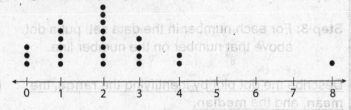

A **dot plot** is a visual way of displaying data.

4	2	1	0	3	2	4	1
1	2	3	8	2	1	0	2
2	3	3	1	1	2	2	0

You can describe the spread, the center, and the shape of a dot plot.

Spread: Range or difference between least and greatest values

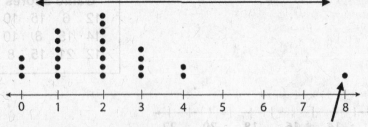

The **shape** of this dot plot is **not symmetrical**, which means there are more dots on one side of the center of the range than on the other side of center.

An **outlier** is a data value much greater or less than other data values.

Measures of **center**:

Mean: $\dfrac{\text{Sum of data values}}{\text{Number of data values}}$

Median: Middle value

Mean, median, and range might be affected by an **outlier**.

Use the dot plot above to answer each question.

1. How would you describe the spread of the dot plot?

   _____

2. What is the mean? What is the median?

   _____

3. What do you think it means if a dot plot is symmetrical?

   _____

Dot Plots and Data Distribution

LESSON 16-4

Success for English Learners

A **dot plot** provides a visual way to display data.

Problem 1

The data below is shown in the
dot plot at the right.

Summer Hours I Spent
Horseback Riding

1, 7, 4, 3, 5, 4, 2,

7, 4, 4, 3, 5, 5, 4

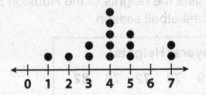

Summer Hours I Spent
Horseback Riding

Problem 2

You can describe the spread, the center, and the shape of a dot plot.

Spread: Range or difference between least and greatest values

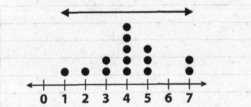

Measures of **center**:

Mean: $\dfrac{\text{Sum of data values}}{\text{Number of data values}}$

Median: Middle value

The **shape** of this dot plot is **symmetrical**, which means
there are about the same number of dots on one side of
the center of the range as on the other side of center.

1. How would you describe the spread of the dot plot?

   _____

2. Find the mean of the data. _____

3. Find the median of the data. _____

4. What does it mean if the shape of a dot plot is **not** symmetrical?

   _____

LESSON 16-5

Histograms
Practice and Problem Solving: A/B

**Use the data in the chart and the description
below to complete Exercises 1–2.**

The data set lists the heights of the Houston Rockets players during the
2011–2012 basketball season.

Players' Heights						
81	80	79	72	72	78	82
80	80	76	87	65	79	82
80	79	81	71	77		

1. Complete the frequency table.
   Use an interval of 5.

2. Complete the histogram.

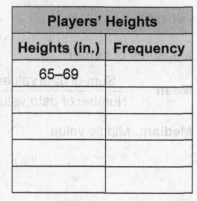

Players' Heights	
Heights (in.)	Frequency
65–69	

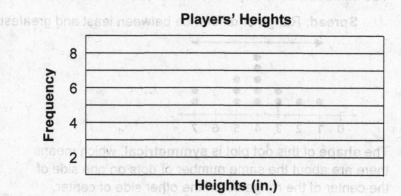

Solve. Use the histogram or the set of data. Tell which you used.

3. Find the range, the median, and the mean of the players' heights.

   a. range

   b. median

   c. mode

4. Based on this data, what do you think is the average height of players
   in the National Basketball Association? Explain how you decided on
   your answer including which display of data you used.

   _____

   _____

   _____

LESSON
16-5

Histograms

Practice and Problem Solving: C

**Use the data set and the description
below to complete Exercises 1–5.**

The data set shows a list of the number of students
at school each day during the month of January.

Students in School				
281	260	279	253	275
278	255	280	220	266
287	252	279	282	293
277	288	254	256	285

1. Complete the frequency table.
   Use an interval of 20.

Students in School	
Number	**Frequency**
220–239	

2. Complete the histogram.

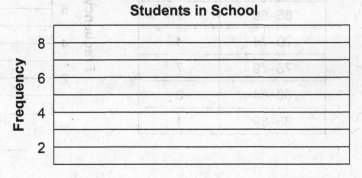

Students in School

3. Where can you find the range, the median, and the mean of the data.

_____

4. Where can you find intervals and frequencies?

_____

5. Besides the histogram, what are some other ways you could display
   these data?

_____

LESSON 16-5 Histograms Practice and Problem Solving

LESSON 16-5 Histograms
Practice and Problem Solving: D

Below is a list of the heights of trees that
are for sale at a nursery. Use the data for
Exercises 1–8. The first one is done for you.

Tree Heights							
70	75	65	70	74	64	77	61
77	73	75	79	68	86	79	75

1. Complete the frequency table.
   Use an interval of 5.

Tree Heights	
Heights (in.)	Frequency
60–64	2
65–69	2
70–74	4
75–79	7
80–84	0
85–89	1

2. Complete the histogram for the data.

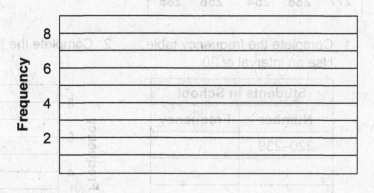

Tree Heights

Answer the questions below. The first one is done for you.

3. What is the range of the tree heights? _____**25**_____

4. What is the median of the tree heights? _____

5. What is the mean of the tree heights? _____

6. Where did you need to look to answer Exercises 3–5?

   _____

7. The nursery wants a sign that tells what trees are available for sale by

   height. What measure of center would you use for the sign? _____

8. In the space below, make a sign for the trees for sale at the nursery.

LESSON 16-5

Histograms

Reteach

Histograms can be used to display data. Use intervals of 10.

Pounds of Newspapers Collected for Recycling

12	28	24	32	35
31	38	55	43	52
42	49	18	22	15
47	37	19	31	37

Pounds of Newspapers

Interval	Frequency
1–10	0
11–20	4
21–30	3
31–40	7
41–50	4
51–60	2

A **histogram** is a bar graph in which the bars represent the frequencies of the numeric data within intervals. The bars on a histogram touch, but do not overlap.

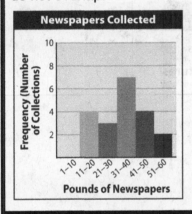

Use the histogram to complete Exercises 1–4.

1. Which interval has the greatest number of collections?

   _____

   _____

2. Were there any collections of less than 11 pounds? Explain your answer.

   _____

   _____

3. Which display can you use to find the median? _____

4. What is the median of the data? _____

LESSON 16-5

Histograms

Reading Strategies: Compare and Contrast Displays

Statistical data can be displayed in different ways. Each of the following displays shows the high temperature on the 15th of each month in one city.

Ordered List

High Temperatures

2 15 18 22 30 30 30 32 45 65 65 90

Line Plot

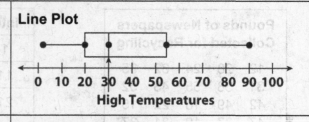

Frequency Table

High Temperatures

Temperatures	Frequency
0–19	3
20–39	5
40–59	1
60–79	2
80–99	1

Histogram

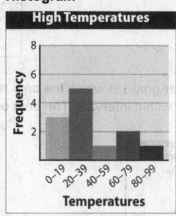

Dot Plot

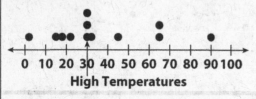

1. Compare and contrast the ability to identify the measures of center with each type of display.

_____

_____

_____

_____

**LESSON
16-5**

Histograms

Success for English Learners

The **histogram** provides a visual way to display data from a chart.

Chart of Temperatures (12 days)			
72	75	68	65
60	76	77	81
79	90	96	102

Problem 1

When you are not looking for the individual values in a data set, you can use a **frequency table** or a **histogram**.

a. frequency table

High Temperatures	
Temperatures	**Frequency**
60–69	3
70–79	5
80–89	1
90–99	2
100–109	1

The data is grouped by intervals instead of individual values.

b. histogram

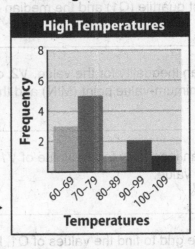

1. Would you use a histogram if being able to identify the median and the mean is important? Explain.

_____

2. What does the shape of the histogram tell you about the high temperatures?

_____

_____

Displaying, Analyzing, and Summarizing Data
Challenge

The box plot has 6 data points between the third quartile (Q3) and the largest value (MAX) of the data set. The minimum value (MIN) of the data set is 21. The interquartile range (IQR) is 27.

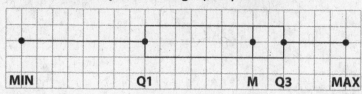

Solve.

1. How many data points are in the distribution? _____

2. Write an inequality for the value, V1, of any of the data points between the first quartile (Q1) and the median (M).

   _____

3. Write an inequality for the value, V2, of any of the data points between the minimum-value point (MIN) and the first quartile (Q1).

   _____

4. Write an inequality for the value of V1 in terms of the minimum data point's value.

   _____

5. Use the grid to find the values of Q1, M, Q3, and MAX.

   Q1:   M: Q3:   MAX:

   _____   _____

6. Given what you have found, create a data set of the values shown in the box plot. Check to make sure that *all* of the values you come up with are consistent with the features of the box plot.

   _____

   _____

   _____

UNIT 1: Numbers

MODULE 1 Integers

LESSON 1-1

Practice and Problem Solving: A/B

1. +85 or 85
2. –3
3. –5
4. +98 or 98
5.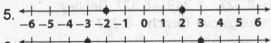
6.
7.
8.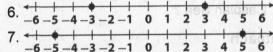
9. –4
10. +2 or 2
11. +535 or 535
12. –8
13. Death Valley: –282; Mount McKinley: +20,320 or 20,320
14. No. There are no whole numbers between 0 and 1, so there are no integers between 0 and 1.

Practice and Problem Solving: C

1. +7 or 7; –3
2. +30 or 30; –12
3. –5; +11 or 11
4. +32 or 32; –32
5. –8.

9. +120 or 120; –120
10. –23; +23 or 23
11. 0; –32
12. –212; –100; no
13. An integer and its opposite are the same distance (in the opposite directions) from 0 on the number line. For example, –7 and 7 are opposites and are the same distance from 0 on the number line.

Practice and Problem Solving: D

1. B
2. B
3. +2 or 2
4. –3
5. +20 or 20
6. –25
7. –38
8. –20

Reteach

1. +3 or 3
2. –10
3. +25 or 25
4. –5

For Exercises 5–8, see number line below.

5. –1; 1
6. 9; –9
7. 6; –6
8. –5; 5

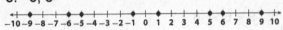

Reading Strategies

1. +25 or 25
2. +1,195 or 1,195
3. +12 or 12
4. –50
5. –87
6. –3,000

Success for English Learners

1. saving money
2. their opposites

LESSON 1-2

Practice and Problem Solving: A/B

1. 10 > –2
2. 0 < 3
3. –5 < 0

4. $-7 < 6$

5. $-6 > -9$

6. $-8 > -10$

7. $-2, 5, 6$

8. $-3, 0, 9$

9. $-1, 1, 6$

10. $1, 0, -1$

11. $2, 1, -12$

12. $-10, -11, -12$

13. $205, 50, -5, -20$

14. $78, 9, -78, -89$

15. $0, -2, -55, -60$

16. $28, 8, 0, -8$

17. $38, 37, -37, -38$

18. $11, 1, -1, -111$

19. Brenda, Tim, Carl, Ali

20. Tuesday, Wednesday, Monday

Practice and Problem Solving: C

1. $7 < 10 > -3 < 0$

2. $-5 < 5 < 8 > -8$

3. $-1 < 2 > -3 < 4$

4. $2 > -1 > -2 < 0$

5. $-9 < 6 > -8 < 7$

6. $2 > -1 < 0 < 1 > -2$

7. $-1, 0, 8, 9$ and $9, 8, 0, -1$

8. $-3, -2, 0, 2, 3$ and $3, 2, 0, -2, -3$

9. $-11, -1, 0, 1, 11$ and $11, 1, 0, -1, -11$

10. $-13, -5, 0, |-7|, 13$ and $13, |-7|, 0, -5, -13$

11. $-8, -7, 0, |7|, |-8|$ and $|-8|, |7|, 0, -7, -8$

12. $-15, -13, 14, |-15|, |16|$ and $|16|, |-15|, 14, -13, -15$

13. Davio, Beth, Abe, Casey, Eric

14. a. $5, -3, 7, -2, 2, -4$

    b. up 7 floors

    c. down 2 and up 2

    d. higher at the finish

    e. the 23rd floor

Practice and Problem Solving: D

1. $>$

2. $<$

3. $<$

4. $-3, 2, 4$

5. $-2, 2, 3$

6. $-1, 0, 3$

7. $-3, -1, 0, 1, 3$

8. C

9. B

10. $-8,327, -1,349; -8,327;$ Bentley Subglacial Trench, $-8,327$

11. Caspian Sea

Reteach

1. $>$

2. $<$

3. $<$

4. $>$

5. $>$

6. $<$

7. $-5, -2, -1$

8. $-5, 0, 5$

9. $-5, -3, 2$

10. $-4, -1, 3$

11. $-5, 0, 3$

12. $-4, -2, 1$

Reading Strategies

1. increase

2. decrease

3. right

4. left

5. -3 is to the left of 3, or 3 is to the right of -3

6. $-3 < 3$, or $3 > -3$

7. -1 is the right of -4, or -4 is to the left of -1

8. $-1 > -4$, or $-4 < -1$

Success for English Learners

1. -3 is to the right of -5 on the number line.

LESSON 1-3

Practice and Problem Solving: A/B

1–4.

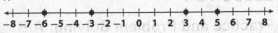

5. 6
6. 3
7. 8
8. 6
9. 3
10. 5
11. The absolute values of 6 and –6 are the same.
12. opposites
13. –20
14. –6
15. –8
16. 20
17. 6
18. 15
19. Monday; the greatest negative number shows the greatest amount spent.
20. $|3 + 10| = |13| = 13$; $|3| = 3$ and $|10| = 10$; $3 + 10 = 13$; $13 = 13$
21. two; possible answer: –4 and 4

Practice and Problem Solving: C

1. 2,300
2. Elan; 2,910
3. Pietro; 2,080
4. Bill, Jorge
5. Bill, Jorge
6. Elan
7. +186
8. 324
9. Their absolute values are the same.
10. –125 and 125; Negative deviations would decrease by 100; positive differences would increase by 100.

Practice and Problem Solving: D

1–4.

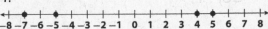

5. 4
6. 5
7. 7
8. 5
9. 4
10. 6
11. same
12. opposites
13. –5
14. –2
15. –3
16. no
17. 5
18. 2
19. 3
20. Monday
21. Thursday
22. absolute value

Reteach

1. c
2. a or d
3. b
4. a
5. c
6. 3
7. 5
8. 7
9. 6
10. 0
11. 2
12. 10
13. $\dfrac{3}{4}$
14. 0.8
15. Sample answer: The absolute value of a number is the number's distance from 0 on the number line. Since the distance is positive or 0, absolute value is always positive or 0. For example $|-5| = 5$ and $|5| = 5$.

Reading Strategies

1. above sea level, scored
2. loss, below sea level
3. rising 17 feet; 17 or +17
4. 5 feet below the surface, –5
5. losing 6 points; –6
6. paying a fee of $35; –35
7. penalty of 5 yards; –5
8. adding 32 MB; +32 or 32
9. award of $50; +50 or 50
10. crediting $60; +60 or 60

Success for English Learners

1. –5, 5
2. 6
3. 4
4. 3
5. 0
6. 2
7. 2
8. They both have an absolute value of 2.

MODULE 1 Challenge

1.
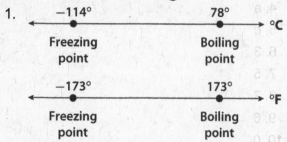

The Celsius degree is larger, or the Fahrenheit degree is smaller.

2. a. –3, –6, –6, –6, –7, –6, –4
   b. –7, –6, –6, –6, –6, –4, –3
   c. 5, 9, 18, 8, 21, 12, 12
   d. 5, 8, 9, 12, 12, 18, 21
   e. none

MODULE 2 Factors and Multiples

LESSON 2-1

Practice and Problem Solving: A/B

1. 1 and 5
2. 1, 3, 5, and 15
3. 1, 2, 3, 4, 5, 6, 10, 12, 15, 20, 30, and 60
4. 1, 2, 3, and 6
5. 1, 2, 3, 4, 6, and 12
6. 1, 2, 3, 4, 6, 9, 12, 18, and 36
7. 3
8. 4
9. 4
10. 3
11. 5
12. 3
13. $44 + 40 = 4 \times (11 + 10)$
14. $15 + 81 = 3 \times (5 + 27)$
15. $13 + 52 = 13 \times (1 + 4)$
16. $64 + 28 = 4 \times (16 + 7)$
17. Since $6 \times (4 + 5) = 24 + 30$, she can make 6 necklaces with 4 jade beads and 5 teak beads.
18. Since $6 \times (2 + 4 + 5) = 12 + 24 + 30$, 6 tanks can be set up with 2 angel fish, 4 swordtails, and 5 guppies.

Practice and Problem Solving: C

1. 250: 1, 2, 5, 10, 25, 50, 125, 250
   45: 1, 3, 5, 9, 15, 45
   30: 1, 2, 3, 5, 6, 10, 15, 30
   GCF: 5
2. 375: 1, 3, 5, 15, 25, 75, 125, 375
   66: 1, 2, 3, 6, 11, 22, 33, 66
   33: 1, 3, 11, 33
   GCF: 3
3. 76: 1, 2, 4, 19, 38, 76
   21: 1, 3, 7, 21
   14: 1, 2, 7, 14
   GCF: 1

4. 1260: 1, 2, 3, 4, 5, 6, 7, 9, 10, 12, 14, 15, 18, 20, 30, 35, 36, 42, 63, 70, 84, 90, 105, 126, 140, 180, 210, 252, 315, 420, 630, 1260

   36: 1, 2, 3, 4, 6, 9, 12, 18, 36

   18: 1, 2, 3, 6, 9, 18

   GCF: 9
5. no, factor of 3
6. no, factors 3 and 5
7. yes, no factors except 1 and 23
8. no, factor of 5
9. yes, no factors except 1 and 29
10. yes, no factors except 1 and 31

Practice and Problem Solving: D

1. 1, 2, 3, and 6
2. 1, 2, 5, and 10
3. 1, 2, 3, 6, 9, and 18
4. 1, 2, 3, 4, 6, and 12; 1, 2, 3, 6, 9, and 18; 6
5. 1, 2, 3, and 6; 1, 2, 4, 5, 10, and 20; 2
6. 1, 5, and 25; 1, 2, 4, 5, 8, 10, 16, 20, 40, and 80; 5
7. 1, 3, 9, and 27; 1, 3, 5, 9, 15, and 45; 9
8. 3; 3; 3; 8
9. 3; 3; 5; 14
10. The GCF is 12, so 12 baskets can be made, each having 2 bottles of shampoo, 3 tubes of lotion, and 5 bars of soap.

Reteach

1. 16
2. 18
3. 28
4. 15
5. $3 \times (3 + 5)$
6. $50 \times (2 + 7)$
7. $3 \times (4 + 6 + 7)$

Reading Strategies

1. Two is a factor of 8 because it divides 8 evenly.
2. Three is not a factor of 8 because it does not divide 8 evenly.

3. 1, 2, 3, 4, 6, and 12
4. 1, 2, 3, 6, 9, and 18
5. 1, 2, 3, and 6
6. 6
7. First, write the factors of each number. Next, identify the factors that the two numbers have in common. Finally, pick the greatest common factor of the factors that the two numbers have in common.

Success for English Learners

1. Step 1: Write the factors of each number.

   Step 2: Name the common factors of both numbers.

   Step 3: Name the greatest common factor of both numbers.
2. The GCF is 8 because 8 is the largest common factor of 16 and 24.
3. Step 1: Write the factors.

   16: 1, 2, 4, 8, and 16

   24: 1, 2, 3, 4, 6, 8, 12, and 24

   32: 1, 2, 4, 8, 16, and 32

   Step 2: Name the common factors.

   1, 2, 4, and 8

   Step 3: Name the GCF, 8

LESSON 2-2

Practice and Problem Solving: A/B

1. 3, 6, and 9
2. 7, 14, and 21
3. 12, 24, and 36
4. 200, 400, and 600
5. 2, 4, 6, 8, 10, 12...; 3, 6, 9, 12...; 6
6. 4, 8, 12, 16, 20...; 5, 10, 15, 20...; 20
7. 6, 12, 18, 24, 30, 36, 42...; 7, 14, 21, 28, 35, 42...; 42
8. 2, 4, 6, 8, 10, 12...; 3, 6, 9, 12...; 4, 8, 12...; 12
9. 5, 10, 15...210; 6, 12, 18...210; 7, 14, 21...210; 210
10. 8, 16...360; 9, 18...360; 10, 20...360; 360
11. Cups: 24, 48, 72; napkins: 18, 36, 54, 72; the LCM is 72, so 3 packages of cups and 4 packages of napkins will be needed.

12. Caps: 3, 6, 9...36, 39, 45; shirts: 5, 10...35, 40, 45; 15 packages of caps will be needed and 9 packages of shirts will be needed.

13. The LCM of 8 and 7 is 56, which is greater than any other LCM of 8 and a number less than 8. This insures that the consumer will have to buy the greatest number of packages of buns in order to use up all 8 hot dogs.

14. The GCF and the LCM are alike, because they are used to find common divisors of two numbers. The GCF and LCM are different in that the GCF is found by looking at the factors of a number, whereas the LCM is found by looking at the multiples of a number.

Practice and Problem Solving: C

1. 4

2. 60

3. 240

4. 240

5. The product of two numbers is equal to the product of their GCF and LCM.

6. 4

7. Answers will vary. Sample answers: (2, 6), (3, 4), (4, 3), (6, 2).

8. $\dfrac{1}{3}, \dfrac{2}{3}, \dfrac{3}{3}, \dfrac{4}{3}, \dfrac{5}{3}, \dfrac{6}{3}, \dfrac{2}{5}, \dfrac{4}{5}, \dfrac{6}{5}, \dfrac{8}{5}, \dfrac{10}{5},$ $\dfrac{12}{5}$

9. $\dfrac{6}{3} = \dfrac{10}{5} = 2$

10. $\dfrac{1}{15}$

11. $\dfrac{1}{15} \cdot x = \dfrac{1}{3}$, $x = 5$;

$\dfrac{1}{15} \cdot y = \dfrac{2}{5}$, $y = 6$;

are answers for Exercise 8.

Practice and Problem Solving: D

1. 4, 8, 12, 16, and 20

2. 13, 26, 39, 52, and 65

3. 250, 500, 750, 1,000, and 1,250

4. 5, 10, 15, 20, 25, 30, 35, 40; 8, 16, 24, 32, 40; 40

5. 6, 12, 18, 24, 30; 10, 20, 30; 30

6. 3, 6, 9, 12, 15; 15; 15

7. 2, 4, 6, 8, 10, 12, 14, 16, 18, 20, 22, 24, 26, 28, 30; 3, 6, 9, 12, 15, 18, 21, 24, 27, 30; 5, 10, 15, 20, 25, 30; 30

8. Count cups by 15's and plates by 10's. Cups: 15, 30; plates: 10, 20, 30; the least number is 2 packs of cups and 3 packs of plates.

9. Count invitations by 12's: 12, 24, 36, 48; count napkins by 24's: 24, 48; the least number is 4 packs of invitations and 2 packs of napkins.

Reteach

1. 2, 4, 6, 8, 10, 12...18; 9, 18, 27, 36 ...; 18

2. 4, 8, 12...; 6, 12...; 12

3. 4, 8, 12, 16, 20...; 10, 20...; 20

4. 2, 4, 6...26, 28, 30...; 5, 10, 15, 20, 25, 30...; 6, 12, 18, 24, 30; 30

5. 3, 6, 9...33, 36...; 4, 8, 12...28, 32, 36; 9, 18, 27, 36; 36

6. 8, 16, 24...112, 120; 10, 20...110, 120; 12, 24, 36...108, 120; 120

7. Pads: 4, 8, 12, 16...100, 104, 108 (27 boxes)

Pencils: 27, 54, 81, 108... (4 boxes)

Erasers: 12, 24, 36, 48, 60, 72, 84, 96, 108... (9 boxes)

LCM is 108, so 108 kits made from 27 boxes of pads, 4 boxes of pencils, and 9 boxes of erasers.

Reading Strategies

1. 5, 10, 15, 20, 25, 30, 35, 40, 45, and 50

2. 10, 20, 30, 40, and 50

3. 10, 20, 30, 40, and 50

4. 10

5. 10

6. Write the multiples of the numbers.

7. Find the least common multiple of the numbers.

8. After you have written the multiples, find the smallest multiple that is common to both lists of multiples.

9. The least common multiple of two numbers is the smallest number that is a multiple of both. For 5 and 7, the multiple of both 5 and 7 that is the least or the smallest is 35.

Success for English Learners

1. Find where on the number line the multiples of 6 and 9 are the same.

2. Answers will vary; the LCM is 24.

MODULE 2 Challenge

1. 70
2. 7
3. 10
4. 56
5. 8
6. 7
7. 728
8. 104
9. 91
10. 56
11. 26
12. 2
13. 1
14. 3,640
15. 364
16. 520
17. 455
18. 280
19. 140

MODULE 3 Rational Numbers

LESSON 3-1

Practice and Problem Solving: A/B

1. $\dfrac{3}{10}$

2. $\dfrac{23}{8}$

3. $-\dfrac{5}{1}$

4. $\dfrac{16}{1}$

5. $-\dfrac{7}{4}$

6. $-\dfrac{9}{2}$

7. $\dfrac{3}{1}$

8. $\dfrac{11}{100}$

9–15.

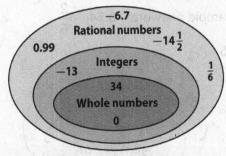

9. integers, rational numbers
10. rational numbers
11. whole numbers, integers, rational numbers
12. rational numbers
13. rational numbers
14. whole numbers, integers, rational numbers
15. rational numbers

Practice and Problem Solving: C

1. $-\dfrac{4}{1}$

2. Sample answer: $\dfrac{0}{5}$

3. $\dfrac{16}{3}$

4. $\dfrac{675}{100} = \dfrac{27}{4}$

5. $\dfrac{17}{8}$

6. $-\dfrac{35}{100} = -\dfrac{7}{20}$

7. $\dfrac{78}{10} = \dfrac{39}{5}$

8. $-\dfrac{48}{5}$

9. rational numbers

10. whole numbers, integers, rational numbers

11. integers, rational numbers

12. rational numbers

13. Sample answers: 9, 11

14. Sample answers: −3, −8

15. Sample answers: −0.54, $-\dfrac{2}{5}$

13–15.

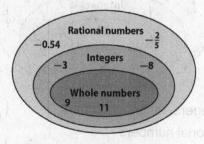

Practice and Problem Solving: D

1. $\dfrac{31}{6}$

2. $-\dfrac{6}{1}$

3. $\dfrac{97}{100}$

4. $\dfrac{18}{1}$

5. $\dfrac{33}{10}$

6. $-\dfrac{17}{8}$

7. integers, rational numbers

8. rational numbers

9. whole numbers, integers, rational numbers

10–12.

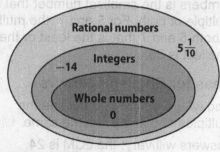

10. rational numbers

11. integers, rational numbers

12. whole numbers, integers, rational numbers

Reteach

1. $-\dfrac{12}{1}$; integers, rational numbers

2. $\dfrac{73}{10}$; rational numbers

3. $\dfrac{41}{100}$; rational numbers

4. $\dfrac{6}{1}$; whole numbers, integers, rational numbers

5. $\dfrac{7}{2}$; rational numbers

Reading Strategies

1. rational number

2. integer; rational number

3. rational number

4. whole number, integer, rational number

Success for English Learners

1. Change the mixed number to an improper fraction, $\dfrac{26}{5}$.

2. Every whole number can be written as a fraction with a denominator of 1.

3. No, some integers are negative. So a number like −2 is an integer, but not a whole number.

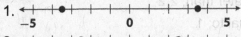

LESSON 3-2

Practice and Problem Solving: A/B

1.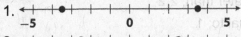

2.

3.

4.

5. −4.25

6. $5\dfrac{1}{4}$

7. $-\dfrac{1}{2}$

8. $2\dfrac{1}{3}$

9. 3.85

10. 6.1

11. A: −15.6; B: −17.1; C: −5.2; D: 6.5; E: 18.5

12. checkpoint C

13. checkpoint E; When you find the absolute value of each elevation, 18.5 is the furthest from 0 (sea level).

Practice and Problem Solving: C

1. $\dfrac{2}{3}$; $\dfrac{2}{3}$

2. $-1\dfrac{1}{7}$; $1\dfrac{1}{7}$

3. 0.89; 0.89

4. −3.47; 3.47

5. $-\dfrac{7}{5}$; $\dfrac{7}{5}$

6. $-5\dfrac{2}{3}$; $5\dfrac{2}{3}$

7. 4.03; 4.03

8. 1.11; 1.11

9. when the rational number is negative

10. |−5.47| = 5.47. The distance from −5.47 to 0 is 5.47 and the distance from 0 to 5.47 is 5.47. So, the total distance between the two points is 10.94.

11. Tuesday and Friday

12. greatest to least: 3.4, 2.1, −1.2, −3.4, −7.1; greatest to least absolute value: 7.1, 3.4, 3.4, 2.1, 1.2

Practice and Problem Solving: D

1.

2.

3.

4.

5. −3

6. 4.5

7. $-\dfrac{1}{3}$

8. 4.0

9. $2\dfrac{1}{2}$

10. $\dfrac{2}{3}$

11. Camille

12. −$7.45

13. $1.50

14. $5.25

Reteach

1. yes; 6.5, 6.5

2. no; $-3\dfrac{2}{5}$, $3\dfrac{2}{5}$

3. Answers will vary. Accept any negative rational number.

4. Answers will vary. Accept any positive rational number.

Reading Strategies

1. positive; 2.7

2. negative; $-3\dfrac{1}{8}$

3. negative; $-\dfrac{2}{7}$

4. positive; 0.9

5. No. All absolute values are positive.

6. It is the distance from 0 and the number and since distance is positive, it is positive.

Success for English Learners

1.
   −3 and −4

2.
   3 and 4

3. $3\frac{2}{7}$

4. $3\frac{2}{7}$

5. They are opposites, and they are the same distance from 0 on the number line.

6. Answers will vary. Sample answer: 2.45 and −2.45; absolute value of both numbers: 2.45

LESSON 3-3

Practice and Problem Solving: A/B

1. 0.375
2. 1.4
3. 3
4. 1.67
5. $\frac{11}{20}$
6. $10\frac{3}{5}$
7. $-7\frac{2}{25}$
8. 0.05, 0.5, $\frac{5}{8}$
9. 1.3, $1\frac{1}{3}$, 1.34
10. −2.67, 2.07, 2.67, $2\frac{7}{10}$
11. 0.422
12. 20
13. 23 or more
14. 0.6, 39 mph
15. $\frac{7}{100}$, 7 cents
16. $\frac{373}{500}$; 0.746

Practice and Problem Solving: C

1. less than; 0.625
2. greater than; 2.2
3. equal to; 1
4. less than; 0.57
5. fraction; $\frac{17}{20}$
6. mixed number; $3\frac{4}{5}$
7. mixed number; $-11\frac{4}{25}$
8. 0.867; yes
9. 0.833; no
10. −5.9, $-5\frac{7}{8}$, 5.78
11. $\frac{3}{7}$, $\frac{4}{9}$, 0.45
12. −0.38, $-\frac{3}{8}$, −0.04
13. blue: $\frac{14}{25}$, 0.56; red: $\frac{11}{25}$, 0.44
14. 7.5 widgets

Practice and Problem Solving: D

1. $\frac{5}{10}$ or $\frac{1}{2}$
2. $\frac{25}{100}$ or $\frac{1}{4}$
3. $\frac{75}{100}$ or $\frac{3}{4}$
4. $\frac{4}{10}$ or $\frac{2}{5}$
5. $\frac{8}{10}$ or $\frac{4}{5}$
6. $1\frac{2}{10}$ or $1\frac{1}{5}$
7. 0.3
8. 0.6
9. 1.4
10. B
11. B
12. basketball game

Reteach

1. $\dfrac{61}{100}$

2. $3\dfrac{43}{100}$

3. $\dfrac{9}{1000}$

4. $4\dfrac{7}{10}$

5. $1\dfrac{5}{10}$ or $1\dfrac{1}{2}$

6. $\dfrac{13}{100}$

7. $5\dfrac{2}{1000}$ or $5\dfrac{1}{500}$

8. $\dfrac{21}{1000}$

Reading Strategies

1. $0.1\overline{6}$; repeating

2. 0.125; terminating

3. $0.\overline{09}$; repeating

4. $0.\overline{2}$; repeating

5. 0.8; terminating

6. $0.\overline{5}$; repeating

7. 0.5; terminating

8. $0.\overline{7}$; repeating

Success for English Learners

1. A terminating decimal ends, while in a repeating decimal one or more digits repeats.

2. Divide the numerator by the denominator.

MODULE 3 Challenge

1. a. The boxes packed on Thursday and Friday will not ship.

   b. The boxes packed on Wednesday will sell for the highest price.

2. The inequality can be corrected in three moves.

$$2 \le -\frac{1}{8} \le -10 \le -0.125 \le -\frac{15}{2}$$

Move 1: Swap −10 and 2.

$$-10 \le -\frac{1}{8} \le 2 \le -0.125 \le -\frac{15}{2}$$

Move 2: Swap $-\dfrac{15}{2}$ and 2.

$$-10 \le -\frac{1}{8} \le -\frac{15}{2} \le -0.125 \le 2$$

Move 3: Swap $-\dfrac{15}{2}$ and $-\dfrac{1}{8}$.

$$-10 \le -\frac{15}{2} \le -\frac{1}{8} \le -0.125 \le 2$$

UNIT 2: Number Operations

MODULE 4 Operations with Fractions

LESSON 4-1

Practice and Problem Solving: A/B

1. $\dfrac{4}{7}$

2. $\dfrac{1}{2}$

3. $\dfrac{4}{15}$

4. 20

5. 12

6. 9

7. $1\dfrac{1}{10}$

8. $\dfrac{4}{15}$

9. $\dfrac{3}{4}$

10. $\dfrac{5}{12}$

11. $4\dfrac{19}{24}$

12. $1\dfrac{23}{45}$

13. 3 h

14. $\dfrac{1}{6}$ of a pizza

Practice and Problem Solving: C

1. $\dfrac{1}{6}$

2. $\dfrac{1}{6}$

3. 14

4. $1\dfrac{3}{10}$

5. $1\dfrac{13}{30}$

6. $\dfrac{3}{4}$

7. flour: 2 c; butter : $1\dfrac{1}{3}$ T; fruit: $2\dfrac{2}{3}$ c; sugar: $\dfrac{1}{2}$ c; salt: $\dfrac{1}{3}$ t

8. $\dfrac{11}{24}$ of the pizza

9. the least common denominator

Practice and Problem Solving: D

1. $\dfrac{1}{2}$

2. $\dfrac{3}{5}$

3. 15

4. $\dfrac{23}{30}$

5. $1\dfrac{1}{20}$

6. $1\dfrac{2}{5}$

7. 6 oz

8. 20 h

9. $\dfrac{1}{9}$ c

Reteach

1. $\dfrac{7}{12}$

2. $\dfrac{2}{9}$

3. $\dfrac{1}{2}$

4. $2\dfrac{2}{5}$

5. $\dfrac{1}{3}$

6. $\dfrac{2}{7}$

7. $1\dfrac{7}{36}$

8. $\dfrac{1}{2}$

9. $1\dfrac{19}{60}$

Reading Strategies

1. $\dfrac{2}{3}$

2. 6

3. $6 \cdot \dfrac{2}{3} = \dfrac{12}{3} = 4$

4. $\dfrac{2}{3}$

5. $1\dfrac{2}{3}$

6. $1\dfrac{4}{7}$

7. $\dfrac{2}{3}$

8. $\dfrac{29}{36}$

9. $1\dfrac{3}{20}$

Success for English Learners

1. When multiplying, you multiply numerators, then denominators. When adding, you change the fractions to fractions with a common denominator and then add the numerators.

2. When multiplying, the GCF helps simplify. When adding or subtracting, the LCM as denominator lets you use smaller numbers.

LESSON 4-2

Practice and Problem Solving: A/B

1. $\dfrac{7}{5}$

2. $\dfrac{4}{3}$

3. $\dfrac{5}{3}$

4. 10

5. $\dfrac{9}{4}$

6. $\dfrac{14}{13}$

7. $\dfrac{12}{7}$

8. $\dfrac{10}{3}$

9. $\dfrac{8}{5}$

10. $1\dfrac{2}{3}$

11. $1\dfrac{5}{16}$

12. $1\dfrac{1}{5}$

13. $\dfrac{1}{12}$

14. $\dfrac{7}{9}$

15. $2\dfrac{7}{9}$

16. $1\dfrac{1}{9}$

17. $1\dfrac{1}{24}$

18. $\dfrac{3}{4}$

19. 24 sandwiches

20. $10\dfrac{1}{2}$ lb

21. 36 points

Practice and Problem Solving: C

1. $\dfrac{7}{3}$; greater

2. $\dfrac{4}{3}$; greater

3. $\dfrac{5}{8}$; less

4. $\dfrac{11}{1}$; greater

5. $\frac{9}{8}$; greater

6. $\frac{4}{13}$; less

7. It is greater than 1.

8. It is less than 1.

9. 1

10. $1\frac{1}{4}$

11. $1\frac{11}{24}$

12. $2\frac{2}{9}$

13. $\frac{5}{6}$

14. $\frac{45}{49}$

15. $\frac{11}{15}$

16. They are greater than 1.

17. They are less than 1.

18. 14; $7\frac{1}{2}$ min

Practice and Problem Solving: D

1. $\frac{3}{2}$

2. $\frac{9}{7}$

3. $\frac{5}{8}$

4. $\frac{9}{1}$

5. $\frac{10}{9}$

6. $\frac{10}{3}$

7. $\frac{7}{4}$

8. $\frac{1}{8}$

9. $\frac{7}{6}$

10. $1\frac{1}{2}$

11. $1\frac{1}{20}$

12. $1\frac{1}{9}$

13. $\frac{9}{25}$

14. $\frac{7}{9}$

15. $\frac{21}{25}$

16. $1\frac{1}{6}$

17. $1\frac{3}{8}$

18. $\frac{13}{14}$

19. $\frac{16}{3}$; 64; $21\frac{1}{3}$; $21\frac{1}{3}$

20. 9 in.

21. $\frac{1}{5}$ h

Reteach

1. $\frac{1}{4} \cdot \frac{3}{1} = \frac{3}{4}$

2. $\frac{1}{2} \cdot \frac{4}{1} = 2$

3. $\frac{3}{8} \cdot \frac{2}{1} = \frac{6}{8} = \frac{3}{4}$

4. $\frac{1}{3} \cdot \frac{4}{3} = \frac{4}{9}$

5. $\frac{2}{5}$

6. $\frac{1}{4}$

7. $\frac{5}{16}$

8. $\frac{1}{4}$

Reading Strategies

1. 3; $\dfrac{1}{2}$

2. $\dfrac{7}{8} \bullet 4 = 3\dfrac{1}{2}$

3. 3

4. $\dfrac{4}{8}$; $\dfrac{1}{2}$

5. $3\dfrac{1}{2}$

6. The answer is the same.

Success for English Learners

1. To find the reciprocal of a fraction you swap or make the numerator the denominator and the denominator the numerator.

2. Find he reciprocal of $\dfrac{1}{3}$ which is $\dfrac{3}{1}$.

   Multiply $\dfrac{5}{8}$ by $\dfrac{3}{1}$. $\dfrac{5}{8} \bullet \dfrac{3}{1} = \dfrac{15}{8}$.

   Then simplify: $\dfrac{15}{8} = 1\dfrac{7}{8}$.

3. The product of any fraction and its reciprocal is 1.

   Sample answer: $\dfrac{2}{3} \bullet \dfrac{3}{2} = \dfrac{6}{6} = 1$

LESSON 4-3

Practice and Problem Solving: A/B

1. $\dfrac{2}{21}$; $\dfrac{21}{2} \times \dfrac{2}{21} = 1$

2. $\dfrac{7}{45}$; $\dfrac{45}{7} \times \dfrac{7}{45} = 1$

3. $\dfrac{9}{26}$; $\dfrac{26}{9} \times \dfrac{9}{26} = 1$

4. $\dfrac{4}{61}$; $\dfrac{4}{61} \times \dfrac{61}{4} = 1$

5. $\dfrac{3}{29}$; $\dfrac{3}{29} \times \dfrac{29}{3} = 1$

6. $\dfrac{8}{61}$; $\dfrac{61}{8} \times \dfrac{8}{61} = 1$

7. $\dfrac{24}{55}$

8. $1\dfrac{1}{13}$

9. $1\dfrac{3}{5}$

10. $1\dfrac{17}{19}$

11. $1\dfrac{16}{19}$

12. $\dfrac{22}{63}$

13. $4\dfrac{20}{39}$

14. $2\dfrac{16}{145}$

15. $1\dfrac{25}{62}$

16. $36\dfrac{5}{6} \div 5\dfrac{2}{3} = 6\dfrac{1}{2}$; No, the slab is not long enough for a 7-ft picnic table since $36\dfrac{5}{6} \div 5\dfrac{2}{3} = 6\dfrac{1}{2}$ ft.

17. $225 \div 13\dfrac{3}{4} = 16\dfrac{4}{11}$; The space is wide enough, but since $225 \div 13\dfrac{3}{4} = 16\dfrac{4}{11}$ in. and $16\dfrac{4}{11} > 16$, the space is not long enough to fit the mirror.

18. $16\dfrac{1}{5} \div 5\dfrac{2}{5}$; 3 costumes

Practice and Problem Solving: C

1. 21 in.

2. He can make 5 pillowcases, and will have $2\dfrac{11}{12}$ yd left over.

3. He has hiked $3\dfrac{11}{12}$ mi.

4. She can make 2 bows.

5. $\dfrac{1}{6}$ oz

6. He can make 14 more bowls. He can make a total of $15\dfrac{5}{8} \div \dfrac{7}{10}$ or 22 bowls in all. $22 - 8 = 14$.

Practice and Problem Solving: D

1. $\dfrac{(9 \times 2)+1}{2} = \dfrac{19}{2};\ \dfrac{2}{19}$

2. $\dfrac{(5 \times 7)+3}{7} = \dfrac{38}{7};\ \dfrac{7}{38}$

3. $\dfrac{(1 \times 9)+8}{9} = \dfrac{17}{9};\ \dfrac{9}{17}$

4. $\dfrac{(14 \times 4)+1}{4} = \dfrac{57}{4};\ \dfrac{4}{57}$

5. $\dfrac{(8 \times 3)+2}{3} = \dfrac{26}{3};\ \dfrac{3}{26}$

6. $\dfrac{(6 \times 8)+5}{8} = \dfrac{53}{8};\ \dfrac{8}{53}$

7. $\dfrac{21}{40}$

8. $1\dfrac{1}{6}$

9. $1\dfrac{11}{12}$

10. $\dfrac{11}{12}$

11. $9\dfrac{3}{5} \div 2\dfrac{2}{5} = \dfrac{48}{5} \div \dfrac{12}{5} = \dfrac{48}{5} \times \dfrac{5}{12} = \dfrac{48}{12} = 4;$
    4 vests

12. $20\dfrac{5}{6} \div 3\dfrac{1}{2} = \dfrac{125}{6} \div \dfrac{7}{2} = \dfrac{125}{6} \times \dfrac{2}{7}$
    $= \dfrac{250}{42} = 5\dfrac{40}{42} = 5\dfrac{20}{21};\ 5\dfrac{20}{21}$ ft long

Reteach

1. $\dfrac{14}{9}$

2. $\dfrac{2}{7}$

3. $\dfrac{3}{32}$

4. $\dfrac{18}{5} \div \dfrac{9}{4}$
   $\dfrac{18}{5} \times \dfrac{4}{9}$
   $\dfrac{72}{45} = \dfrac{8}{5} = 1\dfrac{3}{5}$

5. $\dfrac{3}{2} \div \dfrac{5}{4}$
   $\dfrac{3}{2} \times \dfrac{4}{5}$
   $\dfrac{12}{10} = \dfrac{6}{5} = 1\dfrac{1}{5}$

6. $\dfrac{5}{12} \div \dfrac{15}{8}$
   $\dfrac{5}{12} \times \dfrac{8}{15}$
   $\dfrac{40}{180} = \dfrac{2}{9}$

7. $6\dfrac{1}{4}$

8. $\dfrac{7}{16}$

9. $1\dfrac{2}{3}$

Reading Strategies

1. Draw a single square and label it $\dfrac{1}{2}$.

2. to find the number of $\dfrac{1}{2}$-ft servings in $2\dfrac{1}{2}$ ft.

3. 5

4. 5

Success for English Learners

1. Sample answer: When you divide mixed numbers, you have to change the divisor to its reciprocal and multiply.

2. Change all mixed numbers to improper fractions.

3. You know that $8 \times 7 = 56$, and the area of the rectangle is greater than 56. Since $8\dfrac{1}{2} \times 7$ is greater than 56, then the width would need to be approximately 7 feet.

LESSON 4-4

Practice and Problem Solving: A/B

1. a. $3\frac{1}{3} - 2\frac{5}{6} = 3\frac{2}{6} - 2\frac{5}{6} = \frac{3}{6} = \frac{1}{2}$;

   $\frac{1}{2}$ more apple pie than pumpkin pie is left.

   b. $1\frac{2}{3}$ apple pie plus $1\frac{5}{12}$ pumpkin pie, so $3\frac{1}{12}$ pies in all.

2. a. $2\frac{1}{3} - 1\frac{1}{2} = 2\frac{2}{6} - 1\frac{3}{6} = \frac{5}{6}$; $\frac{5}{6}$ of an inch

   b. $\frac{5}{6} \times \frac{1}{12} = \frac{5}{72}$; $\frac{5}{72}$ ft

3. $3 \times 3\frac{3}{8} = 3 \times \frac{27}{8} = \frac{81}{8} = 10\frac{1}{8}$ ft²,

   $10\frac{1}{8} \div 6 = \frac{81}{8} \times \frac{1}{6} = \frac{27}{8} \times \frac{1}{2} = \frac{27}{16} = 1\frac{11}{16}$;

   2 sheets are needed

4. The difference is $\frac{3}{4}$ mi;

   $\frac{3}{4} \div 6\frac{1}{4} = \frac{3}{4} \times \frac{4}{25} = \frac{3}{25}$

5. $208 + 125\frac{5}{8} = 333\frac{5}{8}$;

   $\dfrac{125\frac{5}{8}}{333\frac{5}{8}} = \dfrac{\frac{1005}{8}}{\frac{2669}{8}} = \frac{1005}{2669}$ or about $\frac{2}{5}$

Practice and Problem Solving: C

1. $2\frac{3}{4} + \left(1\frac{1}{2}\right)\left(2\frac{3}{4}\right) + \frac{7}{8} = 7\frac{3}{4}$;

   $15\frac{1}{2} - 7\frac{3}{4} = 7\frac{3}{4}$ in.

2. $\frac{8}{6} = 1\frac{1}{3}$, $\left(1\frac{1}{3}\right)\left(2\frac{2}{3} + \frac{1}{4}\right) =$

   $\frac{4}{3}\left(\frac{8}{3} + \frac{1}{4}\right) = \frac{4}{3}\left(\frac{32}{12} + \frac{3}{12}\right) =$

   $\frac{4}{3}\left(\frac{35}{12}\right) = \frac{35}{9} = 3\frac{8}{9}$ c

3. He could multiply Laura's answer by $\frac{1}{2}$ since $\frac{4}{8} = \frac{1}{2}$ or he could find $\frac{4}{6}$ or $\frac{2}{3}$ of the sum of the two liquid ingredients; $1\frac{17}{18}$ c

4. $\frac{11}{2} \times 4 \times \frac{5}{2} = 55$ ft

5. $2\frac{1}{5} + 1\frac{1}{10} = 3\frac{3}{10}$, $\frac{33}{10} \times \frac{7}{8} = \frac{231}{80} = 2\frac{71}{80}$

   $3\frac{3}{10} + 2\frac{71}{80} = 6\frac{15}{80} = 6\frac{3}{16}$ h

6. $\frac{1}{5} + \frac{3}{8} + \frac{2}{7} = \frac{241}{280}$,

   $\frac{241}{280} \times 20 = \frac{4820}{280} = 17.21$; $20 - 17.21 = 2.79$; $2.79 left

Practice and Problem Solving: D

1. a. $\frac{5}{6} - \frac{1}{3} = \frac{5}{6} - \frac{2}{6} = \frac{3}{6}$ or $\frac{1}{2}$ pie

   b. $\frac{5}{6} + \frac{1}{3} = \frac{5}{6} + \frac{2}{6} = \frac{7}{6}$; $\frac{7}{6} \bullet \frac{1}{3} = \frac{7}{18}$;

   Terri ate $\frac{7}{18}$ of the pies.

2. a. 1 in.

   b. $\frac{1}{12}$ ft

3. $3\frac{1}{8} + 3\frac{1}{8} = 6\frac{1}{4}$; it will take 2 pieces.

4. $5\frac{1}{2} + 6 = 11\frac{1}{2}$; $\dfrac{6}{11\frac{1}{2}} = \dfrac{6}{\frac{23}{2}} = 6 \bullet \frac{2}{23} = \frac{12}{23}$

5. $208 + 125\frac{5}{8} = 333\frac{5}{8}$; $333\frac{5}{8} \cdot \frac{1}{12} =$

$\frac{2669}{8} \cdot \frac{1}{12} = \frac{2669}{96} = 27\frac{77}{96}$ lb

Reteach

1. $3\frac{5}{8} + 1\frac{3}{4} = 5\frac{3}{8}$; $6\frac{1}{2} - 5\frac{3}{8} = 1\frac{1}{8}$; $1\frac{1}{8}$

Reading Strategies

1. Answers will vary. Students who are good at estimating answers may prefer Method 1, whereas students who prefer a more-formal method of solving problems may prefer the Method 2.

Success for English Learners

1. The common denominator or LCM of 2 and 3 is 6.
2. To solve 1a, subtraction
   To solve 1b, multiplication

MODULE 4 Challenge

1. Find the prices of the rugs by multiplying the area of each rug by $8.

Type of Rug	Length (ft)	Width (ft)	Area (ft²)	Price ($)
Classic	$8\frac{1}{2}$	$10\frac{3}{4}$	$91\frac{3}{8}$	$731.00
Deco	$10\frac{3}{4}$	$9\frac{3}{8}$	$100\frac{25}{32}$	$806.25
Solid	$7\frac{2}{5}$	$8\frac{3}{5}$	$63\frac{16}{25}$	$509.12
Modern	$10\frac{3}{5}$	$9\frac{1}{2}$	$100\frac{7}{10}$	$805.60

Classic $= \frac{17}{2} \times \frac{43}{4} = 91\frac{3}{8} \times \$8 = \$731.00$

Deco $= \frac{43}{4} \times \frac{75}{8} = \frac{3225}{32} = 100\frac{25}{32}$
$= 100.78125 \times 8 = \$806.25$

Solid $= \frac{37}{5} \times \frac{43}{5} = 63.64 \times 8 = \$509.12$

Modern $= \frac{53}{5} \times \frac{19}{2} = 100.7 \times 8 = \$805.60$

The Deco rug is the most expensive. It costs $806.25.

2. The area of the Deco is $100\frac{25}{32}$ sq ft.
   Divide that by $9\frac{1}{2} = 10\frac{185}{304}$ or 10.61 ft long.

3. The product will be $\frac{1}{100}$ if the last fraction written in the pattern is $\frac{99}{100}$. The 99 in the previous fraction's denominator will cross-cancel with the 99 in the last fraction's numerator and you will be left with $\frac{1}{100}$.

MODULE 5 Operations with Decimals

LESSON 5-1

Practice and Problem Solving: A/B

1. 60
2. 60
3. 200
4. 40
5. 50
6. 3

7.
```
       46
  29)1334
    -116
     174
    -174
       0
```

8.
```
       227
  92)20884
    -184
     248
    -184
     644
    -644
       0
```

9.
```
       727
  25)18175
    -175
      67
     -50
     175
    -175
       0
```

10.
$$18\overline{)2902}$$
quotient 161
$$
\begin{array}{r}
161 \\
18\overline{)2902} \\
-18 \\
\hline
110 \\
-108 \\
\hline
22 \\
-18 \\
\hline
4
\end{array}
$$

161 R 4 or $161\frac{2}{9}$

11.
$$
\begin{array}{r}
541 \\
64\overline{)34680} \\
-320 \\
\hline
268 \\
-256 \\
\hline
120 \\
-64 \\
\hline
56
\end{array}
$$

541 R 56 or $541\frac{7}{8}$

12.
$$
\begin{array}{r}
243 \\
215\overline{)52,245} \\
-430 \\
\hline
924 \\
-860 \\
\hline
645 \\
-645 \\
\hline
0
\end{array}
$$

13. 270 students per district

14. about 181 days (181.25)

Practice and Problem Solving: C

1. 60; 59

2. 60; 55.2

3. 200; 225.3

4. 40; 37.0952381

5. 50; 49.05

6. 3; 2.875

7. Estimating to the nearest 10 usually gave a closer estimate.

8. $\frac{2}{9}$

9. $\frac{7}{8}$

10. $\frac{14}{215}$

11. $2,550.00

12. a. about 120.8 days

    b. 30 days

Practice and Problem Solving: D

1. 3; 3; 300 ÷ 30, or about 10

2. 2; 1; 2,000 ÷ 100, or about 20

3. about 35

4. about 20

5.
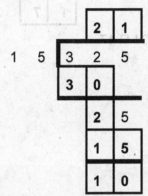

Quotient: 21 R 10

6.
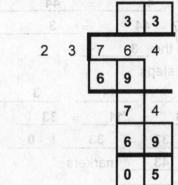

Quotient: 33 R 5

7.

Quotient: 45 R 30

8.

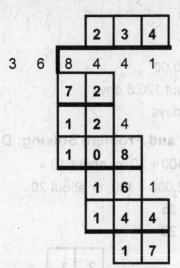

Quotient: 234 R 17

Reteach

$$\begin{array}{r} 43 \\ 11\overline{)473} \\ -44 \\ \hline 33 \\ -33 \\ \hline 0 \end{array}$$

1.

Divide: 47 ÷ __11__ = __4__

Multiply: 11 × __4__ = __44__

Subtract: 47 − __44__ = __3__

Bring down the __3__.

Repeat the steps.

Divide: __33__ ÷ __11__ = __3__

Multiply: __3__ × __11__ = __33__

Subtract: __33__ − __33__ = __0__

Answer: __43__ markers

Reading Strategies

1. 645
2. 120
3. number of items in a group
4. number of groups
5. 43; number of groups
6. 24; number of items in a group

Success for English Learners

1. An overestimate, since 2 > 1.846.
2. Compatible numbers are easy to add, subtract, multiply, or divide.

3. $13\frac{14}{17}$

LESSON 5-2

Practice and Problem Solving: A/B

1. 3.8
2. 3.8
3. 7.9
4. 16
5. 0.44
6. 10.4
7. 11.95
8. 1.84
9. 11.014
10. 1.8 m
11. $12.30
12. 4
13. 5
14. 3
15. $12.99
16. 16.65 ft

Practice and Problem Solving: C

1. 0.666...
2. 1.1666...
3. 3.111...
4. 5.2777...
5. They all have repeating digits.
6. 0.999...
7. 0.575757...
8. 2.111111...
9. 0.333...; 3.333...; 3; $\frac{1}{3}$
10. 0.666...; 6.666...; 6; $\frac{2}{3}$
11. 0.3434...; 34.3434...; 34; $\frac{34}{99}$
12. 1.432432...; 1432.432432...; 1431; $1\frac{16}{37}$
13. Decimals that repeat every decimal place are multiplied by 10. Decimals that repeat every two and three places are multiplied by 100 and 1,000, respectively.

Practice and Problem Solving: D

1.

0.64

2.

0.34

3. 12; 28; 40; 39.65

4. 35; 18; 17; 16.8

5.

	4	7	•	6	5	
+		8	•	0	5	9
	5	5	•	7	0	9

6.

		7	7	•	5	
+		2	3	•	8	7
	1	0	1	•	3	7

7. 27.35

8. 214.3

Reteach

1. 3.75

2. 0.83

3. 4.3, 1.4; 5.7

4. 1.44, 3.8; 10.6

5. 7.3, 8.5; 15.8

6. 12.34, 6.9; 5.44

7. 5, 5.7; underestimate

8. 10; 10.6; underestimate

9. 16; 15.8; overestimate

10. 5; 5.44; underestimate

Reading Strategies

1. It aligns the place values in numbers that are being added or subtracted by lining up the decimal points in the numbers.

2.

3.

4. 7.21

5. 16.62

6. 2.9 as 2.90 and 7.2 as 7.20

Success for English Learners

1. The decimal point is read as "and." For example, "1.05" would be read as "one and five hundredths"

2. The answer will differ from the correct answer, sometimes very little and other times by a lot, depending on how far off the decimal placement is in a problem.

LESSON 5-3

Practice and Problem Solving: A/B

1. 0.12;

2. 0.21;

3. 3.96

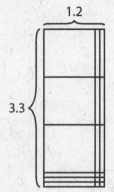

4. 8.61

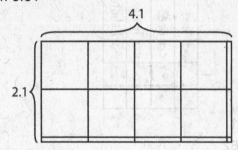

5. 0.02

6. 5.4

7. 0.24

8. 4.64

9. 0.615

10. 0.6432

11. 14.6797

12. 82.8576

13. 17.5 lb

14. $26.25

Practice and Problem Solving: C

1. 1 × 1 or 1; 0.595

2. 3 × 2 or 6; 5.9475

3. 1 × 2 or 2; 1.265

4. 5 × 2 or 10; 8.17626

5. 10 × 5 or 50; 52.74182

6. 6 × 20 or 120; 110.23803

7. 2 × 4 or 8; 4 × 3 or 12; so, 2.4 × 3.8 < 3.5 × 2.8

8. 6 × 4 or 24; 3 × 7 or 21; so, 6.28 × 3.82 > 3.3 × 6.84

9.

Sector	Map Dimensions (cm)	Map Area (cm²)
A	2.5 × 5.8	14.5
B	3.7 × 2.1	7.77
C	4.7 × 3.5	16.45
D	4.2 × 2.8	11.76

a. Change cm² to km².

b. No; The total area is: 14.5 + 7.77 + 16.45 + 11.76 = 50.48 km² which is greater than 50 km².

c. Sectors A, B, and C; Sectors A, B, and D; Sectors A, B, and D; and Sectors B, C and D.

d. The sum of Sectors A, C, and D is 42.71 km². Since these sectors have the greatest areas, their sum maximizes the area studied.

Practice and Problem Solving: D

1. 1.5

2. 3.2

3. 6.3

4. 0.75

5.

6.

7.

8. 1; 2; 3

9. 3; 1; 4

10. 17.875

11. 5.232

12. a. $3.5 \times \$4.95$

b. $14.85

c. $2.475 or $2.48

d. $14.85 + \$2.48 = \$17.33$

Reteach

1. 0.69
2. 0.82
3. 0.05
4. 0.64
5. 0.45
6. 0.84
7. 0.32
8. 0.88
9. 0.16
10. 0.63
11. 0.25
12. 0.18
13. 0.1
14. 0.16
15. 0.09
16. 0.28

Reading Strategies

1.

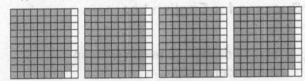

2. $0.89 + 0.89 + 0.89 + 0.89$
3. $0.89 + 0.89 + 0.89 + 0.89 = 3.56$
4. 4×0.89 or 0.89×4
5. $4 \times 0.89 = 3.56$ or $0.89 \times 4 = 3.56$

Success for English Learners

1. Add the decimal places in the factors.
2. left
3. Use estimation and compare it to your answer.
4. no; $1 \times 3 = 3$
5. yes
6. no; $2 \times 3 = 6$

LESSON 5-4

Practice and Problem Solving: A/B

1.

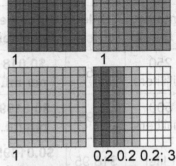

2.

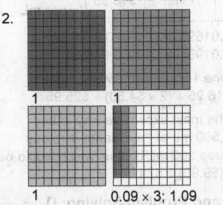

3. 15
4. 13.2
5. 5.44
6. 7
7. 7.5
8. 15
9. About 4; 4.2
10. Between 12 and 18; 14.4
11. About 30; 28
12. About 14; 15
13. 66 images; the exact answer, $66\frac{2}{3}$,

means that last image would not be completely captured.

14. About 0.142 centimeters per year (or a little over a millimeter per year).

Practice and Problem Solving: C

1. Estimate: $8 \div 2 = 4$; Exact Quotient: 3.5
2. Estimate: $14 \div 2 = 7$; Exact Quotient: 6.1111111 or 6.11…
3. Estimate: $55 \div 5 = 11$; Exact Quotient: 10.9
4. <

5. >

6. <

7. =

8.

Size	Amount of Liquid	Sale Price	Price per Milliliter
Small	250 milliliters	$4.50	$0.018 per mL
Medium	500 milliliters	$9.95	$0.0199 per mL
Large	1 liter	$16.95	$0.01695 per mL

a. 0.01695 < 0.018 < 0.0199 or
0.0199 > 0.018 > 0.01695

b. One 1 L and two 250 mL bottles;
$16.95 + (2 × $4.50) = $25.95

c. The most expensive way to buy
1,500 mL of the cleaner is to buy
three 500 mL bottles, which would be
3($9.95) = $29.85.

Practice and Problem Solving: D

1. 0.7

2. 0.9

3. 0.6

4. 0.8

5. 0.05

6. 0.6

7. 6

8. 7

9. 8

10. 11

11. 2

12. 6

13. $0.48 or 48 cents

14. 0.09 in.

15. 2 months

16. 2 lb

Reteach

1. 0.12

2. 0.13

3. 0.08

4. 300

5. 0.2

6. 0.7

7. 50

8. 0.8

Reading Strategies

1–2.

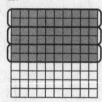

3. 0.20

4. $0.60 \div 3 = 0.20 = 0.2$ or
$3\overline{)0.60} = 0.20 = 0.2$

5–6.

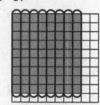

7. 0.09

8. $0.72 \div 8 = 0.09$ or $8\overline{)0.72} = 0.09$

Success for English Learners

1. 3

2. No; 12 divides 36 evenly with no
remainder.

3. Answers will vary. Sample answer: How
much gas will Sari's car use to travel
332.5 miles? (332.5 ÷ 17.5 = 19) e.g. what
is the miles per gallon rate for the total
trip?

LESSON 5-5

Practice and Problem Solving: A/B

1. $3.10

2. 3 vans

3. 7 packs

4. 8 pairs

5. $68\frac{4}{5}$ in.; $5\frac{11}{15}$ ft

6. 12 T

7. $3,565

8. Joey; 0.2 points

9. $4\frac{1}{6}$ c

10. $60\frac{1}{2}$ lb

Practice and Problem Solving: C

1. 59 scarves

2. 2 ft

3. $11.09

4. $7.52

5. 11.585 h; 2.317 h; A, C, D

6. 49; $116.13

7. $0.04; $0.13; 230

Practice and Problem Solving: D

1. $\frac{3}{20}$ mi

2. 11 weeks

3. 6 costumes

4. $26.28

5. 27.6 mpg

6. 15 ft

7. $10\frac{1}{2}$ lb

8. $2\frac{1}{2}$ batches

9. 6 costumes

10. $276.36

Reteach

1. divide; 7 tickets

2. multiply; $36.00

3. divide; 10.97 ft

4. divide; 3

Reading Strategies

1. pumpkin's weight of 31.3 lb and that there are 3 parts; weight of 1 part; divide; 10.43 lb

2. pumpkin's weight of $22\frac{2}{3}$ lb; $\frac{1}{6}$ of weight; multiply; $3\frac{7}{9}$ lb

3. pumpkin's weight of $42\frac{1}{3}$ lb and that each piece will be $2\frac{1}{2}$ lb; number of pieces; divide; 16 pieces

Success for English Learners

1. You place the decimal point right above the decimal point in the number that is being divided.

2. Multiply the answer by 3, and see if it equals $11.61.

MODULE 5 Challenge

1. Multiply the price of each ingredient by the quantity given, then add.

   Beef: $10.65 × 3.25 = $34.61;

   Onion: $2.49 × 0.65 = $1.62;

   Potatoes: $3.29 × 0.2 = $0.66;

   Tomatoes: $8.45 × 0.15 = $1.27;

   Asparagus: $4.99 × 0.33 = $1.65;

   Total cost: $34.61 + $1.62 + $0.66 + $1.27 + $1.65 = $39.81.

2. Subtract the price of beef from the original total: $39.81 − $34.61 = $5.20

   Add the price of the chickpeas and lentils. Multiply the price of each ingredient by the quantity given, then add.

   Chickpeas: $2.49 × 2.5 = $6.23; Lentils: $3.59 × 1.75 = $6.28

   The new total price is $5.20 + $6.23 + $6.28 = $17.71

   Divya saves $39.81 − $17.71 = $22.10 by making the vegetarian version of her meal.

3. $3.49 + 2 × $4.99 + 6 × $0.75 = $17.97. She will spend $17.97 on dessert.

UNIT 3: Proportionality: Ratios and Rates

MODULE 6 Representing Ratios and Rates

LESSON 6-1

Practice and Problem Solving: A/B

1. 9 to 12; 9:12; $\frac{9}{12}$

2. 8 to 16; 8:16; $\frac{8}{16}$

3. 9 to 10; 9:10; $\frac{9}{10}$

4. 10 to 12; 10:12; $\frac{10}{12}$

5. 12 to 9; 12:9; $\frac{12}{9}$

6. Answers may vary. Sample answers: $\frac{8}{6}, \frac{16}{12}, \frac{32}{24}$

7. Answers may vary. Sample answers: $\frac{6}{7}, \frac{18}{21}, \frac{24}{28}$

8. Answers may vary. Sample answers: $\frac{2}{3}, \frac{8}{12}, \frac{12}{18}$

9. Answers may vary. Sample answers: 6 to 8, 9 to 12, 12 to 16

10. Answers may vary. Sample answers: $\frac{10}{14}, \frac{15}{21}, \frac{20}{28}$

11. Answers may vary. Sample answers: $\frac{18}{4}, \frac{27}{6}, \frac{36}{8}$

12. a. 48

    b. 36

Practice and Problem Solving: C

Answers will vary. Check students' work.

Practice and Problem Solving: D

1. 1 circle patch to 3 square patches; 1 to 3

2. 3; 3

3. 3; 12

4. 5 to 1; 5:1; $\frac{5}{1}$

5. 1 to 4; 1:4; $\frac{1}{4}$

6. 4 to 5; 4:5; $\frac{4}{5}$

7. Answers may vary. Sample answers: $\frac{4}{6}, \frac{6}{9}, \frac{8}{12}$

8. Answers may vary. Sample answers: $\frac{6}{8}, \frac{9}{12}, \frac{12}{16}$

9. Answers may vary. Sample answers: $\frac{2}{12}, \frac{3}{18}, \frac{4}{24}$

Reteach

1. 31 to 365

2. 3 to 4

3. Sample answer: 2:3, 4:6. 6:9

4. Sample answer: 4:5, 8:10, 12:15

5. Sample answer: 10:12, 15:18, 20:24

6. Sample answer: 5:7, 15:21, 20:28

Reading Strategies

1. $\frac{3}{4}$; 3 to 4; 3:4

2. 4:9; 4 to 9; $\frac{4}{9}$

3. triangles to squares

4. 5:4

Success for English Learners

1. 15; multiply

2. Sample answer: Multiply $\frac{5}{2}$ by $\frac{3}{3}$ or any representation of 1.

LESSON 6-2

Practice and Problem Solving: A/B

1. 45 mph

2. 95 calories per apple

3. $0.46 per oz

4. a. $0.25 per oz

   b. $0.19 per oz

5. quart

6. Both are the same unit rate.

7. a. $0.19 per oz

   b. $0.16 per oz

   c. the 36-oz box

8. a. 7.5 pages per h

   b. $2.67 per page

Practice and Problem Solving: C

1. 45 mph; 52.9 mph; Ali

2. 95 calories per apple; 62 calories per apple; Oranges

3. a. $0.77 per oz

   b. $0.62 per oz

   c. $0.27 per oz

4. An ounce of paint from a quart costs about twice as much as an ounce from a gallon.

5. 4 times larger

6. a. $5.53 per in.

   b. $7.51 per in.

Practice and Problem Solving: D

1. 25 mi per day

2. 4 emails per min

3. $0.04 per oz

4. a. $0.40

   b. $0.25

5. economy

6. economy

7. a. $0.50 per oz

   b. $1.00 per oz

8. a. $200 per day

   b. $75.00 per room

   c. 16 rooms

Reteach

1. $315 \div 15 = 21$ peanuts a minute

2. $81 \div 9 = 9$ texts per minute

3. $56 \div 2 = 28$ pages per hour

4. 6 oz: $0.90 \div 6 = \$0.15$, 10 oz: $1.10 \div 10 = \$0.11$; 16 oz: $1.44 \div 16 = \$0.09$; The 16-oz can is the best buy.

5. $2.24 \div 16 = \$0.14$; $3.60 \div 20 = \$0.18$; $2.56 \div 16 = \$0.16$; whole wheat

Reading Strategies

1. $1.25 per lb

2. $1.05 per lb

3. small

4. extra large

5. It has the lowest unit price.

6. Flora

7. Dan

8. Flora

Success for English Learners

1. Divide 300 by 5.2 to find the unit rate.

2. No, sometimes the unit price of a smaller size is less.

3. No, sometimes you might not need that much or it might get stale before you can finish it.

4. Sample answer: Bags of apples in three different sizes are on sale at the store. The large 10-lb bag costs $15, the medium 5-lb bag costs $10, and the small 2-lb bag costs $4.50. Which is the best buy? (The large 10-lb bag has the lowest unit price at $1.50 per pound.)

LESSON 6-3

Practice and Problem Solving: A/B

1.

sugar	3	6	12	18	30
milk	2	4	8	12	20

2. Eve's

3. No, the ratios are not the same. 5 to 7 is not equivalent to 15 to 17.

4. $22.50

5. 110 mi

6. a. $\frac{2}{20}$ or $\frac{1}{10}$

   b. $\frac{3}{25}$

   c. Cafe A: 5; Cafe B: 6

Practice and Problem Solving: C

1.

water molecule	2	5	10	20
hydrogen atoms	4	10	20	40
oxygen atoms	2	5	10	20

2. The numbers of atoms of hydrogen and oxygen would be equal.

3. 15H, 5N

4. 5 students, 2 adults

5. 72 mi

6. My Sky

7. Appliance Store; $2.50 per lamp

Practice and Problem Solving: D

1.

club soda	2	4	8	10	20
juice	5	10	20	25	50

2. Erin

3. No, the rates are not the same. 22 to 15 is not equivalent to 5 to 10.

4. $42

5. 28 mi

6. The first sports store sells at the better bargain.

7. Perfect Poultry

Reteach

1. $\frac{2}{3}, \frac{4}{6}, \frac{6}{9}, \boxed{\frac{8}{12}}, \frac{10}{15} ...; \frac{3}{4}, \frac{6}{8}, \boxed{\frac{9}{12}} ...;$
   $\frac{8}{12}, < \frac{9}{12}$

2. $\frac{4}{5}, \frac{8}{10}, \frac{12}{15}, \frac{16}{20}, \frac{20}{25}, \boxed{\frac{28}{35}} ...; \frac{3}{7}, \frac{6}{14}, \frac{9}{21},$
   $\frac{12}{28}, \boxed{\frac{15}{35}} ...; \frac{28}{35}, > \frac{15}{35}$

3. Jack: $\frac{3}{5}, \frac{6}{10}, \frac{9}{15}, \frac{12}{20}, \frac{15}{25}, \boxed{\frac{18}{30}} ...;$

   Evan: $\frac{4}{6}, \frac{8}{12}, \frac{12}{18}, \frac{16}{24}, \boxed{\frac{20}{30}} ...; \frac{20}{30} > \frac{18}{30};$
   Evan's oatmeal is thicker (has more oats).

Reading Strategies

1. Veggie

2. Greens

3. Greens

4. No, it could come from Greens Salad Bar and you have 15 cups of greens or from Veggie Salad Bar and you have only $6\frac{2}{3}$ cups of greens.

5. a. 30 cups

   b. $13\frac{1}{3}$ cups

Success for English Learners

1. 18 sit ups

2. 10 sit ups

3. 9 sit ups

4. Sample answer: table because it is easier to draw; number line because you can see the relationship better.

MODULE 6 Challenge

1. Arabella: $\dfrac{7,229 \text{ ft}}{561 \text{ s}} \cdot \dfrac{1 \text{ mi}}{5,280 \text{ ft}} \cdot \dfrac{3,600 \text{ s}}{1 \text{ h}}$

   = 8.786 mph

   Bettina: first convert 13 min, 12 s to

   $13 \times 60 + 12 = 792$ s

   $\dfrac{3,425 \text{ yd}}{792 \text{ s}} \cdot \dfrac{1 \text{ mi}}{1,760 \text{ yd}} \cdot \dfrac{3,600 \text{ s}}{1 \text{ h}} = 8.846$ mph

   Chandra: $\dfrac{8,214 \text{ ft}}{0.195 \text{ h}} \cdot \dfrac{1 \text{ mi}}{5,280 \text{ ft}} = 7.978$ mph

   Divya: $\dfrac{1.62 \text{ mi}}{732 \text{ s}} \cdot \dfrac{3,600 \text{ s}}{1 \text{ h}} = 7.967$ mph

2. Bettina ran the fastest. Divya ran the slowest.

3. Answers will vary. Sample answer: It is helpful to convert to the same units so that the rates can be compared easily.

4. The first place finisher Bettina would finish in $\dfrac{3.1}{8.846} = 0.3504$ h, or $0.3504 \times 60 = 21.026$ min.

   The last place finisher Divya would finish in $\dfrac{3.1}{7.967} = 0.3891$ h, or $0.3891 \times 60 = 23.346$ min.

   $23.346 - 21.026 = 2.32$ minutes will elapse.

MODULE 7 Applying Ratios and Rates

LESSON 7-1

Practice and Problem Solving: A/B

1. $\dfrac{\text{ounces of water}}{\text{packets of flavoring}} =$

   $\dfrac{24 \text{ oz}}{2 \text{ packets}} = \dfrac{12 \text{ oz}}{1 \text{ packet}} =$

   12 oz of water per packet

2.

Packets of Flavoring	2	5	7	10	12
Ounces of Water	24	60	84	120	144

3.

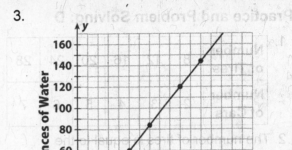
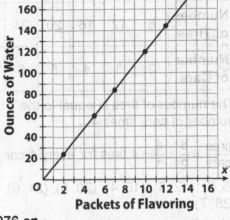

4. 276 oz

5. Yes. You can add nine and a half packets of flavoring to 114 oz of water.

6. $\dfrac{24}{2} = \dfrac{36}{3} = \dfrac{66}{5.5} = \dfrac{108}{9} = \dfrac{180}{15}$

7. It is a multiplicative relationship because the number of packets is multiplied by 12 oz. The line of the graph begins at the origin and is steep.

Practice and Problem Solving: C

1. Sample answer:

A	2	5	7	8	10
B	6	15	21	24	30

2. $\dfrac{A}{B} = \dfrac{2}{6} = \dfrac{1}{3}$. For each 1 A, there will be 3 Bs.

3. Sample answer: An amusement park provides seating on rides in the ratio of 6 children's seats for every 2 adult seats.

4. Sample answer: Multiplication; Each adult seat is multiplied by 3 to find the number of children's seats.

5. Sample answer: No, because it is unlikely an amusement park would have half a child's seat or half an adult seat.

Practice and Problem Solving: D

1.

Number of Tires	8	12	16	20	24	28
Number of Cars	2	3	4	5	6	7

2. The number of tires is equal to the number of cars times 4.

3. $\dfrac{\text{tires}}{\text{cars}} = \dfrac{8}{2} = \dfrac{4}{1} = 4$ tires for every 1 car

4. (8, 2), (12, 3), (16, 4), (20, 5), (24, 6), (28, 7)

5.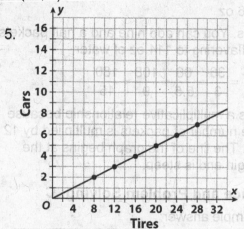

6. $\dfrac{8}{2} = \dfrac{12}{3} = \dfrac{16}{4} = \dfrac{20}{5} = \dfrac{40}{10}$

Reteach

1.

A	6	9	12	15	18	21	24
B	2	3	4	5	6	7	8

2. Sample answer: $\dfrac{6}{2} = \dfrac{3}{1}$, $\dfrac{9}{3} = \dfrac{3}{1}$, $\dfrac{18}{6} = \dfrac{3}{1}$, $\dfrac{24}{8} = \dfrac{3}{1}$

3. $\dfrac{3}{1}$; $\dfrac{69}{23}$

4. 189; $\dfrac{189}{63}$

Reading Strategies

1. Cost to pounds: ($4.50, 3), ($7.50, 5), ($10.50, 7), ($13.50, 9), ($16.50, 11)

   Pounds to cost: (3, $4.50), (5, $7.50), (7, $10.50), (9, $13.50), (11, $16.50)

2. 1 to $1.50; $1.50

3. Flour to baking soda: (6, 3), (8, 4), (10, 5), (12, 6), (18, 9), (24, 12)

   Baking soda to flour: (3, 6), (4, 8), (5, 10), (6, 12), (9, 18), (12, 24)

4. 1 tsp of baking soda to 2 c of flour

Success for English Learners

1. The cost would be on the top of the ratio and the ounces would be on the bottom of the ratio.

2. The ounces would be on the y-axis and the cost would be on the x-axis. The line would be steeper.

3. Sample answer:

Gas (gal)	4	5	6	7	8
Miles	128	160	192	224	256

Ordered pairs: (4, 128), (5, 160), (6, 192), (7, 224), (8, 256)

LESSON 7-2

Practice and Problem Solving: A/B

1. 16
2. 15
3. 9
4. 60
5. 9 in.
6. 12 cm
7. 16
8. $3.08
9. a. 10 mi
   b. 6 in.
   c. 3 in.
10. 1.5 in.

Practice and Problem Solving: C

1. 5
2. 50
3. 28.8
4. 5.7
5. 9 in.
6. 12 in.
7. $6.71

8 a. 0.67 mi/min

   b. Sinead

   c. 362.5 mi; $40 \times 2.5 = 100$.
      $100 + 150 + 112.5 = 362.5$

9. 2.25 cm

Practice and Problem Solving: D

1. 8

2. 8

3. 20

4. 33

5. $\frac{8}{11} = \frac{x}{33}$, $x = 24$; The width should be 24 in.

6. 7.5 cm

7. 200 mi

8. $16.00

9. a. 9 mi.

   b. 5 in.

   c. 1 in. = 1.5 mi

10. 1.3 in.

Reteach

1. $3.06

2. $4.47

3. 6 in.

Reading Strategies

1. a. $0.35

   b. $0.33

   c. $0.30

2. $1.98

3. $2.40

4. $1.20

5. a. $22.60

   b. $113.00

6. a. 9.33 mph

   b. 18.67 mi

7. Jeff

Success for English Learners

1. Yes, $\frac{24}{3} = \frac{8}{1}$. 8 ft^2 per hour is the unit
   rate. 8 (unit rate) $\times$ 9 h = 72 ft^2 per 9 h.

2. No, not a proportion; $\frac{4.50}{18} \neq \frac{9.00}{30}$; $2 x$
   $4.50 = 9.00$, but $2 \times 18 \neq 30$

LESSON 7-3

Practice and Problem Solving: A/B

1. 48 in.

2. $1\frac{1}{2}$ gal

3. 5,000 m

4. 2 kg

5. 20 c; $\frac{4 \text{ cups}}{1 \text{ quart}}$

6. 6 m; $\frac{1 m}{100 \text{ cm}}$

7. 5,280 ft

8. 700 m

9.

Dowel	in.	ft	yd
A	36	3	1
B	66	$5\frac{1}{2}$	$1\frac{5}{6}$
C	90	$7\frac{1}{2}$	$2\frac{1}{2}$

10. a. 44 in.; $3\frac{2}{3}$ ft

    b. $25\frac{1}{2}$ in.; $2\frac{1}{8}$ ft

11. Multiply 3×36 and 2×12 and add the
    products.

Practice and Problem Solving: C

1. 54 in.

2. 0.375 ft

3. 5.43 m

4. 5,100 m; 510,000 cm

5. 26 c

6. 390 cm

7. 5,280 ft; 1,760 yd

8. 7.36 m

9.

Chain	yd	ft	in.
gold	$3\frac{1}{2}$	$10\frac{1}{2}$	126
silver	$4\frac{1}{6}$	12.5	150
bronze	$4\frac{1}{9}$	$12\frac{1}{3}$	148

10. a. 50 cm by 50 cm

    b. 2,500 cm²

    c. No, a square meter is 100 cm × 100 cm = 10,000 cm².

Practice and Problem Solving: D

1. 4 ft
2. 8 qt
3. 3 km
4. 1.5 kg
5. 28 c; 4 cups
6. 5 m; $\frac{1}{100}$ m
7. 15,840 ft
8. 900 m

9.

Trim	in.	ft.	yd.
A	24	2	$\frac{2}{3}$
B	216	18	6

10. a. Use the board to see how many inches long the rug is. Divide the number of inches by 12 to find feet.

    b. 36 in.; 3 ft

11. Multiply 4 × 100 and add 20.

Reteach

1.

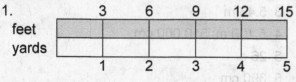

feet		3	6	9	12	15
yards		1	2	3	4	5

2.

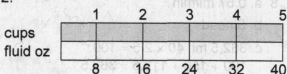

cups		1	2	3	4	5
fluid oz		8	16	24	32	40

3. Sample answers: No, doubling, tripling, quadrupling 5,280 is difficult. Yes, you would double, triple, quadruple 5,280.

Reading Strategies

1. a. 12

    b. $\frac{1}{12}$

2. a. multiply by 12

    b. divide by 12

3. You could show 1 meter and 100 centimeters, 2 meters and 200 centimeters, 3 meters and 300 centimeters and so on.

4. Sample answer:

customary

yd	1	2	3	4
ft	3	6	9	12

Relationship: 1 yd to 3 ft

metric

kg	1	2	3
g	1,000	2,000	3,000

Relationship: 1 kg to 1,000 g

Success for English Learners

1. 198 in.
2. 12.5 yd

LESSON 7-4

Practice and Problem Solving: A/B

1. 36.56 m
2. 148 mL
3. 23.608 kg
4. 4.348 mi
5. 3.958 gal
6. 6.1006 kg
7. 48 ft²
8. 1.1944 L

Practice and Problem Solving: C

1. mile: kick, furlong, cabel

   yard: furlong, cabel, perch, bamboo, cubit

   foot: pes, cubit, span, bamboo

   inch: pes, span

   Sample answer: I chose the units that are close in size to the given unit.

2. a. 1.5

   b. 16.5

   c. 3,280.84

   d. 720

   e. $\frac{1}{10.499}$

   f. $\frac{1}{660}$

   g. $\frac{1}{0.973}$

   h. $\frac{1}{0.75}$

3. 19.636 perches

4. 1.757 bamboos

Practice and Problem Solving: D

1. 2.54; 17.78
2. 0.454; 0.908
3. 29.6; 177.6
4. 3.79; 18.95
5. 0.914; 18.28
6. 28.4; 426
7. $\frac{1}{28.4}$; 3.52
8. $\frac{1}{0.946}$; 21.14
9. $\frac{1}{1.61}$; 2.48
10. $\frac{1}{0.454}$; 13.22
11. $\frac{1}{2.54}$; 19.69
12. $\frac{1}{29.6}$; 2.74
13. 4.2044 m

Reteach

1. 0.305
2. 0.946
3. 0.454
4. 3.79
5. 8.226
6. 113.6
7. 355.2
8. 4.83
9. 10.896
10. 26.53

Reading Strategies

1. 0.454
2. 0.946
3. 7.312
4. 7.58
5. 2.724
6. 3.965
7. 1.0656
8. 4.83

Success for English Learners

1. 1.61; 8.05
2. 3.79; 15.16
3. 28.4; 908.8
4. $\frac{1}{0.914}$; 16.41
5. $\frac{1}{0.454}$; 19.82
6. $\frac{1}{0.946}$; 8.46

MODULE 7 Challenge

1. There are 6 cars in the first section, 12 cars in the second section and 18 cars in the third section.

2. Answers will vary. Sample answer: One way is to move 6 cars from the third section to the first section. Then there will be 12 cars in each section and the ratio will be 1 : 1 : 1.

3. No. To have the ratio of 1 : 2 : 3 the total number of cars must be a multiple of 6. 80 is not a multiple of 6.

4. If 18 cars are added to the third section there would be 6 cars in the first section, 12 cars in the second section and 36 cars in the third section. The new ratio would be 1 : 2 : 6.

MODULE 8 Percents

LESSON 8-1

Practice and Problem Solving: A/B

1. $\frac{3}{10}$; 0.3

2. $\frac{21}{50}$; 0.42

3. $\frac{9}{50}$; 0.18

4. $\frac{7}{20}$; 0.35

5. $\frac{1}{1}$ or 1

6. $\frac{29}{100}$; 0.29

7. $\frac{14}{25}$; 0.56

8. $\frac{2}{3}$; 0.67

9. $\frac{1}{4}$; 0.25

10. 3%
11. 92%
12. 18%
13. 40%
14. 92%
15. 70%
16. 40%
17. 64 students

18. black: 20%; $\frac{1}{5}$; 0.2

navy: 25%; $\frac{1}{4}$; 0.25

brown: 35%; $\frac{7}{20}$; 0.35

other: 20%; $\frac{1}{5}$; 0.2

Practice and Problem Solving: C

1. $\frac{9}{200}$; 0.045

2. $1\frac{19}{100}$; 1.19

3. $\frac{2}{1}$; 2

4. $\frac{7}{1,000}$, 0.007

5. $3\frac{7}{100}$; 3.07

6. $\frac{11}{200}$; 0.055

7. 7.143%
8. 0.75%
9. 0.54%

10. Use more than one grid. For 217% you would use 3 grids, shading in 2 completely and shading 17 squares on the third.

11. Divide a small square on the grid into tenths and shade 7 of them.

12. blue: 30%; $\frac{3}{10}$; 0.3

green: 25%; $\frac{1}{4}$; 0.25

red: 15%; $\frac{3}{20}$; 0.15

white: 30%; $\frac{3}{10}$; 0.3

13. 1 h

14. Add the values 25 + 10 + 10 + 3 = 48, 48% of a dollar.

Practice and Problem Solving: D

1.

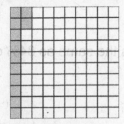

2.

3. $50\% = \dfrac{50}{100} = \dfrac{1}{2}$; 50 hundredths = 0.50

4. $\dfrac{1}{100}$; 0.01

5. $\dfrac{11}{100}$; 0.11

6. $\dfrac{1}{10}$; 0.1

7. $\dfrac{99}{100}$; 0.99

8. $\dfrac{17}{100}$; 0.17

9. $\dfrac{73}{100}$; 0.73

10. $\dfrac{47}{100}$; 0.47

11. $\dfrac{23}{200}$; 0.115

12. $\dfrac{1}{10} = \dfrac{10}{100} = 10\%$

13. 60%
14. 2%
15. 50%
16. 70%
17. 97%
18. 10%

Reteach

1. $\dfrac{43}{100}$

2. $\dfrac{18}{25}$

3. $\dfrac{22}{25}$

4. $\dfrac{7}{20}$

5. 0.64
6. 0.92
7. 0.73
8. 0.33

Reading Strategies

1. 20 to 100
2. 20%
3. 80 to 100
4. 80%

Success for English Learners

1. 0.37; $\dfrac{37}{100}$

   0.06; $\dfrac{6}{100}$ or $\dfrac{3}{50}$

2. Answers will vary, but should reflect that it depends on the situation and numbers and operations involved.

LESSON 8-2

Practice and Problem Solving: A/B

1. 14
2. 11
3. 7.5
4. 162
5. 60
6. 198
7. 7
8. 570
9. 495
10. 70
11. 96
12. 18

13. 13.6

14. 23.1

15. 0.77

16. 475

17. more than 1.8 billion

18. Asia

19. about 1.2 billion

20. about 1.2 billion

21. about 0.3 in.

Practice and Problem Solving: C

1. less than; 25% is equivalent to $\frac{25}{100}$ or $\frac{1}{4}$, a fraction less than 1. A number multiplied by a fraction less than 1 gives a product less than the original number.

2. greater than; 220% is equivalent to $\frac{220}{100}$ or $2\frac{1}{5}$, a mixed number greater than 1. Multiplying a number by a mixed number gives a product greater than the original number.

3. a. $27.36; b. $26.60; c. In a., you find 80% of the original price and then find 90% of the new price so you are finding 72% of the original price. In b., you are finding 70% of the original price.

4. 6,932,164

5. a. 11%; $550

   b. $600

Practice and Problem Solving: D

1. 15

2. $\frac{1}{4}$; 16

3. 3

4. 8

5. 128

6. 6

7. 435

8. 70

9. 125

10. $36

11. 19.24 cm

12. $24.08

13. $15.12

14. $15.12

15. A discount of 16% is the same as 84% of the original price.

Reteach

1. 41%

2. 23%

3. 37.5%

4. First divided 100 by 8 to get 12.5. Then multiplied 3 and 8 by 12.5 to get
$$\frac{3 \times 12.5}{8 \times 12.5} = \frac{37.5}{100}$$

5. Accept all reasonable answers. A good answer might include looking at numbers involved and then choosing which to use.

Reading Strategies

1. 0.35

2. Remove the percent sign. Move the decimal point two places to the left.

3. Multiply the decimal times the number.

4. 0.10

5. 6

6. 12

7. 18

8. 24

9. The answers are multiples of 6.

10. Since 30% is three times as great as 10%, I could multiply 25 by 3 to get 75.

Success for English Learners

1. 12.6

2. 75% is 75 hundredths or $\frac{75}{100}$

3. You can find the percent of a number by using a proportion as in Problem 1 or by changing the percent to a decimal and multiplying as in Problem 2.

LESSON 8-3

Practice and Problem Solving: A/B

1. 40

2. 60

3. $1.35

4. 6

5. 9 text messages

6. 300 people

7. 6.5%

8. 600 people

9. 4,200 people

10. 149 people

11. Yes, Sahil is correct; Possible answer: He knew that 30% is 3 times 10%, so he just multiplied 45 by 3.

Practice and Problem Solving: C

1. $255

2. $62.53

3. 15 red tiles

4. $32.07

5. 50 min

6. 30 min

7. 200 min or 3 h 20 min

8. Check student's work.

Practice and Problem Solving: D

1. 1.8 billion

2. 59%; Asia, 59%

3. 15 mg

4. 1,225 students; 588 boys

5. $35.10

Reteach

1. a. 14

   b. 25

   c. x

   d. $\dfrac{x}{100} = \dfrac{14}{25}$; $25x = 1,400$; $x = 56$

      Answer: 56% of 25 is 14.

2. a. 16

   b. x

   c. 80

   d. $\dfrac{16}{x} = \dfrac{80}{100}$; $80x = 1,600$; $x = 20$;

      Answer: 80% of 20 is 16.

3. 55%

4. 40

5. 300%

6. 140

Reading Strategies

1. •

2. =

3. n

4. $5 = 25\% \cdot n$

5. $40 = n \cdot 160$

Success for English Learners

1. $191.56

2. $1,440

3. $51.84

MODULE 8 Challenge

1. 20% of 30% of 400 is $0.2 \times 0.3 \times 400 = 24$.

   24 is $\dfrac{24}{45} = 53\dfrac{1}{3}\%$ of 45.

2. Kevin completed $0.4(120) + 0.3(170) + 0.1(90) = 108$ pages

   Dashawn completed $0.5(120) + 0.2(170) + 0.3(90) = 121$ pages

3. Whole milk has $8 \times 9 = 72$ fat calories and 150 total calories. $\dfrac{72}{150} = 48\%$ of the calories are from fat.

   An egg has $6 \times 9 = 54$ fat calories and 80 total calories. $\dfrac{54}{80} = 67.5\%$ of the calories are from fat.

   A hamburger has $15 \times 9 = 135$ fat calories and 220 total calories. $\dfrac{135}{220} = 61.4\%$ of the calories are from fat.

   A slice of pizza has $3 \times 9 = 27$ fat calories and 160 total calories $\dfrac{27}{160} = 16.875\%$ of the calories are from fat.

4. 40% of 300 is $0.4(300) = 120$. The maximum number fat calories is 120. Since there are 9 calories per fat gram, the maximum grams of fat is $\dfrac{120}{9} = 13.3$ g.

UNIT 4: Equivalent Expressions

MODULE 9 Generating Equivalent Numerical Expressions

LESSON 9-1

Practice and Problem Solving: A/B

1. 2^4; 16

2. $(3)^3$; 27

3. $\left(\dfrac{3}{5}\right)^2$; $\dfrac{9}{25}$

4. $(10)^2$; 100

5. $\left(\dfrac{1}{6}\right)^4$; $\dfrac{1}{1,296}$

6. $(0.5)^3$; 0.125

7. 1.728

8. $\dfrac{1}{256}$

9. 64

10. −64

11. 1,000,000 cubic millimeters; 100 or 10^2 millimeters

12. $\left(\dfrac{3}{5}\right)^3$; $\dfrac{3}{5}$ volt

13. <

14. =

15. >

16. $81 = 9^2 = 3^4 = 81^1$

Practice and Problem Solving: C

1. $3^5 = (3)^5 = 243$

2. $\left(\dfrac{2}{3}\right)^3 = \dfrac{8}{27}$; $\left(\dfrac{2}{3}\right)^1 = \dfrac{2}{3} = \dfrac{18}{27}$; $\dfrac{8}{27} < \dfrac{18}{27}$

3. $(0.72)^7 > (-7.2)^7$ because $(0.72)^7 > 0$ and $(-7.2)^7 < 0$.

4. a. 4^3 lamps

   b. 4 lamps high, 4 lamps deep, and 4 lamps wide

   c. 2^3 lamps

   d. $4^3 \div 2^3 = 8$

5. $\left(\dfrac{2}{3}\right)^4 = \dfrac{64}{81}$; $\left(\dfrac{3}{2}\right)^4 = \dfrac{81}{64}$; $\left(\dfrac{2}{3}\right)^4 \times \left(\dfrac{3}{2}\right)^4 =$
   $\dfrac{64}{81} \times \dfrac{81}{64} = 1$

6. $(0.5)^3 = 0.125$; $(2)^3 = 8$;
   $(0.5)^3 \times (2)^3 = 0.125 \times (8) = 1$

7. $\left(\dfrac{5}{7}\right)^2$

8. $(0.25)^3$ or $\left(\dfrac{1}{4}\right)^3$

9. $\left(\dfrac{10}{3}\right)^6$

Practice and Problem Solving: D

1. 2, 7

2. $\dfrac{5}{6}$, 4

3. 5, 10

4. 10; 10; 10; 10; 10^4

5. $\dfrac{2}{3}$; $\dfrac{2}{3}$; $\dfrac{2}{3}$; $\left(\dfrac{2}{3}\right)^3$

6. 4; 4; 4; $(4)^3$

7. $(2) \times (2)$

8. $0.25 \times 0.25 \times 0.25$

9. $\dfrac{1}{9} \times \dfrac{1}{9} \times \dfrac{1}{9}$

10. 10^3

11. $3^3 = 27$ baseball cards; $4^3 = 64$ football cards

12. 4,096 mi

Reteach

1. $\left(\dfrac{1}{20}\right)^4$

2. 8^2

3. $(7.5)^3$

4. $(0.4)^1$

5. $\dfrac{1}{8}$

6. 2.48832

7. 729

8. $\frac{16}{9}$

Reading Strategies

1. Two to the fifth power

2. Two is a factor five times:

$(2) \times (2) \times (2) \times (2) \times (2)$

3. $(2)^5 = 32$

4. Three fifths to the fourth power

5. $\frac{3}{5} \times \frac{3}{5} \times \frac{3}{5} \times \frac{3}{5}$

6. No; $\left(\frac{3}{5}\right)^4 = \frac{81}{625}$, but 4 times $\frac{3}{5}$ is $\frac{12}{5}$ or $\frac{1{,}500}{625}$

Success for English Learners

1. 2

2. 7

3. Four to the third power

4. Two to the seventh power

5. a. 7^3

   b. 3

   c. 7

6. a. 5^6

   b. 5

   c. 6

LESSON 9-2

Practice and Problem Solving: A/B

1. Answers may vary. Sample answers:

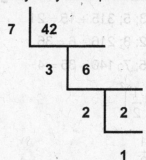

$36 = 3^2 \times 2^2$

2. Answers may vary. Sample answers:

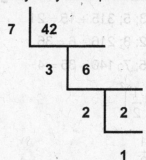

$42 = 7 \bullet 3 \bullet 2$

3. Answers may vary. Sample answers:

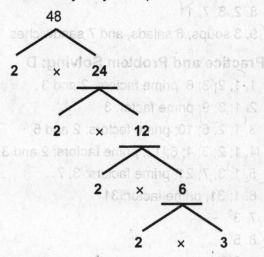

$48 = 2^4 \times 3$

4. Answers may vary. Sample answers:

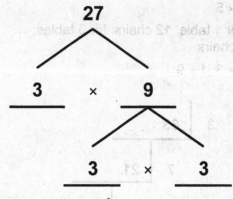

$27 = 3 \bullet 3 \bullet 3 = 3^3$

5. $2^2 \times 11$

6. 5^3

7. 5×17

8. 3×13

Practice and Problem Solving: C

1. 21; 15; 3; 5; $315 \div 15 = 21$
2. 18; 12; 2; 3; $216 \div 6 = 36$
3. 10; 14; 5; 7; $140 \div 35 = 4$
4. $\left(\dfrac{1}{5}\right)^2 \times \left(\dfrac{1}{2}\right)^2$
5. $\left(\dfrac{1}{2}\right)^3 \times \dfrac{1}{3}$
6. 2, 3
7. 3, 5, 7
8. 2, 3, 7, 11
9. 3 soups, 6 salads, and 7 sandwiches

Practice and Problem Solving: D

1. 1; 2; 3; 6; prime factors: 2 and 3
2. 1; 3; 9; prime factor: 3
3. 1; 2; 5; 10; prime factors: 2 and 5
4. 1; 2; 3; 4; 6; 12; prime factors: 2 and 3
5. 1; 3; 7; 21; prime factors: 3, 7
6. 1; 31; prime factor: 31
7. 3^2
8. 5^2
9. 2^3
10. 2×7
11. $2^2 \times 3$
12. 3×5
13. For 1 table, 12 chairs; for 3 tables, 4 chairs
14. 3×3; 1×9
15.

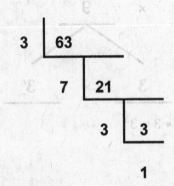

$63 = 3^2 \times 7$

Reteach

1. 1 • 28, 2 • 14, 4 • 7; 1, 2, 4, 7, 14, 28
2. 1 • 15, 3 • 5; 1, 3, 5, 15
3. 1 • 36, 2 • 18, 3 • 12, 4 • 9, 6 • 6; 1, 2, 3, 4, 6, 9, 18, 36
4. 1 • 29; 1, 29
5. $2^2 • 7$
6. $3^2 • 5$
7. $5^2 • 2$
8. $2^3 • 3^2$

Reading Strategies

1. $360 = 2^3 \times 3^2 \times 5$

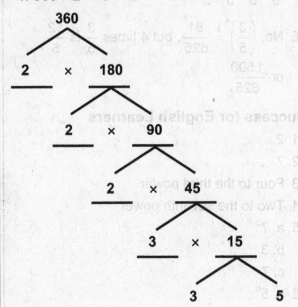

2. $378 = 2 \times 3^3 \times 7$

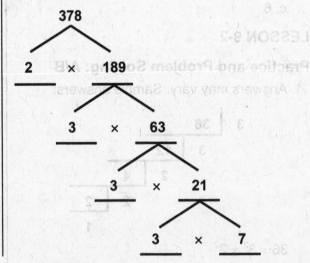

Success for English Learners

1. $24 = 3 \cdot 2 \cdot 2 \cdot 2$ or $3 \cdot 2^3$

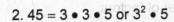

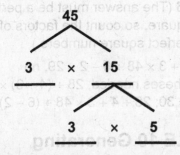

2. $45 = 3 \cdot 3 \cdot 5$ or $3^2 \cdot 5$

LESSON 9-3

Practice and Problem Solving: A/B

1. Multiplication
2. Division
3. Addition
4. Finding a power, exponent
5. Subtraction
6. Finding a power, exponent
7. G
8. F
9. H
10. A
11. C
12. E
13. D
14. B
15. $3 \times 4 + 0.95$
16. $(240 + 360) \div 100$

Practice and Problem Solving: C

1. Answers will vary. Sample answer: $-$, $+$
2. Answers will vary. Sample answer: $-$, $\times$
3. Answers will vary. Sample answer: $\times$, $-$
4. $\dfrac{5}{4}$
5. 5
6. $\dfrac{7}{6}$
7. Undefined
8. $\dfrac{2}{3}$
9. $\dfrac{1}{6}$
10. 8; 9
11. 15; 16
12. $x^2 + (x - 4)^2 = 80$; $2x^2 - 8x + 16 = 80$, or $x^2 - 4x - 32 = 0$. By trial and error, the legs are 4 and 8.
13. $b^2 + (2b)^2 = 100$; $5b^2 = 100$; $b^2 = 20$
14. $b^2 + (b - 5)^2 = 2b^2 - 10b + 25 = c^2$. Students might use numbers instead of b to come up with the general pattern.

Practice and Problem Solving: D

1. multiplication
2. division
3. exponent
4. addition
5. E
6. D
7. F
8. A
9. B
10. C
11. a. $2 \times 13 + 3$
    b. $29
12. Answers will vary. Sample answer: $(2 \times 4) + 8 = 16$
13. Answers will vary. Sample answer: $12 \div 2 - 3 = 3$

Reteach

1. 20; 140; 134

2. 46; 460; 463

3. 30; 40; 33

4. 14

5. 46

6. 97

7. 18

8. 5

9. 35

10. Answers will vary. Sample answer:
$3^2 + (4 \times 5) - 5^2 = 4$

Reading Strategies

1. $(9 \div 3) = 3$; $3^2 = 9$; $9 \times 5 = 45$; $45 + 4 = 49$; $49 - 1 = 48$

2. $(3 \times 2) = 6$; $5^2 = 25$; $8 \div 2 = 4$; $6 + 25 = 31$; $31 - 4 = 27$

3. 40

4. 7

Success for English Learners

1. Answers will vary. Sample answer: (1) In the problem shown, multiplication is done before addition. (2) In the problem, the prices of the types of beads are different, so the number of each bead has to be multiplied by its price.

2. Answers will vary. Sample answer: If the price of each bead is the same, you can then add the number of beads and then multiply by the price.

MODULE 9 Challenge

1.

Product	Number of Zeros in Product	Product as Powers
$100 \times 1{,}000$ $= 100{,}000$	5	$10^2 \times 10^3 = 10^5$
$10 \times 100{,}000$ $= 1{,}000{,}000$	6	$10^1 \times 10^5 = 10^6$
$1{,}000 \times 10$ $= 10{,}000$	4	$10^3 \times 10^1 = 10^4$

To find the product of two powers of 10, $10^a \times 10^b$, find the sum of the exponents,

$a + b$. The answer is a power of 10 with the sum as the exponent, 10^{a+b}.

2. The factors of the numbers are as follows:

9: 1, 3, 9 (3 factors)

16: 1, 2, 4, 8, 16 (5 factors)

25: 1, 5, 25 (3 factors)

6: 1, 2, 3, 6 (4 factors)

15: 1, 3, 5, 15 (4 factors)

20: 1, 2, 4, 5, 10, 20 (6 factors)

  a. The perfect square numbers have an odd number of factors while the non perfect square numbers have an even number of factors.

  b. 36 (The answer must be a perfect square, so count the factors of perfect square numbers.)

3. $28 \div 4 + 3 \times 48 \div 6 - 2 = 29$, no parentheses needed; $28 \div (4 + 3) \times 48 \div 6 - 2 = 30$; $28 \div 4 + 3 \times 48 \div (6 - 2) = 43$

MODULE 10 Generating Equivalent Algebraic Expressions

LESSON 10-1

Practice and Problem Solving: A/B

1. $9 + r$

2. $m \div 4$

3. $5n$

4. $25 \bullet 3$

5. $3 + n$

6. $r \div 8$

7. $7m$

8. $48 - 13$

9. $18 \div 3$

10. $t - 189$

11. $w + 253$

12. Sample answer: the sum of t and 23; 23 more than t

13. Sample answer: n less than 45; 45 minus n

14. Sample answer: $2y - 3$

Practice and Problem Solving: C

1. $2(100) + 60$

2. $t - 25 + 17$ or $t - 8$

3. $44 + 4p$

4. $3a + 4b + 5c$

5. $n + n + n + n$ or $4n$

6. $n \cdot n$ or n^2

7. Sample answer: $3a + 2b + 3c + 3$

8. Sample answer: Josef worked 24 hours on the day shift for d dollars per hour and 8 hours on the night shift for n dollars per hour.

Practice and Problem Solving: D

1. A
2. B
3. B
4. C
5. B
6. A
7. C
8. D
9. B
10. A
11. B
12. C
13. x represents the number of beads Nicole lost.
14. x represents the number of shirts Wilhelm bought.

Reteach

1. Sample answer: When finding the difference in two amounts, you subtract.
2. Since each state gets the same number of senators, you multiply the number of states by the number of senators.
3. $n + 3$
4. $c \div 8$

Reading Strategies

1. Sample answer: 8 less than t
2. Sample answer: n divided by 6
3. Sample answer: the product of 4 and w
4. Sample answer: 8 more than z
5. Sample answer: 9 times m
6. $p + 12$
7. $i - 7$
8. $r \div 3$

9. $z - 1$
10. $19y$

Success for English Learners

1. $m + 5$
2. $18 \div 2$
3. $t - 7$
4. $4r$
5. $x - 9$
6. $21 \div 7$

Sample answers are given for 7–12.

7. 2 less than a
8. the product of 8 and 6
9. p divided by 8
10. the sum of v and 10

LESSON 10-2

Practice and Problem Solving: A/B

1. 12
2. 15
3. 13
4. 54
5. 59
6. 13
7. 27
8. 90
9.

p	$2(13 - p)$
2	22
3	20
4	18

10.

v	w	$3v + w$
4	2	14
6	3	21
8	4	28

11.

x	y	$x^2 \div y$
2	1	4
6	2	18
8	4	16

12. $12.96

13. 345 mph

14. $55

Practice and Problem Solving: C

1.

r	$3.14 \cdot r^2$
2	12.56
3	28.26
4	50.24

2.

z	a	$2z - a$
−4	2	−10
0	2	−2
4	2	6

3.

x	y	$10x^2 \div (y + 1)$
2	1	20
−1	3	2.5
−4	4	32

4. No, with 120 gallons of water, her pickup weighs 6,278.2 pounds.

5. 4.5 mm^2

6. Grayson multiplied 4×3 before squaring 3.

7. Emily added 2 to 36 when she should have multiplied 2 and −2 and then added −4 to 36.

8. Pat substituted 2 for y instead of −2.

9. $4x^2 + 2y = 4(3)^2 + 2(−2)$

$\qquad = 36 + 2(−2)$

$\qquad = 36 + (−4)$

$\qquad = 32$

Practice and Problem Solving: D

1. $3 \times 2 + 4^2$

$\quad 3 \times 2 + 16$

$\quad 6 + 16$

$\quad 22$

2. $2 \times (5 + 3)$

$\quad 2 \times 8$

$\quad 16$

3. $8 + 8 \div 2 \times 4$

$\quad 8 + 4 \times 4$

$\quad 8 + 16$

$\quad 24$

4.

w	$6(3 + w)$
2	30
3	36
4	42

5.

c	$2c + 7$
4	15
6	19
8	23

6.

w	$w^2 - 3$
2	1
3	6
4	13

7. 60

Reteach

1. 10

2. 6; 2

3. 15; 10

4. 3; 9; 18

5. 5; 13

6. 42

7. 9

8. 7

9. 21

10. 0

Reading Strategies

1. $(5 + 14) − 3^2$;

$\quad (5 + 14) − 9$;

$\quad 19 − 9$;

There is no multiplication or division;

10

2. $10^2 - 2(3 \cdot 4 + 6)$;

   $100 - 2(12 + 6)$;

   $100 - 2 \cdot 18$;

   $100 - 36$;

   64

Success for English Learners

Problem 1: 20, 56; 36, 72

Problem 2: 10, 4, 14; 9, 6, 18, 12, 30

1.

r	$2(3 + r)$
2	10
3	12
4	14

2.

c	t	$2c + t$
4	2	10
6	3	15
8	4	20

3.

w	k	$w^2 - k$
2	1	3
5	2	23
8	3	61

LESSON 10-3

Practice and Problem Solving: A/B

1. Commutative Property
2. Associative Property
3. Distributive Property
4. Subtraction
5. $2r + n^2 + 7 - 2n$
6. $3w + 7$
7. $c^2 + 4c - 3$
8. $z^3 + z^2 + 5z - 3$
9. $6c + 4d - 6$
10. $20a - 2b - 1$
11. $40x$
12. $10x + 16y + 14$
13. Sample answer: sides of $2x + y$, $3x$, and $7x - y$, P = $12x$

Practice and Problem Solving: C

1. $8a + a^2 - 10$
2. $v - 6w$
3. $-2c^2 + 4c$
4. $z^3 + 8z^2 + 5z + 7$
5. $6c + 4d - 12$
6. $9a + 6b + 3c - 2$
7. $4x - 1.6$
8. $10x - 2y$
9. $6n + 4(2n) = 14n$
10. $1.5n + 1.25n + 2 = 2.75n + 2$

Practice and Problem Solving: D

1. $5a$ and $2a$; b and $2b$; 43 and 4
2. n, $5n$, and $2n$; $2m$ and $6m$
3. $2g$, $3g$, and g
4. $7x^2$ and $3x^2$; x and $3x$, 2 and 3
5. $r + 5n^2 + 7 - 2n$
6. $v + w + 10$
7. $6c^2 + c$
8. $4z + 3e + 5$
9. $6d + 4c$
10. $12a$
11. C
12. D

Reteach

1. 8
2. 3
3. 1
4. 14
5. $10x$
6. $2m$
7. $12y$
8. $11t$
9. $4b + 6$
10. $6a + 4$
11. $6n - 3c$
12. $10d + e$

Reading Strategies

1. 5
2. because the exponents are different
3. 6
4. $5a^2 + a^2 + 6b - 3b - 2 + 4c$
5. $6a^2 + 3b - 2 + 4c$

Success for English Learners

1. No, because the exponents are not the same.
2. No, because the variables are not the same.
3. Yes, $9a^3$
4. 1

MODULE 10 Challenge

1. equilateral triangle; 10.83 cm^2
2. square; 25 cm^2
3. regular pentagon; 43.01 cm^2
4. regular hexagon; 64.95 cm^2
5. regular octagon; 120.71 cm^2
6. regular decagon; 192.36 cm^2
7. tetrahedron; $s^2\sqrt{3}$
8. cube; $6s^2$
9. octahedron; $2s^2\sqrt{3}$
10. dodecahedron; $3s^2\sqrt{25 + 10\sqrt{5}}$
11. icosahedron; $5s^2\sqrt{3}$

UNIT 5: Equations and Inequalities

MODULE 11 Equations and Relationships

LESSON 11-1

Practice and Problem Solving: A/B

1. yes
2. no
3. no
4. no
5. yes
6. yes
7. yes
8. yes
9. B
10. D
11. Sample equation: $6x = 72$
12. Sample equation: $(6)(5) = (10)(3)(w)$
13. Sample equation: $x - 13°F = 35°F$; $x = 48°F$
14. Sample equation: $16x = \$20$; $x = \$1.25$
15. Sample problem: Twenty-four people were divided evenly into y teams. There were 3 people on each team. Determine whether there were 8 teams or 6 teams.

    Answer: There were 8 teams.

Practice and Problem Solving: C

1. A
2. C
3. D
4. B
5. Sample equation: $7(10 + x) = 112$
6. Sample equation: $y = 11 + \frac{1}{3}(15)$; $y = 16$;

   sea cow = 16
7. Sample equation: $22 = \frac{112}{4} - 6$
8. Sample equation: $4x = 80 + 40$; $x = 30$
9. Sample equation: $3x + 5 = 29$

Practice and Problem Solving: D

1. yes
2. no
3. no
4. yes
5. yes
6. yes
7. A
8. B
9. B
10. C
11. A
12. B
13. (1) $\underline{\$5} + (3)\underline{\$1} + $ Other bill $ = \underline{\$13}$;
    $\$5 + \$3 + x = \$13$; $x = \$5$; The other bill must be a \$5 bill.

Reteach

1. yes
2. no
3. no
4. yes
5. yes
6. no
7. yes
8. yes
9. no

Reading Strategies

1. yes
2. no
3. yes
4. yes
5. yes
6. no
7. no
8. Sample equation: $2 \cdot 13 = 15 + 11$
9. Sample answer: $2 \cdot 13 = 15 + y$; $y = 11$

Success for English Learners

1. Because when the variable in the equation is replaced with 61, it does not make a true statement.

2. Substitute 65 for *a* and check to see if the equation is true.

3. Sample answer: Andrea is given $82 to buy fruit for the class picnic. She spends some of the money on apples and $23 on bananas. Determine whether she spent $61 or $59 on apples.

LESSON 11-2

Practice and Problem Solving: A/B

1. $r = 4$

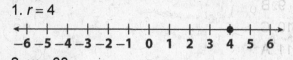

2. $w = 38$

3. $m = \dfrac{5}{8}$

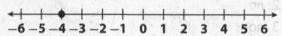

4. $t = -4$

5. $x + 139 = 180$

6. $x = 41°$

7. $x + 18 = 90$

8. $x = 72°$

9. $x = 5$; Sample answer. John has some CDs. If he buys 3 more CDs, he will have 8 CDs. How many CDs did he start with? John started with 5 CDs.

Practice and Problem Solving: C

1. 3.4

2. $\dfrac{7}{9}$

3. $5\dfrac{1}{2}$

4. 17.19

5. −4

6. −40

7. $x + 22 = 90$

8. $x = 68°$

9. Sample answer: $u - 22 = 13$; $u = 35$; Kayla's uncle is 35 years old.

10. Sample answer: $38.95 - 22.50 = g$; $g = 16.45$; Gavin will save $16.45.

11. Sample answer: $s - 10\dfrac{1}{2} = 37\dfrac{1}{2}$; $s = 48$; The board Sierra started with was 48 inches long.

12. $x = 7$; Sample answer: Andy ran 4.65 kilometers. Pam said that if she had run 2.35 fewer kilometers, she would have run as far as Andy. How far did Pam run? Answer: Pam ran 7 kilometers.

Practice and Problem Solving: D

1. $r = 6$

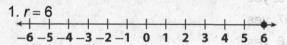

2. $w = -1$

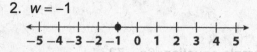

3. $m = 3$

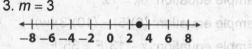

4. $t = 5$

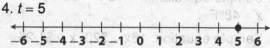

5. $x + 100 = 180$

6. $x = 80°$

7. $23 + n = 40$

8. 17

9. $x = 7$; Sample answer: Joan has some pencils. If she gives away 5 pencils, she will have 2 pencils left. How many pencils did Joan start with? She started with 7 pencils.

Reteach

1. 8

2. 9

3. 5

4. 9

5. 6

6. 8

Reading Strategies

1. Left

2. Add 21.

3. Add 21.

4. 53

5. Right.

6. Add 25.

7. Add 25.

8. 37

Success for English Learners

1. Because the surfer's height, h, plus 14 inches is equal to the height of the surfboard.

2. Substitute 57 for x in the original equation and see if that makes the equation true.

3. Sample answer: $x - 12 = 10$; Add 12 to both sides; $x = 22$.

LESSON 11-3

Practice and Problem Solving: A/B

1. $e = 6$

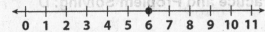

2. $w = 10$

3. $m = \dfrac{1}{4}$

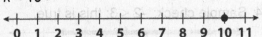

4. $k = 10$

5. Sample answer: $8x = 72$

6. $x = 9$; 9 m

7. $\dfrac{a}{3} = 9$; $a = 27$; 27 pictures

Practice and Problem Solving: C

1. 0.7

2. 27

3. $\dfrac{1}{2}$

4. 75

5. 20

6. $\dfrac{4}{3}$ or $1\dfrac{1}{3}$

7. $A = 144$ in.^{2}; $P = 4s$; $48 = 4s$, so $s = 12$. $A = s^2$, $A = 12^2 = 144$

8. 17 model SUVs; Sample equation: $5m = 85$, $m = 17$

9. 18 min; Sample equation: $\dfrac{n}{3} = 6$, $n = 18$

10. 3 h; Sample equation: $16.50b = 49.50$, $b = 3$

11. $n = 25$; Sample answer: Maria used 12.5 meters of material to make doll clothes for a charity project. Each piece of clothing used 0.5 meter of material. How many pieces of clothing did Maria make? She made 25 pieces of clothing.

Practice and Problem Solving: D

1. $m = 4$

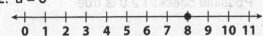

2. $a = 8$

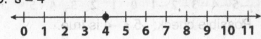

3. $s = 4$

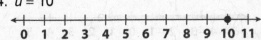

4. $u = 10$

5. Area—60 ft^2; length—12 ft

6. Sample answer: $60 = 12w$

7. 5

8. Jim's garden is 5 feet wide.

Reteach

1. $n = 3$; $3 \cdot 3 = 9\checkmark$

2. $n = 8$; $8 \div 2 = 4\checkmark$

Reading Strategies

1. Divide by 3; $\dfrac{3r}{3} = \dfrac{24}{3}$; $r = 8$; $3 \cdot 8 = 24\checkmark$

2. Multiply by 8; $\dfrac{b \cdot 8}{8} = 16 \cdot 8$; $b = 128$; $\dfrac{128}{8} = 16\checkmark$

Success for English Learners

1. Substitute 8 for *m*. Check whether that equation is true. $4 \cdot 8 = 32$ ✓

2. $\frac{n}{3} = 2$; $\frac{n \cdot 3}{3} = 2 \cdot 3$; $n = 6$; $6 \div 3 = 2$ ✓

3. $5t = 20$; $\frac{5t}{5} = \frac{20}{5}$; $t = 4$; $5 \cdot 4 = 20$ ✓

LESSON 11-4

Practice and Problem Solving: A/B

1.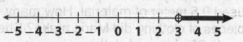

2.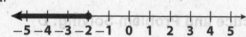

3.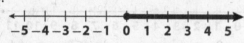

Possible check: $1 \geq 0$ is true.

4.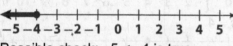

Possible check: $-5 \leq -4$ is true.

5.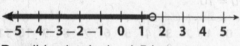

Possible check: $1 < 1.5$ is true.

6. Sample inequality: $1 + x < 5$

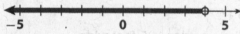

7. Sample inequality: $3 < y - 2$

8. Sample inequality: $t \geq 10$

9. Sample inequality: $b \leq 3$

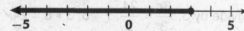

10. Sample inequality: $x \geq -2$

11. Sample inequality: $x < -2$

Practice and Problem Solving: C

1. -1, 0, $4\frac{1}{4}$

2. -3.5, -1, 0

3. Sample check: $4 \geq 1$

4. Sample check: $-4 \leq 0.5$

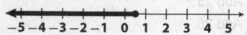

5. Sample check: $-3 < 1 - 3$

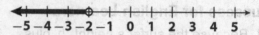

6. Sample inequality: $35 \leq t$; yes

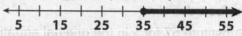

7. Sample inequality: $m \leq 35$; yes

8. Sample answer: $x > 25$; there are more than 25 students in the school band.

9. Sample answer: $x \leq -2.75$; the highest temperature today was $-2.75°C$.

Practice and Problem Solving: D

1.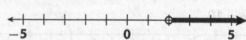

2.

3. Sample check: $0 \geq -2$; this is true.

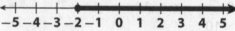

4. Sample check: $-2 \leq 3$; this is true.

5. Sample check: $-4 < -3$; this is true.

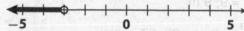

6. Sample inequality: $x < 4$

7. Sample inequality: $-1 > y$

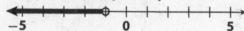

8. Sample inequality: $t > 0$

9. Sample inequality: $m > 2$

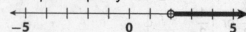

Reteach

1.

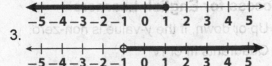

2.

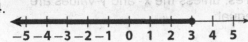

3.

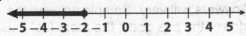

4.

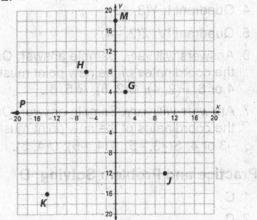

5. Sample inequality: $2 + 3 < y$

6. Sample inequality: $y + 2 \geq 6$

Reading Strategies

1. An inequality is a comparison of two unequal values.

2. The symbol < means less than and the symbol ≤ means less than or equal to.

3. The symbol > means greater than and the symbol ≥ means greater than or equal to.

4. Sample inequality: $x \leq 30$

5. 28 is a solution to the inequality because $28 \leq 30$ is true.

Success for English Learners

1. Yes, $4 \leq 4$ is true.

2. No, $-2 > -2$ is not true.

3. Solid circle; the inequality ≥ means it can be equal to or greater than.

4.

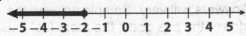

MODULE 11 Challenge

1. $4,700 = 94w$; $w = 50$ ft; $P = 2 \cdot 94 + 2 \cdot 50$; $P = 288$ ft

2. $8,250 = 75l$; $l = 110$ m; $P = 2 \cdot 75 + 2 \cdot 110$; $P = 370$ m

3. $1,586 = 26l$; $l = 61$ m; $P = 2 \cdot 26 + 2 \cdot 61$; $P = 174$ m

4. $8,100 = 90w$; $w = 90$ ft; $P = 2 \cdot 90 + 2 \cdot 90$ (or $4 \cdot 90$); $P = 360$ ft

MODULE 12 Relationships In Two Variables

LESSON 12-1

Practice and Problem Solving: A/B

1. $A(-12, 14)$

2. $B(8, 8)$

3. $C(-12, -4)$

4. $D(0, -14)$

5. $E(14, 0)$

6. $F(0, 0)$

7–12.

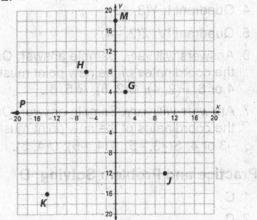

13. Answers will vary. Sample answer: "Go 6 blocks south."

14. Answers will vary. Sample answer: "Go 5 blocks east and 1 block south."

15. Answers will vary. Sample answer: "Go 5 blocks south and 5 blocks west."

Practice and Problem Solving: C

1. Axes labeling may vary. Sample answer:

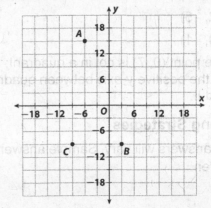

2. Axes labeling may vary. Sample answer:

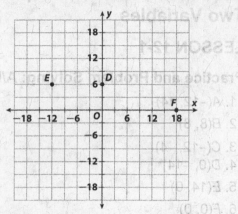

3. Quadrant III; $X(-2, -19)$

4. Quadrant I; $Y(3, 13)$

5. Quadrant IV; $Z(2, -4)$

6. Answers will vary. Sample answer: One of the coordinates of the new point must be 4 or 8. $P(2, 4)$, $Q(2, 8)$, $R(5, 8)$.

7. Answers will vary. Sample answer: One of the coordinates of the new point must be -3 or 4. $S(-3, -5)$, $T(4, -5)$, $U(4, 5)$.

Practice and Problem Solving: D

1. C

2. C

3. B

4. $A(3, -1)$

5. $B(2, 4)$

6. $C(-3, 0)$

7. $D(1, -1)$

Reteach

1. $(-3, +4)$

2. $(+2, -5)$

3. $(+9, +1)$

4. The point $(0, 7)$ is not in a quadrant; it is on the positive y-axis between quadrants I and II.

Reading Strategies

Some answers will vary. Sample answers are given.

1. J

2. r

3. s

4. K

5. Sample answer: L

6. (r, s)

7. Sample answer: M

8. O

Success for English Learners

1. Up or down, if the y-value is non-zero.

2. Quadrants III or IV

3. Yes, unless the x- and y-values are equal.

LESSON 12-2

Practice and Problem Solving: A/B

1. m, money; h, hours worked

2. L, cost of large pizza; M, cost of medium pizza

3. Current

4. Light intensity

5. Answers will vary. Sample answer: close to zero.

6. Answers will vary. Sample answer: 100; $c = \dfrac{L}{10}$.

7. y-axis

8. There is no lap time until the driver drives the first lap, $x = 1$.

Practice and Problem Solving: C

1. Speed; number of passengers

2. Answers will vary. Sample answer: the slower the bus goes, the more fuel it uses.

3. Answers will vary. Sample answer: the more passengers the bus carries, the more fuel that is consumed.

4. Answers will vary. Sample answer: Students should recognize that the fuel consumption is related to *both* the number of passengers and the bus speed. The three variables interact in a complex way that is not completely clear from or explained by this data.

5. For each increase in the independent variable, the dependent variables changes more for line A than it does for line B, except when the value of the independent variables is zero, in which case the value

of line A's dependent variable and line B's dependent variable are the same (22.5 units).

6. For each change in the independent variable, the dependent variable increases by the same amount. However, the value of line B's dependent variable will always be 22.5 units more than the corresponding value of line C's dependent variable.

Practice and Problem Solving: D

1. a. It depends on how long the water has been filling the tank.

   b. $50 \div 10 = 100 \div 20 = 150 \div 30 = 200 \div 40 = 250 \div 50 = 5$; 5

   c. Multiply 60 times 5, which gives 300 gal.

2. 1.61 km per mi

3. 300 sandwiches

4. vertical axis or y-axis

5. 150

Reteach

1. Add 2 to x to get y or $x + 2 = y$.

2. a. $y = 4$

   b. $x = -1$

   c. $y = 2x$

Reading Strategies

1. Cause: increasing number of families requesting assistance; effect: fewer bottles of drinking water per family.

2. Cause: increasing number of voters per hour; effect: the number of hours it takes to vote increases.

3. Cause: car speed; effect: increasing mileage or miles per gallon.

Success for English Learners

1. 50 in.

2. Money collected; cars washed; $300

LESSON 12-3

Practice and Problem Solving: A/B

1. $y = 7x$; 35

2. $y = x - 5$; 1

3. $y = x \div 2$; 2

4. $y = x + 4$; 15

5. 24, 42, 60; $m = 6d$; 60 mi

6. 6, 12, 17, 36; $y = x - 4$; 36 years old

Practice and Problem Solving: C

1. $y = x^2$; 25

2. $y = x \div -4$; 20, −7

3. $y = 0.4x$; 10, 2.4

4. $y = 5x + 2$; 2, 27

5. F represents °F, C represents °C; 68°F; Yes it is a solution because $F = \dfrac{9}{5}(30) + 32 = 86$.

6. $C = \dfrac{5}{9}(F - 32)$; $C = \dfrac{5}{9}(59 - 32) = 15$, so the temperature is 15°C.

Practice and Problem Solving: D

1. $y = x + 2$

2. $y = x \div 5$

3. $y = 3x$

4. $y = x - 2$

5. 100, 120; C

6. 6, 11, 23; B; 33 years old

Reteach

1. $y = 3x$; $y = 18$

2. $y = x - 3$; $y = 12$

3. 8, 18, 40; $y = 2x$; 40 in.

Reading Strategies

1. 8

2. 24

3. 48

4. y stands for ounces; x stands for cups

5. $y = 16$

6. $y = 8(15)$, So 120 ounces is the same as 15 cups.

Success for English Learners

1. The equation shows the relationship between x and y.

2. To substitute a value means to replace the variable in the equation with the value given for it.

3. $y = 12(5)$, $y = 60$; So Mike has 60 inches of rope.

LESSON 12-4

Practice and Problem Solving: A/B

1. 22, 20, 18, 16, 14, 12

2. radios; hours

3. (0, 24), (2, 22), (4, 20), (6, 18), (8, 16), (10, 14), (12, 12)

4. 2

5. The total number decreases.

6. −1; 24

7. Because the total number of radios decreases by h, the number of hours.

Practice and Problem Solving: C

1. 27, 12, 9, 6, 4, 3

2. The number of plant fossils counted daily is decreasing.

3. Rate A for Days 1 and 2 is the greatest decrease in fossils counted.

4. −15 fossils counted per day; −3 fossils counted per day; −1 fossil counted per day.

Practice and Problem Solving: D

1. 10, 13; (0, 4), (1, 7), (2, 10), (3, 13); $y = 3x + 4$

2. 8; (0, 0), (1, 4), (2, 8), (4, 16); $y = 4x$

3. 4, 23; (0, 5), (2, 11), (4, 17), (6, 23); $y = 3x + 5$

4. (4, 2), (8, 4); $y = 0.5x + 0$ or $y = 0.5x$

5. (0, 4), (4, 8); $y = x + 4$

6. (0, 8), (2, 4); $y = −2x + 8$

Reteach

1. $y = 0.5x + 1.5$

2. $y = -\dfrac{3}{2}x + 6$

Reading Strategies

1. 0

2. 300

3.

Tickets (t)	8	10	12	14	16
Total cost (c)	40	50	60	70	80

$t = 5c$

4.

x	4	8	12	16	20	24
y	1	2	3	4	5	6

$y = \dfrac{1}{4}x$

Success for English Learners

1. $y = x + 2$

2. $y = 2x + 1$

MODULE 12 Challenge

1. tables and graph

Table 1

°C	°F
10	50
11	52
12	54
13	55
14	57
15	59

Table 2

°C	°F
10	50
11	51.8
12	53.6
13	55.4
14	57.2
15	59

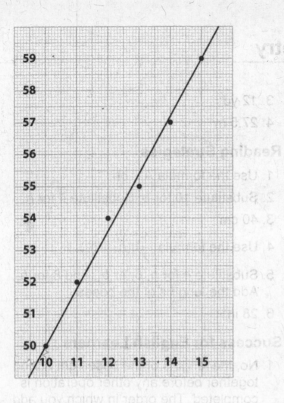

2. Sample answer: The data for Table 2 lie along the straight line because they are computed from the equation. For Table 1, four of the data points are either above or below the line, although they are close to it. The data for Table 1 are approximations because the thermometer can only be read to about the nearest half degree.

MODULE 13 Areas and Polygons

LESSON 13-1

Practice and Problem Solving: A/B

1. 288 ft^2
2. 45 m^2
3. 34 in^2
4. 8 ft^2
5. 27 cm^2
6. 108 in^2
7. 1,200 in^2
8. 84 cm^2
9. 240 ft^2

Practice and Problem Solving: C

1. 38 m^2
2. 60.2 in^2
3. 47.6 cm^2
4. 144 ft^2
5. 26 in^2
6. 36.75 ft^2
7. 0.56 yd^2
8. 686 cm^2

Practice and Problem Solving: D

1. 60 m^2
2. 32 in^2
3. 39 cm^2
4. 30 yd^2
5. 40 ft^2
6. 27 cm^2
7. 4,500 cm^2
8. 75 in^2
9. 25 yd^2

Reteach

1. 96 m^2
2. 48 ft^2

3. 12 yd^2
4. 27.5 m^2

Reading Strategies

1. Use the formula $A = bh$.
2. Substitute 10 for b; Substitute 4 for h.
3. 40 cm^2
4. Use the formula $\frac{1}{2}h(b_1 + b_2)$.
5. Substitute 4 for h, 6 for b_1, and 8 for b_2. Add the lengths of the bases.
6. 28 in^2

Success for English Learners

1. No, the lengths of the bases get added together before any other operation is completed. The order in which you add the lengths of the bases will not change the sum of the bases.
2. Separate the trapezoid into two triangles and a rectangle. Find the area of each part and add the areas together.
3. 26 cm^2

LESSON 13-2

Practice and Problem Solving: A/B

1. 20 cm^2
2. 25 in^2
3. 50 yd^2
4. 7 ft^2
5. 20 ft^2
6. 1.5 in^2
7. 6 ft^2
8. 26 in^2

Practice and Problem Solving: C

1. 17.55 yd^2
2. $8\frac{7}{16}$ ft^2
3. 5 m^2
4. 8 in^2

5. You could change all the areas to one unit, say square inches, by multiplying square yards by 36×36 and square feet by 12×12. Then you could add the areas.

6. 18.7 cm^2

7. $\frac{9}{10} \text{ in}^2$

8. 23.25 cm^2

9. 8.4 in.

Practice and Problem Solving: D

1. 1.5 cm^2

2. 14 in^2

3. 16 m^2

4. 35 ft^2

5. 36 cm^2

6. 48 in^2

7. 28 ft^2

8. 84 ft^2

9. 600 yd^2

Reteach

1. 12 cm^2

2. 6 ft^2

3. 15 m^2

4. 9 mm^2

5. 14 yd^2

6. 20 in^2

Reading Strategies

1. Use the formula $A = \frac{1}{2}bh$.

2. Substitute 10 for b; Substitute 4 for h.

3. 20 in^2

4. 54 m^2

5. 4.5 ft^2

6. Use the same formula but substitute for area and base in the second and third steps. Then solve for the height.

Success for English Learners

1. No, as long as both sides (base and height) meet at a right angle.

2. because of the Associative Property of Multiplication

3. 16 ft^2

LESSON 13-3

Practice and Problem Solving: A/B

1. $600 = \frac{1}{2}b(20)$; The base is 60 ft.

2. $1{,}224 = \frac{1}{2}h\left(70\frac{1}{2} + 65\frac{1}{2}\right)$; The height of the countertop is 18 in.

3. The width of the tabletop 3 ft.

4. The base is 30 cm.

5. The width of the door is 9 ft.

Practice and Problem Solving: C

1. 56 front frames

2. $77.97

3. 20 cm and 5 cm

4. 225 yd

5. 120 triangular pieces

Practice and Problem Solving: D

1. 5 in.

2. $525 = \frac{1}{2}h(30 + 40)$; 15 ft

3. 14 in.

4. 20 in.

5. 5 cm

6. 3 ft

Reteach

1. 10 m

2. 18 cm

3. 8 in.

4. 2 yd

5. 8 mm

Reading Strategies

1. 5 in.

2. 6 cm

Success for English Learners

1. Write the formula for the area of the figure.

2. Substitute in known variables and solve for the missing variable.

LESSON 13-4

Practice and Problem Solving: A/B

1. 5 in^2
2. 7 cm^2
3. 12 ft^2
4. 6 m^2
5. 24 yd^2
6. 17 mi^2
7. 109,600 mi^2
8. 63,800 mi^2

Practice and Problem Solving: C

1. 106 in^2
2. 13.4 m^2
3. 107 ft^2
4. 322 yd^2
5. $48\frac{3}{4}$ m^2
6. 85.5 mi^2
7. 7 ft by 3 ft
8. $99\frac{7}{16}$ or 99.4375 yd^2

Practice and Problem Solving: D

1. 18 ft^2
2. 13 in^2
3. 30 ft^2
4. 68 m^2
5. 8 ft^2
6. 18 m^2

Reteach

1. 15 square units
2. 25 square units
3. 21 square units
4. 34 square units

Reading Strategies

1. length: 7 cm; width: 5 cm
2. $A = l \cdot w$
3. 35 cm^2
4. 18 cm^2
5. Add them.
6. 53 cm^2

Success for English Learners

1. 1,650 ft^2

MODULE 13 Challenge

1. 12 and 28 square units
2. 40 square units
3. Answers may vary, depending on how the triangles are drawn inside ABFG.

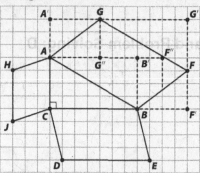

As shown, the triangles and the trapezoid inside ABFG have a total area of about $36\frac{1}{2}$ square units. The area of the large rectangle A'G'F'C is 77 square units; the triangles AA'G, GG'F, ABC, and BFF' have areas of 6, 6, 14, and 14 square units for a total of 40 square units, which gives an area for ABFG of 37 square units. The area of ABFG is about 37 square units, so there is a small difference between the areas of ABFG and the sum of the areas of ACHJ and BCDE.

4. The measure of AB is $\sqrt{65}$ units.

5. Answers will vary, but students should infer that the area of ABFG may not be a whole number like 37 because at least one of the two quantities used to compute the area is irrational. Students might also question whether the sum of the areas of the smaller parallelograms equals the area of the larger parallelogram.

MODULE 14 Distance and Area in the Coordinate Plane

LESSON 14-1

Practice and Problem Solving: A/B

1. $(3, -2)$
2. $(-1, -3)$
3. $(-4, 5)$
4. $(2, 5)$
5. $(2, -6)$, $(-2, 6)$
6. $(4, -1)$, $(-4, 1)$
7. 8
8. 16
9. 10
10. 20
11. 12
12. 10
13. 12
14. 20
15. 16
16. 26
17. First trip: 25 km; second trip: $|-25| + |40| =$ 65 km; third trip: 40 km; total trip: 130 km

Practice and Problem Solving: C

1. $(-4, -7)$
2. $(3, 5)$
3. $|-b| + |5b| = b + 5b = 6b$
4. $|(-3a) - (-6a)| = |3a| = 3a$
5. Answers will vary, depending on which point students start with. Sample answer: Point A results from a reflection across the x-axis of a point with a y-coordinate of -8. The y-coordinate of point B is -4.
6. The coordinates of point A and C are $(10, 8)$ and $(10, -16)$, so the distance between the points is $|8| + |-16|$ or 24. Point B's coordinates are $(-10, -4)$. The point of the line between points A and C is half of 24, or 12. Twelve units "down" from 8 is -4, which is the y-coordinate of point B.

7. From Exercise 6, the shortest distance from point B to the line between points A and C is a line that has a y-coordinate of -4. The x-coordinate of the line between points A and C is 10, so the distance between point B and the line between A and C is $|10 - (-10)|$ or 20.

8. The total distance is given by $4a + 4a + 3b + 3b$, or $8a + 6b$.

Practice and Problem Solving: D

1. 3, 3
2. 3, -3
3. -3, 3
4. -4, -2; -4, 2
5. -1, 6; -1, -6
6. -2, 4, 6
7. 3, -3, 6
8. 4, -5, 9

Reteach

1. $(1, -3)$
2. $(4, 5)$
3. $(-6, -7)$
4. $(-8, 9)$
5. 2
6. 6

Reading Strategies

1. The Library is 6 blocks west of Main Street, or -6; Home is 7 blocks east of Main Street, or $+7$. The distance is $|(-6) - (+7)|$ or 13 blocks. So, the Library is 13 blocks west of Home.

2. The Library is 5 blocks north of Center Street, or $+5$; the Stadium is 3 blocks south of Center Street, or -3. The distance is $|(+5) - (-3)|$ or 8 blocks. So, the Stadium is 8 blocks south of the Library.

Success for English Learners

1. Point B is a reflection of point A across the x-axis.
2. 10 units

LESSON 14-2

Practice and Problem Solving: A/B

1. 5-sided polygon: *ABCDE*; 4-sided polygons: *ABCD*, *BCDE*, *CDEA*, *DEAB*, *EABC*; 3-sided polygons: *ABC*, *ABD*, *ABE*, *BCD*, *BCE*, *CDA*, *CDE*, *DEA*, and *DEB*

2. none

3. one

4. many three-sided polygons

5. Perimeter: $5 + 5 + 6 + 6 = 22$ units; Area: $5 \times 6 = 30$ square units

6. Perimeter: $4 + 4 + 2 + 6 + 2 + 10 = 28$ units; Area: $2 \times 4 + 2 \times 10 = 8 + 20 = 28$ square units

Practice and Problem Solving: C

1. $x + 6$ units

2. $x + y + 8$ units

3. $y + 10$ units

4. $x + y + 16$ units

5. perimeter $ABD = x + y + 8$ units; the sum of the perimeters of the smaller triangles is $x + y + 16$; The sum of the perimeters of the smaller triangles is greater than the perimeter of the larger triangle, since $x + y + 16 > x + y + 8$.

6. 4 square units

7. 12 square units

8. 16 square units

9. 16 square units

10. They are the same.

11. The sum of the perimeters of smaller polygons that form a larger polygon is greater than the perimeter of the larger polygon. The sum of the areas of smaller polygons that form a larger polygon is equal to the area of the larger polygon.

Practice and Problem Solving: D

1.

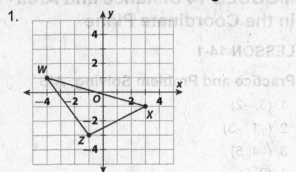

2.

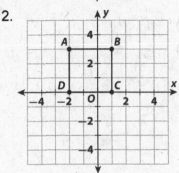

3. (1, 4), (4, 4), (4, 1), and (1, 1); 3, 3, 3, and 3; $3 + 3 + 3 + 3 = 12$ units; $3 \times 3 = 9$ square units

4. (1, 0), (1, –3), (–5, –3), and (–5, 0); 3, 3, 6, and 6; $3 + 3 + 6 + 6 = 18$ units; $3 \times 6 = 18$ square units

Reteach

1. 6, 6, 11, and 11 units; 34 units; 66 square units

2. 7, 7, 7, and 7 units; 28 units; 49 square units

Reading Strategies

1. The side of the solar panel that has corner coordinates of (3, 6) has corner coordinates of (3, 6 + 8) or (3, 14) on its other end.

2. The side that is 6 meters from the edge of the roof and that has corner coordinates of (3, 6) has corner coordinates of (3 + 4, 6) or (7, 6) on its other end. The remaining corner would have coordinates (7, 14) to form a rectangle.

Success for English Learners

1. The vertices of a figure must be listed in the order in which they are connected by the sides of the figure.

2. 35 squares or 35 square units

MODULE 14 Challenge

Sample deck plans:

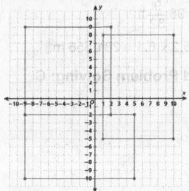

Answers will vary, depending on student examples. Of the 3 designs shown, the deck that measures 14 ft by 8 ft will cost the least because it has the least area.

Mrs. Chirag's design is 10 ft by 12 ft and has a perimeter of 44 ft and an area of 120 ft². The other areas are the answers to Exercises 1–3.

1. Sample answer: 11 by 11, or 121 ft²
2. Sample answer: 14 by 8, or 112 ft²
3. Sample answer: 13 by 9, or 117 ft²
4. Given that the width of the deck can be no more than 20 ft, the deck could be 20 ft by 2 ft and have a perimeter of 44 ft.
5. Practically, the deck has to be wide enough to use, which is based on the Mrs. Chirag's preference.

MODULE 15 Surface Area and Volume of Solids

LESSON 15-1

Practice and Problem Solving: A/B

1. 34 m²
2. 21 yd²
3. A square pyramid has one square base and four triangular faces.
   a. 36
   b. 48
   c. 84
4. a. 248 in²
   b. 1240 in²
   c. $81.25

5. 140.8 in²
6. 360 in²

Practice and Problem Solving: C

1. $A = 2B + Ph$
   $A = 2(6) + 13 \cdot 8 = 116$ m²
2. For the pyramid, $V = \frac{1}{3} Bh$; $48 = \frac{1}{3} B(4)$;
   $B = 36$
   For the base, $s = \sqrt{36} = 6$
   For the height of the triangular face,
   $3^2 + 4^2 = h^2$, or $h = 5$ ft
   For the area of the triangular face,
   area $= \frac{1}{2}(6)(5) = 15$ ft²
   4 triangular faces = 60 ft²
   surface area = base area + area of triangular faces = 36 + 60 ft²;
   Total surface area: 96 ft²
3. Surface area covered in marble = 3,944 ft²
4. Surface area = 87.68 in²

Practice and Problem Solving: D

1. 12; 18; 18, 12, 108;
   $2 \cdot 108 = 216$;
   $15 \cdot 35 = 525$;
   $15 \cdot 35 = 525$;
   $18 \cdot 35 = 630$;
   $525 + 525 + 630 + 216 = 1,896$
2. 16; 6;
   6, 16, 48;
   $4 \cdot 48 = 192$;
   $6 \cdot 6 = 36$;
   $36 + 192 = 228$
3. faces; base(s)

Reteach

1. The area of each base is half of 8 times 3 or 12 square inches. Since the height of the triangle is 3 inches and half of the base is 4 inches, the other two sides of the isosceles triangle are 5 inches in length. Thus, these surface areas are 5 times 12 or 60 square inches, 5 times 12 or 60 square inches again, and 8 times 12 or 96 square inches. The sum of these

surface areas is 60 plus 60 plus 96, or 216 square inches. Since the areas of the two bases are two times 12 or 24 square inches, the total surface area is 24 plus 216, or 240 square inches.

2. The area of the base is 1 times 1 or 1 square meter. The area of each triangular face is half of one times one, or one-half meter. The surface area of the triangular faces is 4 times $\frac{1}{2}$ meter, or 2 meters. Since the area of the base is 1 square meter, the total surface area is 1 plus 2, or 3 square meters.

Reading Strategies

1. Sample answer: **Step 1:** The base of the pyramid is a square, so its length on each side is the square root of 16, or 4 inches. **Step 2:** Therefore, the faces of the triangle each have a height of 5 inches and a base of 4 inches, which gives each face an area of 10 square inches. **Step 3:** Since there are four faces, the surface area of the four triangles is four times 10, or 40 square inches. **Step 4:** The surface area is the sum of the base area, 16, and the triangular surface area, 40, which gives a total of 56 square inches.

Success for English Learners

1. The height and length of the base.

2. Base area $= 2\left(\frac{1}{2} \cdot 1.2 \cdot 4\right) = 4.8 \text{ m}^2$

3. Sample answer: I can see the faces and base and their measure more easily.

LESSON 15-2

Practice and Problem Solving: A/B

1. Answers may vary as to which dimension is length, width, or height. Sample answer: 5, 1, 2, $\frac{2}{5}$, 4, $\frac{4}{5}$; $\frac{8}{25}$ m³

2. Answers may vary as to which is length, width, or height. 6, 1; 3, $\frac{1}{2}$; 2, $\frac{1}{3}$; $\frac{1}{6}$ m³

3. 6 layers × 15 blocks/layer = 90 blocks

4. $V = s^3 = 3^3 = 27 \text{ in}^3$

5. $V = 2\frac{1}{2} \times 4\frac{1}{4} \times 9\frac{1}{4} = \frac{5}{2} \times \frac{17}{4} \times \frac{37}{4} = \frac{3,145}{32}$, or $98\frac{9}{32}$ ft³

6. $V = 7.3 \times 5.2 \times 6.1 = 231.556 \text{ m}^3$

Practice and Problem Solving: C

1. $\frac{1}{10}$

2. 0.5

3. 1

4. 10

5. <

6. >

7. =

Practice and Problem Solving: D

1. 4; 4; 1; 4; 1; 4; 1; 64; 1

2. 5; 3; $\frac{3}{5}$; 5; 1; 4; $\frac{4}{5}$; 60; $\frac{12}{25}$

3. $V = l \times w \times h$; $V = 1,224 \times 660 \times 726 = 586,491,840 \text{ ft}^3$, or about 590,000,000 ft³ of concrete

4. $V = l \times w \times h$; $V = 1 \times 4 \times 9 = 36 \text{ ft}^3$ of chocolate

Reteach

1. $\frac{4}{9}$ yd³

2. 15 m³

3. 150 g/cm³

Reading Strategies

1. cube-shaped, twice the volume, dimensions, length; The volume of the prism is 108, so the volume of the cube is 216, which means its edge is 6 feet.

2. cube-shaped, doubled, volume; If the edge is doubled, the volume increases by a factor of 2³, or 8.

Success for English Learners

1. 60 cubic units

LESSON 15-3

Practice and Problem Solving: A/B

1. 1,800 ft³

2. 6,800 yd^3

3. 270 cm^3

4. 216 in^3

5. 15 ft^3

6. 3 cm

7. 6 in.

8. 8 in.

Practice and Problem Solving: C

1. 0.48 m^3

2. $98\dfrac{9}{32}$ ft^3

3. 2,274.885 cm^3

4. $35\dfrac{55}{64}$ ft^3

5. yes

6. 1,600 ft^3

7. 2.5 in.

8. $3,024

9. 1,797.12 in^3; 1.04 ft^3

Practice and Problem Solving: D

1. 24 ft^3

2. 960 yd^3

3. 120 in^3

4. 160 m^3

5. 90

6. 4 in.

7. 3 ft

8. 6 cm

Reteach

1. 16 ft^3

2. 30 m^3

3. 90 cm^3

4. 1,000 yd^3

5. 27 mm^3

6. 120 in^3

Reading Strategies

1. 4

2. 3

3. 12

4. 4

5. 3

6. 12

7. 24

8. 24 cubic units

9. 3 layers of 12 blocks each; 36 blocks or cubic units in all

Success for English Learners

1. Multiply the length times the width times the height.

2. Volume is measured in cubic units whereas area is measured in square units.

MODULE 15 Challenge

1. 600 m^2

2. 1,000 m^3

3. 10 m

4. 550 m^2

5. 750 m^3

6. 5 m

7. 450 m^2

8. 500 m^3

9. The cubic shape will give the greatest volume.

10. The cubic shape has the greatest surface area.

11. Answers may vary, but students should notice that both products tend to have boxes shaped like rectangular prisms with lengths and heights that are several times greater than their width.

12. No, cube-shaped boxes would have the greatest volume, so they would hold the most product. Answers will vary. Sample answer: Since these shapes are not cubic, the cereal and detergent companies must have other objectives besides fitting the greatest amount of product in the least packaging. For example, the large front and back surface areas may be desirable for product visibility.

UNIT 7: Measurement and Data

MODULE 16 Displaying, Analyzing, and Summarizing Data

LESSON 16-1

Practice and Problem Solving: A/B

1. 5
2. 74 in.
3. 73 in.
4. No; both describe the heights equally well.
5. Mean: 49 °F, Median: 50 °F
6. Mean: 87.5, Median: 88
7. Mean: 69 beats/min, Median: 69 beats/min
8. a. Mean: 53.75 min, Median: 54 min
   b. No; either the mean or median can be used since they are so close in value.
   c. Mean: 58 min, Median: 56 min
   d. Yes; the median better describes the data. The mean is too high since only two of the 9 times are greater than 58 minutes.

Practice and Problem Solving: C

1. Mean: 6.8 in., Median: 6.45 in.
2. Mean: $185, Median: $190.50
3. Mean: 17.6 calendars, Median: 14.5 calendars
4. Mean: 7 km, Median: 5.5 km
5. Sample answer: The median best describes the data set because it is closer than the mean to the number of kilometers that Clara ran the majority of the days.
6. 15
7. 18
8. Answers will vary. Sample answer: 12, 10, 18, 20, 14. The mean is 14.8 and the median is 14. Both measures can be used to describe the data.

Practice and Problem Solving: D

1. a. 48
   b. $\frac{48}{6} = 8$; 8 m
2. a. 6, 7, 7, 8, 9, 11
   b. 7 and 8; $\frac{7+8}{2} = \frac{15}{2} = 7.5$; 7.5 m
3. 6
4. Mean: 20 points, Median: 22 points
5. Median; Sample answer: The median is closer to more of the data values than the mean.

Reteach

1. $11
2. 21 students
3. Yes; 7 + 8 = 15, 12 + 13 = 25, and 4 + 11 = 15. So, the sum of the data values is 15 + 15 + 25 + 15 = 70.

Reading Strategies

1. close together
2. Mean: 100, Median: 98
3. No; both measures describe the scores equally well.
4. spread out
5. Mean: 102, Median: 94
6. Yes; the median is closer to most of the data values.
7. Answers may vary. Sample answer: The mean and median fall in the center of the data when graphed on a number line.

Success for English Learners

1. The data values are written in increasing order from least value to greatest value.
2. Find the mean of the middle two values.

LESSON 16-2

Practice and Problem Solving: A/B

1. 1.4 kittens, or between 1 and 2 kittens

2. 4.36 containers, or between 4 and 5 containers

3. The first bowler's mean number of strikes is about 6.2 per game. The second bowler's mean number of strikes is about 7.2 per game.

   The first bowler's MAD is about 1.1. The second bowler's MAD is about 1.5.

   The second bowler's number of strikes per game varies more widely than the first bowler's number of strikes per game, so the second bowler might be called less consistent.

4-5.

	A	B	C	D	E	F	G	H	I	J
1	8.002	8.002	8	7.997	8.004	7.999	8.002	8.001	7.997	
2	mean =	8.000444								
3	MAD =	0.001951								
4										

Mean: 8.000444 cm
MAD: 0.0039996 cm

Practice and Problem Solving: C

1. No; initial data give the results shown.

mean	14.3
MAD	1.56

2. Answers will vary, but should be realistic, e.g. change the data by varying the amounts on each of the ten days:

15	13	14	14	13	15	15	16	13	13
mean	14.1								
MAD	0.92								

3. Answers will vary, but students should observe that the repairs occur earlier (3.5 hours versus 4.25 hours) on the second day of the race, even though the data is more widely dispersed (MAD of 0.75 on the second day versus a MAD of 0.5 on the 1st day.)

4. MAD = 9

5. Answers will vary. Sample answer: if 241 is changed to 251, a MAD of 10 will result.

6. A value of 256 is added on the 11th day, which results in a MAD of about 10.

Practice and Problem Solving: D

1.

Data	15	11	12	10	12
Distance from the mean	3	1	0	2	0

$$\text{Mean} = \frac{15+11+12+10+12}{5} = \underline{12}$$

Mean absolute deviation (MAD)

$$= \frac{3+1+0+2+0}{5} = \underline{1.2}$$

2.

Data	1.5	1.4	1.7	1.6	1.8
Distance from the mean	0.1	0.2	0.1	0	0.2

$$\text{Mean} = \frac{1.5+1.4+1.7+1.6+1.8}{5} = 1.6$$

Mean absolute deviation

$$= \frac{0.1+0.2+0.1+0+0.2}{5} = 0.12$$

Reteach

1. 0.0192
2. 1.44

Reading Strategies

1. The means of the data elements in each set are the same, but there is greater variability in the values of the elements of the data set that has a MAD of 2.

2. The means of the data elements of the two sets differ, but the amount of variability in the values of the data set elements is similar since both have a MAD of 0.5.

Success for English Learners

1. 5
2. 3, 3, 2, 1, 1, 1, 0, 1, 3, and 7
3. 2.2

LESSON 16-3

Practice and Problem Solving: A/B

1. 61, 61, 62, 64, 64, 66, 69, 69, 70, 72, 73, 74, 78, 78
2. 69
3. 64
4. 73
5.

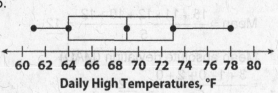

Daily High Temperatures, °F

6. 9
7. 17
8. Class A: 15, 18, 18, 20, 23, 28, 30, 33, 33, 34, 38, 40

   Class B: 18, 20, 24, 26, 26, 27, 28, 28, 29, 29, 29, 30
9. Class: A: median: 29; range: 25; IQR: 14.5

   Class: B: median: 27.5; range: 12; IQR: 4
10. Sample answer: The box plot for Class A would be longer than that of Class B. The box portion for Class A will be more than 3 times as long as that for Class B.

Practice and Problem Solving: C

1. Put the data in order; 40, 40, 41, 42, 42, 42, 43, 43, 43, 44, 47, 47, 48, 48, 48, 48, 48, 49, 50, 50
2. median: 45.5; range: 10; IQR: 6
3.

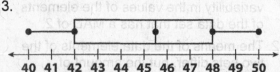

4.

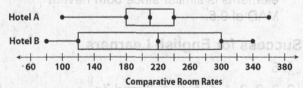

Comparative Room Rates

5. Hotel B
6. Hotel B
7. Sample answer: The interquartile range is smaller for Hotel A than for Hotel B, so Hotel A's room rates are more predictable.

Practice and Problem Solving: D

1. 6, 8, 10, 12, 12, 15, 15, 20
2. 12
3. 9
4. 15
5.

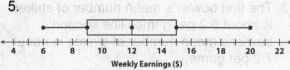

Weekly Earnings ($)

6. 6
7. 14
8. Juan: 1, 2, 2, 3, 4, 4, 6, 6, 8

   Mia: 2, 2, 2, 4, 5, 5, 6, 6, 6
9. Mia
10. Juan
11. Neither, they are both the same, 4.

Reteach

1. 6, 8, 10, 10, 12, 14, 15, 15, 20
2. least value: 6; greatest value: 20
3. median: 12
4. lower quartile: 9; upper quartile: 15
5.

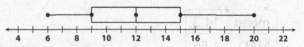

Reading Strategies

1. the middle half of the data
2. The whiskers extend from both ends of the box to the least and greatest values.
3. It divides the set of data in half.
4. least value; lower quartile
5. upper quartile; greatest value
6. median; upper quartile

Success for English Learners

		Median	Least Value	Greatest Value	Lower Quartile	Upper Quartile
1.	Box Plot B	45.5	40	50	42	48
2.	Box Plot C	46	42	50	45	47

3. Box Plot C

LESSON 16-4

Practice and Problem Solving: A/B

1. statistical; Sample answer: miles

2. not statistical

3.

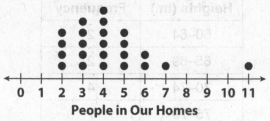

People in Our Homes

4. mean: 4.2; median: 4; range: 9

5. The spread is from 2 to 11, 11 appears to be an outlier. There is a cluster from 2 to 7 with a peak at 4. The distribution is not symmetric.

6. 11; The outlier raises the mean by 0.3 and increases the spread by 4. It does not change the median.

7. Check student's work.

Practice and Problem Solving: C

1.

Cars in the Parking Lot

2. mean: 29; median: 30; range: 32

3. The spread is from 8 to 40, 8 appears to be an outlier. There is a cluster from 28 to 33 with a peak at 33. The distribution is not symmetric.

4. 8; The outlier lowers the mean by 1 and increases the spread by 14. It does not change the median.

5–8. Check student's work.

Practice and Problem Solving: D

1.

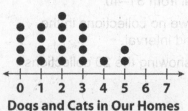

Dogs and Cats in Our Homes

2. mean: 2; median: 2; range: 5

3. B. not symmetric

4.

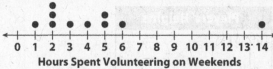

Hours Spent Volunteering on Weekends

5. mean: 4.4; median: 3.5; range: 13

6. B. not symmetric

7. an outlier

Reteach

1.

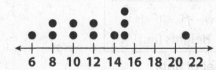

2. 15

3. 12.2

4. 12

Reading Strategies

1. The range is 8. The spread of the data is from 0 to 8 with 8 being an outlier.

2. The mean is 2.1 and the median is 2.

3. Sample answer: There are about the same number of dots on each side of the center of the range.

Success for English Learners

1. The spread of the data is 1 to 7, which is a range of 6.

2. 4.1

3. 4

4. There are more dots on one side of the center of the range than on the other side.

LESSON 16-5

Practice and Problem Solving: A/B

1.

Players' Heights	
Heights (in.)	Frequency
65–69	1
70–74	3
75–79	6
80–84	8
85–89	1

2.

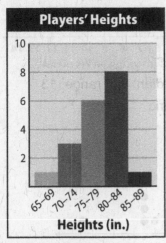

Players' Heights

Heights (in.)

3. a. 22; set of data

b. 79; set of data

c. 80; set of data

4. Sample answer: The average height of players is about 77.9 inches. I used the mean for the Houston Rockets from the data in the chart.

Practice and Problem Solving: C

1.

Students in School	
Number	Frequency
220–239	1
240–259	5
260–279	7
280–299	7

2.

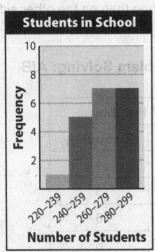

Students in School

Number of Students

3. from the set of data

4. in the frequency table or histogram

5. box-and-whisker plot, dot plot

Practice and Problem Solving: D

1.

Players' Heights	
Heights (in.)	Frequency
60–64	2
65–69	2
70–74	4
75–79	7
80–84	0
85–89	1

2.

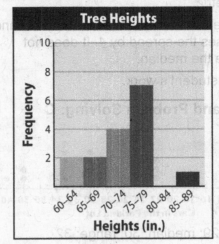

Tree Heights

Heights (in.)

3. 25

4. 74.5

5. 73

6. at the chart of the tree heights

7. range

8. Check students' work. Sample answer: Trees for sale ranging from 61 in. to 86 in.

Reteach

1. the interval from 31–40

2. No, there we no collections in the 1–10-pound interval.

3. the chart showing the 20 collections

4. 33.5

Reading Strategies

1. Sample answer: The ordered list and dot plot make it easy to identify the median, range, and mean. The mean and the range cannot be found using the frequency table and histogram.

Success for English Learners

1. No. They are individual values and not visible in a histogram.

2. Most of the high temperatures are less than 80.

MODULE 16 Challenge

1. 24

2. $Q1 < V1 < M$

3. $21 < V2 < Q1$

4. $V1 > 21$

5. $Q1 = 45$; $M = 66$; $Q3 = 72$; $MAX = 84$

6. Answers will vary, except for 21 and 84. Other points should include five data points between 21 and 45; six data points each in the intervals between 45 and 66 and between 66 and 72; five data points between 72 and 84.

   Sample answer: from 21 to Q1: 21, 24, 27, 30, 33, and 42; from Q1 to M, 48, 51, 54, 57, 60, and 63; from M to Q3, 67, 68, 69, 70, 70, and 71; from Q3 to and including 84, 75, 76, 78, 79, 81, and 84